MW00585741

THE EMOTIONS OF THE ANCI
STUDIES IN ARISTOTLE AND CLASSICAL LITERATURE

It is generally assumed that whatever else has changed about the human condition since the dawn of civilization, basic human emotions – love, fear, anger, envy, shame – have remained constant. David Konstan, however, argues that the emotions of the ancient Greeks were in some significant respects different from our own, and that recognizing these differences is important to understanding ancient Greek literature and culture.

With *The Emotions of the Ancient Greeks*, Konstan reexamines the traditional assumption that the Greek terms designating the emotions more or less correspond to those of today. Beneath the similarities, there are striking discrepancies. References to Greek 'anger' or 'love' or 'envy,' for example, commonly neglect the fact that the Greeks themselves did not use these terms, but rather words in their own language, such as *orgê* and *philia* and *phthonos*, which do not translate neatly into our modern emotional vocabulary. Konstan argues that classical representations and analyses of the emotions correspond to a world of intense competition for status, and focused on the attitudes, motives, and actions of others rather than on chance or natural events as the elicitors of emotion. Konstan makes use of Greek emotional concepts to interpret various works of classical literature, including epic, drama, history, and oratory. Moreover, he illustrates how the Greeks' conception of emotions has something to tell us about our own views, whether about the nature of particular emotions or of the category of emotion itself.

DAVID KONSTAN is a professor in the Department of Classics and Comparative Literature at Brown University.

THE ROBSON CLASSICAL LECTURES

Williams S. Anderson, *Barbarian Play: Plautus' Roman Comedy*, 1993

Niall Rudd, *The Classical Tradition in Operation*, 1994

Alexander Dalzell, *The Criticism of Didactic Poetry*, 1996

M. Owen Lee, *The Olive-Tree Bed and Other Quests*, 1997

David Konstan, *The Emotions of the Ancient Greeks*, 2001

DAVID KONSTAN

The Emotions of the Ancient Greeks
Studies in Aristotle and Classical Literature

UNIVERSITY OF TORONTO PRESS
Toronto Buffalo London

© University of Toronto Press 2006
Toronto Buffalo London
Printed in the U.S.A.

Reprinted in paperback 2007
Reprinted 2008, 2009, 2013

ISBN 978-0-8020-9103-1 (cloth)
ISBN 978-0-8020-9558-9 (paper)

Printed on acid-free paper

Library and Archives Canada Cataloguing in Publication

Konstan, David
   The emotions of the Ancient Greeks : studies in Aristotle and
classical literature / David Konstan.

(Robson classical lectures)
Includes bibliographical references and index.
ISBN 978-0-8020-9103-1 (bound). – ISBN 978-0-8020-9558-9 (pbk.)

   1. Aristotle. Rhetoric.   2. Aristotle – Contributions in psychology.
3. Emotions (Philosophy).   4. Greek literature – History and criticism.
5. Emotions in literature.   I. Title.   II. Series.

B491.P8K65 2006   152.4'092   C2005-906754-3

University of Toronto Press acknowledges the financial assistance
to its publishing program of the Canada Council for the Arts and the
Ontario Arts Council.

University of Toronto Press acknowledges the financial support for
its publishing activities of the Government of Canada through the
Book Publishing Industry Development Program (BPIDP).

For
ALEXANDRA, ZACHARY,
SADIE BLUE, and ANA

Contents

Preface

How provisional ..., how difficult to reconstruct and how exorbitantly specialized of use, are the tools that in any given case would allow one to ask, What was it possible to think or do at a certain moment of the past, that it no longer is?

Sedgwick and Frank 1995: 23

Il y a une psychologie implicite dans le langage.

Lagache 1947: 1

The fact is that once we name an emotion it takes on a life of its own.

W.I. Miller 1997: 31

The premise of this book is that the emotions of the ancient Greeks were in some significant respects different from our own, and that recognizing these differences is important to our understanding of Greek literature and Greek culture generally. What is more, I argue that the Greeks' conception of the emotions has something to tell us about our own views, whether about the nature of particular emotions or the category of emotion itself.

The subject of the emotions has become popular over the last thirty years or so in a variety of fields, including psychology, anthropology, philosophy, sociology, history, and even political science, and more recently still has attracted the attention of students of classical Greece and Rome (e.g., Sorabji 2000, Harris

2001, Nussbaum 2001; on Rome, cf. C.A. Barton 2001, Braund and
Most 2004, and Kaster 2005). In the past, scholars have tacitly
assumed that the Greek terms designating the several emotions
correspond more or less unproblematically to our own categories.
For many purposes, the resemblance is undoubtedly close enough:
discussions of Greek literature retain their validity even if the
subtle differences between Greek and modern anger or shame are
elided. But beneath the similarities there are striking discrepancies, and these too repay scrutiny. When we speak of Greek 'anger'
or 'love' or 'envy,' it is easy to forget that the Greeks themselves
did not use our terms, but rather words in their own language,
such as *orgê* and *philia* and *phthonos*. We cannot take it for
granted that the Greek words map neatly onto our own emotional
vocabulary.

Catherine Lutz (1988: 8) has remarked that 'the process of
translation involves much more than the one-to-one linking of
concepts in one language with concepts in another. Rather, the
process ideally involves providing the context of use of the words
in each of the two languages between which translation is attempted.' Ancient Greece is long dead, and it is not possible to
interview or observe people in emotional situations. We do, however, have detailed analyses of the emotions by Greek orators and
philosophers, and we can see the emotions in action in their
brilliant literary and dramatic works. By making use of these
sources, we can come closer to perceiving the disparities, sometimes subtle and sometimes conspicuous, between their emotional repertoire and ours. And this in turn, I hope, will shed light
not only on their psychology, but on our own as well.

In the first chapter, I review some of the modern controversies
over the nature of the emotions, with particular attention to the
question of whether the emotions are universal and invariant
across cultures, or differ from one society to the next. Given that
my purpose in this book is to investigate the divergences between
the Greek emotional lexicon and ours, I favour the latter view. But
the nature of the disagreement is, I believe, itself enlightening for
our understanding both of classical antiquity and of emotional
theory today.

In the subsequent chapters, I examine most of the emotions

that Aristotle analyses in his treatise the *Rhetoric* (although not in the same order),[1] where possible taking Aristotle as the point of departure for my own discussion. In each case, I look not only to what Aristotle or other philosophers have to tell us about the emotion in question, but also to how it functions in contemporary works of literature, focusing chiefly on the archaic and classical epochs (roughly, the eighth to third centuries BC). Above all, as I have said, I am interested in the ways in which the Greek emotions fail wholly to coincide with their nearest congeners in modern English. My discussions accordingly tend to concentrate on literary passages that are particularly revealing of these differences, rather than offering complete surveys of classical Greek usage in regard to the several emotions (in Greek, *pathê*).

Not all the emotions, moreover, present one and the same kind of problem for analysis. Sometimes the overlap with modern concepts is greater, for example in the case of love, sometimes less, as with anger. There are instances in which there is apparently no corresponding term in one language for what seems to be a basic emotion in the other: such is the case, I argue, with the modern idea of romantic jealousy – an emotion that is not part of Aristotle's inventory. In another case, Aristotle omits to discuss a sentiment – grief – that is central to most modern accounts of the emotions, and here I argue that grief did not fit Aristotle's conception of an emotion. Sometimes Aristotle's analyses are governed or influenced by his systematic philosophical views and do not provide a wholly reliable reflection of contemporary usage, for example in the case of his notion of indignation (this is true also, in part, of his treatment of anger). Then again, Aristotle's discussion of the emotion of gratitude has been almost universally misunderstood by modern commentators, and the burden of my chapter on that topic is a clarification of Aristotle's argument, followed by an indication of its import for the Greek concept generally. The shape of individual chapters is thus determined in part by the case at hand. I hope that the pleasures of variety will in some measure compensate for the lack of a strictly uniform treatment of the various emotions.

I conclude this preface with a mention of one aspect of the classical Greek view of the emotions that may seem provocative.

Aristotle and other Greek philosophers held that animals and small children did not have emotions – or rather *pathê*: it is better to employ the Greek word here – in the proper sense of the term. To us, this may be counter-intuitive,[2] so let me state the case in favour of the Greek approach. The Greeks did not conceive of emotions as internal states of excitation. Rather, the emotions are elicited by our interpretation of the words, acts, and intentions of others, each in its characteristic way. Without pausing here to specify just how each emotion is defined (this is the burden of the chapters that follow), I may say that one consequence of this approach is that it is possible to alter people's emotions by changing their way of construing the precipitating event. If I show you that the insult that has made you angry was unintended, or meant something different from what you understood, or that the enemy you fear has no hostile designs on you, I allay your emotional response. Now, this is not something you can do with dogs or infants. Yes, you can make them feel more secure by holding them, perhaps, or causing them to relax in some other way; you may even show them that you are not threatening or dangerous. But this is not the same as convincing them, by rational arguments, to understand your intentions differently. A second-century AD writer named Achilles Tatius offers an elegant description of the function of words in rousing and allaying emotions in his novel *Clitopho and Leucippe* (2.29):

Leukippe was caught in emotional chaos. She was vexed, ashamed, angered: vexed at being caught, ashamed at being criticized, angered at not being believed. Shame, grief, and anger are three waves rising in the soul. Shame enters at the eyes, where it takes away their freedom of movement; grief lodges in the breast, where it dampens the soul's glow; anger barks around the heart, where it overwhelms reason with its foaming insanity. Speech is the father of all three: like arrows aimed at a target and hitting it dead center, words pierce the soul and wound it in many places. One verbal arrow is insult, and the wound it leaves is called anger; another is exposure of one's misfortunes, and this arrow causes grief; a third is lectures on one's faults, and this wound is known as shame. One quality common to all these weapons is that they pierce deeply but draw no blood. The only remedy for them is counterattack with the same weapons. The wound caused by one sharp tongue is healed by the razor edge of another. This softens the heart's anger and assuages the soul's grief. If one is prevented by *force majeur* from uttering one's defense, the wounds silently fester. Unable to eject their foam, the waves swell up in labor, distended by the puffing breath of words within. (trans. Winkler 1989: 202–3)

The emotions, as opposed to drives and appetites, depend on the capacity for symbolization. For the Greeks, persuasion was central to the idea of an emotion, whether in the law courts, in political assemblies, or in the various therapies that relied on verbal interactions to change the judgments that are constitutive of the passions. A good case can be made, I believe, that such an approach has much to offer our own conception of the emotions as well. The evidence that I am able to muster in support of this claim is in the book before you.

Acknowledgments

This book has been in the works over a number of years, and I have naturally accumulated a huge number of intellectual debts to colleagues around the world. Most of the material in the chapters that follow was tried out in one form or another in lectures, conferences, and colloquia, and I have benefited enormously from the acute and generous comments of my audiences. Others have offered immensely helpful criticism on written versions, whether in manuscript or in the form of articles published in scholarly journals. Almost everyone I know has been subjected in some way to my obsession with the Greek emotions over the years, and even a casual remark in conversation has often helped me see clearly something that until then had been opaque to me. To all these people I am immensely grateful.

Two colleagues – Regina Höschele and Ilaria Ramelli – read every chapter in manuscript, and provided comments with unfailing acumen and generosity. To their encouragement I owe more than I can indicate in this heartfelt acknowledgment of their kindness. Others who deserve special mention are Victor Caston, William Fortenbaugh, Charles Griswold, Robert Kaster, and William Reddy, who read specific chapters and offered advice. I am grateful also to the University of Toronto Press's two anonymous referees, and to Barbara Porter, Suzanne Rancourt, and John St James for their attentive and professional support in seeing this book through to publication.

Although I had worked on one or another aspect of the ancient Greek emotions previously, it was the invitation to deliver the

Robson Lectures at Victoria College in the University of Toronto that provided the impetus to devote an entire book to the subject. Back then, in the autumn of 2001, I had not yet realized the scope of the project: the three original lectures dealt with anger, fear, and jealousy; in addition, I presented a paper on the same occasion to the Classics Department concerning Aristotle's treatment of gratitude. Those four talks have now grown into a dozen ample chapters. I hope that bigger is at least to some degree better in this instance.

Portions of this book have been published in various journals and collections of essays, which are listed in the bibliography. I am grateful to the editors and publishers for permission to use these materials in the present study. Research on this project was made possible by several grants and fellowships, which include two sabbatical semesters from Brown University in 2000 and 2004; a fellowship at the Center for Advanced Study in the Behavioral Sciences at Stanford in 2004–5; a grant from the National Endowment for the Humanities in 2004; a fellowship provided by the National Research Foundation of South Africa in 2003; a William Evans Visiting Fellowship at the University of Otago in 2002; a Leventis Visiting Research Professorship at the University of Edinburgh in 2001, where I organized a conference on Envy, Spite, and Jealousy; an Alexander S. Onassis Foundation Research Grant, for study in Athens, in 2001; and residence as Member of High Table at King's College, Cambridge, in 2000. I also gave a series of lectures on the emotions as Visiting Professor at the Universidade de São Paulo in 2000, and at Washington University in St Louis as Biggs Resident Scholar in 1999. My year as director of the Pembroke Center Seminar at Brown University (2003–4), on the topic 'Shame,' was a special privilege as well, and contributed much to sharpening my ideas on the subject.

Finally, I wish to express my gratitude to my wife, Pura Nieto, who has been my companion through all the labours that resulted in the birth of this book, and to my families in the United States and in Spain, who have always given love and support.

The Emotions of the Ancient Greeks: Studies in Aristotle and Classical Literature

CHAPTER ONE

Pathos and Passion

Each emotion ... is a very exact message. This exactness is comparable to the exactness of color sense in those who are not color blind. (For instance, each person knows instantly and without question whether they are seeing red or blue.)

Isaacs 1998: 13

To recognize that there can exist a color-blindness to blue is as much as to admit that blue exists, which these days seems to me to be more than doubtful.

Tomeo 1986: 6

In an essay entitled 'Is Compassion an Emotion,' Georges Dreyfus observes: '[T]here is, or I should say there was, no Tibetan word for our word *emotion*. I said "there was" because by now Tibetan teachers have been exposed to this question so many times that they have created a new word (*tshor myong*) to translate our *emotion*' (Dreyfus 2002: 31). Whatever the case in Tibetan, ancient Greek had a word that, at least in certain contexts, is customarily rendered in English as 'emotion.' That word is *pathos* (plural *pathê*), the root from which terms such as 'pathology' and 'psychopath' are derived. *Pathos* itself is related to the verb *paskhô*, 'suffer' or 'experience,' and more distantly to the Latin *patior*, from which are derived both the English 'passion' and 'passive' (both roots go back to a prehistoric stem *pa-, with the basic sense of 'suffer'). In classical Greek, *pathos* may refer more generally to what befalls a person, often in the negative sense of an accident or misfortune, although it may also bear the neutral significance of a condition or state of affairs. In philosophical language, *pathos* sometimes signifies a secondary quality as opposed to the essence of a thing (cf. Aristotle *Metaphysics* 1022b15–21; Urmson 1990: 126–7). Psychologically, it may denote a mental activity or phenomenon such as remembering (Aristotle *De memoria et reminiscentia* 449b4–7; cf. 449b24–5 for memory as the *pathos* of formerly perceived or contemplated things). The specific sense of 'emotion' is in part conditioned by this penumbra of connotations: insofar as a *pathos* is a reaction to an impinging event or circumstance, it looks to the outside stimulus to which it responds.

Among the *pathê*, the Greeks included a set of terms that are normally rendered into English by standard equivalents such as 'anger,' 'fear,' 'love,' 'pity,' 'indignation,' 'envy,' and so forth. The *pathê* thus appear to correspond broadly to the kinds of sentiments that we typically or at least sometimes classify as emotions. Often, however, the context will demand some variation. For example, the ordinary Greek term for 'love' is *philia*, but it also does duty for the English 'friendship': we do not usually speak of love in the case of business relationships (cf. Aristotle *Nicomachean Ethics* 8.13). As this example indicates, there is not always a perfect overlap between the Greek and English emotional vocabularies. The tendency to use basic English emotion words as the regular counterparts for Greek terms may lead us, however, to overlook or discount significant differences in the way the respective sentiments are conceived and experienced in the two cultures. It is to these differences that I shall be calling attention in the chapters that follow, in which I examine how the Greeks defined, described, and deployed some of the *pathê* they regarded as basic. It will emerge that their *pathê* do not in fact coincide entirely with the way we understand the relevant emotions. Rather, the way the Greeks conceived the individual emotions and emotion as such will prove to differ in important respects from the way they are characteristically conceived today, both in popular parlance and in scientific literature. The differences, moreover, will turn out to be at least in part systematic, in the sense that there is a broad coherence in the way the ancient Greeks viewed the emotions. This coherence is grounded, I believe, in the social world specific to the Greeks, which was in important ways unlike our own. And yet, despite the disparate cultural contexts, it sometimes happens that the Greeks' way of envisaging the *pathê* has something to contribute to ongoing controversies over the emotions in psychology, philosophy, and related disciplines today.

It may seem strange, even impertinent, to question whether the emotions of the Greeks were the same as ours. We respond profoundly to their epic and tragic poetry, laugh at their comedies, are moved by their love lyrics, and look to their philosophy as a model for our own. How could this be the case if their emotional repertoire was in some important respect different from ours? Besides, emotions such as love, fear, and anger are surely basic human capacities, and their manifestations must be similar everywhere, whether in antiquity or today.

Nevertheless, there are good reasons to suppose that this is not necessarily the case. Let us take an analogy from another sphere of human experience, the perception of colour. Human beings everywhere are capable of sight, although individuals may be partially or wholly blind. If our vision is not defective, we all see more or less the same range of colours. But do we all see blue? More precisely, does what is called blue in contemporary English correspond precisely to some colour label in every other human language? Curiously enough, I believe that I have been witness to a change in the value of 'blue' in my own lifetime. When I was a child, I was taught that the rainbow has seven colours, one of which bore the name 'indigo' (the acronym ROYGBIV represented the colours in order from red to violet). Today, few people think of 'indigo' as one of the basic colour terms in English. Indigo lay between violet and blue, occupying a portion of the spectrum that has presumably now been invaded by its neighbours. Blue, then, should designate a wider spectral range today than it did when indigo still nestled comfortably alongside it.[1]

Now, in the case of terms as close as indigo and blue, we can perhaps accept the possibility of cultural variation, and so too in the field of the emotions. In English, there are several words that overlap with the idea of anger, for example, including rage, ire, wrath, and resentment, and it is plausible that the fine distinctions we draw between these several concepts may not exactly match the vocabulary for anger in ancient Greek, which is also rich and subtle.[2] But sometimes the differences between languages may be more extreme. According to the dictionaries, the Latin word *flavus* denotes a tawny yellow colour, like that of wheat in the field ('golden yellow,' 'flaxen-coloured' are the definitions offered in Lewis and Short's *Latin Dictionary*). And yet the word is etymologically related to the English term 'blue' (MacLaury 1999: 20; cf. Partridge 1959: s.v. 'blue'). The combination 'fl' in Latin frequently corresponds to 'bl' in English, as in *flo* (cf. 'inflate') and 'blow,' or *flos* (whence 'flower') and 'blossom.' Closer to the sphere of colour terminology, 'black' is cognate with *flagro*, meaning 'burn' (compare 'flagrant'). The connection here is perhaps easy to intuit, since things that burn or are near a fire tend to blacken. But what has blue to do with yellow? According to Robert MacLaury (1999: 20), the association between blue and yellow reflects a categorization of colour by way of luminosity rather than spectral proximity, and indeed there are languages today in which blue, green, and yellow form a single category. A dictionary of modern Welsh, for example, defines the word *glas* as (among other things) 'blue,' 'pale,' 'grey,' 'green,' and 'silver' (Evans and Thomas 1989, s.v.).[3] So too, the term *glaukos* in ancient Greek is rendered variously as 'gleaming,' 'blue-green,' 'pale blue,' and 'gray.'[4] 'For physiological reasons,' MacLaury writes (21), 'green and blue appear more similar than green and yellow,' and yet 'culture sometimes overrides neurology.'[5] Colours are complex entities: apart from the frequency of their wavelengths, they are characterized also by differences of hue, saturation, and luminosity (J. Lyons 1999: 45). Just as shifts in colour terminology may occur in more than a single dimension, emotions too may resist being aligned on a single axis or continuum, yielding combinations that to us seem foreign or unnatural.

Of course, we see hues for which we have no label as well as those represented by the basic colour terms in English. Nevertheless, our categories may affect the way we organize a visual field. Suppose that we could view the Parthenon in its original brilliant hues of red, blue, and gold, rather than the pale marble that has come to represent, for us, the austere purity of the classical ideal: would it look the same to us as it did to contemporary Greeks, whose colour terms evidently took account of other factors in addition to position on the spectrum, which is central to modern colour sensibility? It is conceivable that our 'blue' would have been perceived by a classical eye as a mixed or derivative pigment, or that we would pick out a contrast between blues and greens where the Greeks would have seen more of an amalgam.[6] Might not one or more of our basic emotions too have seemed to them a blend of distinct and separable components, and vice versa?[7]

The linguist John Lyons affirms that 'the interdependence between language and culture' is such as to render impossible 'literal translation' in the domain of colour terms (1999: 39). Colour perception, Lyons agrees, is a universal phenomenon, but the identification of individual hues is liable to vary from one society to another. As Lyons puts it: 'I am assuming, then, that color is real. I am not assuming, however, that colors are real'; rather, 'they are the product of the lexical and grammatical structure of particular languages' (1999: 41; cf. Lyons 1995: 197–8). Now, colours seem to be out there in the world, 'neural responses that await a name' (MacLaury 1999: 24, referring to the hypothesis of Berlin and Kay 1969). How much more likely is it that such intangible items as emotions should vary from culture to culture? One might even argue that, unlike colour, the ontological status of emotion itself is as hazy or ambiguous as that of the individual emotions.

I have belaboured the question of the relativity of colour terminology because it is not just popular belief that resists the idea that the emotional repertoire represented by everyday English is necessarily universal. There is also an important current in emotion studies that maintains that a certain array of emotions is innate and hence uniform across cultures. The principle is cautiously formulated as follows (Smith and Scott 1997: 229): 'There is considerable evidence indicating distinct, prototypical facial signals that across a variety of cultures can be reliably recognized as corresponding to at least six different emotions (happiness, sadness, surprise, disgust, anger, and fear), and possibly others, including interest, shame, and contempt' (references suppressed; for lists of ostensibly basic emotions, see Parkinson 1995: 10–12; LeDoux 1996: 112–14; and Konstan 2001a: 4). On this view, anger and fear for the ancient Greeks were and must have been identical to ours, irrespective of the Greeks' own definitions or folk psychology. The modern scientific claim to this effect is associated particularly with the neo-Darwinist school of experimental psychology and with the field of evolutionary psychology, heir to the earlier quasi-discipline of sociobiology.[8]

Charles Darwin's last book, *The Expression of the Emotions in Man and Animals*, published in 1872, was a worthy conclusion to his researches on evolution. In *The Origin of Species*, Darwin had set forth his fundamental hypotheses concerning evolution; in *The Descent of Man*, he extended the idea of evolution to include human beings. With *The Expression of the Emotions*, however, he touched on even more hallowed ground, for he now related the inner or emotional life of human beings to that of the more primitive species from which mankind had evolved. In tracing the expression of emotions in human beings to analogous behaviours in other mammals, Darwin supposed that certain expressive features in humans are as innate and universal as snarling is to dogs. We might agree that all dogs, or at least all dogs of a certain species, snarl in much the same way, and perhaps for much the same reasons, irrespective of the conditions in which they were reared – though this is to ignore the possible effects of training, which can alter ostensibly instinctive behaviour. So too, the human smile and other expressive behaviours were treated by Darwin as invariants over different populations and cultures: 'With all the races of man the expression of good spirits appears to be the same, and is easily recognized' (1998: 211). Darwin confirmed his hypotheses by examining descriptions of human responses drawn from different cultures, particularly those that he and his contemporaries regarded as primitive, and therefore more likely, in his view, to reflect nature: 'My informants,' he continues, 'from various parts of the Old and New Worlds, answer in the affirmative to my queries on this head, and they give some particulars with respect to Hindoos, Malays, and New Zealanders.' Besides the information derived from other peoples, Darwin also observed that '[i]diots and imbecile persons likewise afford good evidence that laughter or smiling primarily expresses happiness or joy' (195). So too, observation of the behaviour of a blind and deaf person suggested to Darwin that this reaction is unlearned and hence instinctive and universal (211).[9]

By classifying the expressions of the several emotions in human beings, and relating these to corresponding expressions in ancestor species, Darwin marked out or delineated a wide range of reflexes that he took to be evidence of inner emotional states. He did not hazard guesses about the origins of many of the expressive features he identified, among them smiling and laughter: '[W]hy the sounds which man utters when he is pleased have the peculiar reiterated character of laughter we do not know ... It is an equally obscure point why the corners of the mouth are retracted and the upper lip raised during ordinary laughter' (206). But he does assign these reflexes a function, in that they serve to communicate joy among 'members of the same social community,' and he adds that the sounds of laughter 'would naturally be as different as possible from the screams and cries of distress' (206).[10]

Darwin related the expressions he examined to a large panorama of emotions, including suffering, anxiety, grief, dejection, and despair, as well as joy, love and devotion, meditation, sulkiness and determination, hatred and anger, disdain, contempt, disgust, guilt, patience, surprise, fear and horror, shame, shyness, and modesty. Since many of these are near relations of one another, they share elements in our expressive repertoire: we may laugh out of joy or upon hearing a joke. Weeping, however, is common to grief and to intense laughter, which are otherwise quite different states. Darwin writes: 'I was anxious to know whether tears are freely shed during excessive laughter by most of the races of men, and I hear from my correspondents that this is the case' (207). But Darwin held that the several emotions are nevertheless broadly recognizable by the complex of reflexes that they generate across the entire species.

Among the devices of which Darwin availed himself, apart from the observation of animal and human behaviour, were the questionnaire – he sent a list of questions to his correspondents in various parts of the world, so that they might report to him on the expressions of the several emotions – and, more especially, the new technique of photography. By recording responses to photographic images, Darwin could determine whether emotional expressions were identified by observers in a uniform way. He is among the earliest scientists to incorporate photographs into his text, or indeed to exploit them for purposes of research. Phillip Prodger (1998: 399) notes that Oscar Rejlander 'presented Darwin with more than seventy photographs of human expression,' and that 'the enthusiasm and imagination with which he embraced Darwin's project transformed the content of the book, and in turn revolutionized the way in which scientists study human behavior.' Darwin was particularly intrigued by a volume published by Guillaume-Benjamin Duchenne, which 'included eighty-four large-format photographs depicting human subjects in various expressive poses' (1998: 404). Duchenne worked at the hospital of La Salpêtrière outside of Paris, and experimented on some of his patients with electric shocks, by which means 'he found that he could artificially stimulate his subjects to produce a variety of facial expressions' (405). These images were sometimes so exaggerated as to amount to caricature (the electric wires used in the experiments were edited out of the published photographs). Darwin also corresponded with the physician James Crichton Browne, who was director of the West Riding Lunatic Asylum in Yorkshire, and although Darwin made use of only one of his photographs in his book, Prodger reports that 'Darwin incorporated so many of Browne's observations in *Expression* that in March 1871 he wrote suggesting that Browne should be credited as a co-author of the book' (1998: 406).

Darwin's influence on the subsequent study of the emotions was enormous. Jon Elster (1999a: 48) writes: 'The psychological analysis of the emotions is little more than a hundred years old. Darwin's *Expression of [the] Emotion[s] in Man and Animals* (1872) and William James's "What Is an Emotion" (1884) are the first studies of the emotions using scientific methodology.' In the article 'Emotion' (part 1 of 'Human Emotion and Motivation') in the *New Encyclopedia Britannica* (1986), Dr Endre Grastyán notes that Darwin's *Expression* 'had a profound influence in systematizing emotion research.' Grastyán himself concentrates almost exclusively on the organic basis of the emotions: 'Investigation into so-called emotional phenomena ... increasingly is being directed toward objective biological evidence' (348), focusing on visible and adaptive responses such as aggression, fright, and fawning, as well as stress responses, involuntary crying and laughing, sleep patterns, and the like. Researchers also began to explore the operations of the sympathetic and parasympathetic nervous systems. Symptoms such as rate of heart beat, blood-sugar levels, production of adrenalin and serotonin, galvanic skin response, and respiration were carefully measured.

Over the past thirty years, Paul Ekman and his associates have continued Darwin's work, developing experiments designed to demonstrate that the basic emotions are universally recognized from facial expressions, irrespective of differences in language and culture. Ekman's *Darwin and Facial Expression: A Century of Research in Review* (1973) was published to coincide with the centennial of Darwin's *Expression*, and Ekman has recently (1998) reissued Darwin's original work, supplemented by an introduction, afterword, appendices, and extensive notes to bring it up to date. Ekman has used more refined techniques than Darwin did, taking larger population samples, making the questionnaires more objective, and employing the results of carefully controlled laboratory experiments. Like Darwin, he too has made extensive use of photography in order to show that certain expressions are universally associated with corresponding emotions. Ekman found it practical to reduce Darwin's large range of emotions to a few basic ones that could be readily discriminated: anger, disgust, sadness, enjoyment, fear and surprise (the two last sometimes conflated into one) are his primary categories, although he suggests as well that contempt and perhaps the complex of shame and guilt have universal expressions (Ekman 1998: 390–1). Ekman remarks, however, that '[j]ealousy seems to have no distinctive expression,' nor does envy (391), both of which, he suggests, are complex or compound emotions.

Jealousy is identified as a basic emotion in the other main tradition indebted to Darwinism, evolutionary psychology, where research on emotions is focused on their role in the evolution of the human species. Psychological traits of modern man, it is assumed, were at some point advantageous to survival, and hence favoured by natural selection. There is a certain temptation in the field to construct narratives – what Stephen Jay Gould has called just-so stories – about how one or another characteristic was adaptive, and to treat this account as confirming the evolutionary hypothesis.

David Buss, a popular exponent of evolutionary psychology, affirms that '[p]eople in all cultures experience love and have coined specific words for it' (1994: 2); hence, love is transcultural, as Darwin too assumed. Love is interpreted as an element of mating strategies: Buss explains, for example, that 'men and elephant seals share a key characteristic: both must compete to attract females' (9).[11] The competition to attract has as its complement the struggle to retain the partner once she has been won: unlike the so-called love-bug, Buss points out (10), '[h]umans do not engage in continuous copulatory embraces for days' as a way of holding on to a mate (it is hard not to think that human evolution took an unfortunate turn here). 'Male sexual jealousy,' then, 'evolved as a psychological strategy to protect men's certainty of their paternity' (16). Buss does not make clear what the evolutionary advantage of such knowledge might be.[12] More importantly, however, Buss's explanation takes it for granted that jealousy is in fact universal. But that very thing has to be demonstrated.[13]

In selecting a small set of basic emotions from the wide array of emotions for which names exist in ordinary language, Ekman and other scientists are following a tradition much older than Darwin. St Thomas Aquinas had identified eleven fundamental emotions, divided into two classes – concupiscible and irascible – and his configuration had considerable influence well into the Renaissance. Although Descartes conceived of his treatise *Les Passions de l'âme* (1649) as a refutation of the Thomistic theory (1988: 195, art. 68), he too presented a scheme of simple or primitive emotions, reduced however to six, namely, surprise or wonder (*l'admiration*), love, hatred, desire, joy, and sadness (1988: 195–6, art. 69).[14] The emotions, Descartes held, are in large part involuntary responses to determinate stimuli. Principal among the external signs of the emotions 'are motions of the eyes and the face'

(219, art. 112), along with changes of colour, trembling, laughter, tears, sighs, and so forth. Descartes emphasizes that 'there is no passion that is not revealed by some motion of the eyes: this is so obvious in some passions that even the most stupid servants can see by the eye of their master' whether or not he is angry with them (220, art. 113). Descartes adds that, although 'one easily perceives these motions of the eyes and knows what they mean, it is not on that account easy to describe them, because each is composed of several alterations,' which are difficult to identify individually. The same is true for facial expressions. It is of course possible to control such responses up to a point; but when an emotion is intense, the best one can do is repress 'some of the movements to which it inclines the body' (183, art. 46); for example, restrain oneself from striking another in a fit of anger or running away under the influence of fear.[15]

It is remarkable that Descartes's theory of the passions was also closely associated, like Darwin's, with a series of visual representations of the emotions, in this case the sketches of the Parisian painter Charles Le Brun, who in the year 1668 – almost twenty years after the publication of Descartes's treatise – delivered his famous 'Lecture on the Passions' before the French Academy. Le Brun illustrated his presentation with drawings of facial expressions, some of them adapted from previous paintings of his while others were prepared specifically for the speech. Christopher Allen observes: 'It is clear that Le Brun regularly conceived figures in his paintings from the outset as epitomizing distinct passions' (1998: 83). According to Allen, 'Le Brun attempts to establish a finite repertoire of human expressions by applying a mechanistic model of affective behaviour, based on the principle of action and reaction' (ibid.). Allen further argues that Le Brun derived the inspiration for his conception of expressive painting precisely from Descartes's theory, which 'emphasized a mechanistic sequence of action and reaction as the basis of the passions ... Before, the passions had been inner movements of the soul, which might or might not manifest themselves adequately on the surface of the body; now the physical manifestation was the primary event, and the artist could expect, by concentrating on the measurable movements of facial muscles, to grasp and convey the essential properties of the passions' (93). Allen contrasts this style of pictorial representation with that of Poussin, a generation earlier. 'For Poussin,' says Allen, 'there is no such thing as joy or sorrow apart from, or prior to, this or that specific joy or sorrow. Everything starts with the particularity of the situation' (87), and it is the complex of responses, subtly varied but always seen as elicited by events, never as isolatable sentiments, that constitutes the fundamental idea or *pensée* of a Poussin painting. In Poussin's method, 'expression involved not only the interrelationship of all his figures, but the involvement of every aspect of the composition' (97).[16]

Darwin knew Le Brun's lecture in a posthumously published and illustrated edition, which may have been more schematic and reductive than the original presentation (see C. Allen 1998: 96); in any case, Darwin did not think very highly of some of the descriptions accompanying the drawings (Darwin 1998: 11; but see p. 7 for a more positive appraisal). Still, the interrelationship between the visual arts and analyses of emotional expression is intriguing. In the seventeenth century, a philosophical treatise on the passions, with a particular emphasis on expression, inspired a series of drawings and, apparently, a new approach to the pictorial representation of the emotions. Two centuries later, the new technique of photography was instrumental in stimulating a novel scientific theory of emotional expression that would largely set the terms for research for a century to come. In both cases, attention to expression in the arts seems to have run parallel to a similar concern in investigations of emotional psychology: both were focused on the individual manifestations of an array of archetypal sentiments. We shall return to this correspondence later in this chapter.

Ekman's project of identifying universal expressions of emotions has been challenged from several quarters. Margaret Mead and Gregory Bateson were among his early critics, maintaining that human behaviour, and emotions in particular, were almost infinitely malleable, and hence that culture was the decisive and indeed the unique determinant of such phenomena (for a summary of this debate, see Ekman 1998). Other anthropologists have joined them in pointing to the wide variation in the meaning of emotion terms across cultures (cf. Russell 1997: 307). To take one example among many, in her book *Unnatural Emotions* (1988), Catherine A. Lutz describes her sojourn with the Ifaluk, a people who dwell on a tiny atoll in the South Pacific. One of the fundamental and most perplexing of the emotional terms that Lutz encountered among the Ifaluk was 'fago,' which she parses as the combined expression 'compassion/love/sadness.' 'This concept required,' she writes, 'more than did most other Ifaluk emotional concepts, an effort to disentangle my own native emotional understanding from theirs' (119). Lutz concludes that 'emotional experience is not precultural but pre*eminently* cultural'; rather than having a more or less uniform content across different societies, the emotions and the meanings attached to them are 'a social rather than an individual achievement – an emergent product of social life' (5).[17]

Cultural history is a kind of anthropology of the past, and students of ancient societies have recently raised similar kinds of doubts about the continuity and universality of emotions. Shweder and Haidt (2000: 401) observe:

Contemporary emotion researchers are likely to find the account of the basic emotions in the 'Rasâdhyâya' [the sixth chapter of the third-century AD Sanskrit book on drama entitled *Nâtyaś âstra*] both familiar and strange. If we compare the Sanskrit list of nine (eight plus one) basic emotions (sexual passion, amusement, sorrow, anger, fear, perseverance, disgust, wonder, and sometimes serenity) with Paul Ekman's well-known contemporary list of nine (six plus three) basic emotions (anger, fear, sadness, happiness, surprise, and disgust, plus interest, shame, and contempt) ..., the two lists are not closely coordinated, although they are not totally disjoint either.[18]

So too, as we shall see in the chapters that follow, the set of emotions that Aristotle treats in his *Rhetoric* also exhibits important discrepancies with modern lists, sometimes cutting across the categories by which we discriminate the emotions. To anticipate, Aristotle seems to divide what we call anger into two distinct emotions; in turn, whereas we typically discriminate guilt and shame, classical Greek appears to collapse the two into a single concept (and yet it has two terms that seem to correspond to our idea of 'shame'). What is more, some emotions that are central to ancient Greek inventories are absent in modern catalogues: an example is *zêlos*, which, as we shall see, connotes a positive spirit of rivalry as contrasted with the negative passion of envy. Pity may be another case: it is universally included in lists of the *pathê*, but figures so rarely in modern accounts that one may wonder whether it is conceived as an emotion at all in contemporary English. In turn, sentiments such as loneliness or sadness are often classified as emotions today but are missing in ancient Greek lists (cf. Wood 1986: 194). More remarkable still is the absence of grief from Aristotle's survey of the *pathê*, although it provides the narrative armature for Martha Nussbaum's neo-Stoic analysis (see below).[19]

Such mergings, separations, hiatuses, and intersections configure the overall picture of the emotions in each given society, and even the idea of emotion itself. We have remarked on the apparent absence of a term for 'emotion' in Tibetan, and on the variety of meanings associated with the Greek word *pathos*: indeed, the use of *pathos* in classical Greek to refer specifically to emotion may have been a relatively late development (Harris [2001: 84] suggests that the term may have aquired this sense as late as 'the 420s and probably later').[20] Even languages that contain words based on the same Latin root as 'emotion' may nuance the concept differently. Although the Spanish 'emoción,' for example, means 'emotion' in psychological parlance, in part under the influence of English usage, 'emoción' and the corresponding verb 'emocionarse' more commonly refer to 'excitement' or 'suspense,' and may thus be included as one of a list of 'emotions,' or 'sentimientos.'[21] One can achieve a proper understanding of these differences only through a close examination of emotional language in cultures foreign to one's own.

The linguist Anna Wierzbicka has mounted the most direct and forceful attack on Ekman's project. Wierzbicka (1999: 168) cites Ekman's claim (1980: 137–8) that '[r]egardless of the language, of whether the culture is Western or Eastern, industrialized or preliterate, these facial expressions are labelled with the same emotion terms: happiness, sadness, anger, fear, disgust and surprise,' and points out that these labels are hardly indifferent to *language*. As Wierzbicka puts it, Ekman

continues to imply that these 'discrete phenomena' can be identified by means of English lexical categories such as 'anger' or 'sadness.' From this perspective, English lexical categories such as 'sadness' or 'anger' appear to cut nature at its joints ..., whereas the lexical categories of languages like Ifaluk or Pintupi ... can only correspond to 'blends.'

The result is that Ekman and his colleagues 'absolutize the English folk-taxonomy of emotions' (171).[22] Wierzbicka's critique has particular saliency for the study of the emotional taxonomies of other cultures, or even one's own at different times or in different social environments.

It may appear that Wierzbicka and Ekman are talking past one another. No one denies that the human face has a variety of expressions, or that some gestures may have natural limits: one can only raise the corners of the mouth so far in smiling, or depress them so far to cause a frown. Such expressions may also serve as elementary cues. As the neuro-physiologist Edmund Rolls puts it (1999: 79):

Although most visual stimuli are not primary reinforcers, but may become secondary reinforcers as a result of stimulus-reinforcement association learning, it is possible that some visual stimuli, such as the sight of a smiling face or of an angry face, could be primary reinforcers. It has been shown that there is a population of neurons in the cortex in the anterior part of the macaque superior temporal sulcus that categorize face stimuli based on the expression of the face (cf. Blonder 1999: 280–83; Laughlin and Throop 1999: 345–46).

There are also data to 'suggest that even very young infants ... are able to discriminate the features of the face that to an adult denote facial expressions' (Nelson and de Haan 1997: 183; cf. 198). But why treat acute gestures as indices of basic or elementary emotions? Extreme cases, as Aaron Ben-Ze'ev (2000: 8) remarks, 'are mistakenly *perceived* to be both typical and frequent because ... they are more noticeable.'

Ekman's Darwinian approach, which seeks to demonstrate that a limited set of emotions is universally recognizable on the basis of extreme or exaggerated expressions, is vulnerable also to the criticism that the information communicated by facial and other gestures is not as consistent as his research method might lead one to believe. A recent volume on *The Psychology of Facial Expression* (Russell and Fernández-Dols eds 1997) proposes to address 'the link between facial expression and emotion ... It is in part a theme of this book that the belief in such a link was not always thus in the past and that it need not be thus in the future' (Mandler 1997: vii). The editors observe: 'By the 1980's, psychologists had largely accepted as a "fundamental axiom of behavioral science" the link between faces and emotions' (Russell and Fernández-Dols 1997a: xi).[23] Some investigators have retreated to the more modest claim of 'a clear and distinct affinity between particular facial expressions and particular categories of emotion' (Frijda and Tcherkassof 1997: 80). Others allow that facial expression may have a communicative function, but deny the connection with emotion. Thus, Fridlund (1997: 104) holds that 'facial displays are simply messages, which influence others' behavior because vigilance for and comprehension of signals co-evolved with the signals themselves'; they are not 'readouts of "emotional state,"' nor are they 'compromise formations of an "authentic" self inhibited by a "social" one' (123). Emotion is thus 'unnecessary to understand how our facial expressions both evolved and operate in modern life' (124).

The most significant critique in Russell and Fernández-Dols volume questions the experimental validity of using extreme expressions stripped of context as cues to descriptions of emotions. Fernández-Dols and Ruiz-Belda (1997: 255–6) recall how Eadweard Muybridge's photographs of galloping horses (1872), made at the request of Leland Stanford, showed that centuries of artistic convention were anatomically wrong; thus, 'we ask a question not unlike that asked by Leland Stanford: What is the actual facial behavior of a happy person, an angry person, and so on?' (256). They go on to suggest that 'smiles, frowns, and other "facial expressions of emotion" do possess an "artistic truth."' That is, if a painter, actor or lay-person sets out to convey happiness or anger by a single image, then a smiling or frowning face is the right image to choose.' But this is not the same as saying that happy people smile or sad ones frown (257). Photographs of people actually experiencing emotions may not correspond to such artistically selected patterns.[24] After reviewing Ekman's and others' experiments, Fernández-Dols and Ruiz-Belda conclude that 'the relationship between happiness and smiles ... is, at the moment, far from clear ... No clear link between happiness and smiles has been found in research on spontaneous facial expressions' (264).[25]

Writing in the same volume, Russell (1997: 295) recalls the experiment by the Russian director Lev Kuleshov (1917), in which the identical deadpan face of an actor set in different situations was described as reflecting a wide range of emotions. The absence of context may leave the observer uncertain as to the emotion expressed, as in this passage from a work of fiction:

But now, as he turned his eyes in Zoffany's direction, he got a shock. The man was gazing at Natalie Arno, had probably been doing so for the past ten minutes, and his expression, hypnotic and fixed, was impenetrable. It might indicate contempt or envy or desire or simple hatred. Wexford was unable to analyze it, but he felt a pang of pity for Zoffany's wife, for anyone who had to live with so much smouldering emotion. (Rendell 1981: 37)

Fernández-Dols and Carroll (1997: 276) conclude that '[k]nowledge of the context can ... lead us to doubt that a genuine (non-feigned) smile expresses happiness, a genuine frown anger, or genuine crying sadness.' Russell (1997: 312), in turn, observes that in experiments in which photographs were combined with stories, '[i]n every case, the modal emotion chosen coincided with the prediction based on the situation rather than on the face' (citing Carroll and Russell 1996). An additional factor is facial mobility. Bavelas and Chovil (1997: 335) point out that 'the literature on facial expression is full of *still photographs* of people with fixed, unmoving expressions' (335). Invoking the theory of discourse analysis, they observe that, although 'facial displays may depict emotional reactions ..., they are not emotional expressions; they signify rather than reveal' (337). They conclude that 'faces in dialogue move rapidly to convey meaning in conjunction with other, simultaneous symbolic acts' (339), a practice that does not lend itself to study by means of still photographs or segments of videotape.

Over the past thirty years or so, investigators in several disciplines have increasingly recognized that emotions typically, and perhaps necessarily, involve a substantial cognitive component. The traditional opposition between reason and emotion is no longer the reigning paradigm in science or philosophy.[26] William Lyons (1980: 70), for example, defines an emotion as consisting of cognitive (or perceptual), evaluative, and appetitive elements, and observes that what differentiates one emotion from another is precisely the evaluative part. Some theorists, in fact, have interpreted emotions as nothing more than judgments – albeit judgments of a particular kind, so as to distinguish them from other cognitive activities. Richard Lazarus (1991: 353) writes that 'cognition is both a necessary and sufficient condition of emotion,'[27] and Robert Solomon (1993: viii; cf. xvii, 15, 60, and 125–6) states baldly that *emotions are judgments* (italics in original). More recently, Martha Nussbaum has defended an extreme cognitivist interpretation in her book *Upheavals of Thought* (2001). Nussbaum describes her view as 'neo-Stoic,' in acknowledgment of the ancient Greek philosophical school whose principal exponents maintained a narrowly intellectualist interpretation of the emotions. In a nutshell, she stipulates that emotions 'involve judgments about important things' (19). We may illustrate her approach with the example of grief, which Nussbaum includes in her own inventory of emotions along with 'fear, love, joy, hope, anger, gratitude, hatred, envy, jealousy, pity, guilt' (24; she later adds wonder and awe to the list, 54). 'The neo-Stoic,' Nussbaum writes, 'claims that grief is identical with the acceptance of a proposition that is both evaluative and eudaimonistic, that is, concerned with one or more of the person's important goals and ends' (41). More simply, mourning just is the awareness that a person whom I love and who has been central to my well-being (or my 'flourishing,' as Nussbaum renders the Greek word *eudaimonia*) is dead. The loss of such an individual is not a neutral event, but bears directly on my sense of what is valuable to me. Thus, the proposition that expresses such a loss carries an intensity that distinguishes the emotion from more narrowly intellectual beliefs, without, however, altering its character as a judgment. The 'real, full recognition of that terrible event ... *is* the upheaval' (45).

One may question whether the intensity characteristic of certain kinds of judgments – namely, those concerning matters that are important for our life goals – can be simply folded into the judgment itself, as opposed to constituting an additional element carrying precisely the affective charge that we associate with the category of emotion. Aristotle, as we shall see, specified that emotions are necessarily accompanied by pain and pleasure, which are not, on his view, judgments but rather sensations.[28] Many modern investigators stipulate that emotions are 'valenced,' that is, positively or negatively inflected (cf. Ortony, Clore, and Collins 1988: 13; Parkinson 1995: 230–6; Isen 2000; Schorr 2001: 31; and Reddy 2001: 21–5),[29] and identify additional components in emotions such as physiological changes, characteristic facial expressions and other surface manifestations, accompanying desires or motives, and so forth. Aristotle himself recognized that emotions involve physical processes in the body (*On the Soul* 1.1, 403a16–27; see Knuutilla 2004: 33–5). Even those who emphasize the centrality of judgment, as in the 'appraisal theory' school of the emotions, affirm that 'emotions are elicited by evaluations ... of events and situations' (Roseman and Smith 2001: 3) – the operative term is 'elicited.' An event 'triggers a process of appraisal and *subsequent* emotion' (ibid.: 7, my emphasis); the judgment is not the emotion itself.

In part as a result of the new turn in modern research on the emotions, the importance of cognition in classical Greek philosophical analyses of the passions has also been recognized in recent years, beginning with the path-breaking study of Aristotle's theories by William Fortenbaugh (1975, 2nd ed. 2002; cf. Sorabji 2000: 19–36). As Richard Lazarus, one of the founders of modern appraisal theory, observes, '[T]hose who favor a cognitive-mediational approach must also recognize that Aristotle's *Rhetoric* more than two thousand years ago applied this kind of approach to a number of emotions in terms that seem remarkably modern' (Lazarus 2001: 40; cf. Hinton 1999a: 6). In the epilogue to the second edition of his book, Fortenbaugh makes clear how radical Aristotle's claim is (2002: 94):

Humans have the capacity to think and therefore can believe that an insult has occurred and that some danger threatens.[30] Animals lack this cognitive capacity and therefore cannot experience emotions as analyzed by Aristotle. Of course, animals can be said to experience *pathê*, for this word has multiple meanings and can be used inclusively to cover both the emotional responses of human beings and the reactions of animals. In addition, emotion words like *orgê* and *phobos*, 'anger' and 'fear,' can be used to describe the behavior of animals, but this is analogical usage.[31]

One of the difficulties with Martha Nussbaum's version of the cognitivist approach, in my view, is that she ascribes emotions, and hence judgment, to animals (2001: 89–138).[32]

Aristotle's analysis, as interpreted by Fortenbaugh (correctly, in my view), raises a further question, which Fortenbaugh does not consider. Granted that a horse fears a snake (for example) only in a derivative or analogical sense of fear, do human beings sometimes react to snakes in this pre-emotional way, or is their response necessarily accompanied by the belief 'that some danger threatens'? Might certain kinds or episodes of human fear be pre-emotional responses? This question will concern us further in the sequel (see pp. 25–6).

Unlike the neo-Darwinian view, the cognitivist model is hospitable to the idea that the nature of the emotions is strongly conditioned by the social environment. Indeed, even such physiological processes as the accelerated heartbeat associated with particular emotions may be a cultural variable. As Hupka et al. (1996: 255, 258) observe in one of several comparative studies:

We found that anger is reported to be felt across the five nations [Germany, Mexico, Poland, Russia, and the United States] in the face, head, and heart. Envy is located in the heart, face, and eyes. Fear is felt in the heart and breath, and jealousy in the heart and face. In brief, the heart is reported to be involved in all four emotions, whereas the other sites are more selectively attributed to the emotions ... The findings corroborate previous research reports of individuals claiming to differentiate different patterns of autonomic nervous system activity for different emotions.'

In Greek popular psychology, endorsed in part by the Stoics, the seat of the emotions and of thought itself tended to be located in the diaphragm or liver rather than the heart or brain. Presumably, the physical experience of certain emotions differed accordingly; I am inclined to wonder, incidentally, whether intense concentration can have been associated with a headache as opposed to tension in the midriff.

Modern appraisal theorists too have begun to insist that 'the appraisal process is more fundamentally social in nature than has generally been acknowledged to date' (Manstead and Fischer 2001: 231). A key focus of recent research in this area looks to the way individuals respond to perceived emotions in others: 'a basic premise for the occurrence of social appraisals is that people are sensitive to the emotional reactions of others and also motivated to know them' (ibid.: 224). Antony Manstead and Agneta Fischer observe, for example, that 'cultures are likely to differ in the extent to which they explicitly value social appraisals,' and this difference may depend in part on 'the way in which the self is conceptualized' (230), that is, whether there exists an 'independent' as opposed to an 'interdependent' sense of self (ibid., citing Markus and Kitayama 1991).[33] Two studies on Dutch versus Spanish emotional responses indicate a 'greater Spanish focus on others' evaluative judgments, in contrast with the greater Dutch focus on autonomous judgments'; the investigators concluded that 'Spanish participants' thoughts during pride and shame experiences were more often other-centered, whereas Dutch participants' thoughts were more often self-centered' (ibid.: 231, citing Fischer, Manstead, and Rodriguez Mosquera 1999 and Rodriguez Mosquera, Manstead, and Fischer 2000). There is at least prima facie reason to suppose that the emotional experience of the ancient Greeks and that of modern Anglo-Saxon cultures may diverge along similar lines. Jon Elster (1999a: 75) has noted that the world implied by Aristotle's account of the emotions in the *Rhetoric* is one 'in which everybody knows that they are constantly being judged, nobody hides that they are acting like judges, and nobody hides that they seek to be judged positively' (cited more fully in chapter 2, p. 75). It is plausible, then, that classical representations and analyses of the emotions would have stressed the interaction or interdependency of emotional responses, and focused as well on the attitudes, motives, and actions of others rather than on chance, mechanical, or natural events as the causes or elicitors of emotion. This approach may have relevance for the modern interpretation of the emotions as well (see below).

Evaluation presupposes values, and insofar as emotions are a function of value judgments, they will vary from one individual to another and according to the collective values of particular communities. If, when people from different cultures confront an apparently similar situation,

they experience a different emotion, it is because they have appraised the situation differently ... For example, if people attribute a negative event such as illness to uncontrollable impersonal forces, such as fate or bad luck, they should feel sad or depressed; if they attribute it to the actions of another person, they should feel angry; if they think they themselves are responsible, they should feel guilty. (Mesquita and Ellsworth 2001: 233)

What is more, the same event may be understood as positive or negative in valence, depending on the value system of the population in question. People prepared to sacrifice their lives for a religious or patriotic cause may regard death as noble or as a sign of martyrdom rather than as an evil to be avoided and lamented. It is possible, nevertheless, to imagine the emotional response of someone from another culture, provided one factors in the relevant description of the event and the value attached to it. As Batja Mesquita and Phoebe C. Ellsworth (2001: 235) put it, '[O]nce the interpretation of the eliciting event is known, the emotional response to it, however strange it seems at first, becomes fully understandable.' It is at the level of evaluation that cultural differences in the determination of the emotions are most salient. Whether or not a given stimulus induces anger or fear or some other emotion depends on whether one judges it to be threatening or insulting, and such an appraisal will involve a whole range of socially conditioned values and expectations.

Although a chasm seems to divide the cognitivist view and that of the neo-Darwinists, the difference is in part a consequence of focusing on distinct moments in the emotional process. Emotions are not indivisible events, at least conceptually. On the one hand, emotions are elicited by a stimulus, which is located in the outside world or else is generated by memory; on the other hand, emotions result in a response, which takes two forms: expression, which may have a communicative function, as Darwin proposed, and action, which is motivated by a wish or desire. Evaluative judgments may be thought of as occurring between the perceived stimulus and the response, as Lyons suggested (unless they are treated as part of the stimulus). As the physiologist Joseph LeDoux puts it: 'At the neural level, each emotional unit can be thought of as consisting of a set of inputs, an appraisal mechanism, and a set of outputs' (1996: 127). Another investigator lists a typical sequence of five components presumed to be constitutive of an emotion: '(1) objects, causes, precipitating events, (2) appraisal, (3) physiological changes, (4) action tendencies/ action/ expression, and (5) regulation' (Planalp 1999: 11; italics in original suppressed).[34] Cognition and appraisal look to the beginning of the emotional process, while expression is relevant to the outcome.[35] It is perfectly possible that the range of expressions is more stereotyped than the variety of emotional stimuli; for example, Russell (1997: 304) distinguishes between dimensions of facial expression, which are physical, 'automatic, and elemental (they cannot be further decomposed), and universal,' and categories of emotion, which 'are complex (they can be analyzed into features), and are, to some degree, variable with language and culture.' The problem lies in assuming that expressions uniquely specify a complete process: it is the process, not just the outcome, that constitutes an emotion.

To be sure, there are some elementary automatisms in human physiology, such as laughter provoked by tickling (to which monkeys too are susceptible) or blinking when an object is thrust before one's eyes, in which the stimulus is closely related to the response. One investigator (Provine 1997: 159) argues that yawning is 'associated with the "emotions" of boredom or sleepiness ..., two behavioral states that fail to make the list of approved emotions, possible victims of science by committee' – with good reason, I would add (Provine lumps together such varied acts as 'yawning, laughing, smiling, tickling, and talking'). The response to a loud noise (sometimes labelled the startle reflex) or to a looming presence may be generated in a similarly automatic way; the latter reaction resembles fear, but perhaps it is better described as analogous to fear, like an animal's or even a human being's instinctive response to a predator. We must be wary of classifying such automatisms as emotions.[36]

Paul Griffiths, in his book *What Emotions Really Are* (1997), proposes to resolve the tension between the neo-Darwinist and cognitive approaches by separating out at least two different classes of emotions – those analysed in the 'affect program' associated with Ekman, and 'higher cognitive emotions such as envy, guilt, jealousy, and love' (9; cf. chapter 6, p. 129). Given this dichotomy, Griffiths concludes that 'the general concept of emotion is unlikely to be a useful concept in psychological theory' (14), since it embraces categorically distinct items; indeed, he proposes that '"emotion" should be eliminated from our psychological vocabulary' (15).

Fear and anger, however, are arguably no less cognitive than envy and guilt, and elementary reflexes may enter into the formation even of highly cognitive emotions. In his well-known analysis of fear, Joseph LeDoux states (1996: 69) that, in general, '[t]he perceptual representation of an object and the evaluation of an object are separately processed in the brain.' More particularly, 'a fear reaction system ... involves parallel transmission to the amygdala from the sensory thalamus and sensory cortex. The subcortical pathways provide a crude image of the external world, whereas more detailed and accurate representations come from the cortex' (165). LeDoux illustrates (284) the process with the reaction to the sight of a snake-like object on the ground: we recoil instantly, and only afterwards discriminate whether the stimulus was alive and dangerous rather than what we know to be a harmless variety or just a stick. Conceivably, animal responses of the sort I have called pre-emotions are primarily mediated by subcortical activity. But this is not enough to account for an emotion like fear. In a culture in which snakes are a delicacy, the final response to the sight even of a dangerous snake might not be fear at all. The dual neural pathways only enable the emotion we call 'fear' when the autonomic reaction of shying away is in synch with a particular learned response to the given stimulus (an analogous split-level process may be at work in constituting the ostensibly higher emotion of pity; cf. Konstan 2001a: 10–11).

One may question whether any definition will include all the sentiments that are popularly classified as emotions. Consider the five components of emotion identified by Sally Planalp: objects or causes, appraisal, physiological changes, action or expression, and regulation. Anxiety, if it is an emotion, may have no specific or identifiable cause; it is doubtful that pity or guilt is necessarily accompanied by physiological alterations; jealousy is acknowledged as yielding no characteristic expression. The situation is still more complicated if one includes emotions identified as basic in other cultures, where, as we have seen, the lists may differ significantly from our own. It has recently been argued that Aristotle's own definition of *pathos* fails to cover all the items he includes in his analysis, and that they are united rather by what Wittgenstein called 'family resemblance' (Fortenbaugh 2003–4), though I argue below that his account is more rigorous than that.

Aristotle's most extensive treatment of the emotions is to be found in his treatise on rhetoric rather than in his book on psychology (*On the Soul*). This circumstance in itself tells us something about the difference between the modern English and ancient Greek ideas of emotion: given that judgment and belief are central to the dynamics of the emotions as Aristotle conceives them, it is natural that an understanding of the *pathê* should form part of the art of persuasion. Aristotle characterizes emotions as consisting of two basic elements: first, every *pathos* is accompanied by pain and pleasure; second, the *pathê* are, in Aristotle's words, those things 'on account of which people change and differ in regard to their judgments.' In a moment, we shall consider this definition more closely; for now, we may remark that one must be alert to the possibility that a focus on the role of emotion in argument conditioned the kinds of sentiments that Aristotle and other students of rhetoric selected for analysis. But it may also be that forensic and deliberative environments were seen as exhibiting intensified scenarios of the way emotions operated in Greek life generally, where they were closely tied to communal interactions and manifested principally in a continuous and public negotiation of social roles. Emotions, seen this way, are not static expressions resulting from impersonal stimuli, as with the patients subjected to electric shock in the photographs published by Darwin, but rather elements in complex sets of interpersonal exchanges, in which individuals are conscious of the motives of others and ready to respond in kind. It is not that Aristotle is right on the emotions and Darwin wrong, but rather that Aristotle's approach may better describe what the emotions meant in the social life of the classical city state, whereas Darwin's may be better suited to the way emotions are perceived in the modern, post-Cartesian universe. Aristotle's view of the emotions depends implicitly on a narrative context.

The narrative context for an emotional display provides information on the stimulus, and thus shifts the emphasis back to the initial moment in the emotional process. The resistance to recognizing the importance of context in the Darwinian tradition may in part be a consequence of its fixation on the terminus of the sequence of events constituting an emotion. The power of scientific paradigms to condition the nature of research programs is well known, and it may be that the coherence and elegance of Darwinian evolutionism is sufficient to explain the narrow focus of subsequent research. But it is worth inquiring whether the bias toward the study of expression might itself have been facilitated by practices and habits of thought in the culture at large.

I do not mean to suggest that the invention of photography alone was sufficient to determine the course of Darwin's research. Photography in any event coincided with a shift towards expressionism in painting, which may also have a bearing on the attention that has been devoted for over a century to the features of the face as revealing of an inner state of feeling. Fredric Jameson (1984: 61) writes of Edvard Munch's famous picture 'The Scream':

The very concept of expression presupposes indeed some separation within the subject, and along with that a whole metaphysics of the inside and the outside, of the wordless pain within the monad and the moment in which, often cathartically, that 'emotion' is then projected out and externalized, as gesture or cry, as desperate communication and the outward dramatization of inward feeling.

The emphasis on expression corresponds, then, not only to an interest in the communicative function of the emotions but also to a Romantic conception of the self as an internal and private locus of feeling, which is exposed particularly in moments of intense passion – a view of the self that was receptive as well to the hermeneutics of Freudian depth psychology (cf. Parkinson 1995: 13–15, 265–72). So too, the Cartesian emphasis on expression again coincided with a view of the self or soul as a distinct internal domain, which one was obliged to read or interpret by means of surface manifestations in the face and body.

In ancient Greece too a development in the interpretation of the emotions may have been accompanied by a like transition in conventions of artistic representation and in the conception of the self.[37] The watershed comes with the Hellenistic era. After Alexander's campaigns, the locus of political power shifted from independent city-states such as Athens to large kingdoms, like that of the Ptolemies in Egypt, governed by Greek elites. The painting and plastic art produced in this period exhibits a tendency towards increased realism or naturalism, abandoning the classical preference for idealized figures in favour of marginal and even grotesque types. At the same time, Hellenistic artists enjoyed representing intense or exaggerated expressions of pain, pleasure, and emotional states.[38] The famous statues of Laocoon and the so-called Dying Gaul illustrate the vividness of such mimesis and its powerful effect on the viewer.

Indeed, modern theories of emotional expression drew inspiration from Hellenistic sculptures, and Darwin himself referred (1998: 183) to the Laocoon group (discovered in 1506).[39] In literature too, where setting and motives are normally transparent, one may perceive the influence of the new expressionism; thus Catullus, a Roman poet steeped in Hellenistic conventions, describes Ariadne at the moment when she awakens to find herself abandoned by Theseus on a deserted island: 'like the stone image of a Bacchant, she gazes, alas, gazes and is tossed by great waves of anxiety' (64.61–2: *saxea ut effigies bacchantis, prospicit, eheu, / prospicit et magnis curarum fluctuat undis*). Ariadne's inner turmoil is revealed by her resemblance to a statue type and analogized to the turbulent waters at which she stares.[40]

By contrast with Hellenistic styles, the art of the classical age seems almost expressionless. A glance at vase paintings, whether of the black-figured variety or the red-figured that superseded it around the year 500, indicates that for all the advances in draughtsmanship over the archaic period, very little effort was expended in representing emotions by way of facial expression. This is as true of funerary monuments and images of war, where one might expect signs of grief or rage, as it is of scenes of marriage or love. When it comes to expressing emotion, classical art appears to be remarkably chaste or reticent.[41]

One can, of course, often infer the sentiment of the characters in a work of art from the context or other elements in the scene. A serious demeanour on a grave stele suggests sadness at loss; similarly, a warrior spearing an enemy might be presumed from the situation to feel hostile or angry, and one plausibly ascribes love to a man presenting a gift to a woman or handsome boy. This dependency on context is the more natural where the story of the characters is known, as in the case of mythological episodes represented in art. It is not arbitrary or wrong to attribute such emotions to the figures in a classical composition. The point is that one arrives at such an interpretation by way of inference from the entire scene, supplemented by whatever one knows of the larger context – a wedding vase, a gravestone – and the background narrative or myth.[42] Expression is minimal, I am arguing, because the information relevant to an understanding of the emotion in question lies in the stimulus and its evaluation, not in the visible sign of an otherwise opaque inner state. So too, Anthony Corbeill (2004: 148), observes:

Although politics in classical Athens also surely depended on ... face-to-face relations, it is remarkable that there is an 'almost complete absence of description of facial expression or gesture in the Attic orators' [citing Evans 1969: 41]. Ciceronian oratory, by contrast, contains constant textual cues to the need for visual vigilance; included especially are references to the visual appearance of the speaker, of the jurors or solo judge, and of the defendant.[43]

Aristotle's cognitively based account of the emotions may be seen as the analytic counterpart to the contemporary cultural disposition to view the emotions as responses to stimuli in the environment, as opposed to self-subsisting inner states that are recognized through their corporeal manifestations. This orientation was abetted by the competitively judgmental world of the classical city-state, in which people seem, as Jon Elster observed, to have been constantly alert to the effect of others' opinions and actions on their social standing or reputation. It was a society in which the self was in large measure conceptualized as interdependent rather than independent, in Manstead and Fischer's terms. If the Hellenistic period was characterized, as many scholars have claimed, by a novel spirit of individualism, it may have been accompanied by a new interest in private sensibilities, in which emotions were imagined as detached from external causes and reducible – at least according to philosophers – to an eliminable disturbance of the soul.[44] What is more, in the suspicious atmosphere of a court society, where people tend to assume a demeanour conformable to the pleasure of the ruler, there is a new premium placed on identifying an inner emotional state from the close examination of outer signs. Forthrightness, or what the Greeks called *parrhêsia*, was now not a civic right, as it had been understood in the Athenian city-state, but the virtue chracteristic of an exceptionally fearless individual (cf. Momigliano 1973 and Konstan 1996). This situation gave rise, among other things, to a genre of treatises on how to distinguish true friends from false. So too, Cicero observes (*Letters to His Brother Quintus* 1.1.15) of provincials who wish to serve a Roman praetor that, though they may be good men, one must judge with care: 'For the nature of each and every one of them is wrapped in folds of pretence and covered, as it were, in veils: their brow, eyes, and expression often lie, but their speech does so almost invariably.' The world of the court had a huge influence on Hellenistic art and literature.[45]

Demonstrating a connection between Aristotle's cognitive approach to the *pathê* and a cultural tendency in classical, as opposed to Hellenistic, Greece to regard emotion as a reaction rather than an inner state to be disclosed will be the argument (in part) of subsequent chapters, in which Aristotle's philosophical account of the individual emotions is compared with contemporary evidence. We may, however, note some broad consequences of the difference between the two orientations. Insofar as attention is fixed on the stimulus of an emotion, there is likely to be less interest in emotional states for which a stimulus is presumed to be either obscure or entirely absent, such as anxiety and generalized resentment. Nancy Sherman (2000a: 155) notes that on Aristotle's 'appraisal-based' view of the emotions, 'emotional shifts are the result of cognitive shifts.' But, she adds, this intellectualist approach constitutes a limitation to his theory: 'What Aristotle doesn't explore is why some emotions don't reform at the beck and call of reason' (156). Sherman extends her critique to ancient Greek and Roman thought as a whole: 'The question Ancient moral psychology leaves us with (though the Ancients never ask it) is, why doesn't persuasion work? That is, why doesn't rational discourse undo irrational emotions?' These are the very questions, as Sherman notes, that 'underlie Freud's project' (157). Thus, although Freud 'allies himself with the Aristotelian view that emotions have cognitive or ideational content,' he departs from this view in a radical way by stipulating that 'ideational content may be unconscious ... Rage at you may really be about rage at myself' (ibid.; see also Sherman 2000b).

In the Hellenistic period, however, some philosophical schools did pose the question of why certain emotional responses seem to be incorrigible. The Epicureans in particular pointed to the repeated social reinforcement of false or vain beliefs, which might be countered by living in Epicurean communities and constantly rehearsing Epicurus's doctrines. In addition, they held that people may be mistaken about the cause of an emotion. Indeed, people generally are consumed by the fear of death, a fear they either conceal or misrecognize. This idea comes very close to describing a state of anxiety, in which the object or stimulus to fear is displaced or unknown (see Konstan 1973 and 2006a; also Gladman and Mitsis 1997). It may be no accident that this view was elaborated by a philosopher writing at the beginning of the Hellenistic era, one who, moreover, discouraged participation in politics and proposed individual peace of mind as the highest good.[46]

The flip side of free-floating emotion is a lack of affect in the presence of an emotional stimulus. The Stoics regarded such *apatheia*, or passionlessness, as the mark of the true sage. We recognize it as well as a sign of modernist literature. In a short story by the Japanese writer Haruki Murukami (2002: 74), Shozaburo discovers that his family perished in the Second World War while he was interned in China:

Shozaburo was now alone in the world. This was not a great shock to him, however; nor did it make him feel particularly sad. He did, of course, experience some sense of absence, but he was convinced that everyone ended up alone sooner or later. He was in his thirties, beyond the age for complaining about loneliness. He felt as if he had suddenly aged several years at once. But that was all. No further emotion welled up inside him.

Is Shozaburo Stoical? Aristotle, at all events, would regard his response as inhuman.

The definition of emotion or *pathos*, however, that Aristotle offers in the *Rhetoric* – the closest he comes to providing such a definition anywhere in his writings (cf. Aspasius 44.20–1) – does not relate emotion to its outer cause or stimulus, but insists rather on its effect on judgment. Let us return once again to Aristotle's definition, which is tantalizingly terse: 'Let the emotions be all those things on account of which people change and differ in regard to their judgments, and upon which attend pain and pleasure, for example anger, pity, fear, and all other such things and their opposites' (2.1, 1378a20–3; for different lists of *pathê*, cf. *Nicomachean Ethics* 1105b21ff.; *On the Soul* 403a16–17).[47] The second component of the definition apparently looks to what modern accounts call the 'hedonic or valence dimension' of an emotion, that is, its positive or negative affect, which corresponds to 'current conceptualizations of the approach-avoidance dichotomy based on two antagonistic or separate motivational systems' (Kappas 2001: 160; references omitted). An instance is Edmund Rolls's definition of emotions as 'states elicited by rewards and punishers, including changes in rewards and punishments' (1999: 60); on this hypothesis, all emotions may be aligned along two axes, representing the presentation or omission of positive or negative reinforcers (see Rolls's chart on p. 63). In regard to Aristotle's account, however, we may note that pleasure and pain are not alternatives: Aristotle is not dividing emotions into two categories in accord with their positive or negative valence. Accordingly, the fact that two emotions are described as opposites does not entail that one of them is accompanied by pain, the other by pleasure: both pity and its opposite, indignation, for example, are characterized by pain. In some emotions, pleasure and pain are combined; others perhaps involve just one of the two sensations.[48]

More remarkable is the first part of Aristotle's definition of emotions, which looks to their effect on judgments. This condition is particularly apposite to Aristotle's immediate concern in the *Rhetoric*, the object of which is to influence the decisions of jurors and legislators (cf. *Rhetoric* 1.1, 1354b8–13 on how the pain and pleasure involved in the emotions obfuscate [*episkotein*] judgment; also 1.2, 1356a15–16: 'for we do not render judgments in the same way when we are suffering and rejoicing, or loving and hating'). Some scholars have supposed, accordingly, that the definition is tailored to the context, and does not represent Aristotle's view on the nature of emotion as such. Thus, Fortenbaugh (2002: 114) comments: 'The definition of emotions given in *Rhetoric* 2 is ... not intended as a general definition covering all the emotions felt by human beings.' But I should like to suggest that, for Aristotle, the manipulation of emotions in forensic and deliberative contexts represents in a concentrated form the way emotions are exploited in social life generally. If Aristotle subsumes emotion under rhetoric, then, it is in part because their effect on judgment was for him a primary feature of emotions in the daily negotiation of social roles.

We have seen that the appraisal theory of the emotions, like Aristotle's, holds that beliefs 'are regarded as one of the major determinants of emotion' (Frijda, Manstead, and Bem 2000: 1; cf. Parkinson 1995: 27–64). However, as Nico Frijda, Antony Manstead, and Sacha Bem point out, '[T]he reverse direction of influence in the relation between emotion and cognition has received scant attention' (ibid.). These same investigators mention Aristotle's view that 'we do not deliver judgments in the same way when we are grieving and rejoicing, or loving and hating' (*Rhetoric* 1.2, 1356a15–16; my translation), and cite further Spinoza's definition of emotions – evidently derived from Aristotle – as 'states that make the mind inclined to think one thing rather than another'

(Spinoza 1989 [1677], Part III: General Definition of Emotions).[49] Popular opinion, in antiquity and today alike, takes it for granted that emotions influence beliefs (cf. Yeats's famous phrase 'passionate conviction' ['Slouching Toward Bethlehem']). To take two ancient examples among many, in Sophocles' *Oedipus the King* (523–4), the chorus comment on Oedipus's rash accusation against Creon: 'but perhaps this reproach arose in fact by dint of anger rather than the judgment of his mind' (*all' êlthe men dê touto touneidos, takh' an d' / orgêi biasthen mallon ê gnômêi phrenôn*). A little later, Jocasta remarks to Oedipus concerning the fallibility of oracles (973–4): 'I told you this a long time ago,' to which Oedipus replies: 'You did, but I was misled by fear' (*oukoun egô soi tauta proulegon palai; / Oed. êudas, egô de tôi phobôi parêgomên*). And yet there has been 'hardly any empirical research' on the subject (Frijda, Manstead, and Bem 2000: 5).

Recently, however, experimental psychologists have begun to examine the conditions under which emotions are likely to motivate beliefs, for example when the object of belief is unfamiliar (cf. Parkinson 1995: 64–7; Forgas and Vargas 2000; and Forgas 2000), as well as the role of affect in the persistence of beliefs (Frijda and Mesquita 2000) and in focusing attention (Clore and Gasper 2000; cf. Brinton 1988, 1994);[50] progress has been made as well in the analysis of just how emotions operate on cognitive functions (Frijda and Mesquita 2000). But this is a far cry from *defining* emotions as the cause of variation in a subject's judgments. The operating definition offered by Frijda, Manstead, and Bem (2000: 5) is rather a typically composite one: 'Emotions can be defined as states that comprise feelings, physiological changes, expressive behavior, and inclinations to act.' Beliefs, on their view, are relegated to a separate category: they impact on emotions as do emotions on beliefs, but they are not constitutive of emotion. I know of no theorist since Aristotle and Spinoza who assigns so massive a significance to the *effect* of emotion on belief. Why define emotions solely by their ability to alter opinion, to the exclusion of all other elements?

I believe that Aristotle's definition may be defended both with respect to his own principles of analysis and for the way it picks out what is in fact the most salient feature of emotions as he understands them. We may begin by considering Aristotle's understanding of 'definition' or *logos*. As we have seen, Aristotle acknowledges that emotions involve physiological changes. In his treatise *On the Soul* (1.1, 403a29–b2), he explains that the natural scientist (*phusikos*) and the critical philosopher (*dialektikos*) will define (*horizesthai*) the *pathê* differently. The critical philosopher defines anger, say, as 'a desire to return pain for pain,' while the scientist relates it to alterations in the circulation of blood and heat around the heart. The scientist, that is, specifies the matter (*hulê*), while the dialectical philosopher limits his account to the form (*eidos*) and formula (*logos*). True, the formula of a thing (*pragma*) is necessarily instantiated in matter; but the description of a house as something that offers protection against the elements is complete (for philosophical or dialectical purposes) even without mention of the materials of which it is built. Similarly, the action of the lancet – that is, cutting – cannot explain what it means to perform a surgical intervention (e.g., drawing water off in the case of dropsy), but the purpose – an action for the sake of restoring health – can do so (cf. *On the Generation of Animals* 5.8, 789b3–15; also *Metaphysics* 8.4, 1044a32–b1 on the different kinds of explanation or *aition*, and 3.1, 996b6–8 on form as the *logos* of a house). These accounts are analogous to the definition of the emotions that Aristotle provides in the *Rhetoric*, in that it too looks to their purpose in the sense of what they are used for.

Aristotle's teleological perspective may seem comparable to that of evolutionary psychology and other functionalist theories, which explain emotions in relation to the survival advantages they confer, such as the capacity to make rapid decisions, focus on relevant stimuli in situations of emergency, or summon up stored information based on prior experience (see Cosmides and Tooby 2000; Izard and Ackerman 2000; and Brandstätter and Eliasz 2001: 4–5). Aristotle, however, is not concerned with how or why the emotions evolved, but rather with the ends to which a knowledge of them can be put; accordingly, he is interested chiefly in their use in persuasion. We have remarked that the purpose of Aristotle's *Rhetoric* is to instruct the orator in ways of influencing political deliberations and the verdicts of jurors. In this context, 'judgment' (*krisis*) evidently refers to decisions concerning policy or matters of law, although in the *Nicomachean Ethics* Aristotle more often employs the term in connection with perceptual discrimination (e.g., 1126b3–4, 1109b20–3, 1119b23–5, 1159a23–4; for the connection with justice, cf. 1134a31–2: '[J]ustice is a discrimination [*krisis*] between what is just and what is unjust,' 1143a19–24). The science of the emotions is thus akin to that of architecture: just as architecture (or house-building, in Aristotle's phrase) informs us how to build a structure that will protect us from the elements, so knowledge of the emotions tells us how to arouse or induce emotions that will dispose others in a way that is to our own advantage. The technique of inducing emotions requires an understanding of the behaviours that arouse them, but its aim is to supplement the other means of persuasion that Aristotle analyses in the *Rhetoric*, exploiting in particular the kinds of belief that are attended by pain and pleasure.

Aristotle offers no explicit indication of how emotions affect judgments, but given his cognitive approach to emotion, we may hazard the guess that the kinds of beliefs that elicit emotions – she insulted me, he intends to do me harm – when excited by the accompanying sensations of pleasure and pain, influence in turn other beliefs or decisions, for example those concerning a defendant's guilt or innocence or the motives of a rival politician. The role of evaluation in emotion is thus not merely constitutive but dynamic: a belief enters into the formation of an emotion that in turn contributes to modifying some other belief or, perhaps, intensifying the original one. In the latter case, the emotion would act on belief in such a way as to confirm the emotion itself.

Although Aristotle does not spell out the implications of this cycle, it would help explain why emotions are sometimes difficult to eradicate: emotions tend to be self-validating because they can affect beliefs in such a way as to reproduce and strengthen the judgment that constituted the original stimulus to the emotion, thus generating a closed or circular cognitive system. We know how people in the grip of emotion will offer a dozen reasons for why they feel as they do – there is nothing more inventive than passion – and these reasons validate or even augment the emotion that produced them. We may illustrate the process by a passage in Virgil's *Aeneid*, in which the hero describes his response upon discovering that Troy has been penetrated by the Greeks and is now in flames (2.314–17):

> arma amens capio; nec sat rationis in armis,
> sed glomerare manum bello et concurrere in arcem
> cum sociis ardent animi; furor iraque mentem
> praecipitant, pulchrumque mori succurrit in armis.

I grab arms mindlessly; not that there is logic in arms, but my heart burns to gather a group for war and race to the citadel with my companions. Rage and anger drive my mind, and it occurs to me that it is beautiful to die in arms.

Rage generates a belief that further motivates Aeneas's battle fury. Emotion provides the impulse, and thought then justifies the act.[51]

In Sophocles' *Oedipus the King* (339–40), Oedipus reproaches the seer Teiresias: 'Who wouldn't be angry at you upon hearing such words, with which you are now dishonouring the city?' Provoked to rage (*orgê*) by Teiresias's stubborn silence, Oedipus then jumps to the conclusion that Teiresias is not only withholding information about Laius's murder but in fact conspired in slaying him (345–9). Anger arising from a perceived insult (Oedipus identifies the city with himself) in turn induces an alteration in judgment that shores up Oedipus's fury. It may be that one cross-cultural constant in emotions is the conspiracy they enter into with reason to provide their own justification.

If we enquire what kinds of beliefs are likely to be able to alter judgments concerning legal guilt or a political course of action, it is plausible to suppose that they will in large part concern the attitudes, motives, and intentions of others. That such judgments are central to Aristotle's analysis is evident both from his descriptions of the causes of the several emotions and from the kinds of emotion that he examines in his treatise on rhetoric, the only text in which he treats the *pathê* in a detailed and systematic way.

Aristotle discusses in the *Rhetoric* anger and the allaying of anger, which he seems to treat as a separate emotion; love and hatred or hostility; fear and its opposite, courage or confidence;

shame and shamelessness; gratitude; pity and its opposite, indignation; envy, emulousness or rivalry, and, finally, the opposite of emulousness, namely, contempt. The emotions in Aristotle's catalogue are directed principally at agents, above all human agents. One does not feel pity, indignation, envy, or emulousness at the successes or failures of inanimate things, nor again gratitude, anger, hatred, or shame, in Aristotle's view. To put it another way, the kinds of sentiments that find a place in Aristotle's discussion of the *pathê* seem to involve an awareness of other subjectivities. This is why such generalized moods as melancholy, the feelings inspired by music, wonder or awe at nature's grandeur (not a sentiment to which the Greeks were especially disposed), and disgust at pallid or slimy things (as distinct from moral disgust) do not count as *pathê* for Aristotle, although they often qualify as emotions in modern inventories (for disgust, see W.I. Miller 1997: 7: 'Disgust is an emotion'; for music, Nussbaum 2001: 249–94). So too, appetites such as hunger and sexual desire are not emotions, but rather factors that may predispose a person to experience an emotion such as anger (cf. Aristotle's discussion in *Rhetoric* 2.2, 1379a9–18).

Fear might seem to be an exception to the above rule. Aristotle himself defines fear as 'a kind of pain or disturbance deriving from an impression of a future evil that is destructive or painful' (*Rhetoric* 2.5, 1382a21–3), and things are frightening when they seem able to destroy us or to inflict harm accompanied by pain. This account does not exclude the possibility that one may fear an overhanging boulder, for instance. And yet, as we shall see (chapter 6), Aristotle's examples suggest that he is thinking chiefly of fear of enemies rather than of inanimate objects.

This disparity between Aristotle's list and more recent typologies of the emotions is not, I believe, a consequence merely of Aristotle's philosophical commitments or his focus on rhetoric. Rather, I would suggest, it derives from the classical view of *pathê* as arising primarily in and from social interactions, a perspective that only recently has begun to receive attention in modern theories of the emotions (cf. Parkinson 1995: 201: '[E]motions can be defined in terms of identity claims which are explained largely in terms of changing social positions'; and Kemper 1978 and

2000). We may particularly note the absence from Aristotle's inventory of such sentiments as sadness, loneliness, or grief, which may result from circumstances beyond anyone's control rather than from a hostile intention on the part of others (on grief, see chapter 12). Such responses to natural loss, as opposed to morally charged social interactions and struggles for status and advantage, are not part of the core set of emotions in the classical period.

In no culture is the emotional vocabulary rigorously consistent, and I do not mean to suggest that Greeks of the classical era systematically differentiated between grief or sadness and emotions proper.[52] I do think, however, that Aristotle's failure to treat these sentiments among the *pathê* discussed in his *Rhetoric* is not an arbitrary omission but rather symptomatic of a Greek habit of thought, which understood emotions as responses not to events but to actions, or situations resulting from actions, that entail consequences for one's own or others' relative social standing. As a result, some sentiments that typically count as emotions in English fall outside the category of *pathê* in classical Greek (Greek of the Hellenistic epoch may differ in this respect). If this is approximately correct, it has significant implications for our understanding of both ancient philosophical accounts of the emotions and literary representations of the emotions in action. It may also, I believe, offer a useful perspective on certain problems in the scientific interpretation of the emotions today.

CHAPTER TWO

Anger

Anger is an emotion that would seem to be universal and unlearned if any emotion is.[1]

Solomon 1984: 242[1]

One emotion that is included almost without exception in both classical and modern inventories of the passions is anger, and it may well seem to be a prime example of an innate and universal emotion. Nevertheless, there is reason to think that the ancient Greek concept is in fact significantly different from the modern. In this chapter, as in many of those that follow, I take as my point of departure Aristotle's account in the *Rhetoric*, which is the most sophisticated and detailed analysis of the emotions to come down to us from classical antiquity. Apart from Aristotle's acumen as an ethical thinker, he was the only one among the major Greek philosophers to accept the emotions as a natural and normal part of human life, attempting neither to abolish them utterly nor to reduce them to mere wraiths of living passion.

Aristotle defines anger as 'a desire, accompanied by pain, for a perceived revenge, on account of a perceived slight on the part of people who are not fit to slight one or one's own' (*Rhetoric* 2.2, 1378a31–3). Why 'accompanied by pain'? Among other reasons, this element is required by the definition of the *pathê* that Aristotle offered shortly before (cf. chapter 1, pp. 33–4): 'Let the emotions be all those things on account of which people change their minds and differ in regard to their judgments, and upon which attend pain and pleasure, for example anger, pity, fear, and all other such things and their opposites' (2.1, 1378a20–3).[2] Pain and pleasure themselves do not count, for Aristotle, as emotions. Rather, they are sensations or *aisthêseis*. A painful sensation may arise either as a result of direct perception, or else by way of *phantasia*, that is, through recollection or anticipation of something perceived. In Aristotle's own words:

Since feeling pleasure is in the perception of some experience [*pathos*], and *phantasia* is a weak kind of perception [*aisthêsis*], some *phantasia* of what one remembers or expects always occurs in a person when he remembers or expects something ... Thus, it is necessary that all pleasures are either present in perception or arise in remembering things that have happened or in expecting things that will happen. (1.11, 1370a27–34)[3]

Anger is accompanied not just by pain but by pleasure, too, which derives from the desire to avenge the slight that has been suffered: for this desire is accompanied by the expectation (*elpis*) of its fulfilment, which we regard as possible – if we did not, we would not be experiencing the emotion that Aristotle defines as anger; and the expectation of revenge is pleasant. As we have seen (chapter 1, p. 34), Aristotle does not differentiate the emotions according to positive and negative valence, but allows for mixed cases ('upon which attend pain *and* pleasure,' he writes, not 'pain *or* pleasure').[4] If the revenge, or anticipation of revenge, is to be pleasant, moreover, it must be perceived, just as the slight was, for otherwise it would not have produced pain: as Aristotle says (2.4, 1382a10), 'All painful things are perceptible [*aisthêta*].' This is why Aristotle insists on 'a *perceived* [*phainomenês*] revenge, on account of a *perceived* [*phainomenên*] slight.'[5]

I assume that the slight or the thought of the slight itself is painful. Why, then, does Aristotle add the phrase 'accompanied by pain'? For two reasons, perhaps. First, the pain associated with the *pathos* anger may not be identical to the pain of the slight itself.[6] Second, Aristotle may wish to differentiate the desire for revenge that is constitutive of anger from related impulses that are not necessarily attended by pain. As we shall see, one way in which hatred is distinct from anger, according to Aristotle, is that 'the one is accompanied by pain, while the other is not accompanied by pain; for one who is angry feels pain, but one who hates does not' (2.4, 1382a12–13; cf. *Politics* 5.8, 1312b25–34). Hatred is a response to what is bad or harmful (*kakon*) in general, not just to a slight, and certain forms of harm – Aristotle singles out vice itself (*kakia*), e.g. injustice or stupidity – are practically imperceptible (*hêkista aisthêta*, 2.4, 1382a9–11), and hence not particularly painful.[7]

There are several elements in Aristotle's account of anger that may seem remarkable: that anger entails, or is reducible to, a desire for revenge; that this desire is provoked by a slight – and only a slight; and that some people, but only some, are not fit to slight another. Let me begin, however, by noting the centrality of evaluation to Aristotle's approach. A slight or belittlement is a complex social event, which takes a considerable measure of judgment to recognize. As opposed to an instinctive response to a hostile gesture, anger involves an appraisal of social roles (who is or is not fit [*prosêkôn*] to offer insult), intentions, and consequences.[8]

As indicated in chapter 1, it is now some three decades since scholars began paying serious attention to the importance of cognition in Aristotle's theory of the emotions (see especially Fortenbaugh 2002 [orig. 1975]), a development that coincided with increased emphasis on cognition on the part of philosophers, biologists, anthropologists, and psychologists, sometimes to the exclusion of all other elements in the constitution of the emotions.[9] This is in sharp contrast to the polarized opposition between reason and passion that has been characteristic of post-Cartesian philosophy and continues to prevail in popular thought (cf. Lewis, Amini, and Lannon [2000: 42], who assert blandly that 'most emotions require no thinking at all').[10] The view that the emotions are irrational coincided with a tendency, beginning at the end of the nineteenth century, to explain emotions entirely in physical terms, thereby ignoring the element of judgment altogether (cf. Grastyán 1986, quoted in chapter 1, pp. 10–11). Following the pioneering work of the physiologist Walter B. Cannon, researchers also began to explore the operations of the sympathetic and parasympathetic nervous systems, and symptoms such as rate of heart beat, blood-sugar levels, production of adrenalin and serotonin, galvanic skin response, and respiration. Finally, the function of the emotions was associated with drives, energy levels, and efforts directed towards the successful attainment of goals. The recent vogue of evolutionary psychology is heir to this research program.[11]

Although Aristotle too, as we have noted, holds that the emotions have a physical basis in the organism (cf. *De anima* 1.1.403a16–b2, esp. 403a25: 'The emotions are reasonings set in matter' [*ta pathê logoi enuloi eisin*]), he does not reduce the emotions to material states such as the temperature of blood around the heart. In the *Rhetoric*, of course, he is interested in the passions above all for their role in persuasion, but there is good reason to believe, as I argued in chapter 1, that his definition of the *pathê* in terms of their effect on judgment is intended to pick out their essential quality.

The weakness in the narrowly physiological view of anger is apparent in the following hypothetical situation. A woman is pushed violently from behind. Instinctively, her muscles tense and her heart beats faster. She may move to escape or defend herself, perhaps aggressively, by striking at her assailant.[12] But is she angry? Very possibly, but if so, it is because she has made a snap but complex evaluation of the event that includes, among other things, a supposition about the motives of the person who shoved her, for example, that the man's action was intended to harm her, and that she had done nothing to deserve it (Aristotle *Rhetoric* 2.3, 1380b16–18, points out that we do not respond with anger when we have done wrong and are suffering justly). If the woman subsequently discovers that the man pushed her by accident, she will very likely cease to be angry.[13] As Aristotle observes in his discussion of calming down, which he treats as the opposite of anger, a slight must be voluntary, and people therefore react mildly towards unintentional offences, or towards people who wished to do the opposite of what they in fact accomplished (2.3, 1380a8–12).[14] But suppose that the man pushed the woman in order to save her life – say she was standing in the path of an oncoming car. In this case, she not only gives over her anger, but presumably feels grateful instead.

Anger, then, involves a judgment of intentions. That is why we do not normally get angry at stones: they can hurt us, but cannot insult us – stubbing is not snubbing (cf. Ben-Ze'ev 2000: 30). Nor can we take revenge on them. In addition, anger depends on values, that is, what one regards as good or bad. Suppose the woman in our thought experiment knew the car was approaching, and intended to commit suicide by hurling herself in front of it. The man, by shoving her, prevented her from taking her life. Is she angry at him? Again, it will depend in part on whether she believes that he was aware of her purpose and deliberately thwarted it. Note how the same act and intention that evoked the woman's gratitude in the previous scenario now rouse her ire.[15]

My story is nevertheless defective in at least one respect as an illustration of Aristotle's theory of anger. For what is extraordinary about Aristotle's analysis is that he limits the causes of anger to intentional offences of a single kind, which are summed up by the term *oligôria* or 'slight.'[16] What, then, is an *oligôria*? Literally, the Greek term indicates a lessening or belittlement, from the root *oligos* meaning 'small' or 'few.' Aristotle defines a slight as 'the activation [or activity: *energeia*] of a belief about something seeming worthless' (*energeia doxês peri to mêdenos axion phainomenon*, 2.2, 1378b10–11). To see how severe a restriction this is, consider the three classes of slight that Aristotle enumerates. The first is *kataphronêsis* or contempt, which he defines as the belief that something is of no value; it follows a fortiori that we slight a person whom we treat with contempt, since slighting is just the active belief that a thing is or seems worthless. The second category of slighting is more interesting. This is *epêreasmos* or 'spite,' which Aristotle defines as 'blocking the wishes [*boulêseis*] of another not in order to have something for oneself but rather so that the other not have it' (2.2, 1378b18–19). In this case, the slight, Aristotle explains, lies precisely in that the offender seeks no personal advantage. The only explanation for such a gratuitous hindrance of another's wishes, according to Aristotle, is that one neither fears him nor seeks his friendship; he is thus useless, whether for good or ill, which is just Aristotle's definition of worthlessness. If the motive were self-interest, it would not be a clear case of belittlement, since one can impede another person's plans out of selfishness and still respect him or her. And if that were the case, then the act, according to Aristotle, would not produce anger, for anger results from a slight and nothing else.

So too with Aristotle's third category of slighting, namely, *hubris* or arrogant abuse, which is defined as speaking or acting in ways that cause shame to another, not so that something may happen to you or because something has happened, but for the sheer pleasure of it (2.2, 1378b23–5) – a pleasure that derives from a sense of superiority, not from gain.[17] If the abuse is in return for an injury, it does not count as insolence but rather as revenge. The kind of affront that provokes anger, Aristotle explains, must be neither in reprisal for an offence nor beneficial to the offender, but purely a function of arrogance (2.2, 1379a29–32) – that is, a form of belittlement.[18]

It is evident that the causes of anger, in Aristotle's view, are far more limited than is the case in English.[19] Anger is not a response to harm as such, even when the harm is intentional. It is not that one is indifferent to deliberate injury, of course; but one reacts to it, if I understand Aristotle correctly, not with anger but with hatred or hostility (*misein*), unless it is the sort of injury that constitutes an affront. Aristotle is intensely conscious of the difference between these two emotions, which overlap in English to a far greater extent than in Greek, to go by Aristotle's descriptions. Let me offer some illustrations.[20]

Aristotle observes that rejoicing at the misfortune of another is the sign either of an enemy or of one who is slighting you (2.2, 1379b17–19). These are alternatives: an enemy may be expected to take delight in your ruin without it following that he or she despises you as being of no account. When an enemy behaves in this way, accordingly, one does not necessarily react with anger. In a similar vein, Aristotle points out that no one slights a person he fears (2.3, 1380a22–3), because fear is a sign of one's own weakness, and this is incompatible with contempt for the other. Of course, we can certainly hate such a person, and normally do. As Aristotle says, 'No one likes [*philei*] a person he fears' (2.4, 1381b33). For the same reason, we are not angry with those who fear us, since their fear demonstrates their respect for us (hence, they cannot slight us), though we may certainly dislike them. What is more, Aristotle says that 'it is impossible to be afraid of and angry with someone at the same time' (2.3, 1380a33). The reason for this, I presume, is that we acknowledge, by our fear, the superior status of the other, who is accordingly in a fit position to deliver a slight. Nor can we return anger for anger, according to Aristotle, since those who are angry at us do not appear to act out of contempt, but are responding precisely to our disdain for them (2.3, 1380a34–5); yet anger is listed as one of the three primary causes of enmity (2.4, 1382a1–2). The result of a slight or put-down is that we find ourselves diminished in esteem, and in order to turn the tables on the offender, we must first restore the original equilibrium through an act of revenge. Until that happens, we are not in a position to diminish the other, and hence inspire her or his anger.

The sharp distinction that Aristotle draws between anger and hatred or enmity may seem surprising, but it follows from his understanding of the nature of the two emotions.[21] Enmity, according to Aristotle, is the opposite of friendship or affection; whereas friends desire the good of the other, the object of hatred is to inflict harm (2.4, 1382a8). The object of anger, however, is to cause pain to the other.[22] A slight makes one feel small, and the only way to get even is to induce a similar feeling in the other. It follows that, for an angry person to get revenge, the original offender must be aware of it (*aisthesthai*), since there is no such thing as unperceived pain (hence the stipulation in the definition of anger that the revenge, like the slight itself, must be perceived), whereas to one who hates it is a matter of indifference whether an enemy is aware or not of the damage done to him. That is why we may wish that people whom we hate should die, but when we are angry, what we desire is that the other person feel in return (*antipathein*) the kind of diminishment that provoked our anger in the first place (2.4, 1382a14–15). The death of the other would render that impossible.

Anger is also more personal than hatred. Aristotle asserts that one can be angry only at an individual – at Cleon, for example – and not at a class of people or at mankind generally (2.2, 1378a34–5), whereas hatred or dislike may be directed against a group, e.g. thieves or slanderers (2.4, 1382a4–7). It is understandable, then, that hatred need not be accompanied by pain in the way that anger over an intentional slight must be. Hatred for Aristotle signifies a settled antagonism that is lasting and not subject, as anger is, to being healed by the passage of time (2.4, 1382a7–8).[23]

So far, I have discussed only one aspect of Aristotle's conception of anger: that it is produced by a slight, and only that. We have yet to consider the implications of the connection with revenge, and of the implicit distinction between those who may appropriately belittle another, and those who may not. We shall return to these issues shortly. But even on the basis of what we have already noted, it would seem that Aristotle's notion of anger relates to our own in something like the way that indigo does to blue: they overlap in part, but do not have the same extension (see chapter 1, p. 5). Now, Aristotle is a professional philosopher, and he is within his rights to define a concept more narrowly or widely than obtains in popular usage (we shall see below that he has, to a certain degree, availed himself of this privilege). Hence, we must inquire whether classical Greek literature bears out the distinction he draws between anger and hatred, and the limited scope that this contrast leaves for the emotion anger. To test it, we shall examine a poetic text in which anger is universally recognized as playing a central role.

At the beginning of Greek literature stands Homer's *Iliad*, and, as is well known, the first word of this epic poem is anger, or rather, wrath: the term *mênis* has a solemn and perhaps religious register, and is often associated with divine anger (Considine 1986: 54).[24] Among mortals, the word is employed of Achilles' anger against Agamemnon, who took from Achilles the girl he had won as a war prize. There can be no doubt that what provokes Achilles' rage, or *kholos* – the standard term for anger in the Homeric epics (e.g., 1.224, 283) – in this part of the epic is precisely his sense of having been slighted; as he says to his mother, Thetis, 'wide-ruling Agamemnon has dishonoured me [*êtimêsen*]' (1.356; cf. 1.412; 1.244: Agamemnon 'failed to honour the best of the Achaeans'). To Agamemnon, he declares: 'Call me a coward, a no-account, if I ever again submit to anything you say' (1.293–4). And when Agamemnon sends an embassy to Achilles' tent, offering to compensate Achilles with boundless gifts, Achilles' final word is: 'My heart swells with anger when I recall those things, how Agamemnon treated me shamefully before the Achaeans as if I were some vagabond without honour' (9.646–8).

Achilles returns to battle after he learns that Patroclus has been slain by Hector; he will not rest or take food until he has killed Hector in return. What motivates his hostility in this portion of the epic? One of the sections (7.3) in Oliver Taplin's fine study of the *Iliad* is entitled 'Anger Displaces Anger' (1992: 193; the section runs from p. 193 to p. 202). Taplin argues that Achilles' rage after the death of Patroclus remains unchanged in substance, but is transfered from one object to another.[25] Taplin opens his discussion with a citation of Achilles' address to his mother in *Iliad* 18.94–126, in which Achilles, stricken with grief at the loss of his friend, utters the wish that strife (*eris*) might perish among gods and mortals, and also *kholos*, or anger, which, Achilles says, 'is far sweeter than dripping honey in the breasts of men'; so it was, he says, when Agamemnon, lord of men, angered him just now (*eme nun ekholôsen*, 107–11). Taplin comments on this passionate plea (199): 'In sum, Achilleus renounces all the ἔρις (*eris*) and χόλος (*cholos*) which have pervaded the *Iliad* since its very beginning ... Thus, half-way through a speech, the passions of book 1 are renounced: the *mênis* poem is over.' Taplin continues (199–200): 'When Achilleus turns his attention to Hektor in 114ff., he shows no awareness that what has happened is not that he has given up *eris* and *cholos* altogether, but that Hektor has replaced Agamemnon as his target. The timing of this realization by the audience may vary; but there will be no shortage of *eris* and *cholos*, verbal and physical, in books 20 to 22. There are verbal signals even sooner,' Taplin concludes (citing 18.337 and 19.116).

Hector has done Achilles, and the Achaeans generally, great harm, as Achilles himself acknowledges. At the moment of his triumph over Hector, when he is at his most savage and has wished aloud that he might be capable of devouring Hector's body for what he has done to him (22.346–7), he recognizes his stature as a warrior who has damaged the Greek side more than all the other Trojans combined (22.378–80). Achilles has every motive for hating his opponent. But if anger is, as Aristotle defines it, a response not to injury but to insult, and more particularly to dishonour or belittlement, in what sense has Hector provoked this emotion in Achilles? True, Achilles taunts the dying Hector for having forgotten, when he slew Patroclus, that a greater spearman remained behind (22.331–5). But we can hardly conclude from this that Hector's act was a sign of contempt for Achilles. Warriors slaughter whom they can.[26]

Was Aristotle wrong, then, about the motives for anger, when he restricted them to a narrow range that belies the ample and complex character of the emotion? Of course, the term that Aristotle subjected to analysis, as I have mentioned, was *orgê*, not the Homeric *kholos* (*orgê* does not appear in archaic epic); we have no more reason, a priori, for assuming that *orgê* and *kholos* coincide in meaning that we do for assuming that one or both coincide with the English term 'anger' (cf. Harris 2001: 51: 'It would be extremely perilous to assume that there was one constant meaning that was attached to *cholos* or to *orgê* or to *ira* in all ages'). Nevertheless, I believe that Aristotle's discussion is in fact illuminating for the interpretation of the *Iliad*, and that Achilles does respond differently to Agamemnon's affront and to the pain that Hector inflicts on him.

Contrary to what Taplin suggests, there are in fact no references to Achilles' *kholos* in books 20 to 22 of the *Iliad*, and indeed only one in the last five books, apart from a single occurrence that looks back to the original quarrel between him and Agamemnon (*kekholômenos Atreïôni*, 24.395).[27] Moreover, when Achilles 'turns his attention to Hector,' in his speech to his mother, he does not mention his own anger. He simply declares that he will return to battle in order to slay Hector, and with that he is prepared to accept whatever Zeus and the other gods have in store for him – for his mother has just told him that Hector's death is the prelude to his own (18.96). Not even Hercules, he observes, escaped his fate, but destiny and the anger of Hera conquered him. Here the word *kholos* does indeed occur (18.119), but as frequently in the *Iliad*, the subject of the emotion is a god, and the gods – especially Zeus and Hera – are notoriously sensitive when it comes to human overachievers and other obstacles to their ambitions, which they tend to treat as personal affronts.

It is not that Homer rigorously eschews the word *kholos* in connection with Achilles' feelings concerning Hector, subsequent to his reconciliation with Agamemnon in book 18 and his ostensible renunciation of anger. Homer is neither a philosopher nor a pedant, and the use of emotion terms in Greek cannot be neatly circumscribed any more than it can be in English or any other language. Thus, Achilles' grief for Patroclus is compared to that of a lion whose cubs have been stolen by a deerhunter; a 'bitter *kholos* seizes him' – that is, the lion – as he searches for the tracks of the man (18.322). It may be that the lion feels insulted that a mere deersman should have injured him, and that by treachery rather than in open combat.[28] But the adjective 'bitter' (*drimus*) suggests the root meaning of *kholos* as 'bile' (compare 'choleric' and 'melancholy'), and as applied to an animal the term apparently signifies violent fury, irrespective of whether it is provoked by harm or scorn (for *drimus* used of *kholos*, cf. Hippocrates *Airs, Waters, Places* 10). So too, in the single use of the term in book 22, Hector's determination (*menos*, 22.96) to face Achilles is compared to the *kholos* (94) that seeps into a snake as it lies in wait (*menêisi*), munching its own poison. Hector himself is not described as angry; but then he is afraid of Achilles, and anger, according to Aristotle, is incompatible with fear.

Achilles, however, does feel anger. He decides to sacrifice twelve Trojan youths on the pyre of Patroclus, so enraged is he that Patroclus has been slain (*sethen ktamenoio kholôtheis*, 18.337); this is the same formula that recurs at 23.23, which is the only time in the final five books of the poem in which *kholos* over Patroclus's death is ascribed to Achilles.[29] Achilles' passion here evidently derives from his pain at the loss of his friend (and guilt, perhaps, over his failure to bring him home, 326–7); it is not said to be directed specifically at Hector, although he has just vowed to kill him for what he has done (334–5). Be that as it may, Zeus, in his earlier prophecy of Patroclus's (and Sarpedon's) death, explicitly asserts that Achilles will slay Hector because of his anger over Patroclus (*tou de kholôsamenos ktenei Hectora dios Akhilleus*, 15.68), and in the battle round the body of Patroclus, before Achilles has learned the news of his friend's death, Menelaus doubts that Achilles, without armour, can join the fighting, 'angry though he may be at godlike Hector' (*mala per kekholômenon Hektori diôi*, 17.710).

These third-person descriptions of his motives do not prevent Achilles from repeating a second time, in book 19, that he has desisted in his anger towards Agamemnon, and that it is wrong 'to rage forever' (*aiei meneainemen*, 19.67–8) – and this moments after we are told that '*kholos* seeps into him' (19.16) at the sight of his new armour. The word 'seeps' (*edu*), used also of the snake's *kholos* in book 23, again suggests something like raw battle fury, I think, rather than the focused anger aroused by an insult or personal offence.[30]

And yet, I believe that Aristotle's analysis of *orgê* points the way to a different, and perhaps richer, appreciation of the emotional dynamics of the epic. I should like to maintain that there does occur a shift in the poem from anger on Achilles' part, which was provoked by Agamemnon's arrogance and disdain for his best fighter, to a desire for retaliation against Hector that responds rather to the pain that Hector has caused him. Despite a couple of references to Achilles' *kholos* against Hector, the poet insists on the harm – *kaka* and similar expressions – that Hector has done to Achilles and the Greeks generally as the motive for Achilles' revenge. What is more, anger as a motive for combat is explicitly disparaged after Achilles 'renounces all the ἔρις (*eris*) and χόλος (*cholos*) which have pervaded the *Iliad* since its very beginning' (Taplin). When Achilles, after his return to combat, meets Aeneas on the battlefield in book 20, he taunts Aeneas, in the martial repartee known as 'flyting,' with his inferior status in the royal line of Troy. Aeneas responds by reciting his lineage, and then reminds Achilles that such wrangling is for women, 'who get angry over some quarrel [*eris*] that eats their hearts out and go out into the middle of the street to hurl abuse at one another, whether true or not; for their anger drives them to it' (20.253–5). Men, however, decide their conflicts not with words, says Aeneas, but with steel, or rather bronze (257; cf. Harris 2001: 28).

There is more than one kind of pain in the *Iliad*. Achilles experiences both the resentment induced by an undeserved slight – that is, Aristotle's *orgê*, the epic name for which is *kholos* – and the fury unleashed by the death of his dearest comrade, in the heat of which his earlier anger withers. There is no exact term in Homer for the latter sentiment. Sometimes *kholos* serves, as we have seen, but it does not capture the grim duty to the deceased and appreciation of the opponent's valour that mark Achilles' return to battle, and it falls short too of defining the demonic, 'berserker' violence of Achilles' peak moment or *aristeia*. Achilles is right to say that he has abandoned *kholos* in the ordinary sense after the death of Patroclus. 'Anger' is too weak a term, or the wrong term, for the emotion that displaces it. When Achilles declares that, despite the way Agamemnon angered him (*ekholôsen*, 18.111), he is prepared to repress the fury in his breast (*thumon eni stêthessi philon damasantes*, 18.113 = 19.66) and go forth against Hector for slaying his dearest friend, the scholia – marginal notes in the manuscripts that preserve the comments of ancient critics – observe: 'of the two emotions besetting Achilles' soul, anger [*orgê*] and grief [*lupê*], one wins out ... For the emotion involving Patroclus is strongest of all, and so it is necessary to abandon his wrath [*mênis*] and avenge himself on his enemies' (schol. bT ad *Il.* 18.112–13). The scholia have got it right. Perhaps they were composed under the influence of Aristotle's analysis of anger as resulting from a slight, rather than harm as such, but if so, it only confirms the value of taking Aristotle's view into account.[31]

At the end of book 9 of the *Iliad* – the 'Embassy' to Achilles – Ajax makes a final attempt to assuage Achilles' wrath and bring him back to battle:

But Achilles, cruel as he is, harbours in his breast an arrogant temper [*thumos*], nor does he care about the love of his companions, we who honoured him beyond all others by the ships. Pitiless! And yet a man accepts compensation [*poinê*] for the murder of a brother or a child who has died, and the murderer remains among his people when he has paid handsomely, while the heart and proud temper of the other are appeased, when he has accepted the compensation. But the gods have placed in your breast an implacable and evil temper for the sake of a single girl. But here we are offering you seven outstanding girls and much else besides: adopt a sympathetic temper. (9.628–39)

To this, Achilles famously replies:

Ajax, son of Telamon, descended of Zeus, ruler of peoples, all that you have said seems to me in accord with your [or my] temper. But my heart swells with *kholos* when I recall those things, how the son of Atreus treated me as a fool in front of the Achaeans as if I were a vagabond without honour. But go and report this message: I shall not turn my thoughts to bloody war until divine Hector, the son of wise Priam, arrives at the tents and ships of the Myrmidons as he slaughters the Achaeans. (9.644–53)

In a recent book on ransom and revenge in the *Iliad* (2002), Donna Wilson attempts to resolve the apparent inconsistency between Achilles' words here and subsequent passages in which he suggests that he might have returned to battle sooner if Agamemnon had treated him more decently (11.609–10, 16.71–3, 84–6). Wilson solves the dilemma by distinguishing (7–10) between the terms *poinê* and *apoina*, 'penalty' and 'ransom': 'Although Achilleus feels he is owed *poinê* for the seizure of Briseis, Agamemnon offers him *apoina*. Accordingly, Achilleus in Books 11 and 16 can legitimately discount the previous offer, since Agamemnon's gifts are inevitably unacceptable in form and function' (10). Ajax, for his part, 'misses the point of the quarrel. He fails, moreover, to account adequately for Achilleus' singular demand: the life for which Achilleus seeks to secure *poinê* is his own' (106).[32] I agree with Wilson that Ajax misunderstands the reasons why Achilles remains uncompromising in his anger at Agamemnon, but it seems to me that her explanation is mistaken. Ajax supposes that the issue between Achilles and Agamemnon is the seizure of the girl Briseis, and in this respect comparable, though lesser in degree, to the loss of a relative through violence. Such aggression may be resolved, as Ajax says, by means of suitable compensation. Achilles does not deny that this is so. Rather, he distinguishes an attack that deprives a man of someone dear to him from the humiliation he has suffered at the hands of Agamemnon, which is the source of his anger. The latter requires, as Aristotle explains, that the offender be aware of and feel in return the kind of mortification that provoked the anger in the first place: it is not simply a matter of compensation. Ajax's analogy is thus irrelevant to Achilles' anger, insofar as it was produced by a slight and not by mere harm to himself or a dear one. But it corresponds perfectly to the pain that Achilles experiences upon the death of Patroclus, and thus anticipates the finale of the *Iliad*, when Achilles will in fact accept a ransom for the body of Hector: Hector has not insulted Achilles and hence is not the object of his *kholos* in the same way that Agamemnon is. As the scholia put it (ad 9.646–7), Achilles 'again recalls Agamemnon's *hubris*, indicating that he indeed would like to yield, but the magnitude of the *hubris* does not permit it.'[33]

In rejecting Ajax's argument from compensation in cases of homicide, Achilles is not claiming that the anger he harbours is too great for such a solution. He is indicating rather that Ajax has offered examples of harm, while his own anger is a response to an intolerable slight. Harm causes pain, grief, even perhaps a kind of rage, but not anger in the Aristotelian sense – nor, I would say, in the Homeric sense. It really is the case that, in book 18, 'the *mênis* poem is over,' as Taplin puts it; from here on, it is about revenge for another kind of injury, and the emotion that drives it is different as well.

A slight, as we have seen, consists according to Aristotle in the active belief that another person is of no account. The response to such an act is to restore the opinion of one's worth by an act of reprisal (getting even [*antipoiein*] itself is not arrogance but requital, and hence does not necessarily invite further acts of revenge: *Rhetoric* 2.2, 1378b25–6). Anger is just the desire to restore the state of affairs prior to the insult by depreciating the offender in turn. Not every slight inspires anger, however, on Aristotle's view, but only those 'on the part of people who are not fit to slight one or one's own.' Who, then, is fit to belittle another? It is time to return to this proviso in Aristotle's definition of anger.

For Aristotle, what counts as belittlement depends on status: if your position is inferior, it is no insult to be reminded of it. Like many other Greeks of his time, Aristotle is intensely conscious of rank and social role. One may speak to a slave in ways that would constitute an intolerable affront if one were addressing a fellow citizen. Slaves are not in a position to take offence, but must be careful to appease their masters' anger by humbling themselves, confessing that they are at fault, and not talking back (*Rhetoric* 2.3, 1380a15–18): back-talk, indeed, constitutes a slight, and hence exacerbates the master's ire, since slaves who speak up in their own defence presume to treat the master as an equal. Such attitudes are so deep seated that they seem to correspond to natural uses of language; thus, the grammarian Demetrius, in his treatment of forceful expression or *deinotês* in his essay *On Style*, observes almost in passing (7): 'Giving orders is succinct and terse, and every master is monosyllabic to his slave, whereas supplication and lamentation go on at length.'[34] If Achilles really had been 'some vagabond without honour,' he could not have been angry at the way Agamemnon treated him.[35]

Since anger is defined as a desire for revenge, moreover, Aristotle concludes that anger can only arise where revenge is possible: 'No one gets angry at someone when it is impossible to achieve revenge, and with those who are far superior in power than themselves people get angry either not at all or less so' (*Rhetoric* 2.2, 1370b13–15).[36] To take one example among many, in the first book of the *Iliad* the priest Chryses and his patron god Apollo react very differently to Agamemnon's refusal to free Chryses' daughter (this episode triggers the quarrel between Agamemnon and Achilles). Chryses pleads and offers a ransom; when he is threatened and harshly dismissed, he obeys in fear, although he suffers inwardly (*Iliad* 1.33–4). He appeals to Apollo to take revenge in his behalf (42), but is not said to experience anger in his own right. Apollo, however, is 'angry in his heart' (*khôomenos kêr*, 44) and immediately punishes the Greeks for this slight to his divinity; he is, of course, entirely capable of doing so.

As a test case for differential responses to insult as a function of social roles and power, let us consider the nature of women's anger. Women may, of course, bicker among themselves, as Aeneas observes to Achilles; so too can slaves. But could women experience anger at their husbands or fathers, men whose authority over them was, if not equal to that of a master over a slave, nevertheless tantamount to that of an aristocratic ruler, in Aristotle's analogy (*Nicomachean Ethics* 8.10, 1160b32–3)?

Women do not constitute a homogeneous group, and their actual power will vary according to their class or wealth; Aristotle observes, for example, that heiresses may exercise an undue domination over their husbands. In order to explore the world of women's anger, I examine two works from the Athenian tragic stage that offer contrasting paradigms of a marital crisis.

Euripides' *Medea* is unforgettable for the savage vengeance that the heroine takes upon her husband Jason for deserting her in order to marry the daughter of Creon, the king of Corinth, where he and Medea find themselves in exile. Medea's anger is highlighted at the beginning of the play when her nurse, who speaks the prologue, reveals her fear that Medea may harm her own children: 'Fierce is the temper of tyrants, and though they start small, because their power is great they curtail their anger with difficulty' (119–21; cf. the chorus's comment at 176–7). These are the words of a slave who recognizes that wrath is the prerogative of the mighty. Jason too denounces Medea's savage anger, which he reproves as an uncontrollable evil (446–7; cf. *kholos*, 590). He claims that he has attempted to assuage the anger of the Corinthian royal house against her (455–6), and he advises Medea to give over her anger for her own good (615). At least in regard to their children, Jason appears to have been as good as his word, since the messenger who reports the deaths of Creon and his daughter, incinerated by Medea's poisoned gifts, describes how Jason first allayed the princess's anger and irritation (*orgas ... kai kholon*, 1150) towards them. Like the nurse, Jason sees anger as the right of kings, and he rebukes Medea for harbouring a sentiment that is incompatible with her humble situation as a foreign woman in a distant land. Like a slave's anger, Medea's can only lead to trouble.[37]

Medea has, we may believe, every reason to be upset, and Jason's excuses for contracting a politically advantageous alliance may seem mere sophisms, given the oaths he swore when she gave up everything to save his skin in Colchis. But Medea smarts particularly for what she sees as Jason's disdain for her. 'Go on, insult me!' (*hubrize*, 603), she tells him, and throughout the play she is concerned to laugh in triumph over her enemies rather than the reverse (cf. 383, 404, 797, 1049, 1162, 1355). Medea is not just hurt and fearful, she is humiliated and dishonoured (*ētimasmenê*, 20; cf. 33, 417, 438, 696). She is herself a princess, and Jason, an exile like her, is not fit to slight her.

But anger, according to Aristotle, requires not just pride but power. Contrary to Jason's warning, Medea can afford to be angry because she is capable of revenge. In the event, she murders Creon and his daughter, and leaves Jason childless but alive to savour his loss – which is just what anger seeks, says Aristotle. For her part, Medea escapes safely to Athens in an airborne chariot, courtesy of her grandfather, the Sun God: 'You were not about to lead a pleasant life after dishonouring my bed,' she gloats (1354–5). One should know better than to slight a woman like her.[38]

I have neglected, so far, to discuss one passage in the play that casts a different light on women's anger. In order to allay Jason's suspicions concerning her plans for revenge, Medea asks him to forgive her former anger, out of respect for the love they had for each other (869–71). Jason magnanimously consents, letting slip the patronizing platitude that it is natural for females to work up anger (*eikos gar orgas thêlu poieisthai genos*, 909; the following two lines, which are suspect, indicate that this is particularly so when their husbands decide to marry another woman). How does this disposition to anger on women's part square with their ostensible lack of power relative to men?

Aristotle holds that the emotions, including anger, are natural and necessary; a person who fails to respond angrily to a slight is not so much tolerant as stupid and servile (*Nicomachean Ethics* 1126a4–8). But too quick a temper is as much a fault as no temper at all, and Aristotle takes irascibility to be a sign of moral incontinence and vacillation (*NE* 1103b19). The inability to govern one's passions bespeaks softness and a lack of self-control, and this, in popular ethics as well as in Aristotle, was imagined to be characteristic of women (cf. *NE* 1145b12–14, 1150b14–16; Plutarch *On Controlling Anger* 8, 457A–B, on women's greater disposition to anger as a consequence of their weaker natures; Harris 2001: 264–74). Thus, while some people, Aristotle says, approve of a fierce temper as a masculine trait and a qualification for ruling others (*NE* 1226b1–2), it may also be seen as an unstable and effeminate quality, as the term *malakos* or 'soft,' which Aristotle employs here, suggests.[39]

Such contradictions are inherent in any world view that ascribes essential psychological differences to human beings on the basis of gender, race, or other traits. If women display anger despite their powerlessness, it must reflect an infantile inability to control themselves, which proves that they are unfit to rule and so justifies their socially subordinate position.[40] The irony is that

Jason is wrong, and he will pay dearly for his mistake. For Medea is able to avenge the slight, as her anger testifies, which is grounded not in petty jealousy but in a proud sense of honour.

In Sophocles' *Women of Trachis*, Hercules, enamoured of the princess Iole, destroys her city, takes the girl captive, and brings her home to Trachis, where he intends to instal her in his house alongside his legitimate wife Dejanira. At first, Dejanira is deceived about her husband's purpose by a herald who seeks to soften the news, and she is moved to pity the proud young captive who has been sent on ahead. However, she soon learns the truth, and in despair at losing Hercules' love sends him a tunic dipped in what she believes is a love potion, but in reality is a fatal poison that causes the death of the hero. Dejanira first recognizes the possibility of her error when she observes the corrosive effect of the toxin on a piece of cotton, once it is exposed to sunlight, and she is understandably distraught. The chorus submit that 'anger is gentle toward those who slip up involuntarily,' but Dejanira replies: 'One cannot say so who is party to the evil, only if nothing weighs on you at home' (727–30). At this point, enter Hyllus, the son of Hercules and Dejanira, furious at his mother. Only later, after Dejanira has slain herself, does Hyllus learn that her act was unintentional, and that he drove her to suicide 'on account of his anger' (*kat'orgên*, 932–5).[41]

It is understandable that Dejanira fears Hercules' anger, given what she has done (at 1036, Hercules says she rendered him furious [*ekholôsen*] with pain). But why is she at no point angry at him for bringing another woman into her home? Her situation is not so different from Medea's. Both women were won in combat, after a fashion; both were brought to live in a foreign city; both discover that their husband has preferred another woman (and a younger one). Indeed, both respond by sending a poisoned garment, which in the one case destroys the rival princess and her father, in the other the offending spouse. To be sure, the deed was involuntary on Dejanira's part, whereas it was deliberate on Medea's.[42] But why was it involuntary for Dejanira?

One can, of course, reply that that is how the stories go. Euripides portrays a proud woman's vengeance, Sophocles a timid but desperate wife who accidentally destroys the man whose love she sought to rekindle. From the beginning of the play, Dejanira is represented as good but naive. She is carried off by Hercules after he defeats the river god Achelous in a wrestling match, and from that time on she has worried loyally during his long absences, although she feels, she says, like a remote pasture that the farmer has ploughed but once (27–33). Unlike Medea, Dejanira never speaks of dishonour. She knows that Hercules has had adulterous affairs (459–62), but she accepts it passively: 'It is not decent [kalon] for a sensible woman to be angry,' she affirms (552–3).[43] Or, with Aristotle: 'No one gets angry at someone when it is impossible to achieve revenge, and with those who are far superior in power than themselves people get angry either not at all or less so.' With Hercules all-powerful and Dejanira all too vulnerable, he is not of the class of people who are 'not fit to slight' her.

It is true that the personalities of Euripides' and Sophocles' heroines are different; so too are their resources. I am suggesting that these two circumstances are not wholly independent. The capacity for anger depends on status, and where power is unevenly distributed between men and women, anger will be similarly asymmetrical. Medea is the exception, a proud princess and a sorceress, and for just this reason her anger is represented as monstrous. By deliberately murdering her own children, she exhibits the danger of feminine anger. The initial conditions, so to speak, of the two tragedies determine whether and by whom anger can be expressed and acted on. Aristotle's analysis enables us to see how it works.[44]

If the wife of Hercules is not in a position to feel anger at the behaviour of her husband, what will have been the reaction of people who have been conquered in war and are consequently without hope of resisting or avenging the actions of the victors? Euripides composed several tragedies concerning the plight of women in the aftermath of the Trojan War, when the men of the city had been massacred and the women and children were on the point of being distributed as slaves among the Greek leaders. Below, I examine Greek attitudes towards the mass annihilation of defeated populations, and the emotions that drove or permitted such brutality on the part of the conquerors (cf. also chapter 9, pp. 194–8). Here, however, I should like to focus on the anger, or absence of anger, on the part of the vanquished, in the light of Aristotle's understanding of the close connection between anger and the power to exact revenge.

Euripides' *Hecuba* is a study in the suffering of a queen reduced to servitude. The embers of what was Troy are still smouldering, her husband has been slain, and she awaits news of who her new master will be. In the course of the play, she becomes aware of two further losses that augment her anguish. First, the Greek army decides to sacrifice her young daughter Polyxena to the ghost of Achilles; and later she learns that the body of her son Polydorus, whose safety she had entrusted to an allied king, has washed up on shore, the boy having been treacherously murdered by the very man who was supposed to protect him in the event of Troy's capture. Hecuba responds differently, however, to each of the disasters. She argues vigorously against the slaughter of Polyxena when Odysseus declares the will of the Greeks, but in the end resigns herself, as she must, to the event; her submission is in part eased because Polyxena herself, with regal pride, accepts her death as preferable to a life of slavery. When Polymestor, the Thracian king who slew her son, comes to Troy together with his young sons, Hecuba succeeds, with the help of the other Trojan women, in avenging the crime by killing the children and blinding the unsuspecting father, who was unaware that his perfidy had come to light. What is more, she defends her action before Agamemnon, the leader of the Greek host, and gains his verdict in her favour (1243–51). In what respects do Hecuba's sentiments differ in regard to the two bereavements?

One line of interpretation of the tragedy has been to see Hecuba as the victim of a cumulative sequence of ordeals that ultimately reduce her to near-savage viciousness, symbolized by the prophecy uttered by the blind Polymestor of her metamorphosis into a howling dog (1270–3; cf. Nussbaum 1986: 397–421). Thus, William Arrowsmith, in the introduction to his widely read translation of the play (1958: 3–4), writes:

[T]he figure of the suffering Hecuba loosely presides, giving at least the feel of unity to the various episodes as they occur.[45] Carefully, if not elaborately, her progress, from grief to despair, toward the final atrocity is traced under the rhythm of the descending blows, each one heavier than the last; but the emphasis is not so much on the psychology of the change within Hecuba as the way in which, confronted by her tormentors, she is forced to yield, one by one, her values, her self-respect, and the faith which makes her human.

Alternatively, the cruelty of Hecuba's retaliation against Poly-mestor has been understood to be motivated in part by her re-pressed hostility towards the Greeks: she takes it out on the Thracian king because he is the only available target, but the intensity of her vengeance is redoubled by her displaced rage against Odysseus and the rest for the murder of Polyxena. But while the deaths of Polyxena and of Polydorus are both sources of agony for Hecuba, they are not equivalent in their moral significance, and might thus be expected to elicit different emotional responses on the Greeks', or at all events Aristotle's, view of the passions.

In reply to Hecuba's desperate plea for her daughter's life, in which she proposes, among other things, that if a woman must be sacrificed, then Helen would be a more appropriate victim than Polyxena, Odysseus cautions her not to let passion (*to thumoumenon*) mislead her into considering him an enemy (299–300). Hecuba appeals to Odysseus's pity, and reminds him of his debt to her for having concealed his identity when he was spying inside Troy, thereby saving his life. Against this, Odysseus advances pragmatic reasons of state for honouring military heroes; besides, speaking ghosts have intrinsic authority (no one in the play doubts that Achilles really appeared from the grave). Polyxena, in turn, beseeches Odysseus to be considerate of a mother's passionate feelings (*thumoomai*), while to her mother she pleads, 'Do not, poor woman, fight against those in power' (402–4). Polyxena recognizes that Hecuba is in no position to rage against the victorious Greek army, do what they will (*thumos* and its cognates in this period sometimes approximate the idea of anger). She is free only to lament, not to seek reprisal, and avenging Polyxena's death does not cross Hecuba's mind in the play.

The case is entirely different with respect to Polymestor. Hecuba is intent on avenging the deaths of her children (she uses the plural, 749–50); she would, she says, gladly remain a slave her whole life for the sake of vengeance (756–7; cf. 882). In appealing to Agamemnon to be partner to the retaliation (789–90, 842–3), Hecuba insists on the wrong that Polymestor has done her, violating the laws of guest friendship that are sustained by the gods: 'We ourselves are slaves, and weak no doubt; but the gods are strong as is the law that governs them' (798–800). Though Agamemnon hesitates to take action against an ally of the Greeks, he nevertheless agrees that Polymestor deserves punishment (852–3). What is more, Hecuba and the other women are capable of exacting it on their own, if only Agamemnon will give them passive cover (870–5); with superior numbers and cunning they can defeat a man (884), says Hecuba (she adduces in evidence the stories of the Danaids and the Lemnian women). Later, she gloats over having made Polymestor pay the penalty (*dikên de moi dedôke*, 1052–3), as he emerges raging (*thumoomai*) from the tent where she and the other women took out his eyes and killed his sons. When Agamemnon sees what has happened to him, he declares: 'Miserable Polymestor, who has destroyed you, who has blinded your eyes and bloodied the pupils, and slain these your sons? Whoever it was bore a fierce anger [*kholos*] toward you and your children' (1116–19), thus acknowledging the close connection beween anger and revenge. Towards the end of the tragedy, when Polymestor groans aloud at the loss of his children and his eyes, Hecuba exclaims: 'You are in pain? What then, do you think I felt no pain for my son?' 'You rejoice in your arrogant abuse [*hubris*] of me, you criminal,' Polymestor shoots back, to which Hecuba replies: 'And should I not rejoice at avenging myself on you?' (1255–8). Getting even, as Aristotle says, is not arrogance but requital.

The Greeks have harmed Hecuba, but they have not wronged or slighted her. They treat her harshly, but she is a slave, no longer a queen. The Greeks owe nothing to Hecuba: they have conquered her city, and their power over her is complete. She thus has no motive for anger – slaves, as Aristotle says, must rather take care to appease their masters – nor is she in a position even to imagine exacting vengeance. If, as Aristotle stipulates, anger is just a desire for revenge, and one only desires what is possible, then on these grounds too Hecuba cannot be angry. As both Odysseus and Polyxena herself remind the miserable queen, there is no place for passionate fury. This is not subversive irony on Euripides' part, as most commentators on the play have supposed (e.g., Mossman 1995: 56): Odysseus's counsel is grim but practical (cf. Konstan 1997a).

The situation is entirely different with the murder of Polydorus. Polymestor was a friend and ally of the Trojan royal family, and has betrayed their trust. Hecuba is justifiably outraged, as Agamemnon acknowledges; what is more, she finds herself in a position to retaliate, despite the fact that she is a woman and a slave. All the conditions for anger are thus realized. As for the awful act of slaying Polymestor's children while leaving him sightless but alive to experience his anguish, this is just what Aristotle affirms to be the objective of anger, as distinct from enmity: revenge for an insult, as opposed to harm as such, demands that the offender suffer in return the pain that he or she has inflicted. The same intention was evident in Medea's vengeance upon Jason.

In her study of *Hecuba* as a revenge tragedy, Judith Mossman (1995: 207) argues that 'the Polyxena-action must be seen as subordinate to, but contributing to the effect of, the revenge plot,' although the symmetry of the two episodes 'encourages us to contrast Hecuba's reaction to Polyxena's death with her response to her discovery of Polydorus.' The contrast, I would add, is the clearer if we consider Hecuba's sentiments and behaviour from a Greek perspective on the emotions, using Aristotle as our guide: anger consists in a realizable desire for revenge; the unique stimulus to anger is a slight on the part of those not fit to slight one or one's own. The first movement of the play is a study in loss and grief; here, the response of Hecuba and the other Trojan women is lamentation. The second movement, however, centres on anger and retaliation. Of course, Euripides' portrait of Hecuba's emotional state is far richer and more nuanced than the schematic difference I have outlined (this is my sop to critics who abhor reductionism). But as with the *Iliad*, so too with Euripides' *Hecuba*, a sensitivity to the specific character of anger in Greek culture helps us to discriminate motives that are less transparently distinct to us than to them. Hecuba is not just subjected to a series of 'descending blows, each one heavier than the last'; rather, she suffers helplessly in the first major movement of the play, and successfully avenges the acknowledged wrong she has endured in the second. Two situations, two responses: part of the power of Euripides' tragedy is that each movement is brilliantly articulated according to its own moral and emotional logic.

Having relied implicitly so far on Aristotle's analysis of anger, or rather *orgê*, as a guide to the sense of the concept in classical Greek generally, I must now enter a caveat: important as Aristotle's discussion in the *Rhetoric* is for an understanding of ancient anger, there is nevertheless reason to believe that his specification of a slight as the only cause of anger is too narrow, and fails to cover the range of stimuli recognized in contemporary litera-ture.[46] For example, William Fortenbaugh observes (2002: 117) that '[f]rom Stobaeus and Seneca, we learn that Theophrastus conceived of anger as a desire for revenge on account of injus-tice.'[47] Theophrastus was Aristotle's successor as head of the Lyceum, and he might have wished to correct Aristotle's account by enlarging the scope of the emotion. The passages themselves, however, do not indicate a sharp difference of view. The citation preserved by Stobaeus (a late Greek excerptor) runs:

Wise people ought to do nothing in anger [*orgê*]. For temper [*thumos*] is irrational, and never acts with forethought, but rather, intoxicated by contentiousness, acts randomly and on impulse. Therefore you must not take revenge at once on mistakes [*hamartêmata*], whether of slaves or others, so that you may always do what looks best to reason and not what is dear to temper. Thus you will not cause grief to yourself in harming others. For to avenge oneself by harming oneself is to pay a penalty as much as to exact one. Therefore one must seek to defend oneself at leisure rather than chastise one's enemy swiftly but without profit to oneself.

Theophrastus's main object here is to discourage taking action in a fit of passion (cf. *On the Senses* 45, where Theophrastus com-pares an angry person's judgment to that of a child); there is no reason to think that Aristotle would disagree.

Seneca, as a Stoic, takes a hard line against anger (*On Anger* 1.12.2–5):

A good man will carry out his duties clearheaded and unafraid ... My father will be killed? I shall defend him; he has been killed? I shall carry out [my duties][48] because I ought to, not because I am grieving. 'Good men are angry for injuries done to their dear ones [*irascuntur boni uiri pro suorum iniuriis*].' When you say this, Theophrastus, you look to cast scorn on more powerful principles and turn away from the judge in order to play to the crowd. Since everyone gets angry when a misfortune of this kind befalls their own, you imagine that people will judge that what they do should be done, since all people pretty much judge an emotion they recognize to be justified. But they act the same if hot water is not adequately supplied, if a glass is broken, if their shoe is splashed with mud. It is not filial piety but weakness that inspires such anger, just like children who weep equally whether they lose their parents or their toys. To be angry in behalf of dear ones is the mark not of a dutiful soul but a weak one.

Theophrastus's 'injuries' do not seem to be confined to slights, but to include harm generally, thus encroaching on the kind of acts that, for Aristotle, generate hatred or hostility rather than anger. But Theophrastus was undoubtedly thinking of undeserved offences, which is what the Latin word *iniuria* normally connotes. A little further on, Seneca reports (3.14.1): '"It cannot happen," Theophrastus says, "that a good man does not grow angry at evils [or at evil men: *malis*]."'

The Stoic Chrysippus, however, explicitly described *orgê* as 'the desire to take vengeance against one who is believed to have committed a wrong contrary to one's deserts.'[49] As Harris (2001: 61) observes, '"Injustice" has replaced "slight."'[50] And yet, Aristotle himself had already asserted that 'anger resides in a perceived injustice [*adikia*]' (*Nicomachean Ethics* 5.8, 1135b25–9; cf. n. 18 above).

Anger at injustice is, moroever, a fundamental theme in the speeches of Athenian pleaders in the fifth and fourth centuries BC. Jurors and citizens are again and again invited to feel anger for a wrong committed against another party, irrespective of direct harm or insult to themselves. In an oration by Lysias, for example, the plaintiff admonishes the jurors (15.9):

And if any one of you, gentlemen of the jury, thinks that the penalty is great and the law too harsh, you must recall that you have not come here as lawmakers on these matters, but rather to vote according to the established laws, nor to pity those who do wrong, but rather to be angry with them and to come to the aid of the entire city.

The opposition between pity and anger here is revealing.[51] Elsewhere, Lysias puts into the mouth of a defendant (1.28) 'I believe you know that those who do not act justly do not acknowledge that their enemies are telling the truth, but rather, by lying and scheming in this way, they instil in the wrongdoers anger against those who do act justly' (cf. 21.21, 32.19). Clearly, anger is rightly directed against genuine malefactors. Another speaker in Lysias (6.17) affirms: 'This man has been far more impious than Diagoras the Melian [famous for his atheism]. For Diagoras was impious in words concerning other people's rites and festivals, while this man was so in deeds and concerning matters in his own city. It is right then, Athenians, to be more angry at citizens who do wrong than at foreigners in these things.' The historian Thucydides sums it up (1.77.4): 'It seems that men are more angry when they are wronged than when they suffer violence' (cf. 5.46.5).

Demosthenes fulminates against a law that will result in the jurors seeming to 'take their oath, impose penalties, pronounce their verdicts, grow angry, and do all that they do in vain' (24.90). Demosthenes comments specifically on the usefulness of civic anger against the unjust, since people are then likely to be more careful about unlawful behaviour (24.143). Indeed, the term *orgê* may be used in a way that is virtually equivalent to a negative verdict or condemnation, as when Demosthenes says that the laws authorize the jury to utilize anger that is proportionate to the offence (24.118; cf. 24.218, 25.6).[52] As Danielle Allen (1999: 194) observes: 'The Athenians had no doubts about why they punished: it was simply because someone was *angry* at a wrong and wanted to have that anger dealt with.'[53]

Litigants were wary, of course, of seeming to disdain members of a democratic jury, who were generally of humble station. Socrates, in Plato's *Apology* (35B–C), professes to fear that his failure to appeal to the jury's pity may be taken as a sign of arrogance, with the result that the jurors will condemn him in anger (met' orgês). In Aristophanes' Wasps (243, 404, 424, 646, 727, 1083), the jurors are fiercely proud of their disposition to anger; since they belong to the poorest class of citizens, we may suppose that they are at least in part motivated by a sensitivity to slights. Aristophanes himself boasts (1030) of having an anger like that of Hercules, thanks to which he has stood up squarely to opponents like Cleon (MacDowell glosses orgê here as spirit or courage; cf. Peace 752, Lysistrata 550 and 1113). But anger against malefactors was not restricted to reactions to personal affronts, unless we maintain – with a certain plausibility – that any offence against the law was ipso facto regarded as a disparagement of the dêmos or civic body.

Anger may also be a response simply to personal harm. Thus, Demosthenes (8.57) speaks to the Athenians of 'the anger that it was natural that you feel if you were hurt in the war' (cf. 16.19, 19.302). Thucydides represents the Spartan Archidamus as cautioning that 'orgê besets all those who perceive with their own eyes and right before them that they are enduring something unpleasant [aêthes]' (2.11.6). One might suppose that Achilles' response to the slaying of Patroclus was this sort of anger, but in the orators, at all events, there is always the implication that the source of anger is unfair mischief, and not damage as such, and this seems the prevailing conception.

If indeed orgê was frequently a response not just to a slight but to an unjust act, why did Aristotle fail to mention this in his analysis of anger in the Rhetoric (we have seen that he acknowledges it in the Nicomachean Ethics)? The reason, I believe, is that he appropriated this dimension of orgê for another emotion, which he elevated to the status of a primary pathos. I am referring to the term nemesan, or 'be indignant.' I discuss why Aristotle introduced this concept among his basic emotions, and allowed it to encroach in this fashion on the territory of anger, in the chapter devoted to indignation and envy. Here, it may suffice to note that anger at unjust behaviour and anger at a slight both look to maintaining a proper relationship among the members of the city-state society. Both involve moral judgments, as opposed to reactions to impersonal events. You can no more grow angry at an object for violating the law than you can for its having deliberately insulted you.

Anger was perceived to have a negative side. It is an impatient emotion, and leads to precipitous action. Demosthenes comments: 'It is the part of angry people to do some harm swiftly to the one who has hurt them, but of those who have been wronged to avenge themselves when they have the wrong-doer in custody' (24.175). Appealing to the courts rather than relying on individual vengeance is a sign that one is able to control one's anger and respond not just to the personal affront but to the offence against the law. This is not to say that the desire for vengeance is abandoned; rather, it is pursued by different means. Anger might also distort deliberation, whether in the courtroom or the assembly. Antiphon, in his speech on the murder of Herodes (72), writes: 'There is no one who judges well when angry. For it corrupts that very thing by which one deliberates, that is, a person's judgment [gnômê]. It is a large task, gentlemen, as days go by to free one's judgment from anger and find the truth of what happened.' Aristotle himself worried about this problem in the opening chapter of the *Rhetoric*, where he remarked that 'one ought not to warp a juror by leading him to anger or envy or pity' (1354a24–5).[54] It was a view the Stoics would develop with characteristic rigour and consistency, as part of their attack on the passions generally. Thus, the Stoic philosopher Chrysippus (third century BC) affirmed that 'anger is blind; it often prevents our seeing things that are obvious and it often gets in the way of things which are <already> being comprehended ... For the passions, once they have started, drive out reasoning and contrary evidence, and push forward violently towards actions contrary to reason' (Plutarch *On Moral Virtue* 10, 450C = *SVF* 3.390; quoted in Harris 2001: 370).

The volatile nature of anger made it particularly problematic in war. Thucydides (2.11.4) cites the warning of Archidamus, the Spartan king, that 'events in wars are unpredictable: many things result from a small cause and undertakings are based on anger.' He explains (2.11.6–8) that when the Athenians see the Spartans ravaging their land, they will be overcome by anger, 'and will employ reason minimally and passion (*thumos*) maximally,' and so will fail to fight effectively. So too Diodotus observes in his speech opposing the slaughter of the Mytilenaeans (3.42.1): 'I believe that two things are most opposed to good counsel, haste and anger, of which the one tends to be accompanied by thoughtlessness, the other by amateurishness and snap judgment.'[55] Xenophon, in his continuation of Thucydides' history called the *Hellenica* (5.3.5–6), describes a scene in which a general leads his troops against a city in a fit of rage (*orgistheis*), with the result that he himself is slain and his men massacred. Xenophon draws the lesson (5.3.7) that masters ought not even to punish slaves in anger, and that by doing so they frequently suffer more harm than they inflict; indeed, 'to attack opponents in anger and without intelligence [*gnômê*] is a complete mistake, for anger is without forethought, but intelligence looks as much to avoiding harm to oneself as to doing harm to one's enemies.'

Aristotle does not dwell, in the *Rhetoric*, on the adverse consequences of acting under the influence of anger, although he was well aware of them. When he comes to examine the virtues in the *Nicomachean Ethics* (2.8, 1117a5–15), he observes that 'when human beings are angry, they feel pain, and when they avenge themselves, they feel pleasure; those who fight for such reasons are warlike, yes, but they are not courageous: for they do so not for the sake of what is good or in the manner dictated by reason [*logos*], but rather out of emotion [*pathos*].'[56] So too, he includes anger among the forms of wickedness (*mokhthêriai*), along with self-indulgence (*akolasia*) and cowardice, that are responsible for unjust actions (*adikêmata*) – in the case of anger, for example, striking another person. I imagine that Aristotle is thinking here rather of a disposition to excessive anger (what he calls *orgilotês*, or irascibility, 4.5, 1125b29), but it is revealing that the bare term *orgê* can carry such a negative connotation.[57]

There is one military context in which anger is invoked as a legitimate motive, and that is in the treatment of the inhabitants of conquered cities. It is a commonplace that, in ancient Greece, those who were vanquished in war were wholly at the mercy of the victors, and that there were no constraints, apart from spontaneous pity or calculated self-interest, that prevented the conquerors from annihilating or enslaving the entire population.[58] While this was by no means always the price of defeat, it was common enough that it stood as a real possibility in the minds of the warring parties. The Athenians voted angrily (*hupo orgês*, Thucydides 3.36.2) for the extermination of the men and enslavement of the women and children of Mytilene, an allied city during the Peloponnesian War, after putting down a revolt there, and changed their minds just in time to prevent the massacre (only a thousand ringleaders were put to death: Thucydides 3.36–49; for the Athenians' angry reaction to defiance on the part of a weaker foe, cf. 4.123.2–3). The Thebans and Corinthians urged a similar reprisal against Athens itself after its defeat in the war, and the city was only spared thanks to the opposition of the Spartans (Xenophon *Hellenica* 2.2.19–20). Isocrates, in his *Panegyric* to Athens (181), observes of the Trojan War that 'because of the seizure of one woman, all Greeks grew so enraged on behalf of those who were wronged [i.e., Menelaus and Agamemnon] that they did not cease from making war until they had utterly laid waste the city of the man who had dared to offend against them.'

Polybius, writing in the second century BC, describes how Antigonus Doson of Macedon destroyed the city of Mantinea and sold the population into slavery. He explains that when the Mantineans went over to the Spartans, they slit the throats of the Achaeans in their midst, in violation, Polybius says, of the laws common to mankind. They thus deserved any amount of anger (2.58.8), and indeed there was no way they could have paid a sufficient penalty. Towards the end of the Second Punic War (201 BC), when Scipio had already crossed into Africa and Carthage had sued for peace, a Roman supply convoy was driven ashore by a storm and impounded by the Carthaginians. Scipio was infuriated, Polybius relates (15.1.2), by this treacherous behaviour even more than by the material loss, and sent envoys to demand the restitution of the ships and their cargo. The Carthaginians dismissed the envoys, and subsequently ambushed their ship as it approached the Roman camp. In response to this double breach of faith, Scipio decided no longer to take under his protection even cities that voluntarily surrendered, but rather enslaved their populations, thereby manifesting the anger (*orgê*) he bore towards the enemy as a result of the Carthaginians' perfidy (15.4.2).

Treachery on the part of an enemy can be interpreted as a sign of contempt, and hence a motive for Aristotelian anger in the narrow sense: why else would one flagrantly violate a truce and the prevailing rules of warfare, unless one thought the enemy too weak or cowardly to avenge such insolence? In any case, anger and the desire for revenge that is intrinsic to it were deemed to constitute an appropriate response to a betrayal of trust in the classical Greek world.[59]

In the cases mentioned above, the decision to eradicate a conquered population does not derive from a judgment of its indelibly vicious nature, but from a particular violation of good faith. The Greeks of the classical period were prone to vaunt their superiority over barbarians, and some thinkers, like Aristotle, held that non-Greeks were by nature suited to servitude (*Politics* 1.2, 1252a31–4). But while attacks on foreign cities and villages were sometimes motivated by a desire to take captives along with other forms of wealth, the Greeks did not typically seek justification for such violence in the evil character of the people: self-interest and the right of the victor sufficed for that. When there was some doubt or debate over whether to annihilate a city, however, it was anger at the enemy's guilt – not the demonization of the 'other' – that provided the motive, or the excuse, to do so.

A vicious feature of this way of justifying mass slaughter is precisely the connection with juridical practice, in which anger on the part of jurors was understood to be a legitimate response to wrongdoing. As a result, the Greeks were less inclined than we are to invoke legal norms as a check on military violence. The speaker who, according to Thucydides, argued for a more lenient policy towards Mytilene, by which the city would be spared complete annihilation, sought precisely to change the issue from one of justice, by which standard the Mytilenaeans might be said to deserve the harsher fate, to one of political advantage, where he could maintain that a milder policy would encourage other rebellious states to surrender rather than fight to the bitter end (Thucydides 3.44.4; cf. Aristotle *Rhetoric* 1.3, 1358b20–9; Konstan 2001a: 80–3; and below, chapter 10, p. 205). There was thus no place from which to condemn the immorality of extermination as a violation of rights; it was in effect simply a large-scale instance of capital punishment, likewise motivated by indignation and an impulse for revenge.

The world implied by Aristotle's account of anger is hierarchical, consisting of people who are superior or inferior in regard to strength, wealth, or status. The point of *hubris*, for example, is to demonstrate one's superiority to another; hence, it is characteristic of the rich and also of young people (2.2, 1378b28), who presumably are physically strong and at the same time need to prove themselves. This is why people who have doubts about themselves, in regard to looks or occupation or whatever they take seriously, are particularly prone to anger, while those who are confident that they excel (*huperekhein*) are not (*Rhetoric* 2.2, 1379a36–b2). People who really do excel, however, whether by virtue of family, power, wealth, or indeed a particular skill such as oratory (which is joined closely here to the ability to govern), expect deference (*poluôreisthai*) from their lessers (*hêttones*) on account of their superiority (2.2, 1378b34–9a6), and are especially likely to become angry if they suffer a slight instead. So too we tend to be angry at those who oppose us, if they are our inferiors, or do not repay us in kind, as though we were their inferiors, and above all at a slight received from people of no account (*en mêdeni logôi*), for, as Aristotle says, 'we have assumed that anger over a slight is directed to those who ought not [*mê prosêkontes*] to do so, and inferiors ought not to slight [their betters]' (2.2, 1379b11–13).

We might describe the social situations in which anger is triggered or allayed in Aristotle's account as informed by an acute sense of honour, with its intense regard for status, protocols of conduct, and the opinion of others – Aristotle specifies, for example, that we are more disposed to anger when a slight is delivered in the presence of those with whom we compete, those whom we admire or wish to be admired by, or those before whom we feel shame or who feel shame before us (2.2, 1379b24–6). Aristotle himself says that disrespect (*atimia*) is a part of *hubris*, and that to dishonour (*atimazôn*) a person is to slight him, for what is worthless has no value (*timê*), whether for good or ill (2.2, 1378b29–31).[60] He cites in illustration Achilles' resentment against Agamemnon: 'He dishonoured me,' and 'treated me as a fool in front of the Achaeans as if I were a vagabond without honour [*atimêtos*]' (*Iliad* 1.356, 9.648, etc.). The allusion to Homer suggests, I think, that the use of the word *timê* in the context of slights and anger may have had a poetic ring, since in prose usage the term referred primarily to political rights and offices or to economic value. But honour captures well the extreme sensitivity that Aristotle reports towards offences against one's dignity and esteem in the eyes of one's fellow-citizens, provided that we do not assimilate the idea to the complex of honour and shame that has become popular in so-called Mediterranean anthropology in the past two or three decades, with its particular emphasis on the need to control the sexual comportment of the women in one's family. Athenian literature of the classical period offers little evidence of an obsessive preoccupation with dishonour in this narrow sense of defilement.[61]

Although the cause of anger is a slight on the part of someone who ought not to have rendered it, such as an inferior or a friend or beneficiary who might be expected to have a thought for one's dignity, Aristotle recognizes that there are certain states in which we are more or less disposed to be sensitive to such affronts, irrespective of their source.[62] When we are enjoying ourselves at a party or feeling particularly prosperous, we are not inclined to anger (2.3, 1380b2–5). Contrariwise, we are more irritable when we are suffering (*lupoumenos*, 2.2, 1379a11) because of something we want and lack, and are particularly prone to anger towards those who obstruct the fulfilment of our desire, as when we are thirsty, sick, poor, in love, and so forth. It may be that our condition of want exposes us the more to insult, just to the extent that a person fails to respect our need,[63] but it is important to distinguish between the suffering that results from lack, as in thirst, ill health, poverty, and the like, and the pain that accompanies anger. Pain of one kind makes us more susceptible, perhaps, to feeling pain of another, but the two have different causes in this case, and are not the same pain.[64]

Anger for Aristotle, then, is anything but a reflex to pain or harm, even when the cause is intentional. Aristotle envisages a world in which self-esteem depends on social interaction: the moment someone's negative opinion of your worth is actualized publicly in the form of a slight, you have lost credit, and the only recourse is a compensatory act that restores your social position. Anger is precisely the desire to adjust the record in this way.

Discussions of anger in the Hellenistic age and later typically stress the need to control or eliminate it.[65] Such advice is usually addressed to people in power, and is concerned with 'the great wrath of kings nurtured by Zeus,' as Aristotle puts it (2.2, 1379a4–5), citing a verse of Homer's *Iliad* (2.196). For such a public of princes and noblemen, it was important to advise restraint; anger, in particular, could vent itself in destructive rages against people helpless to resist.[66]

This is not the implied audience of Aristotle's treatise on rhetoric. Aristotle was writing for potential orators before the assembly and above all in the courts, which were at their most active and popular in the fourth century. While defendants and prosecutors in the courts may have come mainly from the wealthier classes, the jurors were ordinary citizens, and predominantly poor, as Aristophanes' *Wasps* indicates. These were not people whose anger reflected the caprices of omnipotence: they were far more likely to suffer an indignity than inflict one, and it was their emotions that the aspiring orator had to manipulate. They lived in a democracy, of course, but it was a democracy in which one had to maintain at every turn one's dignity and status. Equality resulted not just from political rights but from continual and universal vigilance to protect one's reputation and economic position. Every public interaction was a scene of potential gains, losses, and settlings of accounts; an insult was a put-down, and one was obliged to get even. Jon Elster (1999a: 75) deftly characterizes the social world implied by Aristotle's description of the emotions as 'intensely confrontational, intensely competitive, and intensely public; in fact, much of it involves confrontations and competitions before a public. It is a world in which everybody knows that they are constantly being judged, nobody hides that they are acting like judges, and nobody hides that they seek to be judged positively. It is a world with very little hypocrisy, or "emotional tact."'[67] In this volatile environment, in which equality was an ideal but never a given, and had constantly to be asserted and defended if the image of a society of equals or similars was to be maintained, anger was obligatory, 'insofar as the individual citizen who was sensitive to his honor and guarded it with anger was also guarding his personal independence, greatness, and equality' (D. Allen 2000: 129).[68]

But it was not precisely our anger. As Catherine Lutz has observed (1988: 8):

The process of coming to understand the emotional lives of people in different cultures can be seen first and foremost as a problem of translation. What must be translated are the meanings of the emotion words spoken in everyday conversation, of the emotionally imbued events of everyday life, of tears and other gestures, and of audience reaction to emotional performance. The interpretive task, then, is not primarily to fathom somehow 'what they are feeling' inside ... but rather to translate emotional communications from one idiom, context, language, or sociohistorical mode of understanding into another.

The *orgê* of the Greeks, like anger today, was conditioned by the social world in which it operated. It is the task of the philologist to help reveal its lineaments.

CHAPTER THREE

Satisfaction

It is revealing that the word for self-esteem in Japanese is *serufu esutiimu*. There is no indigenous term that captures the concept of feeling good about oneself.

Nisbett 2003: 54

The definition of the emotions that Aristotle gives in his *Rhetoric* runs, as we have seen, as follows: 'Let the emotions be all those things on account of which people change and differ in regard to their judgments, and upon which attend pain and pleasure, for example anger, pity, fear, and all other such things and their opposites' (2.1, 1378a20–3). The opposite of an emotion, it would appear, is itself an emotion, rather than, say, the absence of that emotion.[1] Having begun his analysis of the several emotions in the *Rhetoric* with anger or *orgê*, Aristotle in fact proceeds immediately to discuss the *pathos* that he designates as the opposite of anger. Commentators and translators seem agreed in rendering this passion, which Aristotle calls *praotês*, as 'calmness,' 'calming down,' or the equivalent. But in what sense is calmness an emotion? Has Aristotle been misled into designating calmness an emotion by his habit, common to the ancient Greeks generally, of thinking in polar contrasts?[2] In this chapter, after reviewing earlier interpretations, I argue that the relevant emotion is – or at least should be – the elation or positive disposition consequent upon a compliment or other gesture that results in an enhanced opinion of a person's worth. Such a belief may be activated when an angry person is appeased, and this is the case with which Aristotle is chiefly concerned: hence the association with calming down. But, I suggest, *praotês* need not be restricted to this scenario. In the course of the discussion, I consider too the place of positive evaluations of worth, or self-esteem, in classical Greek thought, and how it might have played a role in the constitution of an emotion.

Here is how Aristotle introduces the new *pathos* that is to be the opposite of *orgê* (I have for the moment transliterated, rather than translated, the Greek word *praotês* and related forms, since their meaning is precisely what is in question):

Since being angry [*to orgizesthai*] is the opposite of *to praünesthai*, and *orgê* the opposite of *praotês*, we must now consider in what state people are *praoi*, and towards whom they are *praoi*, and by means of what they become *praoi* [*praünontai*]. Let, then, *praünsis* be a settling down and quieting of *orgê*. If, then, people are angry at those who slight them, and a slight is a voluntary thing, it is clear that people are *praoi* in turn towards those who do no such thing or do such things involuntarily or who seem to be such. (2.3, 1380a6–12)

What, then, does *praos* (plural *praoi*, the adjective corresponding to the abstract noun *praotês*) mean in this context?

As I have indicated, commentators and translators more or less universally take the term to mean something like 'calm' or 'tranquil.' Thus, W. Rhys Roberts (1984), in the Bollingen translation of the complete works of Aristotle, renders the above passage as follows (the italics in the following versions are mine, intended to highlight the relevant terms): 'Since *growing calm* is the opposite of growing angry, and *calmness* the opposite of anger, we must ascertain in what frames of mind men are *calm*, towards whom they feel *calm*, and by what means they are made so. *Growing calm* may be defined as a settling down or quieting of anger,' and so on. So too, in a recent Portuguese translation by Isis Borges da Fonseca (2000), the chapter on *praotês* is entitled 'Da Calma,' and the opening phrases are rendered: 'Como estar *calmo* é o contrário de estar encolerizado, e a cólera se contrapõe à *calma*, deve-se examinar em que estado de ânimo as pessoas são *calmas*,' etc.

Franz Sieveke (1980: 91) translates the beginning thus: 'Da nun die Erregung des Zornes der *Besänftigung* entgegengesetzt ist und der Zorn der *Sanftmut*,' etc. Antonio Tovar (1953: 101) provides as a title for the section 'De la calma o serenidad,' and renders the opening: 'Puesto que a enojarse es contrario *aplacarse* y la ira es contraria de la *calma*, corresponde tratar en qué disposición están los *no airados* y respecto de quiénes lo son y por qué causa.' H.C. Lawson-Tancred, in the Penguin translation (1991: 147), has: 'Now since being angry is the opposite of *being calm*, and anger the opposite of *calmness*, we must grasp in what condition men are calm,' etc., and continues a little further: '*Let calming, then, be a suspension or placation of anger*' (emphasis in original). To take one more example from an older translation, Adolf Stahr offers (1862: 125): 'Das Zürnen ist der *milden Stimmung* und der Zorn der *Milde* entgegengesetzt,' etc.

Edward Cope, in his seminal commentary on the *Rhetoric* (1877), introduces the section under discussion with the words 'Analysis of *praotês*, patience,' and remarks that '*praotês* then, here, as a *pathos* – in the Ethics it is a *hexis* or virtue – is this instinctive *affection*, feeling, emotion, in a mild, calm, subdued state (opposed to *orgê* an emotion in a state of excitement); placidity of temper' (32). Most recently, George Kennedy (1991) entitles the chapter under discussion '*Praotês*, or Calmness,' and translates: 'Since becoming calm is the opposite of becoming angry, and anger the opposite of calmness ...,' etc.

Calmness, however, or mildness, gentleness, patience, good temper, to cite the list of equivalents provided by Grimaldi (1988) in his epigraph to this chapter, is problematic as an emotion. Kennedy (1991: 130), in his headnote on *praotês*, defends its status as a *pathos* by disputing the rendering as 'calmness,' despite his own translation:

Aristotle regards *praotês* as the emotion opposite to anger. It is often translated 'mildness,' which seems rather a trait of character or absence of an emotion, while Aristotle views it as a positive attitude toward others and experience, involving an emotional change toward a tolerant understanding: in colloquial English, 'calming down' is perhaps the closest translation, but there is no single English word that quite captures the meaning. The appearance of mildness, gentleness, patience, tractability, good temper are all aspects of it.

The variety of terms to which Kennedy resorts reflects his honest recognition that 'calming down' will not do in a good many of the illustrations of *praotês* that Aristotle provides; but even if it did fit more or most of them, it is not clear that the process of becoming calm is a *pathos* in Aristotle's sense of the term, any more than the process of growing angry is one, as opposed to anger or *orgê*. As we saw in the previous chapter, Aristotle defines *orgê* as 'a desire, accompanied by pain, for a perceived revenge' (for the rest of the definition, see below); this scarcely describes 'an emotional change.'

Cope states the case against *praotês* as an emotion most clearly in his final comments on the section, and it is worth citing his words *in extenso* (1877: 42):

I have already hinted a doubt in the notes on the preceding chapter whether *praotês* is properly ranked amongst the *pathê*. I think that it can be made plainly to appear that it is not. It is introduced no doubt for the purpose of giving the opposite side to the topics of anger, because the student of Rhetoric is in every case required to be acquainted with both sides of a question. And this purpose it may answer very well without being a real opposite of *orgê* or indeed a *pathos* at all. If we compare *praotês* with the other *pathê* analysed in this second book, we find that it differs from all of them in this respect – that the rest are emotions, instinctive and *active*, and tend to some positive result; wheareas *praotês* is inactive and leads to nothing but the allaying, subduing, lowering, of the angry passion ... It seems plain therefore that it is in reality, what it is stated to be in the Ethics, a *hexis*, not a *pathos*, of the *temper* ... It is accordingly represented in the Ethics as a virtue, the mean between irascibility and insensibility ... The true *pathos* is the *orgê*, the instinctive capacity of angry feeling.

Over a century later, however, Grimaldi, in his commentary (1988: 49), sees no difficulty in taking mildness as the opposite of anger, and, as an opposite, identifying it as an emotion: '[I]ts opposition is of the same character as the opposition found between pity and indignation, fear and confidence, shame and shamelessness, kindness and unkindness ... The opposition A. speaks about in all the above is contrary opposition, i.e., two positive terms denoting extremes of difference within the same genus.'³

Now, calmness, insofar as it is the negation or elimination of anger, is in fact not comparable to the opposition between pity and indignation, on which Aristotle particularly insists. As we shall see in more detail in later chapters, Aristotle defines 'being indignant' (*to nemesan*) as 'feeling pain at someone who appears to be succeeding undeservedly' (*Rhetoric* 2.9, 1837a8–9). Pity, in turn, is defined as 'a kind of pain in the case of an apparent destructive or painful harm in one not deserving to encounter it, which one might expect oneself, or one of one's own, to suffer, and this when it seems near' (2.8, 1835b13–16). Reduced to basics, the contrast is between pain at undeserved good fortune and pain at undeserved misfortune (2.9, 1386b9–12). Both emotions, Aristotle specifies, are characteristic of good men, since people ought not to fare ill or well undeservingly. Aristotle notes, however, that some take *phthonos*, commonly rendered as 'envy,' as the opposite of pity, on the view that *phthonos* 'is related to and is indeed the same thing as *to nemesan*' (2.9, 1386b16–17). The Stoics, indeed, characterized pity simply as pain at another's ill fortune, and envy as pain at another's good fortune (e.g., Andronicus *On the Emotions* 2 p. 12 Kreuttner = *SVF* 3.414; cf. Cicero *Tusculan Disputations* 3.21 and *On the Orator* 1.185, 2.206, 2.216). But in fact, Aristotle says, they are different: although *phthonos* too is 'a disturbing pain arising from the well-being' of another (2.9, 1386b18–19; cf. 2.10, 1387b22–4), it arises not because the other person is undeserving, but simply because he is our equal or similar (2.9, 1386b19–20), and yet has gained an advantage over us.

Whether we take indignation or envy as the opposite of pity, each member of the opposed pair has an independent definition; neither is described simply as the absence or abatement of pity. They are incompatible with pity because the eliciting circumstances are mutually exclusive: someone is either suffering or prospering, not both simultaneously. So too of the contrast between fear and confidence or *tharros*. Fear, according to Aristotle, is 'a kind of pain or disturbance deriving from an impression [*phantasia*] of a future evil that is destructive or painful' (2.5,

1382a21–3), whereas confidence arises when there is hope accompanied by an impression of imminent safety, and frightening things are either non-existent or remote. The things that inspire confidence (ta tharralea) also include the prospect of amelioration and assistance, and the knowledge that one has neither wronged another nor been wronged, and that any rivals we may have are either weak or friendly, or that we have more or stronger allies on our side (2.5, 1383a16–25). Here again, the contrasting emotions are conceived as responses to opposite kinds of stimuli: fear is aroused by things that portend harm, whereas confidence derives from what presages security. Of course, these are normally mutually exclusive, but while the absence of what is frightening is a condition for confidence, confidence is not simply reducible to the suspension of fear (people with no experience of danger are 'emotionless' [apatheis, 1383a28] in the sense, presumably, that they are not given to fear). The case of love and hatred, to which we shall return below, is also analogous to these.

Neither kindness nor unkindness is an emotion for Aristotle; the section (2.7) of Aristotle's Rhetoric in question, as we shall see (chapter 7), in fact treats rather gratitude (kharin ekhein) and ingratitude (akharistia) for a favour rendered. Here, indeed, it may be doubted whether Aristotle thinks of thanklessness as a full-fledged emotion. Rendering people ungrateful (akharistoi) involves convincing them that the service they received was not a genuine favour (2.7, 1385a33–b2), and depends essentially on negative arguments. Aristotle does not describe a set of graceless acts that would elicit the contrary of gratitude, although one could perhaps fill out Aristotle's account by suggesting that a positive feeling of ingratitude is aroused by a false or pretended service that was in fact undertaken for selfish reasons. Again, Aristotle seems to treat shamelessness simply as the absence of shame: 'Let shame be a pain or disturbance concerning bad things that appear to lead to a loss of reputation [adoxia] ..., while shamelessness is a contempt [oligôria] and indifference [apatheia] concerning these same things' (2.7, 1383b12–15). Aristotle goes on to indicate in some detail the kinds of circumstances that induce shame, and then concludes briskly (2.7, 1385a14–15): 'So much for shame; as for shamelessness, clearly we can deal with it on the basis of what is opposite.'

Once more, it is possible to imagine an opposite emotion to shame that has a more positive content: if shame results from the kinds of evils that bring about infamy, its contrary might be a *pathos* resulting from those goods that are conducive to a superior reputation or *doxa* (nothing prevents there being more than one opposite to a given term: cf. *Topics* 2.7, 113a14–15: 'It is clear from what has been said that there may be several opposites to a single thing'). In this case, one might label the emotion opposite to shame pride, as do some modern theorists of the emotions (e.g., Nathanson 1992: 86; cf. M. Lewis 2000; Ben-Ze'ev 2000: 491, 512; and Manstead and Fischer 2001: 231; and see below, chapter 4, p. 100). Why Aristotle does not include a discussion of pride or self-satisfaction among the *pathê* he examines in the *Rhetoric* is a separate question, which will be considered in the chapter devoted to shame. His discussion of *anaiskhuntia* or shamelessness, at all events, is meagre and negative.

Aristotle's account of *praotês*, however, is neither. On the contrary, *praotês* on its own receives more discussion than gratitude and ingratitude combined, and more than is devoted to some other major passions such as envy and emulation (*zêlos*). Granted, Aristotle begins by considering ways to counter anger by redescribing the nature of the offence that has aroused it. Anger, for Aristotle, is, as we have seen (chapter 2), a response to a slight or put-down (*oligôria*), and only that; as he defines it, *orgê* is 'a desire, accompanied by pain, for a perceived revenge, on account of a perceived slight on the part of people who are not fit to slight one or one's own' (2.2, 1378a31–3). This is, as I remarked in the chapter on anger, a very restricted conception of the stimulus to anger, not only in comparison with the range of 'anger' in English but even in relation to Greek usage of the term *orgê*, which was understood, as Aristotle himself notes in the *Nicomachean Ethics* (5.8, 1135b25–9), as a response also to injustice. Nevertheless, it is clearly the view that Aristotle adopts in the *Rhetoric*, and the relevant one for interpreting his notion of *praotês*. Thus, among the strategies for diminishing or eliminating anger that Aristotle mentions is demonstrating that a supposed slight was not such in fact, by showing, for example, that it was involuntary or unintended. Alternatively, one may argue that the agent of an ostensible slight says or does the same things in respect to him- or herself ('for no one is believed to slight himself,' 2.3, 1380a13–14), or make it clear that the offending party has confessed and is sorry, which undoes the social effect of the belittlement. The tactic is not dissimilar to that which Aristotle recommends in regard to diminishing gratitude by redescribing the nature of the service in such a way as to show that it was selfishly motivated, unintentional, or the like, and hence not a true favour (see chapter 7). Aristotle goes on to say that we are *praoi* towards those who humble themselves before us and do not contradict us, for by this 'they are seen to concede that they are our inferiors, and those who are inferior feel fear, and no one who feels fear offers a slight' (2.3, 1380a23–4). The context here is perhaps ambiguous: is Aristotle referring to apologetic behaviour subsequent to some ostensible belittlement, in which the self-abasement of the offender is designed to prove that no offence could have been intended? Or does he mean that a humble attitude elicits *praotês* in general, irrespective of whether there has been an offence? Probably the former, since Aristotle adds that anger is allayed towards those who humble themselves, citing in evidence the fact that dogs do not bite those who sit down, though perhaps here one is not obliged to think of an abatement of a prior belligerence.

But Aristotle then affirms that people who are serious or eager about something are *praoi* towards those who are similarly disposed, for they believe that they themselves are being taken seriously and not being treated with contempt (2.3, 1380a26–7); this does not obviously refer to a case in which an offender exhibits some form of contrition, but rather to respectful comportment in and of itself. So too, we are *praoi* towards those who have obliged us, or begged and pleaded with us, since they are humbler; or again, towards those who are never arrogant or insulting towards people like ourselves (2.3, 1380a27–31). In these instances, we are *praoi* just because of the consideration, or rather the deference, of others, and not necessarily because of some supposed appeasement. *Praotês*, it would appear, is elicited by reverence or other admiring or self-abasing signals on the part of others that elevate our standing or esteem.[4]

Such an account of *praotês* is not wholly surprising in the context of Aristotle's analysis of anger. If anger is a response to a slight, as Aristotle holds, and if, moreover, a slight is the activation (or activity) of a belief or *doxa* about a thing's seeming to be worthless (2.2, 1378b11), then the opposite of anger should, or at least could, be a response to the activation of a *doxa* about a thing's (or a person's) seeming to be of great value. *Praotês*, then, might be defined as 'a desire, accompanied by pleasure, to treat someone kindly, on account of a perceived gesture of respect.' It would derive from the sense of an increase in one's status or *doxa*, as opposed to its diminishment, as in the case of *orgê*. As an emotion, we might perhaps think of it as the disposition to do a service for another that results from praise or some other act that enhances a belief in one's worth.

A *pathos* of this sort as the opposite of anger would be the counterpart to pride as the opposite of shame: a positive emotion deriving from an amelioration of one's reputation or status (see chapter 4 below). The difference between the two would be analogous to that between anger (*orgê*) and shame itself (*aiskhunê*): the one is triggered by a deliberate insult, the other by an evil or misfortune. *Praotês* would differ also from affection or *philia*, which Aristotle treats next in order, in the same way that anger differs from hatred or *misos*. Affection, as defined in the *Rhetoric*, consists in wishing good things for another's sake and acting, to the best of one's ability, to obtain them for the other (2.4, 1380b35–81a1). It is an altruistic emotion, stimulated by an appreciation of the other's character (or charm or usefulness), rather than by his or her obsequiousness or signs of admiration or regard. *Praotês* thus occupies a distinct niche in Aristotle's system of the *pathê* (once we appreciate that the subject of section 2.7 of the *Rhetoric* is gratitude rather than benevolence, it is clear that there is little overlap between it and *praotês* either).

At this point in his exposition of *praotês*, Aristotle reaffirms that 'in general, one must investigate what things make us *praoi* [*ta praünonta*] on the basis of their opposites' (2.3, 1380a31), that is, by contrast with the things that are conducive to anger,[5] and he proceeds to enumerate the kinds of people with whom we are disinclined to grow angry, for example, those we fear or before whom we feel ashamed, or those who feel shame before us, as well as the states of mind in which we are prone to *praotês*, such as when we are at play or are successful or have recently avenged ourselves on someone else. Nor do we get angry, Aristotle says, at those who are ignorant or insensible of our revenge, such as the dead (the orator is being advised, I presume, to show that the object of a jury's anger is beyond the reach of vengeance). Aristotle concludes by reasserting that to render people *praoi* (*katapraünein*) one must make those with whom they are angry appear frightening or deserving of their shame or ingratiating (*kekharismenoi*) or unwilling or remorseful in regard to what was done (1380b31–4).

Clearly, Aristotle's focus is on anger, and his treatment of *praotês* is largely conceived as a means of checking anger in others. A show of deference can have that effect, but so too can a menacing posture: as Aristotle says, 'It is impossible to be frightened and angry at the same time' (2.3, 1380a33–4). The primacy of anger is not surprising in a treatise on rhetoric, since this was the emotion that pleaders chiefly sought to arouse against their opponents, just as they solicited the pity of the jurors for themselves and their clients. As Danielle Allen puts it (2000: 148), 'The language of anger and pity defined the contours of the competition between prosecutor and defendant' (cf., e.g., Lysias 32.19, Demosthenes 21.127). Allen adds: 'Other emotional concepts could be used to flesh out the core ideas of "anger" and of "pity" in the process of trying to establish desert. The ideologies of hate, envy, and fear ... could be grafted onto the ideology of anger' (149). But anger, or rather *orgê*, was crucial, and speakers naturally tried to direct it away from themselves in the same measure as they attempted to elicit pity for their side. Hence, the importance of techniques of anger management.

Aristotle himself, as Cope points out, offers a different account of *praotês* in the *Nicomachean Ethics*, where it is treated as the mean between the excess of *orgilotês* or irascibility and the deficiency of *aorgêsia*, an 'absence of anger' or insensibility to insult (2.7, 1108a4–9; 4.5, 1125b26–26b10), although, in fact, Aristotle concedes, the mean state has not a proper name of its own, and Aristotle imports *praotês* as something of a makeshift (1125b27–8); he also affirms that *praotês* is closer to the deficiency than the excess, and hence may serve as anger's opposite. In these contexts, where Aristotle is speaking also of such mean states as courage (*andreia*), liberality (*eleutheriotês*), and high-mindedness (*megalopsukhia*), *praotês* assumes the character of a disposition rather than a *pathos*: 'The person who is *praos* tends to be unperturbed and is not led by emotion but rather as reason directs' (1125b33–5). So too, in the *Topics* (4.5, 125b20–7) Aristotle asserts that one must not classify a disposition (*hexis*) under the genus represented by a capacity (*dunamis*), and gives as examples of this error the subsuming of *praotês* under the category of mastering anger, or courage under the mastery of fears: 'for a courageous or *praos* person is called emotionless [*apathês*], whereas one who has mastery does experience [*paskhein*] the emotion but is not led by it.' Aristotle adds that if a courageous or *praos* person were to experience the relevant *pathos* (fear and anger, respctively), he would likely not be dominated by it. However, this is not what is meant by being courageous or *praos*, but rather being entirely insensible with respect to such things, that is, to fear or anger.

An emotion or *pathos* for Aristotle, however, is always a response to some stimulus, not simply a trait of character: the very term *pathos*, as we have seen (chapter 1, p. 3), is related to *paskhô*, 'suffer' or 'experience.' Insofar as *praotês* may be conceived of as an emotion, accordingly, it must occur in reaction to some external impetus, just as anger arises in response to a slight. As we noted in the discussion of anger, Aristotle's system of the emotions is particularly attentive to status and to the everyday social interactions that subtend and modify it. Fear, shame, pity and indignation, emulousness and envy all centre on the individual's relative position or reputation in society. Anger, in particular, had a key function in this environment. If anger was a response to a loss of face or *doxa* as the result of an affront, then *praotês* as an emotion was elicited by behaviour that enhanced public respect and esteem.

Even fear as a cause of *praotês* has a place, perhaps, in Aristotle's conception of 'calmness' as an emotion. Not every slight, as we have seen, results in anger. Aristotle specifies in his definition of *orgê* that it arises 'on account of a perceived slight on the part of people who are not fit to slight one or one's own.' People do not necessarily react with anger when they are slighted by those who are stronger or better placed in society, in part because of fear. Thus, if one can demonstrate that the author of an ostensible impertinence is of a class superior to your own, then your status will not have been damaged, since it was already inferior, and the emotion of *praotês* – the sense of being conciliated in respect to an imagined attack on one's status – ensues.

Aristotle's account of *praotês* as an emotion is not wholly free of contradiction. He sometimes speaks as though *praotês* were simply the absence or abatement of *orgê*, a neutral state of calm free of pain or pleasure and not a *pathos* in its own right. In this regard Aristotle was in accord with contemporary usage. Jacqueline de Romilly (1974: 100) notes that *praotês* enjoyed a particular vogue in the fourth century BC, and adds that it would eventually 'lead to Polybian *philanthropia* and to Roman *clementia.*' Indeed, Demosthenes and others had already associated the word *praos* with *philanthrôpos* ('humane') and *epieikês* ('decent,' 'fair') as indicating a patient and gentle disposition (e.g. Demosthenes 8.33), not a sentiment elicited by mollification or regard. Does Aristotle's account of *praotês* as an emotion (as I have recon-structed it), that is, as a wish (accompanied by pleasure) to treat kindly those who have shown one deference or respect, find confirmation in the literature of his time? Is there, indeed, any evidence that such a *pathos* – an emotion of proud elation in response to a gesture of obsequiousness or respect – for which Aristotle appropriated the term *praotês* in the *Rhetoric*, was recognized at all (perhaps identified by other words)?

Such evidence as there is is exiguous. In the sixth oration in the corpus of Lysias, the speaker argues that Andocides, who had been accused of sacrilege and has surrendered himself to the verdict of the court, is now behaving like a citizen with full rights, 'as though it were not because of your *praotês* and want of time that he has not paid the penalty you set' (34). *Praotês* here could well mean 'gentleness,' as Stephen Todd (2000: 71) renders it. But the author might also be intimating that the Athenians have re-sponded to Andocides' implicit humility and for that reason have adopted a generous attitude towards him. In another speech dubi-ously attributed to Lysias (20.21), the speaker notes that some of the guilty have fled, while fear has induced others not to remain in Athens but rather to serve as soldiers, 'so that they might render you more *praoi* or influence these men [i.e., the prosecutors].' The speaker adds that Polystratus, the defendant, submitted to a trial at once, though he was innocent of wrongdoing. Being *praos* here is not a matter of a permanent disposition, but rather a response to ingratiating behaviour; by implication, the jurors ought properly to feel this way towards Polystratus himself, because of his humble behaviour in presenting himself before the court, but not towards the others, who either ran off or else acted in fear. In the *Memorabilia* of Xenophon (2.3.16), Socrates urges reconciliation with one's brother: 'Do not shrink back, my good man, but try to render the man *praos* [*katapraünein*], and very soon he will heed you; don't you see how concerned for honour and magnanimous he is?' Here again, *praotês* is induced by humble behaviour that augments the self-esteem of the other and for this reason renders him gentle. A few other passages are perhaps subject to a similar interpretation (e.g. Plato *Euthydemus* 288B, *Republic* 572A, Herodotus *Histories* 2.121δ). But the texts I have examined do not demonstrate conclusively, so far as I can judge, that *praotês* was generally understood to be an emotion elicited by deference and appeasement.

Aristotle's system of the emotions invites, I believe, or at least allows a place for, a positive *pathos* opposed to anger that takes the form of a pleasurable response to a gesture that enhances one's status or self-esteem. I think that there are hints of such a meaning in Aristotle's exceptional treatment of *praotês*, which is conditioned by his definition of anger or *orgê*. But it comfortably coexists with the notion of appeasement, and Aristotle does not distinguish clearly between the two ideas. Perhaps the best name for the sentiment of *praotês* as Aristotle conceives it, then, is 'satisfaction,' which suggests both compensation for an injury or insult and the self-esteem deriving from an affirmed sense of self.

Even if the analysis I have proposed is not quite Aristotle's, I venture to hope that it is at least Aristotelian.[6] Still, it is worth inquiring why Aristotle did not develop the self-affirming aspect of *praotês* further, and why a specific emotion of this kind does not figure among the *pathê* commonly recognized by the Greeks, whereas anger, its ostensible opposite, occupies so prominent a position. It may be that, in the fiercely competitive world of the classical Greek city-state, gestures intended to augment the reputation of another – the opposite, that is, of a slight – were so rare that there was no need to give a special name to the response that they elicited. In many societies today one may observe a comparable reserve in the lavishing of praise and commendation. In the following chapter, we shall see that a similar restraint may have inhibited the emergence of a positive conception of pride, which is often included in modern inventories of the emotions.

CHAPTER FOUR

Shame

La vergüenza es un sentimiento universal.

Marina 1996: 146

[T]he Balinese no more feel 'guilt' than we feel *lek*, the Balinese emotion closest to our 'shame.'

Rosaldo 1984: 142

Shame has had a bad press for the past century or so. As Thomas Scheff remarks (1997: 205): 'Over the last 200 years in the history of modern societies, shame virtually disappeared. The denial of shame has been institutionalized in Western societies.'[1] Its status as a moral emotion has been impugned by critics, among them theologians and anthropologists, who consider it a primitive precursor to guilt: shame, the argument goes, responds to the judgments of others and is indifferent to ethical principles in themselves, whereas guilt is an inner sensibility and corresponds to the morally autonomous self of modern man.[2] The shift from a shame culture to a guilt culture, in the formula made popular by Ruth Benedict (1946), is taken as a sign of moral progress. Thus, the warrior society represented in the Homeric epics – a shame culture, according to E.R. Dodds (1951) – slowly gave way to a guilt culture, which began to emerge in fifth-century democratic Athens but did not achieve a fully developed expression in the classical world until the advent of Christianity.[3]

Psychologists either ignored shame or treated it as characteristic of an early stage in the socialization of the child,[4] at least until Helen Block Lewis, in a highly influential study (1971), insisted on the importance of shame in adult life. By characterizing shame as the experience of the utter worthlessness of the self, however, in contrast to guilt, which is limited to a negative feeling about a particular act (40), Lewis too contributed to the general belief that shame is something we would be better off without.[5] True, guilt can get out of hand and become transformed into a generalized emotion or guilt complex, a psychic condition that has in part been fostered in Western culture by the Christian emphasis on original sin.[6] In addition, permissive attitudes towards children and a naive belief in the essential goodness of human nature have led to a disparagement of guilt as a pernicious form of conscience. Even so, guilt retains a certain dignity as a sentiment, while shame seems at best infantile and other-directed.[7] Thus, Stephen Pattison (2000: 129) remarks, 'While guilt may have a very constructive role in creating and maintaining social relationships and moral responsibilities, shame has a much more dubious effect.' And Zygmunt Bauman (2001) writes:

Just half a century ago, Karl Jaspers could still neatly separate 'moral guilt' (the remorse we feel when we do harm to other human beings, whether by what we have done or by what we have failed to to) from 'metaphysical guilt' (the guilt we feel when harm is done to a human being, although this harm is in no way related to our action). This distinction has lost its meaning with globalization. John Donne's phrase, 'Do not ask for whom the bell tolls: it tolls for thee,' represents as never before the solidarity of our destiny, although it is still far from being balanced by the solidarity of our sentiments and actions.[8]

Like many other cultures, Greece and Rome did not have distinct terms for what we call shame and guilt, and they seem to have made do with one concept where we recognize two.[9] Such a view of the matter, however, presupposes a natural correspondence among psychological ideas across linguistic and social boundaries. Thus, the Greek term we customarily translate as 'shame' is imagined to match, more or less, the English concept, unless perhaps, in the absence of a word for guilt, Greek shame had a somewhat wider extension so as to include some (or all) of the modern notion of guilt. Alternatively – and this is the more common assumption – the ancient Greeks simply failed to achieve a notion of guilt, which is in turn a sign of the poverty of their moral vocabulary and their incomplete psychological development. As we have seen, however, the ancient Greek emotional lexicon does not map neatly onto modern English concepts.[10] Rather than assume that the Greeks' emotional terminology for shame was either fuzzier or more primitive than our own, we may better appreciate their idea of this emotion and its ethical significance by paying close attention to their vocabulary. Here again, moreover, we can avail ourselves of Aristotle's subtle analysis of shame (or, more precisely, of *aiskhunê*), which, I argue, offers new perspectives on several problems and paradoxes that arise within modern treatments of shame and related sentiments. In the discussion that follows, then, I begin by examining the meanings and connotations of certain Greek words. I beg the reader's indulgence for what may seem an excessively lexical or philological emphasis (it will be relatively brief, but those who wish to go straight to Aristotle may flip to p. 98). The payoff, I hope, will be a richer sense of the significance of shame both in ancient Greek society and in our own.

As it happens, there are two Greek words that are typically rendered as 'shame' in English: *aidôs*, which has received some scholarly attention recently (notably Cairns 1993), and *aiskhunê* (sometimes transliterated as *aischyne*). These terms are by no means entirely synonymous, and it is a weakness in Bernard Williams's fine book on shame in Greek antiquity (1993) that he lumps *aidôs* and *aiskhunê* together, although he provides an excellent defence of shame as a moral sentiment and challenges the 'progressivist' hypothesis of a great conceptual shift from ancient to modern ethical thought, with its new concentration on guilt (7). Thus, in an endnote Williams observes (194 n. 9): 'There are two Greek roots bearing the sense of "shame": *aid-* ... and *aiskhun-* ... I have not been generally concerned to separate uses of the two kinds of word. Not much turns on the distinction, for my purposes, and, in particular, many of the variations are diachronic,' with *aiskhunê* taking the place of *aidôs* as the latter became increasingly obsolete over the sixth to fourth centuries B.C.[11] Williams cites the brief lexicographical analysis by George Shipp (1972: 191), who notes that the two roots are in fact differentiated in Herodotus, where terms based on *aid-* carry the sense 'respect the power of,' while the *aiskh-* words mean 'be ashamed.' Herodotus, however, wrote in the Ionic dialect. Shipp maintains that, in the Attic dialect, which was the predominant vehicle of literature in the classical period, '*aiskhunomai* [the verbal form] took over both senses.' This evolutionary story cannot be right. As Cairns points out (1993: 138), in Homer *aiskhunomai* already serves as an equivalent to *aideomai*, the verbal form of *aidôs* (cf. *Odyssey* 7.305–6, 21.323–9). What is more, Shipp's claim ignores the fact that *aidôs*, which, along with its associated verbal form *aideomai*, continues to occur in the classical period (especially in poetry), also acquired two senses.[12]

Douglas Cairns, who has written the definitive study of *aidôs*, offers the following as a preliminary definition of the term (1993: 2): '[L]et *aidôs* be an inhibitory emotion based on sensitivity to and protectiveness of one's self-image'; Cairns suggests that the verbal form *aideomai* roughly means 'I am abashed.' The standard Greek-English lexicon (Liddell, Scott, and Jones 1940) defines *aidôs* as 'reverence,' 'awe,' 'respect,' and a 'sense of honour'; the term does not normally designate the feeling of shame for acts committed. In Homer, where *aidôs* and its relatives occur frequently, '*aidôs* is always prospective and inhibitory' (Cairns 1993: 13); 'it does not approximate to our notion of the retrospective "bad" or guilty conscience' (145). More crisply, Cairns affirms that '*aidôs* is not shame' (1993: 14).[13]

Aiskhunê, on the contrary, is defined in Liddell, Scott, and Jones (s.v.) as 'shame,' 'dishonour,' as well as a 'sense of shame' and 'honour'; in this latter sense, we are told, it is 'like *aidôs*.' When a term is said to bear contradictory senses such as 'honour' and 'dishonour,' one begins to suspect that a problem of interpretation may be lurking. The vast new *Diccionario griego-español* (1980–) reports that *aiskhunê* may denote 'disfigurement or ugliness,' as well as a sentiment induced by public disapprobation, citing Euripides, *Andromache* 244: 'Shameful things [*aiskhra*] entail *aiskhunê*.' Thucydides (2.37) contrasts offences against the law, which result in punishment, with those against unwritten customs, which engender *aiskhunê*. But *aiskhunê* is also 'a restrictive virtue' (*una virtud restrictiva*), and in this connotation it means 'shame or honour [*vergüenza, honor*] in the sense of respecting one's commitments at all cost, principledness [*pundonor*] and at times almost heroism.' Thus, Thucydides (1.84.3) is cited for the view that '*aidôs* partakes most of modesty, courage [*eupsukhia*] of *aiskhunê*,[14] testifying incidentally to a still lively awareness of a distinction between the two terms in the classical era.[15]

Although some scholars hold that there is 'no discernible difference' in Aristotle's use of the terms *aidôs* and *aiskhunê* in his ethical writings (Grimaldi 1988: 105),[16] a close analysis reveals that he in fact respects their distinct ranges of meaning, normally limiting *aidôs* to the prospective or inhibitory sense. While this is not the place for a thorough survey of Aristotle's usage, we may take as an illustration an important passage in the *Nicomachean Ethics* (1128b32–3), often supposed to show the interchangeability of the two: 'If shamelessness [*anaiskhuntia*] is a bad thing and also not feeling *aidôs* [*to mê aideisthai*] at doing shameful things, then it is not any more honourable for someone who does such things to feel *aiskhunê* [*aiskhunesthai*],' that is, after the deeds have been done. In this passage, *aidôs* is clearly understood to inhibit bad behaviour, while *aiskhunê* reflects back on it with regret.

But if *aidôs*, complex though it may be in its own right, is nevertheless a reasonably coherent concept,[17] what shall we say of *aiskhunê*, which seems to have both a prospective and a retrospective dimension, signifying equally 'shame' and a 'sense of shame'?[18] The two meanings are ostensibly quite diverse: why should they cohabit in a single concept? To be sure, they also overlap in English: 'Have you no shame?' means 'Have you no sense of shame?' (so too in the negative compound 'shameless'). But Greek appears to have had available a vocabulary by which to distinguish the two senses. Indeed, the two concepts would seem to be psychologically discrete, 'shame' being an emotion while a 'sense of shame' is more like an ethical trait.[19]

Greek philosophers and rhetoricians too seem regularly to have classified *aiskhunê* as an emotion or *pathos*, whereas the status of *aidôs* was more ambiguous. It is *aiskhunê*, not *aidôs*, that Aristotle chooses to analyse in the *Rhetoric*, his most extensive and penetrating discussion of the emotions. True, Aristotle at times lists *aidôs* among the *pathê* (plural of *pathos*), and Douglas Cairns states categorically (1993: 5): '[T]hat *aidôs* is an emotion is, I take it, uncontroversial; Aristotle regards it as more like a *pathos*, an affect, than anything else.' But the question is not quite so straightforward. For while *pathos* often approximates the English 'emotion,' it can have a much wider extension (see chapter 1, p. 4). What is more, precisely in those passages where Aristotle identifies *aidôs* as a *pathos*, it is clear that he is using *pathos* in the broad sense to include a variety of psychological states. Thus, in the *Eudemian Ethics* (1220b37–21a12) we find included under the *pathê*, along with *aidôs*, such items as courage, moderation, justness, and liberality, which Aristotle normally treats as virtues (cf. also *Eudemian Ethics* 1233b16–34b14, 1233b26–35). Indeed, already in antiquity the scholar Alexander of Aphrodisias (or someone writing in his name), commenting on Aristotle's discussion, wondered whether *aidôs* could properly be classified as a *pathos*.[20]

The Stoics, in turn, cite the unusual form *aidêmosunê* as a form of *sôphrosunê*, 'modesty' or 'self-control' – usually one of the four cardinal virtues – and define it as 'a careful knowledge of appropriate blame.'[21] Typically, the Stoics contrasted *aidôs* with *aiskhunê*, treating the former as a healthy sentiment (*eupatheia*) characteristic of the sage, whereas *aikshunê* was classified among the vicious emotions to which everyone except the sage is subject (*SVF* 431.1–9 = Diogenes Laertius 7.115). Thus, *hagneia*, 'purity' or 'chastity,' turns up in the same category as *aidôs*, namely, *eulabeia* or 'caution,' the wise man's equivalent of the fear (*phobos*) to which ordinary people are exposed.[22] *Aiskhunê*, in turn, is precisely 'a fear of disgrace.'[23] It is true that Aristotle at one point in the *Nicomachean Ethics* (1128b12–13) says of *aidôs*: 'It is defined as a kind of fear [*phobos*] of disgrace [*adoxia*]' – or at least, he adds, it is something like fear [*paraplêsion*] – and as a species of fear it ought, in Aristotle's terms, to be an emotion.[24] If so, however, it is one that looks to future rather than to past or present events, as Aristotle's definition of fear in the *Rhetoric* stipulates (2.5, 1382a21–2): 'Let fear be a kind of pain or disturbance deriving from an image [*phantasia*] of a future evil that is destructive or painful.' In this, as we shall see, *aidôs* is quite distinct from *aiskhunê*.[25] My guess is that Aristotle is casting about here for an adequate determination of the psychological status of *aidôs*, and brings in fear as a rough approximation in part because it is prospective.

The Christian bishop Nemesius of Emesa, writing in the fourth century AD, locates *aidôs* under the Stoic rubric of fear – an emotion or *pathos* – rather than caution, and defines it as a 'fear of the expectation of blame,' though Nemesius adds the proviso that 'this is the finest emotion [*pathos*].'[26] But this is clearly a mistake in regard to orthodox Stoic doctrine. More interesting, however, is the distinction that Nemesius draws between *aidôs* and *aiskhunê*. Nemesius defines the latter as 'a fear in the case of a shameful thing that has been done,' and remarks that it is not unpromising in respect to salvation. He then adds that '*aidôs* differs from *aiskhunê* in this, that a person who feels *aiskhunê* is shamed [*kataduetai*] for things he has done, whereas a person who feels *aidôs* fears that he will land in some kind of disgrace; the ancients [i.e., Greeks of the classical era] often call *aidôs aiskhunê*, but in this they misuse the terms.' Nemesius is the first, so far as I have discovered, to distinguish explicitly these two meanings of shame – the feeling of being ashamed and a sense of shame – as well as the first to differentiate between *aidôs* and *aiskhunê* on the basis of this distinction.

Nemesius is certainly wrong about the semantics of *aidôs* and *aiskhunê* in classical Greek: we have seen that both meanings of shame coexist in the term *aiskhunê* (see further below).[27] But the distinction that Nemesius draws between two concepts of shame, one retrospective and oriented towards the past, the other prospective and oriented towards the future, has had a considerable influence on later thought. Kurt Riezler (1943: 462–3), for example, notes that French, Greek, and German all have two words for shame, and explains: '*Pudeur* means a kind of shame that tends to keep you from an act, whereas you may feel *honte* after an act.' While he acknowledges that '[t]he Greek distinction between *Aidos* and *Aischyne* does not correspond to the French,' he nevertheless cites the definition provided by the great Renaissance humanist Stephanus in his *Thesaurus* of the Greek language: '*Aidôs* is shame that derives from reverence, whereas *aiskhunê* is shame that derives from immorality.'[28] More recently, Melvin Lansky (1996: 769) notes that English 'shame' can refer to a desire to 'disappear from view' or to 'comportment that would avoid the emotion (the obverse of shamelessness),' and adds: 'Many languages have separate words for the emotion,' citing French *honte* 'for the emotion itself; *pudeur*, for the defense' (769).[29] Thomas Scheff (1997: 209), in turn, differentiates the Greek terms *aiskhuynê* and *aidôs* under the rubrics 'disgrace' and 'modesty,' and compares them with the Latin *foedus* versus *pudor*, French *honte* versus *pudeur*, German *Schande* versus *Scham*, and Italian *vergogna* versus *pudore*, while noting that this distinction is absent in English.[30] None of these contrasts captures the value of the Greek concept of *aiskhunê*, to which I now turn.

The fullest and clearest analysis of shame, as of a variety of other emotions, bequeathed to us by the ancient Greeks is to be found in the *Rhetoric* of Aristotle, as we have seen, since Aristotle, like a number of his successors, regarded the job of exciting or assuaging the passions as a part of the art of persuasion. Aristotle's definition of *aiskhunê* in this treatise runs as follows (2.6, 1383b12–14): 'Let *aiskhunê*, then, be a pain or disturbance concerning those ills, either present, past, or future, that are perceived to lead to disgrace, while shamelessness is a disregard or impassivity concerning these same things.'

Aristotle's inclusion of future ills, along with past or present ills, in the definition of *aiskhunê* as a cause of shame may seem surprising, since if we feel shame at something still to come it might be supposed that we would avoid the situation or behaviour that will induce the emotion. But Aristotle's definition makes it clear that he draws no distinction between prospective or restrictive shame, on the one hand, and retrospective or remorseful shame, on the other.[31] A key element in the definition is the term 'perceived' or 'imagined' (the Greek word, *phainomena*, may also mean 'are seen'). We remember past events, sense present ones, and anticipate future events, and things good or ill may 'appear' to us in all three modes. If the ills we perceive or imagine are of the kind that bring about a loss of reputation or disgrace (*adoxia*), we respond with the emotion of shame.[32] Of course, such phenomena, if they are memories, can no longer be altered or avoided, save insofar as one can perhaps change the opinions that others hold of them and thus limit the damage to one's status or repute. By contrast, one will ordinarily try to prevent foreseen events of this type from being realized. But envisioning an anticipated ill evokes the emotion of shame just as much as recollecting a past one does, and the very same sentiment that galls us in the case of things that have been done moves us also to avert them, if we can, in the future.[33]

It seems to me that Aristotle has, in a stroke, resolved the problem of two kinds of shame – retrospective and inhibitory – or recast the question in such a way that the distinction between them is otiose. It is not that *aiskhunê* includes both kinds of shame, one properly denoted by *aiskhunê* and the other by *aidôs*, as Nemesius proposed. Whatever the case with the French *honte* and *pudeur*, the German *Scham* and *Schande*, or the Spanish *pudor* and *vergüenza*, classical Greek did not divide the conceptual sphere of shame between two distinct terms. Nor is *aiskhunê*, as Aristotle defines it, a complex idea, as the English 'shame' is said to be, embracing within itself the two distinct notions of the experience of shame and a sense of shame. The emotion, as Aristotle understands it, is uniform; what varies is simply the timing of the perceived ills. The lexicographers are thus wrong to split *aiskhunê* into subdefinitions, for there is nothing to disambiguate.

The opposite of shame, in turn, is simply 'shamelessness' (*anaiskhuntia*), a failure of sensitivity to the relevant kinds of ills, whether past, present, or future. Whereas 'shamelessness' in English is ordinarily taken to be the antonym of a sense of shame, as opposed to the feeling of being ashamed, for Aristotle, again, there is no need to differentiate the two connotations. His interpretation of *aiskhunê* as a unitary sentiment allows him to treat shamelessness as an insensiblity to all evils, regardless of tense, that tend to a loss of reputation or disgrace. A person who is not ashamed of having committed such an act will not refrain from committing it in the future.

Shamelessness, as Aristotle defines it, does not seem to be a distinct emotion that is shame's opposite, but rather a lack of feeling or insensibility (*apatheia*) in respect to the kinds of ills that arouse shame. In the *Rhetoric*, as we saw in the preceding chapter (pp. 81–3), Aristotle tends to pair contrasting emotions, such as love and hatred, fear and confidence, or pity and indignation. Anger's opposite is given as 'calmness' or, if it is a true emotion, as a sense of enhanced esteem in response to a gesture of respect or self-abasement; pity, in turn, is defined as pain at the undeserved misfortune of another, while its opposite, indignation, is pain at another's undeserved good fortune. It is not difficult to construct an emotion that is the contrary of shame as Aristotle conceives it: for example, one might define it as 'pleasure concerning those goods that are perceived to lead to a good reputation or approval.' Such a sentiment we might well label something like 'pride.' Many modern investigators, in fact, couple shame and pride as opposites. Thus, Donald Nathanson (1992: 86) writes: 'Shame, of course, is the polar opposite of pride.'[34] Classical Greek, however, seems to lack a basic emotion term corresponding to a positive sense of pride, though the negative sentiment of arrogance is well attested (e.g., in the form of *hubris*).[35] While it is beyond the scope of this book to consider all the reasons why Aristotle and his contemporaries may not have identified pride as an emotion, perhaps one factor is that in the competitive world of Greek city-state society, people were more likely to be struggling to preserve their status under the critical gaze of their fellow citizens than to be basking in their admiration (cf. chapter 2, p. 75). They were concerned to protect their reputations, not to make others feel good about themselves. Praise was easily read as flattery. The pride the ancients meditated on was that which goes before a fall.[36]

Returning to Aristotle's definition of *aiskhunê*, it is important to note that shame is not conceived as a response to perceived ill repute or disgrace (*adoxia*) as such, but rather to those ills that lead to such a state. It is true that, a little later, Aristotle recapitulates the definition in an abbreviated form: 'Since *aiskhunê* is a perception [or impression: *phantasia*] of disgrace, and this on its own account and not for what results from it ...,' etc. However, the wording of the initial and fuller description is, I think, significant. Shame arises not at the contemplation of loss of honour in the abstract, but from specific acts or events that bring about disgrace. Aristotle immediately offers examples of the kinds of ills he has in mind:

> If shame is as we have defined it, then it follows that we feel shame for those kinds of ills that seem disgraceful, either for ourselves or those we care about. Such are all those actions that arise out of vice, for example throwing away one's shield or fleeing; for they come from cowardice. Also confiscating a deposit, or wronging someone; for they come from unjustness. And sleeping with the wrong people, or those who are related to the wrong people, or at the wrong time; for they come from sensuality.

Other examples of vices are wrongful gain, illiberality or servility, effeminacy, small-mindedness, meekness, and conceitedness, each manifested in visible outward behaviour, such as making a profit off the poor, lack of generosity, flattery, lack of endurance, and blowing one's own horn. All these actions are evidence of personal defects, and it is these in turn that, when recognized, lead to a loss of esteem and status. There are thus three elements that together prompt the emotion of shame: a particular act (throwing away one's shield in battle); the fault of character that is revealed by the act (cowardice); and the disgrace or loss of esteem before the community at large.

With this schema, Aristotle seems to bridge the difference that modern investigators suppose exists between shame and guilt, according to which guilt is elicited by a specific act of wrongdoing, while 'we feel shame about the very essence of our selves' (Morrison 1996: 12). Shame, for Aristotle (and I would say for Greeks in the classical period generally), results from imagining particular acts or events, whether committed or intended, for example doing someone an injustice or failing to help another when it is in one's power to do so. It is possible to make amends for such offences, whether by apologizing or by some other form of compensation. They are limited acts, and do not necessarily entail an annihilation of one's sense of self. At this level, Aristotle's discussion encompasses the modern idea of guilt. Shame-inducing behaviour, however, in addition to being unjust or inappropriate, also testifies to a character flaw or moral failing, and in this respect it is damaging, like modern shame, to one's self-esteem, or at least to one's self-representation in the world. But to what degree? It is only a particular trait or vice that is exposed, for example avarice or boastfulness, and this need not destroy a person's standing completely. The close connection between shame and honour in fact allows for gradations in the phenomenological effects of shame. There is no reason why it must be experienced as an assault on one's essential being, and Aristotle, for whom shame was a fact of everyday life, does not suggest such drastic consequences.

To the causes of shame indicated above, Aristotle adds the condition of not sharing in those advantages which most or all of one's peers enjoy, whether fellow citizens, age-mates, or relatives, for example, the same level of education or culture.[37] Such a deficiency could be the result of a personal failing, but there might also be other reasons for it. It is doubtless productive of shame to appear boorish in cultivated company, even if it is not one's own fault. Here, then, Aristotle recognizes that shame may arise from circumstances beyond one's control, in contrast to modern guilt, which is commonly taken to presuppose moral responsibility.[38] Nico Frijda (1993: 367) reports, however, that despite current theories, his research indicates that while responsibility perhaps pertains to the way we experience guilt, it is not necessarily a component of the antecedent appraisal; that is, one can feel guilty for hitting or narrowly missing a child who jumps in front of one's car without believing one is at fault. So too, 'Norm violation does not seem prominent in the causation of guilt emotions that emerged after serious loss for which the subject is not responsible; for instance, when a relative has died, towards whom they felt they should have been more kind or caring.'[39] The borderline between modern guilt and shame seems fuzzier than one might imagine, and it may well be reasonable, with Aristotle, to see both culpable and morally blameless behaviours as eliciting a single emotion.

Aristotle adds, however, that all such defects are the more shameful 'if they are perceived to occur on one's own account; for it is all the more a consequence of vice, if one is oneself responsible for what has happened, is happening, or is going to happen.' In his discussion of shame, then, Aristotle is not indifferent to the question of accountability. Rather, it figures as an exacerbating condition in relation to those kinds of ills that do not derive from vice or ethical deficiency. It would appear, then, that responsibility plays a primary role in Aristotle's concept of shame. While Aristotle acknowledges that certain behaviours, though strictly speaking beyond one's control, may elicit shame if the deficiencies they expose are closely related to character (and hence are easily imagined to be moral shortcomings), he is not concerned with trivial accidents that indicate nothing about the ethical self (we may recall that the Greek word for character is *êthos*, whence the term 'ethical').[40]

Bernard Williams (1993: 78) writes that '[t]he basic experience connected with shame is that of being seen, inappropriately, by the wrong people, in the wrong condition. It is straightforwardly connected with nakedness.'[41] Now, Aristotle indeed observes that one feels shame more intensely when the acts that evoke it are 'in the eyes [sc., of others] and in public; whence the proverb that "*aidôs* is in the eyes."'[42] But rather than being fundamental to shame, exposure is treated as an aggravating factor, like responsibility in the case of deficiencies relative to one's peers. I doubt that nakedness and sexuality in general played so central a role in Greek shame as modern critics sometimes suppose; after all, Greek males in the classical period exercised naked in public.[43] As we have seen, Aristotle mentions sexual misconduct among the acts that can lead to shame, but his concern is with the character flaw to which such behaviour testifies, not with sex as such.[44]

For Aristotle, shame has to do above all with loss of reputation or *adoxia*, and since, Aristotle argues, 'no one worries about reputation [*doxa*] except via those who have an opinion of it [*hoi doxazontes*], it follows that we feel shame before those people whom we take seriously.' Examples are those whom we admire or who admire us, those with whom we compete, and older or cultivated people, along with righteous folk not inclined to pardon or forgive. The opinions of others are clearly relevant to shame, but they must be opinions of those we have reason to respect. This again indicates the fundamentally ethical character of shame, as Aristotle understands it. Aristotle goes on to say, however, that we feel shame also before those likely to divulge what we have done; 'for not proclaiming it is the same as not believing [dokein] it.' Here, Aristotle's shame seems to part company with a wholly interiorized sense of guilt. Whatever we may feel at the knowledge that we have inflicted a secret injury on another, it only becomes shame in the fullest sense when the evidence of our vicious character has reached the ears of those whose opinions we value. But this is not to say that we may not disapprove of our private vices. Such a condemnation of our own behaviour, however, would take the form of a moral judgment rather than an emotion, comparable to the response of those before whom we feel shame. If Aristotle had considered the judged rather than the judging self, the emotion he would have ascribed to it would, I expect, be shame.[45]

Aristotle's analysis of *aiskhunê* plausibly represents, I believe, the quality of the emotion among Greeks of his time. To take one particularly illuminating example, at the beginning of a court-room speech that the orator Antiphon composed for the defence against a charge of unintentional homicide in the year 419 BC, the speaker declares (6.1): 'The nicest thing, gentlemen of the jury, for a human being is never to be in jeopardy on a capital charge, and in one's prayers this is the thing to pray for. But if one is obliged to be in jeopardy, then at least that the following obtain, which I deem crucial in such a matter: that one know in one's own mind that one has not erred, but that even if some misfortune arises, it is without vice (*kakotês*) or shame (*aiskhunê*), and by accident rather than by injustice.' A deed may seem to others to be the sign of a defect in character, and hence productive of shame, but true shame arises only if one knows oneself to be at fault. Shame is aroused, as Aristotle observes, by an action of the kind that exposes a defect in the agent, but the agent is not wholly at the mercy of public opinion.

Aristotle's discussion, moreover, sheds a different light on problems attaching to the modern idea of shame, such as the tension between its inhibitory and its a posteriori manifestations, the relation between judgments concerning specific actions and those concerning the self as a whole, and the role of responsibility versus events beyond our control. The Greek concept no doubt is consistent with a society that placed a high value on public honour and reputation;[46] it may also be that different values and practices in child-rearing favoured a more positive role for shame, in contrast with modern accounts that emphasize its devastating effects on the self and the importance of encouraging self-esteem in the child. The very idea of a 'self' may have differed in antiquity from the way it is conceived and experienced today.[47] Without entering into these complex questions, I should like to conclude by examining the role of *aiskhunê* in two contrasting literary texts that are particularly indicative of the different ways in which ancient and modern shame are conceived.

After the death of Achilles at Troy, his arms were awarded as a special prize to Odysseus. Ajax, enraged at what he considered an insult to his own valour, undertook to kill the Greek leaders he held responsible, including Odysseus himself along with Agamemnon, the chief commander of the Greek expedition, and his brother Menelaus. The goddess Athena, however, muddled the wits of Ajax, so that he mistakenly took captive, tortured, and finally slaughtered a herd of sheep rather than his enemies. Sophocles' tragedy *Ajax* dramatizes the aftermath of these events, in which Ajax comes to his senses, realizes his blunder, and then, deceiving his comrades about his intentions, seeks out an isolated place and slays himself. The play concludes with a debate between Odysseus, Agamemnon, Menelaus, and Teucer, Ajax's half-brother, over whether to permit the burial of Ajax's body after his attempt at vengeance.

In an illuminating study, Melvin Lansky (1996: 761) argues that Ajax's shame 'leads to narcissistic rage,' and remarks that 'classicist critics, for the most part, have failed to distinguish an adherence to the heroic code from pathological shame and vengefulness' (765).[48] In the text, however, neither Ajax nor anyone else indicates shame as the reason for his suicide, although the chorus of Ajax's companions connect the rumour concerning his actions with their own *aishkunê* (173–5). How then are we to decide Ajax's motive? It is true that Ajax sings (403–4): 'Where can one flee? Where can I go and stay?' But the reason why he wishes to hide is that 'the whole army would kill me sword in hand' (408–9); not shame but prudence moves him. Again, he dreads to face his father, who brought home great spoils in his campaigns (462–3); but the reason why is that he must return naked, without the armour of Achilles that, in his view, he most deserved (464). The closest Ajax himself comes to suggesting shame as a motive is in the remark (473–4) 'It is ugly [or shameful: *aiskhron*] for a man to desire a long life, when he is inalterably embroiled in evils.'[49]

There is, however, another possible motive for Ajax's suicide, and that is anger – the same anger that inspired his attempt to murder the Greek generals (cf. verse 41, Athena speaking; 776–7, Agamemnon speaking). Aristotle defines anger, as we have seen, as 'a desire, accompanied by pain, for a perceived revenge on account of a perceived slight' (2.2, 1378a31–2). Ajax sought to exact revenge for what he perceived as a derisive insult, but failed because of a temporary spell of insanity. Nothing in the play suggests that he regrets the attempt, or that he sees it as indicative of a flaw in his character. Thus, there is no basis for shame; the disgrace that he acknowledges derives exclusively from the award of Achilles' arms to Odysseus.[50] He is distressed because his life is now in danger, and despite his enduring anger he no longer has an opportunity to avenge himself. Aristotle does not specify the emotion involved in such frustrated rage; perhaps he would just label it anger. But it is not shame or *aiskhunê*.[51]

A tragedy in which shame clearly does serve as a motive to action is Sophocles' *Philoctetes*. When the play opens, Philoctetes has been alone for ten years on a deserted island, suffering from an excruciating wound in his foot and surviving only by his skill at archery. He had been bitten by a snake when he accidentally intruded upon a sacred precinct on the island of Chryse, where the Greek armada had put in on its way to Troy, and he was subsequently abandoned on Lemnos by his comrades because of his continual cries of pain and the reek of the suppurating lesion. The Greek forces at Troy, in the meantime, have learned from a seer that Troy will fall only to Philoctetes' bow, and Odysseus is sent, along with Achilles' son Neoptolemus, a new recruit to the army, to fetch it and, if possible, Philoctetes himself as well.

Neoptolemus's role will be to feign sympathy for Philoctetes on the basis of their common hatred for the Greek leaders, motivated on Neoptolemus's part (he pretends) by the award of Achilles' arms to Odysseus, which he himself ought rather to have received as his father's heir. But the need to resort to deceit (*dolos*) troubles the idealistic young warrior: 'Why by treachery, necessarily, rather than lead him by persuasion?' he asks. To which Odysseus replies: 'He cannot be persuaded; nor can you take him by force' (101–3). For Achilles' son, force and persuasion are proper methods of compulsion, whereas he regards deception as shameful. Odysseus does not soften the element of dishonesty in his scheme: rather, he plainly calls it an act of theft (55, 57), and sees Neoptolemus as the robber of Philoctetes' bow (77). He explains:

I know that you are not by nature disposed to say or plan such ignoble things, but it is sweet to gain the prize of victory. Be bold. We shall seem just afterwards. Now, for my sake, give yourself to shamelessness [*anaides*] for a brief part of a day, and then for the rest of time be called most pious of all mortals. (79–85)

When Neoptolemus innocently asks, 'Don't you believe that it is shameful [*aiskhron*] to tell lies?' (108), Odysseus replies that lies are justified when survival depends on them.

Neoptolemus finally agrees to carry out the scheme, but it is clear that it sits badly with him, and once he has obtained the bow by insinuating himself into Philoctetes' confidence, he begins to suffer pangs of conscience: 'Everything is difficult,' he tells Philoctetes, 'when one has abandoned one's own nature and does what is unseemly' (902–3). Philoctetes assures him that he is doing nothing unworthy of Achilles in helping a good man, but Neoptolemus replies, 'I shall appear shameful [*aiskhros*] – this is what has pained me for some time now' (906), and he adds: 'Can I be caught out being ignoble a second time, concealing what I ought not and uttering the most shameful [*aiskhista*] of words?' (908–9). Philoctetes homes in on his qualms: 'How you have deceived me! Are you not ashamed, you scoundrel, to look upon me, your trophy, a suppliant? You have deprived me of my life by taking my bow' (929–31). When Neoptolemus maintains a stony silence, he exclaims: 'He swore to take me home, but he is taking me to Troy; he gave me his right hand!' (941–2). And when Neoptolemus at last bursts out, 'A terrible pity has overcome me for this man, not just now, but long since,' Philoctetes replies: 'Pity me, my child, by the gods, and do not open yourself to the reproach of mankind by robbing me' (965–8; cf. 1136).

Nevertheless, prompted in part by Odysseus, who enters opportunely at this critical moment, Neoptolemus makes off with the bow, leaving Philoctetes to lament his fate alone. But in a new and unexpected twist, just when things seem most bleak for Philoctetes, Neoptolemus returns, pursued by an amazed and outraged Odysseus, to give back the weapon. To Odysseus's demand for an explanation of his behaviour, Neoptolemus replies: 'I have come to undo the errors I committed earlier.' 'What error?' Odysseus asks; 'When I submitted to you and the whole army,' Neoptolemus says, 'and seized a man by shameful deception and treachery' (1224–8). And again: 'I acquired his bow shamefully and unjustly' (1234); 'I committed a shameful error and I shall try to undo it' (1248–9; cf. 1282–3, 1288). With this, Neoptolemus restores the bow to Philoctetes, who henceforth has no cause to blame him (1308–9), although when Neoptolemus persists in the attempt to persuade Philoctetes to sail to Troy, the latter exclaims: 'You say this and feel no shame before the gods?' To this Neoptolemus replies: 'Why should one feel shame for helping another?' (1382–3).

What induces shame in Neoptolemus is the act of entrapping Philoctetes through deceit or treachery. The act, in turn, is taken to reveal a flaw in character, in accord with Aristotle's analysis of the sentiment: as the son of Achilles, Neoptolemus should be above such behaviour, and in consenting to oblige Odysseus in this way he shows that he has abandoned his own nature, as he puts it. Neoptolemus's awareness of this lapse into vice causes him to feel shame in anticipation of the deed, while Odysseus is coaxing him into it; at the moment of the theft of the bow itself; and again later, and most intensely, when he has succeeded in stealing it from Philoctetes, just as Aristotle gives us to understand. His shame deeply affects Neoptolemus's sense of self, but there is nevertheless a way to negate or nullify it, which is precisely by returning the bow and fulfilling the promise he made to Philoctetes in order to win his confidence, namely, that he would take him home – and not to Troy.

Neoptolemus's change of heart in the course of the action is not, however, due simply to the fact that shame is greater for actions done than for those that are still merely prospective. Neoptolemus has also been moved to pity Philoctetes, since his suffering and misfortune have been unmerited (see chapter 10, p. 212). In addition to feeling pity, Neoptolemus has come to respect the rough nobility and endurance of Philoctetes; he is now capable of regarding the man he is manipulating not as a stranger but as a friend. To a degree, his pretence has got the better of Neoptolemus, and the bond he feigned with Philoctetes has become real. But his newfound respect for Philoctetes means that Philoctetes' view of him matters. While lying was always contrary to Neoptolemus's moral code, Odysseus took a different view, and so Neoptolemus had no reason to feel shame before him. But in proportion to his positive regard for Philoctetes, Philoctetes' judgment of his conduct is increasingly important to him. Aristotle, as we have seen, maintained that 'we feel shame before those people whom we take seriously,' for it is their opinion of us that we care about. Neoptolemus's shame is sharpened because the vice in his character, as exhibited by the action performed contrary to his own principles, has now been made manifest to a morally serious witness. Unlike Odysseus, the wizened Philoctetes shares the belief of Neoptolemus that 'it is shameful to tell lies.'[52]

In his complex analysis of the things that arouse laughter, Plato observes that it is legitimate to experience pleasure at the misfortunes of enemies, but not at those of one's friends (*Philebus* 48B, 49C–D; cf. Xenophon, *Memorabilia* 3.9.8, and pseudo-Plato, *Definitions* 416; see chapter 5, n. 4). So too, as long as Neoptolemus had no personal relationship with Philoctetes, he could place the duty to obey his superiors (925–6) above his sense of shame at tricking, if not an enemy, at least a stranger. But when his natural sense of the ignominy of deception is compounded by the awareness that he has behaved treacherously towards a person who had trusted him, and whose character, moreover, he has learned to respect, he experiences the full charge of shame that his conduct entails.

Richard Shweder and Jonathan Haidt (2000: 406) observe that 'the contemporary Hindu conception of *lajja* (or *lajya*) ... is often translated by bilingual informants and dictionaries as "shame," "embarrassment," "shyness," or "modesty"; yet ... every one of these translations is problematic or fatally flawed.' They go on to remark on 'how hazardous it can be to assume that one can render the emotional meanings of others with terms from our received English lexicon for mental states' (407).[53] This is perfectly just, but a careful examination of the value of emotion terms in other languages can also enrich and clarify our own emotional vocabulary.

Shame was a vigorous emotional category for the ancient Greeks. Although it has tended to be suppressed in contemporary American society, or else treated as a morally deficient emotion (we are ashamed of shame), writers in classical Greece saw it as fundamental to ethical behaviour.[54] And yet, we may have difficulty recognizing the Greek concept as 'shame,' since its phenomenology and modes of expression differed from our own. What Ajax feels in the play described above is shame for us, but not, perhaps, for him, just as we may perceive the colour blue in an ancient painting where a native of the culture would have identified a different complex of hues, defined not just by a shift in spectral range but by visual elements that have ceased to enter into the classification of basic colour terms in modern English (see chapter 1, pp. 5–7).[55] And just as one may gain in visual sensitivity by learning to apprehend an alternative colour system, so too, by attending to the meanings and contexts of ancient terms, we may expand our awareness of how the emotions function, even in our own social world. I venture to hope that this discussion of Greek terms for shame has made a contribution in that direction.

CHAPTER FIVE

Envy and Indignation

Envy ... is that one emotion in all human life about which nothing good can be said.

Friday 1997: 9

Feelings of envy are ... closely linked to feelings about fairness.

Frank 1988: 15

In this chapter, I discuss in tandem two emotions that Aristotle analyses in his treatise on rhetoric. The two are commonly translated as 'envy' (the Greek term is *phthonos*) and 'indignation,' and they have a good deal in common, on Aristotle's description, though Aristotle insists that there is a fundamental difference between them. In what follows, I argue that historically they are even more closely related than Aristotle suggests, and I attempt to explain how and why they diverged to the extent of constituting two distinct sentiments in Aristotle's catalogue. I also maintain that 'indignation,' as Aristotle defines it, was not commonly conceived of as an independent emotion in Aristotle's time. This, then, is a case in which Aristotle seems to have introduced an emotion, and treated it as basic, for reasons that have more to do with his own systematic exposition than with actual usage. I shall try to indicate why he might have been moved to do so, and what relationship his account has with popular conceptions of envy and indignation. Let us begin, then, with 'indignation.'

The term in Aristotle's *Rhetoric* that I have provisionally translated as 'indignation' is in fact not a noun at all, but rather a verbal expression, *to nemesan*. This is a nominalized infinitive – *to* is the Greek definite article, and *nemesan* is an infinitive verb – corresponding to the abstract noun *nemesis*; we may render *to nemesan* as 'being indignant.' We shall consider in a moment why Aristotle avoids the noun in favour of the verbal form. At all events, Aristotle defines *to nemesan* as 'feeling pain at someone who appears to be succeeding undeservedly' (2.9, 1837a8–9). So understood, it is, Aristotle says, the opposite of pity, which he defines in the same treatise, as we have seen, as 'a kind of pain in the case of an apparent destructive or painful harm in one not deserving to encounter it, which one might expect oneself, or one of one's own, to suffer, and this when it seems near' (2.8, 1835b13–16; see further chapter 10). Put schematically, *to nemesan* is pain at undeserved good fortune, whereas pity is pain at undeserved misfortune (2.9, 1386b9–12). Both emotions, Aristotle goes on to say, are marks of a good character, since people ought neither to prosper nor to suffer undeservingly: for what runs counter to worth, Aristotle explains, is unjust. This is why, Aristotle concludes, we ascribe *to nemesan* to the gods, the point being that it entails an assessment of fairness or lawfulness. As the emotion we feel when others unfairly acquire what they have done nothing to earn, *to nemesan* may be taken as a rough equivalent to the English 'indignation.'

Aristotle goes on to note, however, that according to some, not only *to nemesan* but also *phthonos* – the term commonly rendered into English as 'envy' – is the opposite of pity, on the grounds that *phthonos* 'is related to and is indeed the same thing as *to nemesan*' (2.9, 1386b16–17). But in fact, Aristotle avers, the two are different. For, as he explains, although *phthonos* too is 'a disturbing pain arising from the well-being' of another (2.9, 1386b18–19; cf. 2.10, 1387b22–4), it arises not because the other person is undeserving, but simply because he is our equal or similar (2.9, 1386b19–20); and such a person (we feel) ought not to have an advantage over us. In his fuller definition of *phthonos* in the chapter devoted to that emotion (2.10, 1387b23–5), Aristotle states that '*phthonos* is a kind of pain, in respect to one's equals, for their apparent success in things called good, not so as to have the thing oneself but [solely] on their account' – that is, because they have a good that we do not, irrespective of its use to us.[1] It is this indifference both to desert and to one's own need that renders *phthonos* an emotion unsuited to a decent (*epieikês*) person. As Aristotle conceives it, *phthonos* is motivated by a small-minded concern for image – it is characteristic, he says, of people who are *philodoxoi* ('enamoured of popular opinion') and *mikropsukhoi* ('small-souled,' 2.10, 1387b33–4). So petty a sentiment seems little more than spite or malice (cf. Milobenski 1964: 62–5; Cairns 1993: 194 n. 51). Indeed, among all the emotions Aristotle discusses in detail in the *Rhetoric*, including anger and calming down, love and hatred, fear, shame, gratitude, pity, *to nemesan* itself, and *zêlos* or emulation, *phthonos* is the only one that he treats as unqualifiedly negative. So too, the psychologists J. Sabini and M. Silver (1986: 169) have remarked that of the seven deadly sins – greed, sloth, wrath, lust, gluttony, pride, and envy – the six 'other than envy *involve acts having goals which are not in themselves evil but which have been done inappropriately or to excess* ... Envy is out of place on this list, as it does not appear to point to a natural goal. This is the paradox of envy.'[2]

Despite the confidence with which Aristotle distinguishes *to nemesan* from *phthonos*, against the view of those who identified them, in the later rhetorical and philosophical tradition it was in fact the contrast between pity and *phthonos* or 'envy' that prevailed – irrespective of the question of desert – rather than that between pity and *to nemesan*.[3] The Stoics, for example, described pity as pain at another's ill fortune, while envy is pain at another's good fortune (e.g., Andronicus, *On the Emotions* 2 p. 12 Kreuttner = *SVF* 3.414). Cicero effectively transposed Aristotle's dictum concerning pity and *to nemesan* when he wrote (*Tusculan Disputations* 3.21) that 'to pity and to envy [*invidere*] befall the same person, since the same person who is pained at the adverse circumstances of another is pained also at the favourable circumstances of another' (cf. *On the Orator* 1.185, 2.206, 2.216; Ben-Ze'ev 2000: 338–40). Consequently, Cicero concludes in a Stoic vein, a wise man will be subject to neither sentiment.

The Stoics, to be sure, rejected all emotion as incompatible with virtue, and were not interested in defending the value of those emotions based on an assessment of desert, such as pity and *to nemesan*, over ostensibly non-moral passions such as *phthonos*. But there was another reason why Aristotle's contrast between pity and *to nemesan* gave way to that between pity and envy: for the term *nemesan* and its associated noun, *nemesis*, were archaic even by Aristotle's time, except in certain contexts, and were no longer central to the Greek emotional lexicon (the more exhaustive Stoic lists, running to a hundred and more *pathê*, do include *nemesis*). *Nemesis* yielded to *phthonos* as pity's opposite by default, as it were. But the replaceability of the one term by the other nevertheless suggests that there is more to be said than Aristotle allows for the similarity between the two in his own time and earlier. In what follows, I trace the evolution of the two terms and lend support to the view of those who, according to Aristotle, maintained that *phthonos* was 'indeed the same thing as *to nemesan*.' This is a case, then, in which the emotional vocabulary of the Greeks themselves is shown to have a history. And like most historical developments, this one too, I believe, was a product of politics and social antagonisms.

I have preferred to speak of *to nemesan* or 'being indignant' in connection with Aristotle's analysis, rather than use the simple noun *nemesis*, because, as I have indicated, Aristotle himself eschews the latter term in the *Rhetoric*. The reason why is evident from a passage in the *Eudemian Ethics*, where Aristotle avails himself of the word *nemesis* to indicate the virtuous mean between two extremes: the excess is *phthonos* or 'envy,' while the deficiency, according to Aristotle, has no name in ordinary Greek (1220b34–21a10). Aristotle goes on to explain that *phthonos* – the emotion associated with the *phthoneros* man – consists in being pained at those who are doing well and deserve to, whereas the nameless *pathos*, characteristic of one who delights in the misfortune of others (the *epikhairekakos* man, in Aristotle's phrase), consists in being pleased at those who are faring ill even though they do not deserve such misfortune. Aristotle labels the man who strikes the mean between these extremes *nemesêtikos*, and adds that 'what the ancients called *nemesis*' consists in 'being pained at [others'] faring ill or faring well contrary to desert, and being pleased at these same states when they are merited.' This is why, Aristotle says, people think that Nemesis is a goddess (*Eudemian Ethics* 1233b16–34).

It is clear that Aristotle is self-consciously appropriating an archaic word to designate the emotion associated with the character type he calls *nemesêtikos*, so as to have a noun that answers to the vice of *phthonos*. In contemporary diction, Nemesis normally referred to the divinity who for at least two centuries had had a major cult centre in the Attic deme of Rhamnous (for a catalogue of all references to the personified deity, see Hornum 1993: 91–152; the goddess is discussed further below). As defined in the *Eudemian Ethics*, moreover, *nemesis* is a curiously complex emotion, involving both a painful and a pleasurable response to states that may be either good or bad: pleasurable if they are deserved, otherwise painful. So interpreted, *nemesis* encroaches on pity, as Aristotle conceives it, since both entail pain at the undeserved misfortune of another. Aristotle's effort to contrast *nemesis* with *phthonos* in this treatise appears to be something of a dud.

In the *Nicomachean Ethics* (1108b1–10), Aristotle introduces the noun *epikhairekakia*, roughly 'Schadenfreude,' to name the opposite pole to *phthonos*, with *nemesis* again serving as the mean. Here, however, *nemesis* is restricted to being a painful response to another's undeserved good fortune, while *phthonos* is extreme in responding painfully to any good fortune, deserved or not (on pain at others' good fortune, cf. Isocrates 15.149). The *epikhairekakos* person, finally, is so far from feeling pain as actually to take pleasure – at the ill fortune of another, clearly, and irrespective of desert, though Aristotle does not say so explicitly.[4] The reason for this reticence is, I think, that the appropriate opposite to *epikhairekakia* should be pleasure taken in another's justified misfortune, and this sense clashes with the more restricted definition of *to nemesan* given in the *Rhetoric*. So much for Aristotle's rather confusing attempts to adapt the opposition between *nemesis* and *phthonos* to his tripartite model of mean and extremes (further discussion in Milobenski 1964: 74–88).

Not just the noun *nemesis*, but also the verb *nemesan* and the adjectives derived from it were old-fashioned in Aristotle's time, and where they, or *nemesis*, do occur after the archaic period, it is in a limited set of contexts and formulas that suggest fossilized locutions. Leaving aside cases in which Nemesis refers to the goddess, whether in cult or mythology, it and related terms frequently describe the attitude of a deity or deities.[5] Apart from these instances of divine *nemesis*, the most common uses are in the formulas *ou nemesêton* or *anemesêton* (parallel to the expression *ou nemesis*) meaning 'there is no blame attaching' to such and such a word or deed. Here again, the reference is often to things said of the gods, in the hope that they will not take offence.[6] These and similar uses represent a substantial percentage of all occurrences of the root *nemes-* (apart from the proper name Nemesis) in classical and Hellenistic literature down to the first century BC. There are about one hundred such instances in all, of which thirty-three are to be found in Aristotle alone and another dozen in Plato – amounting together to nearly half the total; outside these two, there are some ten or fifteen occurrences in prose. Later, *nemesis* regains a certain popularity with archaizing or moralizing authors, such as Diodorus Siculus and Dionysius of Halicarnassus (especially in his *Roman Antiquities*), as well as with Plutarch and writers of the Second Sophistic. By way of comparison, the root *phthon-* is found seventy-eight times in Demosthenes alone (a few of these in the morally neutral form *aphthonia* or 'abundance').

In Homer, as is well known, *nemesis* is generally aroused at behaviour that runs contrary to socially accepted norms.[7] These norms are not universal in the sense of applying equally to all, but take account of role and status. When Thersites addressed his rude complaint to Agamemnon, the Achaean troops 'raged and grew indignant [*koteonto nemessêthen t'*] in their hearts' (*Iliad* 2.222–3). Achilles' far harsher rebuke of Agamemnon in book 1 evoked no such response in them; here, however, the defiant insubordination of a common soldier excites their pique (cf. Quintilian, *Inst. Or.* 11.1.37). In a contrary vein, Diomedes silences his henchman Sthenelus's irritation at Agamemnon's reprimand (4.413–17): 'I do not *nemesô* at Agamemnon, shepherd of the peoples, for stirring the well-greaved Achaeans to do battle, for just as the glory will be his if the Achaeans should conquer the Trojans and capture holy Troy, so too vast grief is his if the Achaeans should be conquered.' Diomedes recognizes that

Agamemnon's position of responsibility entitles him to speak in ways that might well have caused offence on the lips of another Greek leader.

Sometimes the bare verb, without an explicit object, leaves the motive for the sentiment vague, as when Apollo feels *nemesis* (*nemesêse*) and shouts encouragement to the Trojans as the Achaeans advance upon the walls of the city (*Iliad* 4.507–8). It is reasonable to suppose, however, that, as a god, he is indignant that a mortal army should threaten the city that he favours. When Hera asks Zeus to share her indignation (*Zeu pater, ou nemesizêi?*) at Ares for supporting the Trojan side (5.757–8), she protests that Ares has no sense of what is right (*themista*, 761). Ares, in turn, appeals to Zeus in similar terms after he is wounded by Diomedes at the instigation of Athena (5.872); his point is that it is beyond the province of a mortal to injure a deity.[8] Rutherford, who re-marks (1992: 146 ad 19.121) that 'the sense of divine retribution, common in later Greek and more or less universal in modern usage, is not Homeric,' suggests that passages in which a god expresses displeasure at mortal behaviour, as Apollo does in *Iliad* 24.53, 'perhaps show the germs of the later meaning.' But such instances are perfectly in line with the gods' tendency to take offence at mortal audacity or insolence.

Nemesis is sometimes paired in archaic poetry with *aidôs*, and the two terms are commonly interpreted as designating the exter-nal and internal responses to a violation of customary rules (cf. Hesiod, *Works and Days* 195–200, where, in response to the decline in human morality, Aidos and Nemesis are said to leave the earth and join the other gods on Olympus). Walter Leaf ob-served more than a century ago (1888: 10 ad 13.122): 'It is clear that the word [*nemesis*] is "objective," expressing the indignation felt by other men. *aidôs*, on the other hand, is subjective, the shame felt by the offender.' So too, Stanford (1959: 231 ad 1.350) explains: 'Two complementary qualities restrained the fierce self-centred heroes – *aidôs*, which is a feeling of reverence for certain conventions and privileges of gods and men; and the fear of *nemesis*, *i.e.* just indignation against violations of *aidôs*, includ-ing public censure and generally punishment as well.'[9] The verb *aideisthai*, however, commonly takes a person as direct object, and both sentiments are best treated as other-regarding, the one indicating respect, the other disapproval. Both, moreover, involve considerations of status. At times the verbs *nemizesthai* (middle voice) and *aideisthai* seem all but synonymous.[10] Indeed, one can feel *nemesis* in regard to oneself, by imagining how one would respond if others behaved that way; Achilles cuts short a quarrel between Ajax and Idomeneus by inviting them to do just that (*Iliad* 23.473ff.; cf. Cairns 1993: 98).[11]

The noun *phthonos*, by contrast, is not found in archaic epic, didactic, or hymnal poetry – that is, the oral hexameter tradition that the Greeks identified collectively under the rubric *epos*. The verb *phthoneô* does indeed occur, but is relatively rare: there are just two instances in the *Iliad*, and these within two lines (4.55–6). In return for the destruction of Troy, Hera surrenders to Zeus two of her favourite cities and declares: 'If I *phthoneô* and do not allow [*eaô*] you to demolish them, I shall not succeed, for all that I *phthoneô*, for you a far stronger than I.' The meaning of *phthoneô* here would seem to be 'refuse,' though the stronger sense of 'begrudge' is also compatible with the context.

The *Odyssey* offers eight occurrences of *phthoneô* (including the compound *epiphthoneô* at 11.149, again opposed to *eaô*). For example, Alcinous, king of the Phaeacians, says to his daughter Nausicaa, when she asks permission to wash her clothes at the seashore: 'I do not *phthoneô* you the mules that you request, nor anything else' (6.68). Here, the sense of *phthoneô* is hardly more than 'deny' or 'decline to give' (so too at 1.346, 11.381, 17.400, and 19.348). In one case, the term seems more charged than the bare idea of 'refusal' would suggest. When Odysseus, dressed in rags, seeks entry to his own house and is blocked by the mendicant Irus, who claims sole right to beg inside, Odysseus asserts: 'I do you no harm in deed or word, nor do I *phthoneô* what you are given, though you have plenty; this threshold can hold both of us, and there is no need for you to *phthoneein* others' (18.15–18). Here it would seem that the term assumes the connotation of 'begrudge' or 'resent,' but this sense may be an effect of the context rather than the sign of a true lexical shift.[12]

No form of *phthonos* occurs in Hesiod's *Theogony*. The abstraction thus lacks a genealogy and even the minimal degree of personification that this entails, which is the more curious, given the vast array of psychic and other concepts that are so dignified, including *nemesis* itself (223–30):

And baneful Night also bore Nemesis, a misery [*pêma*] for mortals, and after her Deceit and Love and destructive Old Age, and she bore Strife, fierce of temper. Then hateful Strife bore painful Toil and Oblivion and Famine and tearful Aches and Battles and Wars and Slayings and Murders and Feuds and Lies and Equivocal Words and Lawlessness and Madness, all related to one another.

This is rather unsavoury company for Nemesis, though in keeping with her genesis from Night, and it is plausible to suppose that Nemesis here bears the negative sense of 'resentment' or even 'hatred' rather than 'righteous indignation.'

In the *Works and Days*, the verb *phthoneô* occurs once (26), and here it is associated with what Hesiod calls 'good Strife,' which stirs potters, carpenters, beggars (a reminiscence of the *Odyssey*?), and singers to healthy rivalry with each other. It is more or less synonymous with *speudô*, *zêloô*, and *koteô*, which too are evidently positive terms for competitive effort (for *zêloô* in a negative sense, see 195–6). The contrast between the benign sense of *phthoneô* here and the unappealing characterization of the personified Nemesis is striking.[13] The verb is occasionally used in the neutral sense of 'I don't mind' into the classical period.[14]

The noun *phthonos* makes its first appearance in epinician or victory poetry, and it is prominent, along with its cognates, in the odes of Pindar.[15] Correspondingly, there is sharp decline in *nemesis* and its relatives, in comparison with their frequent appearance in archaic poetry.[16] If there was a transition from *nemesis* to *phthonos*, the moment at which to locate it is at the end of the sixth and beginning of the fifth centuries BC.

That *nemesis* fell out of favour just as *phthonos* became popular, if it is not sheer coincidence, might be taken to reflect a shift in social values from the archaic world of the epic to that of the newly emerging city-state. This would be the more likely if the two terms were always as different in meaning as Aristotle makes them out to be, the former signifying justified indignation and the latter a wholly invidious form of resentment. We have seen, however, that the evidence of Homer and Hesiod speaks against such a sharp contrast. What is more, it is clear that *phthonos* was not regarded as a uniformly negative emotion even in the classical period.

As Aristotle indicates, the contrast between pity and *phthonos* (rather than *to nemesan* and *phthonos*) was a commonplace in his time. As Pindar puts it (*Pythians* 1.85), '*phthonos* is better than pity [*oiktirmos*],' the point being that success is preferable to failure, despite the envy it may entail.[17] When the Athenian soldiers in Sicily were facing defeat, Nicias attempted to reassure them by observing that they were more deserving of the gods' pity than of their *phthonos* (Thucydides 7.77.4).[18] Lysias, in his funeral oration (2.67), contrasts envy for others' goods with pity for those who have been wronged – the latter clearly considered the more virtuous sentiment (cf. 24.2). Pity, in turn, was associated with unmerited misfortune – as opposed to misfortune per se – well before Aristotle, although Aristotle was perhaps the first to make this a formal part of the definition, and the connection between pity and desert underlay appeals to pity in forensic and deliberatory rhetoric.[19] To take one example among many, Isocrates (*On the Chariot* 48.6) asserts that 'one must pity those who are unjustly at risk.'[20]

It is not surprising, then, that *phthonos* too – as pity's opposite – should be linked with desert.[21] Isaeus can say of his clients (6.61): 'Thus, *they* do not deserve *phthonos*, but much rather, by Zeus and Apollo, these others do, if they acquire what does not belong to them.' *Phthonos* is legitimate when directed at those who do not have title to the goods they possess. Demosthenes, in his speech *Against Meidias* (21.196), assails his opponent: 'You would have discovered a great rule, or rather a great art, if in so short a time you could win for yourself two things that are absolutely opposite to each other: *phthonos* for your way of life, and pity for your lies. But pity doesn't fit you in any way, but just the opposite: hatred and *phthonos* and anger. That's what you deserve for what you do.' Meidias, according to Demosthenes, has earned *phthonos*, because his arrogance and privilege are not warranted.[22] Towards such an individual, *phthonos* is perfectly appropriate, even required. Isocrates, in his speech, *Panathenaicus* (23), speaks of others as 'unjustly feeling *phthonos*' towards him (*adikôs ... phthonountas*), and proposes to teach them that 'they hold this view neither justly nor rightly' (*hôs ou dikaiôs oude prosêkontôs ... tautên ekhousi tên gnômên*). The implication is that their opinion of him would have been justified if, by his behaviour, he had in fact flaunted his superiority. The function of *phthonos* is to preserve the proper hierarchy in society. If a person attempts to exceed his station, he rightly incurs *phthonos*, as does an inferior who pretends to equality with his betters (e.g., the gods). Again, when Isocrates, in his letter to Philip of Macedon (22), complains that he as much as Philip is a victim of *phthonos*, the suggestion is that he, like Philip, is entitled to regard; this is why the sentiment is malicious in their case.[23] Clearly the term does not mean 'envy' in these contexts, if by envy we understand a gratuitous or improper resentment at another's well-being. So too the verb *phthoneô* may carry the sense 'feel righteous indignation at.'[24]

To be sure, Demosthenes can also affirm to the Athenians (20.140): '*Phthonos* is an absolute sign of vice [*kakia*] in human nature, and he who harbours it has no pretext by which to obtain sympathy,' in accord with Aristotle's own harsh evaluation of this sentiment (cf. 165; also Plato, *Timaeus* 297D: 'No *phthonos* concerning anything ever arises in a good man'; and Isocrates, *Antidosis* 142 on *phthonos* directed at those who are morally superior). We can explain the apparent contradiction in these uses of *phthonos* by observing that it was never a compliment to characterize someone as *phthoneros*, that is, temperamentally given to resenting others' well-being, and manifestations of *phthonos* could be taken as a sign of such a disposition. But this does not mean that *phthonos* is invariably illegitimate. The rich and powerful might attempt to stigmatize all *phthonos* as invidious, but in the world of democratic Athens, the way to avoid *phthonos* was to make proper use of one's advantages in the service of the community at large.[25] *Phthonos*, then, was not simply a moral flaw, but had a constructive social function as well.[26] As the philosopher Hippias of Elea (a contemporary of Socrates) said, 'There are two kinds of *phthonos*, one just, when a person feels *phthonos* in regard to bad people who are held in esteem, the other unjust, when one feels it in regard to good people' (fragment B16 Diels-Kranz; quoted by Stobaeus 3.38.32 from Plutarch's lost essay *On Slander*).

If *phthonos*, so understood, seems to approximate the sense that Aristotle ascribes to *to nemesan*, namely, a response to undeserved prosperity (*eupragein anaxiôs*), Aristotle himself acknowledges that *to nemesan*, in turn, is not simply indignation at the illegitimate acquisitions of another, but is also modulated by what we may call class entitlement. Thus, he says, 'the *nouveaux riches* [*neoploutoi*] who acquire office by means of their wealth offend more than the *anciens riches* [*arkhaioploutoi*] ..., the reason being that the latter seem to have what is truly theirs, but the former do not' (*Rhetoric* 2.9, 1387a22–5). As Aristotle explains, 'What is ancient seems practically natural' (1387a16). The traditional elites are perceived to deserve wealth and office, and hence escape reproach even when they have done nothing to earn them. This connection between *nemesan* and status is not very different from the way the term is used in Homer.

All in all, then, *nemesis* appears to overlap considerably with *phthonos* in classical Greek. Both terms represent an emotional response based on the judgment that a person, whether an equal or an inferior, is getting above himself. It is true that, at least in democratic Athens, *phthonos* tended to be associated particularly with what we might call 'upward resentment,' that is, the anger of the lower classes towards the rich, whereas in Homer, *nemesis* seems more often to express 'downward resentment' on the part of superiors – whether gods or mortals – towards inferiors who overstep their station.[27] Aristotle himself points out (*Rhetoric* 2.9, 1387b5–8) that those who are worthy of good things and in fact possess them are particularly *nemesêtikoi* – prone to feel *nemesis* – because it is unjust that lesser people should be deemed deserving of comparable goods. But Aristotle also notes that the successful tend to be *phthoneroi* (*Rhetoric* 2.10, 1387b28–9; for the *phthonos* of kings, cf. Herodotus 3.80, 5.92.ζ–η; Demosthenes 11.12; Cairns 2003: 242). The difference between upward and downward resentment does not seem adequately to distinguish the two terms on an abstract conceptual level, although, as we shall see, it provides a clue to the different connotations and uses of *phthonos* itself in Aristotle's own time.

It is not clear why the term *nemesis* and its congeners fell out of favour in the classical period. Perhaps they merely sounded poetic, like *aidôs* itself, and came to be restricted to more elevated registers of diction, even though the meaning of the terms remained familiar and usable. We cannot simply assume, as I have indicated, that *nemesis* was so closely bound up with the values of archaic epic poetry that it became obsolete as an idea in the society of the classical city-state. As for *phthonos*, the reasons for its absence in archaic hexameter poetry, and the morally neutral or, in Hesiod, evidently positive significance of the verb *phthoneô* in contrast to its frequently pejorative sense in the classical era, are lost in the prehistory of the Greek language. Glenn Most (2003) has argued that heroic epic self-consciously banished envy as a motive to the margins of the heroic community (e.g., the beggar Irus), preferring to ascribe to the warriors themselves a spirit of noble rivalry. But the absence of the noun in Hesiod, who, as Most notes, did not share the heroic ethos of the Homeric epics, suggests that *phthonos* may not have had the ethically charged meaning that it acquired in the classical period, and may have been something of a latecomer as a central term in the Greek moral vocabulary, displacing, as it came into use, *nemesis* and its relatives. Since our knowledge of everyday Greek in the period during which the epics were being actively composed is practically nil, it is idle to speculate on whether *phthonos* was a common term outside the epic tradition, and if so, precisely where and in which dialects.

If *nemesis* came subsequently to be associated more exclusively with divine censure than it had been in archaic poetry, the reason may well be the rise to prominence of the local cult of the goddess Nemesis in the Attic deme of Rhamnous (see especially Stafford 2000). The status of Nemesis as a minor deity in myth seems to have been ancient. A tradition perhaps going back to the *Cypria* in the epic cycle makes her the mother of Helen; she sought to avoid Zeus's embrace by changing her shape (like Thetis), but when she assumed the form of a goose, Zeus metamorphosed into a swan and overpowered her. Hence it happened that Helen was hatched from an egg.[28] But it is plausible that the Athenian victory over the Persians at Marathon, located near the deme of Rhamnous, was perceived as a god-sent curb on the Persians' overweening ambitions, comparable to Apollo's resentment at the Achaeans' attack in the *Iliad*. In her indignation at the Persians, Nemesis enacted *nemesis*, and this gave a boost, as Stafford argues (2000: 88–9), to her status as emblem of divine retribution.

The importance of the cult of Nemesis ensured that *nemesis* would remain a live idea in ancient Greece. As a personified concept, however, Nemesis was no longer just an emotional response to the violation of social limits, but a complexly motivated figure who could feel the very sentiment she stood for. The epigraphical evidence suggests also 'a frightful being who can snatch away any success or good fortune a human being has obtained, a sort of *malocchio*' (Hornum 1993: 9), and one epitaph for an eighteen-year-old boy from the imperial period refers to her as *phthonerên Nemesin* ('envious Nemesis').[29] Unlike Nemesis, *phthonos* seems never to have had a rite or mythology of its own, but it too might be momentarily personified. In Sophocles' *Philoctetes*, the hero, about to suffer a bout of his disease, hands over to Neoptolemus the bow he had received from Hercules with the words (774–8) 'Come then, take it, son; and pray [*proskuson*] to Phthonos that this weapon may not bring grief to you, nor be what it was for me and him who owned it before me.' As an object of prayer, Phthonos acquires a human character, and one can appeal to it not to exercize the very emotion it names – that is, resentment that a man should possess a weapon greater than that which pertains to mortals.[30] The analogy with divine Nemesis is clear, but the positive sense of *phthonos* was not protected in the long run, as *nemesis* was, by official worship.

That the gods were believed to be capable of *phthonos* has scandalized critics both ancient and modern. Plato, for example, declares (*Phaedrus* 247A7) that 'envy stands outside the chorus of the gods.'[31] Yet Herodotus put into the mouth of Solon the statement that 'the divine is wholly *phthoneron*' (1.32.5–6; cf. 8.109), and comparable sentiments are expressed by other contemporary writers.[32] Inordinate success or ambition, like that of Croesus in

Herodotus's tale, invites the gods' resentment because it threatens to cross the line between mortal and divine. Though described as *phthonos*, this top-down indignation is no different from that expressed by the older term *nemesis*. As Douglas Cairns (1996: 18) observes: 'There is in many a passage a strong connexion between "thinking more than mortal thoughts" and divine *phthonos*' (cf. 18–22 for further examples; Hornum 1993: 9). It is just in relation to the gods that the moral distinction drawn by Aristotle between *nemesis* and *phthonos* has least salience.[33]

We have seen that, in the *Eudemian Ethics*, Aristotle explains the worship of Nemesis by her connection with justice, and that, in the *Rhetoric*, he says that *to nemesan* is ascribed to the gods for much the same reason. Aristotle himself conceives of the divine as wholly contemplative in nature (*Nicomachean Ethics* 10.8, 1178b8–23), and hence devoid of emotion. His association of *nemesis* with divinity serves to underscore the distinction he draws between *to nemesan* as a virtuous sentiment and the vice of *phthonos*, once he had resuscitated the archaic expression *to nemesan* as a technical term to denote a morally acceptable opposite to pity as he defined it. But if religious personification helped to enhance the moral aspect of *nemesis*, it is equally true that *phthonos* suffered the opposite process of pejoration from its neutral or even positive sense in archaic poetry to its status as a moral failing in philosophy and rhetorical topoi of the classical period, where it is censured for being directed indiscriminately at all excellence or superiority.[34] Even in these cases, it is usually implicit that *phthonos* is not so much wrong in principle as unjustified in the particular instance, since the individual in question is in truth both exceptional and a benefit to the community. Aristotle himself notes, as we have seen, that people feel *phthonos* only at the success of those who are or seem their equals (*Rhetoric* 2.10, 1387b25–6) and are near themselves in station (1388a6–9), the logic being that equals *deserve* to prosper equally.[35]

Why did *phthonos* acquire so negative a reputation in the classical period? The answer requires situating *phthonos* in the ideological struggles between the elites and the masses in the Greek world, and especially in Athens, from the sixth to the fourth centuries. It seems particularly to have been a charge levelled at the poorer classes by the rich – hence its 'bottom-up' character in forensic and philosophical discourse, as well as in aristocratic lyric poetry.[36] No doubt the term circulated in all levels of society and had a certain semantic homogeneity across the culture.[37] But, from Pindar onward, an elite disdain of lower-class resentment at what they conceived of as their legitimate privileges seems to have prevailed in conditioning its moral significance.

There is an analogy, indeed, in the complex senses of the term 'envy' in modern English. We have cited Sabini and Silver's observation that envy stands out as perverse even in the company of the six other capital sins, and it gives rise to some of the harshest judgments in the whole range of the emotions. The popular writer Nancy Friday (1997: 9) reports: 'Envy, I would learn, is that one emotion in all human life about which nothing good can be said'; according to the philosopher Richard Wollheim (1999: 91), envy is an example of an emotion that is 'invariably malformed'; and the social theorist and psychologist Robert Solomon observes (1993: 207): 'Envy is an essentially vicious emotion, bitter and vindictive.'[38]

Yet some investigators argue that envy is not a wholly negative sentiment, but may – as in ancient Greek usage – have a socially constructive function. The socio-linguist Anna Wierzbicka (1999: 234) judges that '[e]nvy, which used to be regarded as one of the seven deadly sins ..., appears to be now seen as a less grave offense; after all, it can be said to imply only a desire for equality, which is one of the key modern ideals.' So too, the economist Robert Frank (1988: 15) affirms that 'it may pay people to feel envious, because feeling that way makes them better bargainers ... Feelings of envy are also closely linked to feelings about fairness.' And the sociologist J.M. Barbalet (1998: 106), after citing Adam Smith's (1982: 243) characterization of envy as the 'odious and detestable passion,' comments that '[e]nvy is not thought of today as a shameful thing ... Envy is simply the emotional form of a desire for benefits which others are believed to possess.'[39] Indeed, nearly four centuries ago Descartes (1988: 262 art. 182) had already written: 'What one commonly calls envy is a vice that consists in a perversity of nature, which makes certain people angry at the good that they see coming into the possession of other men. But I use the word here to mean a passion that is not always vicious. Envy, then, insofar as it is a passion, is a kind of sadness mixed with hatred that occurs when one sees a good coming into the possession of those who, one thinks, are unworthy of it' – a sense very like Aristotle's definition of *to nemesan*.

Why should envy have such different, and apparently contrary or incompatible, meanings in Anglo-American culture? It may be that the term is changing valences as modern society becomes more egalitarian in its ideology, as Wierzbicka and others suggest. Perhaps, too, the idea of envy both reflects and confirms polarized social roles within the modern, politically democratic state. Thus, Arlie Hochschild (1975: 291) observes: 'While the moral injunction against envy applies to winners and losers alike, envy is unequally distributed among winners and losers. In other words, the socially induced feeling and the rule against it are systematically discrepant.' Envy is both a natural response to systemic inequality and a stigmatized feeling at the level of individual morality (Lansky [1997: 330] observes that 'disowning is a major clinical feature of envy'). To seem anything other than petty, envy must, according to Hochschild, find expression in a social movement (292). An analogous social dynamic – but in the reverse direction – may have contributed to the complex sense of *phthonos* in classical Athens.

Aristotle, like Plato, Isocrates, and many other prominent Greek intellectuals, regarded democracy with a certain suspicion, especially in the extreme egalitarian form it had assumed in Athens in the fifth and fourth centuries BC. It was thus natural that he should have regarded *phthonos* as a vice endemic to democracy, one that is excited by the prosperity of those we deem our equals (Isocrates [*Nicocles* 18] affirms that 'those who live under monarchies have no one toward whom to feel *phthonos*,' since they do not compare themselves with the king or imagine that they are on the same level as he).[40] As such, however, it was unsatisfactory as the opposite emotion to pity, which for Aristotle was a moral sentiment responding, as we have seen, not to suffering as such but to unmerited misfortune. It is for this reason, I believe, that Aristotle appropriated an old-fashioned term for moral indignation, one that had acquired a particularly high-minded tone through its association with the cult of Nemesis at Rhamnous, and elevated it to the first rank among the emotions that an orator must learn to manipulate, thereby sealing the reduction of *phthonos* to a wholly unworthy sentiment – the only one in Aristotle's catalogue that is not appropriate under any circumstances.[41] Furthermore, the decision to treat *to nemesan* as the opposite of pity had an impact on Aristotle's account of another emotion in the *Rhetoric* – the one he treats first and at greatest length, namely, *orgê* or anger. For if *nemesis* was the opposite of pity, then there was no room for anger to occupy this position, even though in the courts and other deliberative contexts it was most commonly anger – certainly not the archaic term *nemesis* – that speakers contrasted with pity (see chapter 2, pp. 66–9). I suspect that, in the *Rhetoric*, Aristotle deliberately limited the causes of anger to personal slights, as opposed to injustices in general, at least in part because he wished to reserve the idea of outrage at an undeserved advantage for the *pathos* that he chose to label *to nemesan*.

In this chapter, I have attempted to show that the opposition between *nemesis* and *phthonos* to which Aristotle testifies, and which many modern scholars accept as the full story, masks a complementary similarity between the two sentiments, insofar as both denote a resentment at people who 'get above themselves' and violate the status rules of a highly class-conscious society. This is why *phthonos* in classical prose and poetry could substitute for *nemesis* in archaic epic as the term for divine displeasure at human immoderation (religious formulas tend to preserve antiquated diction). The further evolution of the two words, and their polarization as moral concepts, was not due to an original difference in meaning (at least so far as one can determine from surviving texts), but was shaped by cultural and historical factors, including the rise of the cult of Nemesis and the politically charged use of *phthonos* in the ideological discourse of the polis. Even so, the affinity between the two concepts was never wholly eclipsed in classical Greek.

CHAPTER SIX

Fear

Fear – of death, of pain, of disgrace – is the main ground of courage.

W.I. Miller 2000: 201

The unique function of fear is to motivate escape from dangerous situations.

Izard and Ackerman 2000: 260

Of all the emotions analysed by Aristotle, fear would appear to be the most universal, identical, more or less, not only across human cultures but pertaining to the higher animals as well. We might doubt whether a charging bull is angry, at least on Aristotle's conception of anger as a response to a slight or, more generally, to injustice, which requires a capacity to evaluate the intentions of others in reference to a moral code. So too with shame and envy, which depend on complex cognitive judgments. We have little hesitation, however, about ascribing fear to a deer in flight. In moving from these socially conditioned emotions to fear, then, it may seem that we are changing in some measure the object under investigation.

Paul Griffiths (1997: 8–9), indeed, includes fear among 'short-term, stereotypical responses involving facial expression, autonomic nervous system arousal, and other elements,' as opposed to 'higher cognitive emotions such as envy, guilt, jealousy, and love' (Griffiths, however, lumps anger in with fear in the former category, along with surprise, joy, and disgust).[1] David Scruton, by contrast, has coined the term 'sociophobics' in order to identify the 'study of human fears as these occur and are experienced in the context of the socialcultural systems' (1986: 9), in the belief that the emotions, including fear, are 'not innate ... any more than language is' (18). Scruton points out that '[m]uch of our fearing is not for self at all, but for others, and these fears can easily reach or surpass the intensity of those for ourselves' (8). 'Fearing for' should involve cognitive processes as much as love does, though one may question whether it is the same emotion as direct fear.[2]

Let us turn, then, to Aristotle, in order to see whether his discussion sheds light on the cognitive status of fear (later, we shall have occasion to consider his views on indirect fear, in particular in connection with tragedy). Aristotle's definition of fear (or, rather, of *phobos*) runs as follows:

Let fear be a kind of pain or disturbance deriving from an impression [*phantasia*] of a future evil that is destructive or painful; for not all evils are feared, for example whether one will be unjust or slow, but as many as are productive of great pain or destruction, and these if they are not distant but rather seem near so as to impend. For things that are remote are not greatly feared. (*Rhetoric* 2.5, 1382a21–5)

In illustration of the last clause, Aristotle points out that all people know they will die, but because death is not near, they do not fear it (Cephalus in the first book of Plato's *Republic* expresses a similar view; cf. 330D).[3] It follows from Aristotle's definition of fear, moreover, that frightening things (*phobera*) are just those that seem to possess the power to destroy or to inflict the kind of harm that entails intense pain. Correspondingly, signs or tokens (*sêmeia*) of such things are also frightening, for then the frightening thing itself seems near; danger, Aristotle adds, is just the approach of what is frightening (1382a25–32). Note that, although we fear pain, according to Aristotle, it is not pain that is frightening but rather those things that portend it, for example a poisonous snake or a poised spear.[4] The track of a snake in the sand, or a rattling sound, are frightening in turn because they indicate that a snake is nearby. Fear involves knowledge and inference.

Aristotle's account of fear shares a number of elements with his analysis of pity, as his definition of pity makes clear: 'Let pity, then, be a kind of pain in the case of an apparent destructive or painful harm of one not deserving to encounter it, which one might expect onself, or one of one's own, to suffer, and this when it seems near' (2.8, 1385b13–16). Both emotions are described as pain caused by the proximity of something destructive or harmful. The differences between the two are equally revealing, however. First, fear arises from a direct impression of something bad, and is not mediated by inference from the suffering of another to what we might ourselves experience (we shall see below that Aristotle himself gives reason to qualify this description of fear). Second, in the case of fear there is no reference to merit or desert: criminals fear punishment even if they deserve it, whereas pity entails an assessment of whether the other is suffering justly or not. Fear, then, does not involve the complex moral judgment that Aristotle ascribes to pity and to pity's contrary, *nemesis*, or indignation.

This is not to say that cognition plays no role in Aristotle's account of fear. In modern scientific literature on the emotions, cognition is used in various senses.[5] At one extreme, it refers to ethical evaluations such as those Aristotle associates with pity. At the other, it designates bare perception, which is itself a function of elaborate processes in the cerebral cortex (Rolls 1999: 6). Between the extremes of moral evaluation – 'this is wrong' – and simple perception – 'this is painful' (assuming for a moment that perceptions may be rendered propositionally) – we may distinguish a third kind of judgment of the form 'this is harmful.' This latter evaluation normally depends on experience; as Aaron Ben-Ze'ev (2000: 52) puts it, we do not fear motorcycles unless we have 'some knowledge about the dangers of motorcycles.' Aristotle himself observes that there are two ways in which people become insensible (*apatheis*) to frightening things: either because they have no experience of the danger, for example, the perils of seafaring (or of motorcycles), or because they have the resources to deal with it (1138a28–9). Already in antiquity, Aspasius, who wrote the earliest surviving commentary on any of Aristotle's works (mid-2nd century AD), criticized the view of the peripatetic philosopher Andronicus, who held that 'an emotion arises because of a supposition [*hupolêpsis*] of good or bad things' (Andronicus's formula apparently cuts the difference between utilitarian and ethical judgments). In reply, Aspasius affirmed that 'certain emotions are generated simply by impressions [*phantasiai*],' that is, they arise 'as a result of perception (*aisthêsis*) when something appears as pleasant or painful'; hence they are prior to any supposition. Although Aspasius does not mention fear,[6] one can see how he might have arrived at his conclusion, since fear, according to Aristotle, arises from a *phantasia*; but Aristotle specifies, as we have seen, that 'it is an impression of a future *evil*,' not of pain per se, that generates fear. At least in regard to fear, then (and, we may add, the other emotions that Aristotle discusses in the *Rhetoric*), the truth lies more with Andronicus than with Aspasius.

The process of identifying a thing as frightening, as Aristotle immediately makes clear, involves sophisticated social judgments as well. Among the causes of fear, for example, Aristotle includes anger or enmity on the part of people who have the power (*dunamenoi*) to inflict harm or pain (2.5, 1382a32–3). Hatred or enmity, as we saw in chapter 2, involves a disposition to cause harm, whereas anger is by definition a desire for a perceptible kind of revenge. The ability to do harm, then, is not in itself frightening, unless it is accompanied by a hostile intention. But this means that, to feel fear, we must understand the nature of anger and hatred, which themselves depend on complex judgments (e.g., the significance of a slight or insult, and the contexts in which a given gesture counts as such).

Broadly speaking, according to Aristotle, those people are frightening who are unjust or arrogant, who fear us or are our competitors, whom we have wronged or who have wronged us, and indeed anyone who is in a position to do us a bad turn, since, Aristotle says, human beings will usually take advantage of others if they can (2.5, 1382b8–9). The chief catalyst of fear in all these cases is the superior strength of the other party (2.5, 1382b15–19). So too confidence (*to tharsos*), which Aristotle characterizes as the opposite of fear, derives from the knowledge that any rivals we may have are either weak or of a friendly disposition, or else that we have more or stronger allies on our side (2.5, 1383a22–5). Aristotle adds that confidence is inspired also by inference and comparison. Thus, we shall be confident if we believe that we have defeated people who are equal to or stronger than our enemies and rivals, or that we have more wealth, friends, land, and matériel for war (2, 5.1383a32–b3) than they do.[7] In turn, people are rendered fearful if they are reminded that more powerful people than they have suffered reversals, since this causes them to recognize their own vulnerability (1383a.8–12) – an inference from the fate of others that is reminiscent of Aristotle's analysis of pity.

William Fortenbaugh describes well the complex role of ratiocination in Aristotle's conception of fear (2002: 103). A frightened soldier, he explains,

> sees a cloud of dust on the horizon and connects the cloud with an advancing army. He thinks the army hostile and capable of taking his life, which he values dearly. Making these connections is the work of *logos* [reason] (428a24); it also sets the stage for a further exercise of *logos*. As Aristotle tells us, fear makes men ready to deliberate (*Rhet.* 1385a5). Believing themselves in danger, men desire safety and engage in practical deliberations ('whether to do this or that?'). That too requires *logos*, in which animals have no share.[8]

Like anger, hatred, shame, and envy, fear, for Aristotle, was not an instinctive aversion but a socially conditioned response in which relations of power and judgments concerning the status and attitudes of others play a crucial role – a subject for 'sociophobics,' if you like. Aristotle's conception of fear pertains to that same world of intense competition and struggle for dominance that we have identified as the context for most of the emotions that he discusses in the *Rhetoric*.

To understand better how an apparently visceral reaction like fear can depend essentially on reasoning and evaluation, we may appeal to the neurological analysis proposed by the physiologist Joseph LeDoux. LeDoux recognizes that emotions have an important cognitive dimension, but he maintains that '[t]he perceptual representation of an object and the evaluation of an object are separately processed in the brain ... It is, indeed, possible for your brain to know that something is good or bad before it knows exactly what it is' (1996: 69). Thus, a snake-like object may cause us to recoil before we determine, by slower neural pathways, whether the stimulus was in fact a dangerous reptile rather than, say, a stick (contra Rolls 1999: 6, 97, 104). At this point, we can correct our instinctive reaction (284). By 'good or bad,' LeDoux means simply 'positive or negative,' that is, productive of aversion or attraction. LeDoux does not indicate, however, what relation must obtain between the two neural events in order for a response to qualify as fear. Is it enough to rear back at a snake-like thing, even if one subsequently recognizes that it is not in fact harmful, or indeed that it constitutes a tasty dinner item? Or must the initial reaction be confirmed by the judgment that the object was in fact dangerous if we are to speak of fear proper, and not just an instinctive reflex like the so-called startle response that is consequent upon a sudden loud noise? For Aristotle, at all events, the reflex alone is not an emotion: for it to be a *pathos* requires that one also have evaluated the object as being harmful, and hence involves higher-order neural processes.[9]

Fear for Aristotle is (to repeat his definition) a 'pain or disturbance deriving from an impression of a future evil.' The impression includes the judgment or, perhaps more accurately, it is an impression of something already evaluated as harmful. Such an impression is disturbing, and the result is fear. Fear, then, just is the disturbance associated with the impression of harm, just as anger is the desire for revenge in response to a slight. Opinions may, of course, differ about what constitutes harm: Socrates and later thinkers such as the Stoics and Epicureans denied that death was an evil, and to one who holds this view, the approach of death is not a cause of fear. But if one considers a given event to be harmful, and the threat of it to be imminent (for example, an attack on the part of a powerful enemy), then one fears it. Fear is not the sign of a moral or other deficiency; it just is the response to a credible danger. Indeed, failure to experience fear in such circumstances would testify rather to a cognitive deficit. Aristotle makes this clear in his analysis of courage, where he argues (*Nicomachean Ethics* 1115b23–8) that 'it is for the sake of what is noble that the courageous man stands fast and does what courage requires. Of those who go to excess, there is no name for the man who acts out of lack of fear [aphobia] ..., but such a person would be either mad or insensible to pain, if he feared nothing, whether an earthquake or seawaves, as they say is the case with the Celts.'[10] So too, when Socrates, in Xenophon's *Memorabilia* (4.6.10), asks Euthydemus: 'Don't you think that it is useful to be ignorant when it comes to terrible and dangerous things?' Euthydemus replies: 'On the contrary.' 'Then, those who are not afraid of such things because they do not know what they are are not courageous at all?' asks Socrates. 'Right, for on that basis, many madmen and cowards would be deemed courageous' (in the continuation, Socrates concludes that those who know how to make the right use of terrible and dangerous things are truly courageous). Again, Socrates says to Pericles, son of the famous general, in reference to the decline of Athens's martial confidence after losses in battles to the Boeotians:

Confidence [to tharros] instils carelessness, negligence [rathumia], and heedlessness, whereas fear makes people more attentive, more obedient, and more orderly. You can judge this by what happens on ships: whenever the sailors fear nothing, they are bursting with disorder, but when they fear a storm or enemies, they not only do all that they are commanded but silently await instructions, just like members of a chorus.[11]

Far from being irrational, as Aristotle puts it, 'fear makes people deliberative [bouleutikos]' (*Rhetoric* 2.5, 1382a5).

During the famous battle at Thermopylae, in which three hundred Spartans lost their lives defending a pass against the invading Persians, a certain Aristodemus, Herodotus tells us (7.229–31), missed the fighting because of eye trouble. Upon returning alive to Sparta, he was the object of 'reproach and dishonour' (oneidos, atimiê), and was dubbed 'he who trembled' (ho tresas, 231). Later, however, at the battle of Plataea, Aristodemus removed the stigma, for he was far the best among the fighters, in Herodotus's judgment (9.71). The Spartans, however, refused to grant him this honour, because 'he clearly desired to die, on account of the censure that attached to him, and only by raging madly and leaving the battle formation did he demonstrate great deeds; Posidonius, however, was a commendable man although he did

not wish to die, and precisely to this extent he was the better.'
Herodotus hints that envy might have motivated the Spartans'
preference, but it is clear that courage was perceived not as a
disregard for death, but as vacuous without the fear of it.

The idea that fear is simply the response to danger, above all in
the form of an enemy in a position to do one harm, makes a
difference to how we understand the nature and function of fear
in Greek literature. We may take as our first example the duel
between Hector and Achilles at the beginning of the twenty-
second book of the *Iliad*. Hector stands alone outside the walls of
Troy, waiting nervously as Achilles races towards him for the
final showdown after the slaying of Patroclus. Hector's mother
and father have attempted in vain to dissuade him from facing his
more powerful (*pherteros*) adversary (40), but Hector is determined. Were it for martial pride alone, he might have retreated
into the safety of the city, but he is ashamed (105) at the losses he
caused to the Trojan side by keeping the army in the field after
Achilles' return to battle, and rather than face the Trojan men and
women he prefers to take his chances with Achilles. Caught
between shame and fear, Hector indulges in a strange reverie: he
imagines that he might lay down his armour and promise Achilles
to yield up Helen and all Troy's riches to the Achaeans. But he
knows that such a gesture is futile. The issue between him and
Achilles has transcended the original cause of the war, and Achilles, he reflects, will kill him shamelessly, naked as he is, like a
woman (124–5). And so he decides to fight, but as Achilles draws
near, his armour blazing like the sun, a trembling seizes him and,
unable to stand his ground, he flees in fear (*bê de phobêtheis*, 137).[12]

Fearing and avoiding a stronger opponent is natural; only shame
at a previous lapse in judgment – not shame at taking flight itself –
prevents Hector from seeking refuge within the walls of Troy.
When Nestor, beset by the Trojans, proposed flight (*phobos*) to
Diomedes (8.139), the greatest Achaean warrior after Achilles,
Diomedes hesitated at the thought that Hector would boast to the
Trojans that he, Diomedes, had been put to rout in fear of him
(*phobeumenos*, 149), but in the end he yielded to Nestor's good
judgment and turned his horses to flight (*phugade*, 157 answering
to *phobonde*, 139). A scholiast remarks of this passage, 'A timely

retreat brings no shame'; so too Agamemnon asserts (14.80): 'There is nothing invidious in fleeing harm [*kakon*].'[13] Momentarily paralysed by two conflicting emotions, Hector fantasizes a way of saving his life while retaining his honour, but he immediately realizes that this is impossible and decides to stand firm. As Achilles approaches, however, Hector's resolution, which had been prompted by shame, yields to fear (danger, as Aristotle says, is the approach of what is frightening, while 'things that are remote are not greatly feared'), and he takes to his heels.[14] We may recall Aristotle's definition of the emotions as 'those things on account of which people change their minds and differ in regard to their judgments.'[15]

Jean Delumeau, in his study of episodes of mass fear in Europe from the fourteenth to the eighteenth century, observes that the chivalric code treated fear as shameful, and it is rarely mentioned in knightly literature (1978: 14, citing Delpierre 1973: 7). As opposed to this 'archetype of the fearless knight' (15), it is the humble who are fearful (16). Even after the French revolution, when the humble classes took power, they mimed the fearlessness of the nobility (17). As a result, Delumeau asserts, a conspiracy of silence has surrounded the history of fear. Only with modern warfare has a real change occurred:

It is probable that knights in times past, impulsive, accustomed to war and duels, who hurled their doomed bodies into the fray, were less conscious than soldiers of the twentieth century of the dangers of combat, and so less susceptible to fear. In our times, at all events, fear before the enemy has become the rule. On the basis of surveys taken in the American army in Tunisia and the Pacific during the Second World War, it turns out that only one in a hundred men asserted that they had never been afraid. (21)[16]

The medieval contempt for fear has its roots in antiquity, according to Delumeau: 'Fear proves souls ignoble' (*degeneres animos timor arguit*), says Dido to her sister Anna (Virgil, *Aeneid* 4.13, cited in Delumeau 1978: 15), although, curiously enough, she begins her speech by confessing that 'dreams are terrifying me' (9), and goes on to express her anxiety for Aeneas. So too, the Homeric scholia (ad 13.95) remark that 'it is a Greek trait to appeal to shame; among the barbarians, Hector appeals not to what is shameful but rather to fear' (cf. *Iliad* 12.250) as a means of encouraging them to fight (he threatens to stab laggards with his spear). Fear is already considered a sign of a debased spirit.[17]

Homer's Hector, however, is not a coward. His fear is the register of Achilles' superior power, as Aristotle might express it. Not to fear, in his circumstances, would be to fail to take account of the realities. Achilles himself is afraid (*deisas*, 21.249) when he is caught in the flood of the river Scamander: mortals cannot normally prevail against an irate god (the river is personified in this episode). Aristotle's cognitive account of fear, according to which fear is produced by an impression of imminent harm, permits us to appreciate Hector's reaction to the advancing Achilles as compatible with courage. Shortly afterwards, when he believes, mistakenly, that his brother Deiphobus (really Athena in disguise) is at hand to help him, Hector announces that he will cease running away in fear (22.250). This again is to be expected, since the odds are now closer to being equal. Whatever the case for medieval knighthood, in archaic and classical Greece heroes were not supposed to be fearless in the face of a hostile and superior force.[18]

This is not to say, of course, that fear is never a sign of cowardice: if one's own side is not inferior, then fear is evidence of undue timidity, and Hector himself reproaches Polydamas for such trepidation (*deos*, 12.246).[19] Obviously, there is room for error in evaluating the balance of power: a disposition to fear will cause one to overestimate the capacities of the enemy. Habitual success or failure, in turn, also condition one's judgment: 'If fear is accompanied by a certain expectation that one will suffer a destructive experience, it is obvious that no one fears if he believes that there is nothing he can suffer' (Aristotle, *Rhetoric* 2.5, 1382b29–31). As a consequence, Aristotle continues, neither those who have continually enjoyed good fortune nor those who believe they have already endured the worst are inclined to feel fear (in this, too, fear is analogous to pity as Aristotle describes it). A given event or perception in itself is neither terrifying nor the reverse; what response it elicits depends on the disposition and expectations of the perceiver.[20] As Keith Oatley (1992: 19) observes: 'There is no physical situation that will reliably initiate particular emotions, because emotions depend on evaluations of what has happened in relation to the person's goals and beliefs.' Oatley adds, however, that 'it would be strange not to feel fear in response to a believable threat of torture.' Or, we may add, to the impression produced by the approach of a wrathful Achilles.

The idea that fear arises from a credible threat of harm also lies behind the Greeks' notion of political stability. In general, the Greeks tended to favour parity between contending parties as a strategy for maintaining equilibrium, whether among states or social classes. In his twenty-third oration, Demosthenes articulates a doctrine of balance of power among the Thracian kingdoms in the north as a way of protecting Athenian interests in the area:

Consider that this is also advantageous to our citizens dwelling in the Chersonese [in Thrace], namely, that none of the Thracians be strong, for trepidation [*tarakhê*] and suspicion towards one another on their part is our greatest and surest safeguard for the Chersonese. But this decree, which grants safety to the commander in charge of Cersobleptes' operations [Cersobleptes was one of the kings] but creates fear and apprehension [*phobon kai deos*] in the generals of the other kings lest they incur blame [i.e., with us Athenians], renders the latter weak and the former, though he is a single individual, strong. (103)

Demosthenes imagines the other kings remonstrating with the Athenians over the decree (106): 'You, Athenians, not only failed to help us when we were wronged, but also created an extraordinary fear in us, should we attempt to defend ourselves' (cf. also 23.140, 175). Superior power on the side of Cersobleptes instils fear in his potential enemies. There is no suggestion that the other Thracians are a particularly timid or pusillanimous lot. Their fear is the natural consequence of their perception of danger, or, in Aristotle's terms, the 'proximity of what is frightening,' the latter being a function of relative strength. Later, Demosthenes explains that 'when Cersobleptes stood in fear' (23.170), it was possible to compel him (*anankazein*) to share authority in Thrace, since he was sensible of the power of Athens. As the Athenians put it in the Melian dialogue recorded by Thucydides, there is no shame (aiskhunê) in yielding to superior force, only to an equal (5.101).

We may observe that Demosthenes is not recommending a balance of terror. Provided that no regime or combination of regimes is too strong, none will have cause to fear the others. Since fear, according to Aristotle, is the perception of greater might in an antagonist, it is not normally reciprocal, although of course mutual apprehension may arise if one or both parties is mistaken about the resources of the other. The Greeks did not have the modern strategic goal of Mutual Assured Destruction (or MAD), in which dread restrains both sides from aggressive action. Where forces are equal, neither party is afraid, and that is precisely what guarantees the peace.

This way of conceiving fear helps us to understand as well the famous passage in which Thucydides analyses the fundamental causes of the Peloponnesian War. According to Thucydides (1.23.6), 'the truest rationale [prophasis]' for why the Athenians and Lacedaemonians dissolved the peace that had obtained between them, though it was 'least evident in their statements [logôi],' is that 'the Athenians had grown powerful and induced fear in the Lacedaemonians, thus compelling them to wage war' (Thucydides observes that 'the publically proclaimed reasons on either side' emphasized particular treaty violations; cf. 1.88.1). In ascribing the Spartans' authentic motive to fear, Thucydides is not substituting a psychological for a political or economic cause of the war, as Francis Cornford (1907) supposed. The Lacedaemonians' alarm is the subjective correlate of the expansion of the Athenian empire and the consequent disequilibrium of power among the Greek city-states. It is the objective situation that compels them formally to terminate the peace, if they are not to submit to Athenian hegemony.[21] So long as power was proportionate, neither side had reason to fear. An increasing power gap between states did not constitute adequate justification for a declaration of war, any more than it does in today's political climate; this is why the Spartans represented themselves as responding to Athenian infringements of the treaty rather than their growing empire. Had it been for the infringements alone, the Spartans might have felt anger, if they imagined that their power had been scorned, or antagonism on account of the harm they suffered. Given how things stood, however, the relevant emotion was fear.[22]

When the Corinthians raised a huge fleet against Corcyra, Thucydides reports, the previously neutral Corcyreans grew frightened at their preparations (1.31.2; cf. 1.42.2) and decided to ally themselves with Athens and petition its help. The Athenians responded positively – a decision that led directly to hostilities between themselves and the Lacedaemonians – and in the opening phase of the naval battle, the mere sight of the Athenian ships induced fear in the Corinthians, even though they withheld their forces from combat (1.49.4). On both sides, fear derives from the perception of greater strength – numerical or tactical – in the opponent.

Since fear depends on an estimation of relative strength, it may be augmented or reduced by arguments for the superiority of one's own or enemy forces. Thucydides provides us with a textbook illustration of the rhetorical strategies employed in such situations. When Cnemus, Brasidas, and the other Peloponnesian generals perceived that their men feared a naval encounter with the Athenians after a previous defeat (2.86.5), they sought to demonstrate that the fear was unreasonable: 'The previous sea battle, Peloponnesians, offers no legitimate grounds for being afraid [to ekphobêsai], if indeed any of you fears the impending one' (87.1). The generals begin by attributing the earlier failure to poor preparation, bad luck, and inexperience (87.2). They continue:

What you lack in experience, you more than make up for in daring. Their proficiency, which is what you most fear, will allow them to put what they have mastered into practice in the crunch [en tôi deinôi] only if it is accompanied by courage and presence of mind [mnêmê], because without spirit no amount of skill avails in danger. Fear knocks out presence of mind [phobos gar mnêmên explêssei], and skill without mettle is useless. Put your greater daring in the balance against their greater experience, and against your fear [dedienai] arising from your earlier defeat put the fact that you were unprepared that time around. (87.4)

The generals conclude by reminding the men of their superiority in numbers, and encouraging them to sail out with confidence (*tharsountes*, 8), which, as Aristotle says, is the opposite of fear.

Initially, the Peloponnesians are intimidated by the enemy's perceived mastery of seacraft and their prior success. The generals respond with three kinds of counter-argument. First, they explain away the Peloponnesians' defeat as a result of unreadiness and bad luck. Second, they stress the advantages – greater boldness and numbers – which compensate for the Athenians' skill. Finally, they assert that the enemy's reverse fear of Peloponnesian superiority, above all in the matter of courage or boldness, will neutralize their skill itself. This last is a clever move: the advantages on either side are asymmetrical – daring versus skill – and the opponent's fear of ours nullifies theirs.

In alleging that fear will block the Athenians' ability to recollect the skills they have learned, the generals acknowledge that fear may, in the face of what is terrible (*deinon*), befuddle wits rather than render people more reflective (cf. the observation of a state trooper in a modern mystery novel: 'Fear makes people forget how to think' [Lehane 2001: 231]). This is plainly not the kind of fear that besets the Spartans at this juncture: their fear invites reasoned discourse about whether, in the circumstances, it is wise to engage the Athenians or put off the fight for a more favourable moment. The fear that may arise in the heat and confusion of battle has a different effect, more akin to panic: one tip-off is the use of the verb *ekplêssô*, which along with the related noun *ekplêxis* (cf. English 'apoplexy') is a key term in descriptions of panic. We shall return to the distinction between panic and Aristotle's account of fear later in this chapter.

Fear may be a deterrent to battle, especially if the disparity of forces is great. Again, it may provoke war, as in the Spartan case.[23] And it may also be, as in the episode we have been considering, a factor in the fighting itself. We recall that, according to Aristotle, fear arises from an expectation or impression of future harm, which typically involves a judgment of an adverse relationship of power. Aristotle does not specify the kind of response that fear provokes, however, save in one respect. To experience fear, Aristotle says, 'people must have some hope of safety [*sôtêria*] in the matter over which they are contending'; it is in proof of this claim that Aristotle adds: 'fear makes people deliberative [*bouleutikos*],' for, as he notes, 'no one deliberates over things that are hopeless' (1382a5–8). Keith Oatley (1992: 20) observes: 'When frightened, we evaluate a situation in relation to a concern for safety and become ready to freeze, fight, or flee.' Which of the three behaviours we adopt depends on a judicious calculation of possibilities that fear itself encourages. Greek fear, as Aristotle analyses it, is not instinctive avoidance. As he awaited the onset of Achilles, Hector took counsel with himself, like a good Aristotelian. He was not desperate, but had 'some hope of safety.' In the end, he ran. No doubt the proximity of harm was a factor in his deliberations. But in Homer too, fear involves cognitition.

Returning to Thucydides' sea battle, Phormio, the general in charge of the Athenian fleet, 'was also anxious [*dediôs*] because of his men's state of dread [*orrôdia*]' (88.1), which derives precisely from the enemy's numerical advantage. 'I have summoned you together, soldiers, because I saw that you were in fear of the quantity of enemy ships, and I did not think it right that you should be in dread of what is not in fact terrifying' (89.1). Phormio reminds his men that the Peloponnesians will be the more nervous because they lost the previous engagement. If they are superior on land, the Athenians have the edge at sea: what is more, 'they have no advantage when it comes to spirit – we are both more experienced and more confident' (89.3). Then, as though he were responding directly to the Peloponnesian generals' exhortation, Phormio insists that his men need not fear the Peloponnesians' daring: 'You inspire much more fear in them, and more credible fear, both because you have already defeated them and because they cannot believe that you will not oppose them in a way worthy of great achievement' (89.5). Fear, then, will sap the Peloponnesians' courage rather than impair the Athenians' seamanship. 'When they calculate [*logizomenoi*] these things,' Phormio continues, 'they are afraid of us more for want of probability than relative preparation' (89.6). Phormio lists several practical considerations that favour the Athenians, and concludes by reminding them: 'This is a decisive engagement for you, in which you will either destroy all hope the Peloponnesians may have in their fleet, or else foster in the Athenians a fear of the sea' (89.10). In the event, the Peloponnesians emerged victorious from the battle.

Phormio and the Peloponnesian generals are as adept in the rhetoric of fear as courtroom pleaders were in the tactics of pity and anger. Since fear depends on the relative degree of power, each seeks to represent his own side as the stronger, so as to encourage the troops to fight rather than flee. In addition, they suggest that, once the fleets are engaged, the enemy's fear, grounded in the calculation of probabilities, will handicap them still further, precisely in their strong point – the Athenians' skill and the Peloponnesians' daring, since fear is the opposite of confidence. Like Homer, Thucydides too illustrates how fear not only depends on judgments but colours them as well. The prior fear on the part of the Peloponnesians and Athenians leads them to magnify the threat represented by their opponents; by reducing their fear, and indeed inducing the contrary emotion of confidence, the generals seek to alter their perception of the enemy's capabilities (again, we recall Aristotle's definition of the emotions as 'all those things on account of which people change their minds and differ in regard to their judgments,' *Rhetoric* 2.1, 1378a20–1). The subtle interaction between fears and impressions, along with the second-order tactic of imagining the other's fear to stimulate one's own confidence, lends Thucydides' text its corruscating brilliance.[24] The speeches he records (or invents) depend entirely on *logos*, that is, arguments concerning the objective balance of forces. They are anything but the 'rah! rah!' of a football coach's pep talk.[25]

In his comic parody *The Frogs*, Aristophanes has the tragic poet Aeschylus boast that, in his day, sailors limited their chatter to the rowers' chant *rhuppapai* (1073). When it comes to fear, however, Aeschylus is as subtle a reasoner as Euripides or Thucydides. Of all Greek tragedies, the one in which fear is most central to the theme is Aeschylus's *Seven against Thebes*. The first words that the chorus of Theban women utter upon learning that the enemy army is approaching are 'I cry out at great frightening [*phobera*] troubles' (78). As the din of arms reaches them, they exclaim, 'I dread [*dedoika*] the clamour' (103), and protest their 'fear [*phobos*] of martial arms' (121). To Athena and Poseidon they pray, 'Grant us release from our fears' (132), and in their anxiety they break into an inarticulate wail: *e he e he* (150, 158).

The reigning king Eteocles, by contrast, like a good general, seeks from the beginning to inspire confidence in his men (*eu tharseite*, 34), and he is disgusted that the women, 'hateful to all sensible people' (*sôphronôn misêmata*, 186), are producing the contrary effect with their frantic prayers (cf. *tharsos*, 184): 'When triumphant,' he declares of women, 'their confidence [*tharsos*] is insupportable, but when frightened [*deisasa*] they are a still greater evil to home and city' (189–90). In reply, the chorus explain once more that they were frightened (*edeis'*, 203) at the noise of the enemy (cf. *phobôi*, 214). Eteocles warns the women: 'Do not fear overmuch' (*mêd' agan huperphobou*, 238), to which they reply yet again that the din of battle caused them to mount the acropolis 'in panicky fear' (*tarbosunôi phobôi*, 240; cf. *dedoik'*, 249). Fear (*phobos*) seizes their tongues (259) and causes them to cry out. Eteocles bids them, 'Be silent, and do not frighten [*phobei*] our own men [*philoi*]' (262). His style of prayer, he asserts, brings 'confidence to our men [*philoi*] and rids them of fear of the enemy [*polemios phobos*]' (270).

At the end of this exchange, Eteocles announces his plan to select seven leaders, including himself, to oppose the enemy at each of the gates (282–4). The chorus continues to fear: they cannot sleep for *phobos* (287), they compare themselves to a dove terrified (*huperdedoiken*, 292) for its young at the approach of snakes (cf. *protarbô*, 332), and they conjure up awful images of defeat in war. Eteocles' warnings seem to have been futile. At this point, the messenger returns, and in the most famous but also most puzzling scene in the play he announces the names of the seven enemy champions selected by lot and describes the shield of each (375ff.).

The first is Tydeus and his haughty insignia. Eteocles replies, 'I cannot tremble [*tresaim'*] before a man's paraphernalia' (397), and selects Melanippus to oppose him: 'Ares will decide the result with a toss of the dice' (414), he says, indicating thereby that the two heroes are equally matched. The chorus make it known that they, for their part, continue to tremble (*tremô*, 419). Next comes Capaneus: who, the messenger asks, will face him without shrinking (*mê tresas*, 436)? (He is opposed by Polyphontes.) To stand against the third, Eteoclus, the king picks Megareus, who 'is not frightened [*phobêtheis*] of the roar' (475) of whinnying horses and will not desert the gate at which he is posted. The enemy Hippomedon 'glances fear' (*phobon blepôn*, 498), and boasts that Fear itself is at his gate (500); Hyperbius is selected to oppose him. Next comes Parthenopaeus, against whom Eteocles appoints Actor. The sixth champion is Amphiareus, the only one who is reverent rather than boastful; as his counterpart, Eteocles chooses Lasthenes, likewise a prophet and exemplary for justice and piety. Last is Polyneices, Eteocles' brother, whom Eteocles himself will face at the seventh gate: 'Who else more justly?' (673).

Here, at last, the chorus leaves off fearing, its concern now fixated on the pollution associated with fratricide (677–82, etc.). 'I have shuddered' (*pephrika*, 720), they sing, at the god destructive to the house, and they conclude their ode: 'Now I tremble [*treô*] lest the Fury accomplish it' (790–1). When the messenger returns, his first word to the chorus is 'Be confident!' (*tharseite*, 792), for the enemy has been defeated. He then announces the double fratricide, and in its final song the chorus dilates on the theme. The tragedy as we have it concludes (though some think this a later interpolation) with the arrival of Antigone and Ismene and Creon's proclamation that the body of Polyneices shall be left unburied.

Many critics have felt that Eteocles' harsh treatment of the Theban women is a sign of his tyrannical temper; after all, he himself brought on the war by refusing to share the throne of Thebes with his brother, as he had sworn to do. Christopher Dawson (1970: 5), however, argues that it is Eteocles' 'sense of the need for civic responsibility that accounts in large measure for his violent attack on the Chorus of young women ...; all he is trying to do may be undone by the irrational emotions of women.' This interpretation presupposes a sharp differentation between male and female psychology in the play, in which women lack the self-control and courage characteristic of men. If the women seem to give over their fear before the outcome of the battle is known, it is only because their anxiety is now focused on the stigma of fratricide, which displaces the threat posed by the invading army (Dawson 1970: 14–15).

I should like to suggest another way of understanding the women's change of attitude, based on what we have so far seen of the Greek conception of fear. If, in the first half of the play, the women are frightened by the enemy forces at the gates, it is because they believe that they can conquer the city, an inference based on their numbers and the din they raise. Eteocles has confidence in his troops, but he fears that the women's lamentations will discourage them; he therefore attempts to browbeat them into silence or else into adopting a more constructive way of supplicating the gods. In this, he fails utterly. In the scene of the shields, however, Eteocles demonstrates that, despite the vaunting of the enemy champions and the arrogant emblems on their bucklers, there are Theban heroes, including himself, equal to each opponent and prepared to defend the gates. By retaining his equanimity before the symbolic menace of the besiegers, and meeting the practical danger that they pose by a judicious strategy of defence, Eteocles makes it clear that the forces are in fact equal on both sides, a situation that in principle favours the defenders. The function of the shield episode, on this reading, is to make this parity manifest to the women, who constitute the only internal audience in the scene.[26] And it works: at the conclusion of the scene, they give over their fear of military defeat. Eteocles' responses to the messenger are thus analogous to Brasidas's and Phormio's hortatory speeches in Thucydides, counteracting fear by logistical arguments, whereas the women occupy the place of the Athenian and Peloponnesian marines in Thucydides' narrative.

Once freed of fear, the women turn their attention to the issue of fratricide, which figuratively reflects the symmetry and parity of the opposing sides. This new crisis involves miasma, or pollution, rather than the physical annihilation of the city, and the women respond to it not with fear but with horror (pephrika). The shift in emotional register in the Seven against Thebes is analogous to that in the Iliad from anger to fury (cf. chapter 2, pp. 52–3): a new kind of concern elicits the reaction appropriate to it. In the detective novel Darkness, Take My Hand (Lehane 1996: 272), the private investigator Angela Gennaro protests to her partner, Patrick Kenzie: 'I'm so tired of being scared, Patrick. I'm so tired of all that fear turning into anger. I'm exhausted by how much all of it makes me hate.'[27] For us, it is natural to conceive of the emotions as labile and readily convertible into one another. Our metaphors of 'pouring out feelings,' Sally Planalp (1999: 107) suggests, reflect an underlying conception 'that the body is a container and emotions are fluids inside it.'[28] On a cognitive view such as Aristotle's, however, a change of emotion is correlated with the different conditions that elicit it.

At the beginning of the play, the chorus of Theban women are panicky, and they clearly overestimate the threat to the city: their misapprehension is a consequence of their ignorance of war but also of their fear. As Aristotle says, emotion affects people's judgments, and the erroneous judgments, in turn, augment the emotion. Eteocles is right to worry that they may communicate their fear (that is, their judgment of the power of the enemy) to the Theban army, which will damage its effectiveness. But the women's terror is not just a sign of feminine irrationality. Eteocles himself would be afraid if he thought the odds against him were insuperable, just as Hector was afraid in the *Iliad*. If he calms the women down, it is by showing them that he is equal to the challenge and is not daunted by the enemy's boldness, any more than Thucydides' Phormio was. Were the women anxious over the mere possibility of defeat, Eteocles' confident preparations would have no effect on them.

My attempt to analogize the chorus of frightened Theban women to soldiers hearing a pre-battle exhortation may appear outlandish. Yet the women do cease fearing when Eteocles explains his strategy and pooh-poohs the braggadoccio of the enemy. The cognitive understanding of fear was, I suggest, so deep a part of Greek sensibility that it even shaped the argument of Aeschylus's tragedy.[29]

The contexts in which I have examined fear have all been military. Since fear involves a judgment of an enemy's superiority, citizens in a democracy were unlikely to acknowledge it in respect to their political equals (save in conditions of class warfare or tyranny), and mentions of fear occur most often in reference to foreign states. Fear is pervasive in Thucydides' history (the root *phob-* occurs 183 times; 160 times in Polybius; 34 times in Herodotus) and in those orators who occupied themselves with foreign affairs (201 times in Demosthenes, 58 in Isocrates), while it is relatively rare in those who dealt chiefly with private cases (*phob*- is absent in Isaeus; of the sixteen occurrences in Lysias, eight are concentrated in his funeral oration). The Greek cities were more or less continually engaged in warfare, and were prepared to meet a rival state courageously if the battle were on equal terms. But where calculation revealed a wide difference in power, it was appropriate to be conscious of harm or destruction.

I have been arguing that, on the view that Aristotle articulates explicitly but which represents a generalized Greek outlook in his time, the impression that causes fear derives from a judgment about the world, namely, that someone with a motive to harm you is in a position to do so. It follows that fear is not necessarily a sign of cowardice but rather an inevitable response (unless one is wholly insensible) to a plausible threat of danger. Managing fear thus involves evaluating the relative balance of forces among opponents, an exercise in calculation (*logismos*) and argument. There is also the further implication that one is not simply afraid: a person is always afraid of something. So stated, the Aristotelian view of fear would seem to dismiss the possibility of two affects closely connected to fear: panic and anxiety.

Fear, as Jean Delumeau puts it (1978: 30), 'relates to what is known,' whereas anxiety relates 'to the unknown.[30] Fear has a determinate object that one can confront. Anxiety does not, and is experienced as a painful anticipation before a danger that is the more terrible for not being clearly identified.'[31] Outside the *Rhetoric*, Aristotle does allow the possibility of fear in the absence of a perceived cause. In his treatise *On the Soul* (1.1, 403a23–4) he observes that 'even though nothing frightening befalls them, people do find themselves experiencing the feelings of someone who is afraid.' Although such fear, detached from a specific object, resembles the modern conception of anxiety, Aristotle does not develop the idea of a free-floating state of apprehension detached from an impression of specific harm. It was the Epicureans, with their hypothesis that irrational fears and desires have their roots in an unacknowledged fear of death, who distinguished two types of fear, the one responding to a concrete object, the other to a vague and indefinite impression. In the second century AD, a great inscription was erected in the town of Oenoanda (now in southwestern Turkey), summarizing Epicurean doctrine; one of the still legible portions reads (35 II Smith): 'As a matter of fact this fear is sometimes clear, sometimes not clear – clear when we avoid something manifestly harmful like fire through fear that we shall meet death by it, not clear when, while the mind is occupied with something else, it (fear) has insinuated itself into our nature and [lurks] ...'[32] The fear of death is of this latter kind, since, as the Epicureans put it, 'Death is nothing to us' (Epicurus, *Letter to Menoeceus* 124; *Principal Doctrines* 2; Lucretius 3.830; cf. chapter 1, p. 32; Konstan 1973).

In his brief essay *On Dreams*, Aristotle points out that, while asleep, people see images in the absence of an external stimulus, and he observes that, under the influence of emotion, a slight resemblance in an object to something we fear or love may cause us to take it for that thing: 'The more one is under the sway of the emotion [*empathesteros*],' the smaller the resemblance needed to generate the deceptive impression (3, 460b3–8). In the case of the emotions, as opposed to dreams, note that there is *some* external stimulus, even if we mistake its nature; in addition, the imagined object is itself specific rather than general. A fearful man may imagine that someone rushing towards him intends him harm, but he is not necessarily in a state of indeterminate anxiety (though the envisioned threat may amplify the pre-existing fear, suggesting the possibility of a spiral of dread). It is Aristotle, I believe, rather than the Epicureans, who best captures the way fear was conceptualized in archaic and classical Greek literature. Fear is fear of something, and whether that thing is really frightening remains open to debate.[33]

Panic, as opposed to anxiety, was an experience the Greeks recognized well: the term was believed to derive from sudden manifestations of the feral deity Pan (half goat, half man in appearance), which struck terror into onlookers. The Byzantine lexicon called the Suda (s.v. *panikôi deimati*, π 201) notes that women celebrate Pan noisily (hence his association with clamour), and adds that 'people ascribed things that were without cause to Pan.' The absence of an identifiable cause is an element in many modern accounts of panic, which tend to treat it either as a pathology or as a physiological reflex. Thus, Jon Elster (1999: 313) includes '[p]anics or phobias that lack cognitive support' in a list of 'putatively irrational emotions.' Robert Handly and Pauline Neff (1985: 4, 26) identify panic with physiological symptoms such as sweaty palms, rapid heart beat, and a feeling of faintness, and regard both panic and phobia as 'a reaction to an irrational fear.'[34] In antiquity, however, panic was understood not as an individual disorder but, typically, as a collective response to an indistinct threat arising in a specific kind of situation. Philippe Borgeaud, who devotes a chapter of his book on Pan to panic, concludes (1988: 88–9) that

a panic is always an irrational terror involving noise and confused distur- bance that unexpectedly overtakes a military encampment, usually at night. Its suddenness, its immediacy, is stressed ... Furthermore, there is a stress on the lack of any visible cause, a lack that leads to fantasy; the victims of panic are in the grip of the imagination, which is to say, of their worst fears. Any noise is immediately taken as the enemy in full attack.[35]

So too, the Suda (ibid.; quoted by Borgeaud, 92) explains that panicky fear 'occurs among armies, when horses and men are suddenly alarmed [*ektarakhthôsi*], although no cause is evident.' As William Miller observes (2000: 207) in his exploration of cour- age, 'Fear ... is contagious. If the contagion is especially virulent and spreads rapidly, we speak of panic.' Miller adds: 'Once we are alarmed or given over to fear we are very susceptible to interpret- ing events in line with our worst expectations. Thus it is that in battle, any unexplained rapid movement to the rear can set off a panic.'

Panic so described is less a spontaneous outbreak of fear than a reaction to an obscure event (noise or commotion) that is taken to be a sign (*sêmeion*) of a genuine danger. There is a plausible Aristotelian interpretation of the phenomenon: in the initial alarm, the menace is exaggerated (as Aristotle suggests, when one is frightened one more readily interprets things as dangerous); the confused reaction of the crowd in turn generates more pandemo- nium, and thus compounds the stimulus that produced the fear. The emotion arising from the initial impression of imminent harm becomes part of the reason why 'people change their minds and differ in regard to their judgments' of the event itself, in this case intensifying the original *pathos* (see chapter 1, p. 37). On such an account, panic retains a cognitive element.

Nevertheless, the Greeks regarded some kinds of fear as resulting less from deliberation than a kind of shock or *ekplêxis*, which drives out reflection and either causes an instinctive impulse to flee or leaves one dazed. It may be produced by music, for example, and thus seems closer to an *aisthêsis* (in Sophocles' *Ichneutae* 314–18, the satyrs experience *ekplêxis* when they first hear the lyre and Silenus runs away terrified). So too, highly effective oratory may 'stun' an audience.[36] Josephus (*Jewish War* 5.469–72) describes how, when a fire suddenly breaks out, *ekplêxis* 'enters' (*empiptei*) the Romans (*explêxis* tends to assail you; cf. Aeneas Tacticus 27.9, Pausanias 10.23.5–8). In Sophocles' *Trachinian Women* (21–7), Dejanira says she was too stricken with fear (*ekpeplêgmenê phobôi*) to observe the wrestling contest between her two suitors, Hercules and the river god Achelous (cf. Euripides fr. 67 [*Alcmaeon*]: 'When someone gets up to speak at a trial on a matter of life and death, *phobos* impels a human's mouth to *ekplêxis* and prevents the mind from saying what it wishes'). We may recall that *ekplêssô* is the term the Spartan generals use when they predict that the Athenians will be scared witless in the coming naval battle. Such a reaction is not strictly a *pathos* in the sense Aristotle gives the term in the *Rhetoric*.

It may be that the women in Aeschylus's *Seven against Thebes* too should be regarded as suffering under the impact of panic rather than fear proper (as I have been defining it). They refer repeatedly to the din and hubbub of the attacking army, and Eteocles is worried that their inarticulate cries will sow fear in his troops. As W.I. Miller (2000: 207) says, when fear is infectious, 'we speak of panic.' The boundary between rational fear and wild fright is not strictly policed either in Greek or in English, and Aeschylus's representation of the women's fear may well blend elements of both. Yet the women in the play do engage in argument and are open to correction; theirs is not simply a blind terror. A reading that takes account of the Greek tendency to think of emotions as cognitively motivated, and that does not take for granted the modern opposition between reason and passion, offers the possibility of a richer interpretation of the tragedy.

Phobos is clearly not the only Greek word that broadly corresponds to the English 'fear.' Robert Zaborowski (2002) has catalogued all the words that plausibly can be related to the idea of fear (and also of courage) in the Homeric epics, and has come up with forty-three different terms (deriving from twenty-two distinct roots), including, besides *phobos*, the nouns *deos*, *aidôs*, *sebas*, *thambos*, *oknos*, *tromos*, and *tarbos*, and the verbs *atuzesthai*, *rhigein*, *perideidein*, and *ekplêssô*, the last of which he relates particularly to panic. Zaborowski sorts these terms in various ways, for example whether they are experienced predominantly by groups or by individuals, whether they elicit a positive or negative reaction, and also according to the kinds of stimuli and physical responses that characterize each. Some of these, like *oknos* or *tromos*, refer to acts such as shrinking back or trembling, and hence designate symptoms of fear (or of other emotions) rather than fear itself. Others, like *aidôs* and *sebas* ('awe' or 'reverence'), undoubtedly share some features with fear, and may even be described as forms of *phobos* by ancient writers,[37] but seem to belong to a distinct semantic sphere. A lexical survey reveals certain affinities among items in the emotional vocabulary, but may also bring under a single umbrella notions that are in fact dissimilar.[38]

Although the term that Aristotle analyses in the *Rhetoric* and elsewhere is *phobos*, however, the noun *deos* and the related verb *dedoika* largely overlap with it. Indeed, Protagoras, in Plato's dialogue by that name, declares that *phobos* and *deos* are strictly synonymous (358E5–7), although the linguistic stickler Prodicus professes to see some difference between them (cf. *Philebus* 12C), and the two are often paired in the way that 'trial and tribulation' are in English, with no ostensible distinction in sense (e.g. Lysias, *Oration* 20.18). On the basis of her study of *deos*, *phobos*, and their congeners in Thucydides, however, Jacqueline de Romilly (1956: 119) took the side of Prodicus and the later Greek grammarian Ammonius, who wrote a treatise on differences between similar words: Ammonius explains that '*deos* is a presentiment of evil [*kakou huponoia*], whereas *phobos* is a sudden quivering [*parautika ptoêsis*].' Thus, Romilly writes: 'Opposed to emotional and irrational *phobos*, which suddenly seizes body and soul, is *deos*, an intellectual kind of apprehensiveness which involves calculation relative to the future and measures that are taken as a result.'[39] Romilly notes (119–20) that *deos*, accordingly, is connected with verbs of thinking (e.g. at 2.5.5., 3.93.1, 5.71.3, 8.109.1), whereas *phobos* is rather associated with words indicating alarm or perturbation (*tarakhê*, 3.79.3); *deos* implies action, but *phobos* leaves one defenceless (6.36.2); *deos* often has a happy outcome, but *phobos*, in general, a negative one: 'Although clearly the same reality can be evoked by either word, and sometimes is by both, it is certain that Thucydides, in selecting one or the other, means to emphasize either the affective aspect and the presence of an emotion, or else the intellectual aspect and the presence of foresight.'

Romilly is careful to note exceptions to her rules,[40] but in fact Ammonius is simply wrong: there is no cognitive difference between *phobos* and *deos* in ordinary Greek usage. *Deos*, as well as *phobos*, may be paired with alarm (*tarakhê*: Lysias 6.35); one may feel *phobos* just as much as *deos* before the gods or the laws of the city (Lysias 32.17, 14.15 respectively; for *deos* and virtue, 2.57).[41] There attaches, I think, a slightly more elevated tone to *deos*, which thus more easily assumes the sense of reverent awe, but I can find no context in which the two terms are not effectively interchangeable. *Phobos*, at all events, does not normally designate an irrational or panicky terror in Thucydides or elsewhere: as we have seen, it is most often a stimulus to argument and debate.

We began with Aristotle's definition of fear as 'a kind of pain or disturbance deriving from an impression of a future evil,' and saw that such impressions result from complex judgments concerning the state of mind and intentions of others, as well as inferences from the experience of people similar to or stronger than oneself (likewise in the case of confidence). The fear inspired by tragedy, according to Aristotle, also involves this sophisticated cognitive operation. What befalls a tragic hero, who is (as Aristotle says) greater than we are, can happen to us, even though no such catastrophe seems imminent. That is why, as Aristotle puts it in the *Poetics*, 'fear pertains to a person who is similar to ourselves'

(13, 1453a5–6), whereas pity responds to undeserved suffering. Now, we have seen that pity too, according to the *Rhetoric*, is evoked by misfortunes 'which one might expect onself, or one of one's own, to suffer' (2.8, 1385b14–15), and hence depends on a sense of one's own vulnerability. How, then, does tragic fear differ from pity?

The answer, I think, is just that this fear is not mediated by a judgment of desert.[42] As Stephen Halliwell (1998: 176) observes, tragic fear is, at bottom, 'an emotion felt at one's own prospective experience' – and, like ordinary fear, I would add, is unregarding of merit. Halliwell goes on to state that such fear 'differs from ordinary fear by virtue of being focussed on the experience of others.' Where I disagree, however, is with Halliwell's further claim that 'Aristotle's discussion of the nature of fear … does not rule out the possibility that its object can in some cases be the prospect of *others'* sufferings.' Halliwell explains: 'For this to be so, we can deduce, one condition must be satisfied: the prerequisite of strong sympathy. Once this exists, we can feel fear for others analogous to fear for ourselves.'[43] As we shall see (chapter 10, pp. 211–12), Aristotle restricts such sympathy to the pain or pleasure we share with dear ones. Characters on stage are not our intimates. There is thus, I think, no basis in Aristotle's account of the tragic emotions for vicarious fear or 'fearing for' others. Spectators fear for themselves, because they realize that they are equally liable to misfortune.

The Greeks were great debaters. The speeches in Homeric epic and in historians such as Thucydides, the contrapuntal exchanges or *agônes* of tragedy and comedy, the orations delivered in court and in the assembly and theorized in rhetorical treatises such as Aristotle's all testify to the pervasive role of argument in Greek society. The regime of the word conditioned the Greek conception of the emotions along with other areas of life. While it is true that Aristotle's analysis of the emotions in the *Rhetoric* looks to the practical needs of the public speaker, the idea that the emotions respond to deliberation was ingrained in Greek psychology. This was as true of fear as of ostensibly more cognitive passions like anger and pity. In this respect, Greek *phobos* differed subtly from 'fear' in modern English. Fear too has had a history.

CHAPTER SEVEN

Gratitude

Gratitude is an emotion, the core of which is pleasant feelings about the benefit received. At the cornerstone of gratitude is the notion of undeserved merit. The grateful person recognizes that he or she did nothing to deserve the gift or benefit; it was freely bestowed.

Emmons 2004: 5

To requite a benefit, or to be grateful to him who bestows it, is probably everywhere, at least under certain circumstances, regarded as a duty.

Westermarck 1908: 154; quoted in Gouldner 1996: 59

In the chapters of the second book of the *Rhetoric* that are conventionally numbered two to eleven, Aristotle analyses, as we have seen, the several emotions or *pathê* that an orator should be able to arouse and assuage. In chapter 2, he treats anger, or *orgê*, in 3 what I have called satisfaction, in 4 love and hate, in 5 fear, in 6 shame, in 8 pity, in 9 indignation (*to nemesan*), in 10 envy, and in 11 the emulous impulse he calls *zêlos*. Chapter 7 (1385a16–b11) too examines a *pathos* – but which? This is the question that occupies the first and principal part of this chapter; the second part considers some ways in which Aristotle's analysis and Greek usage generally shed light on a current problem in the philosophy of the moral emotions.

To go by all translations and all commentaries but one (Rapp

2002: ad loc.) on this section of the *Rhetoric*, the *pathos* in question would seem to be entirely clear, for they are unanimous on this score.[1] Here, for example, is the first sentence of chapter 7 in Roberts's translation, published in the Bollingen series edited by Jonathan Barnes (p. 2207): 'To take Kindness next: the definition of it will show us towards whom it is felt, why, and in what frames of mind.' And the chapter concludes in Roberts's version: 'So much for kindness and unkindness.' The subject of the chapter, then, is precisely kindness. Or again, consider George Kennedy's translation of the opening and closing sentences (1991: 149): 'To whom people show kindliness and for what reasons and in what state of mind will be clear [to us] after having defined *kharis*.' And (151): 'This finishes the discussion of being kindly and being unkindly.' Kennedy's headnote to the chapter reads:

Kharis has a number of meanings in Greek – 'kindliness,' 'benevolence,' 'good will,' 'a favor,' 'gratitude,' 'grace' ... Aristotle's definition in section 2 makes it clear that he is speaking about an altruistic feeling of kindliness or benevolence that at a particular time gratuitously moves a person to do something for another.

Or take Cope's commentary (1877: 87): '$\chi\acute{\alpha}\rho\iota\varsigma$, the $\pi\acute{\alpha}\theta o\varsigma$, or instinctive emotion, of which this chapter treats, represents the tendency or inclination to benevolence, to do a grace, favour, or service, spontaneous and disinterested to another, or to our fellow-man. It also includes the feeling of gratitude, the instinctive inclination to *return* favours received.' In what amounts to a translation of the opening sentence (88), Cope writes: 'The object of benevolence, the circumstances and occasions (on which it is exercized), and the dispositions, characters, and moods of mind (of those who exercize it), will be evident when we have defined benevolence.' To be absolutely unambiguous, Cope adds that '"gratitude" and "ingratitude" are not distinctly noticed in the chapter.'[2]

Nor is this interpretation of the subject of chapter 7 of Aristotle's *Rhetoric* a novelty. While I have not examined every translation ever produced (the number is very large, and many are difficult to obtain), it is clear that the modern consensus began at least as early as the Renaissance.[3] For example, Ermolao Barbaro, in his Latin translation published in Basel in 1545, has (387): 'to which men, and in which matters, favour is seen to occur [gratia fieri videatur], and how those who do a favour [gratiam faciunt] are disposed, will be clear from the definition of the matter.'[4] The commentary, which was provided by Daniel Barbaro, worries at the fact that in defining gratia or kharis, Aristotle includes the definiendum in the definition (426); but he rescues Aristotle from this elementary logical error by claiming that the kharis that is defined and that in the definition have different senses.[5] Clearly this distinction is contrived, though Barbaro was right to identify a problem here.[6]

In what follows, I argue that the emotion in question, however, is not kindness, kindliness, benevolence, 'favour' or anything of the kind.[7] Spontaneous munificence (as opposed to the generosity that accompanies love or affection) is not an emotion for Aristotle, for it fails to conform to the precondition for any pathos, namely, that it be a response or reaction to some stimulus or event. All the emotions analysed by Aristotle are so motivated, from anger, which is provoked by a slight, to shame, indignation, fear, pity, and the rest. The pathos that Aristotle examines in chapter 7 is rather the gratitude that is elicited by a favour. Kindness, I am afraid, must be expunged from the list of Aristotelian pathê.

There is unfortunately no other way to make the case I am proposing than by a close scrutiny of Aristotle's text, sentence by sentence.[8] Luckily, he devotes only a brief paragraph to gratitude, and the exersise is not without interest for the insight it provides into his method of argument. The chapter, then, begins as follows: 'Those towards whom people have kharis and in what circumstances [or for what things] and how they themselves are disposed, will be clear when we have defined kharis.' What does 'having kharis' – kharin ekhein – mean? It means to feel gratitude, and only that (e.g. Rhetoric 1374a23).[9] It never in all of Greek literature means to show favour towards someone, be kindly, do a service, or anything of the sort. The way to say 'do a favour' in Greek is kharin pherein, tithesthai, and so on, or with the verb kharizesthai. By way of illustration, here is Plutarch's account of Cato's response to Lucius Caesar's offer to intercede in his behalf with Julius Caesar (*Cato Minor* 66.2): 'If I wished to be saved by the benefaction [*kharis*] of Caesar, I should approach him myself. But I do not wish to owe gratitude [*kharin ekhein*] to a tyrant for something in which he violates the law, and he violates the law by saving me as my master, though it is not right for him to have despotic power.' In the first use, *kharis* means 'saved by Caesar's grace,' in the second, it means '*gratitude*.' Again, compare Pericles' account of the Athenian view of friendship in his famous funeral oration, as reported by Thucydides (2.40.4): 'The firmer friend is the one who has treated the other well, with the result that, through his goodwill [for the one] to whom ne has given it [the favour], he keeps it [the gratitude] owed.'[10]

Aristotle next offers a definition of the term *kharis*, on the basis of which, as he says, the significance of *kharin ekhein* will become manifest: 'Let *kharis*, then, in accord with which one who has it is said to have *kharis*, be a service to one who needs it, not in return for anything, nor so that the one who performs the service may gain something, but so that the other may.' Here, I expect, is the chief source of the misunderstanding of this chapter. It is true that, in several other chapters on emotions, Aristotle uses the formula *estô dê* ('let such and such be ...') to introduce the definition of the *pathos* under consideration, for example in the case of anger (1378a31), love (*philein*, 1380b35), fear (1382a21), shame (1383b13), and pity (1385b13).[11] In chapter 7, however, Aristotle offers a definition not of the emotion itself, that is, gratitude, which is signified in Greek by the compound expression *kharin ekhein*, but of the constituent term *kharis*. It is not difficult to see why, if we translate literally. Roberts offers the following, which is fairly representative: 'Kindness – under the influence of which a man is said to be kind – may be defined as helpfulness toward someone in need, not in return for anything, nor for the advantage of the helper himself, but for that of the person helped.' The redundant and awkward formulation 'Kindness – under the influence of which a man is said to be kind' is evidently an attempt to escape the definitional problem signalled by Daniel Barbaro in his commentary of 1545. What the text says, however, is this: 'Let "a benefaction," then, in respect to which the one who has it [i.e., receives the benefaction] is said to feel gratitude, be a service to one who needs it, not in return for something, nor so that something should accrue to the one who does the service, but rather that it should accrue to the other.' As I understand him, Aristotle is here offering a punning explanation of how the phrase *ekhein kharin* ('have *kharis*') came to mean 'feel gratitude': one receives or has a favour (*kharis*) from another, and in turn is said to feel or have gratitude (again, *kharis*). Barbaro was right that the two uses of *kharis* here are different; he failed, however, to recognize the force of the expression *kharin ekhein*.[12]

The next few phrases expand on the conditions in which a favour is likely to inspire gratitude. Thus, 'the favour [*kharis*] is great if it is for someone in serious need, or in need of great or difficult things, or at a time that is such [i.e., urgent], or if he [who provides the service does so] alone or first or chiefly.' *Kharis* here presumably refers to the service performed. Aristotle next specifies the nature of needs: 'needs are desires [*orexeis*], and of these above all those that are accompanied by pain if it [i.e., the thing desired] is not realized. Cravings [*epithumiai*] are desires of this sort, for example erotic passion, and those desires connected with bad states of the body and with danger: for in fact those who are in danger and in pain do crave.'[13] The text continues: 'Thus, people who stand by those in poverty or exile, even if they do a small service, yet because of the magnitude of the need and the urgency of the occasion, are pleasing [*kekharismenoi*], like the man who gave the mat in the Lyceum [the reference is unkown]. It is most necessary, then, to receive the service [*ekhein tên hupourgian*] in regard to these things, and if not to these, then to equal or greater things' (text according to Kassel 1976). There are two points that invite elucidation. The first is the meaning of the participle *kekharismenoi*. Roberts, for example, translates: 'Hence those who stand by us in poverty or in banishment, even if they do not help us much, are yet *really kind* to us,' and so on (my emphasis).[14] This interpretation favours the idea that kindness is the subject of this passage. However, it is highly dubious. The perfect participle is connected rather with the passive voice of the verb, and invariably bears the sense 'pleasing' (over 50 occurrences in this sense in the fifth and fourth centuries BC; for Aristotle, cf. *Parts of Animals* 645a4–10), which puts the focus on the recipient's attitude. The second point concerns the meaning of the phrase *ekhein tên hupourgian.* Again, Roberts translates: 'The helpfulness must therefore meet, preferably, just this kind of need,' which, while it rather fudges the Greek, suggests that *ekhein* bears the sense of 'do' or 'provide' a service. This yields an odd construction, rather like taking *ekhein kharin* in the sense of 'do a favour.' Hence, I have preferred to render it 'receive a service.'[15]

Aristotle proceeds: 'Thus, since it is clear to whom and for what things *kharis* occurs, and how they are disposed, it is obvious that *kharis* must be elicited on the basis of the following: by showing that the one party either is or has been in pain and need of this sort, and that the other party has rendered or is rendering such a service in such necessity.' It is clear that the first clause – 'to whom and for what things *kharis* occurs, and how they are disposed' – answers to the clause with which the chapter begins: 'toward whom people have *kharis* and for what things and how they themselves are disposed.'[16] On my reading, then, *kharis* here must be understood as 'gratitude,' a perfectly good meaning of the term, rather than a 'kindness' or 'service,' even though when Aristotle defined *kharis* ('let *kharis* ... be,' etc.) he took it in the latter sense.[17] The balance of the sentence surely favours gratitude. Aristotle is offering advice on how to produce *kharis* in an audience. In actual courtroom situations, litigants often emphasize the benefactions they have bestowed on their fellow citizens or the city in an effort to elicit the jurors' gratitude and make it clear that they have employed their wealth properly and for the public weal (cf. chapter 5, p. 121; Fisher 2003). Rarely would one try to induce in an audience a sudden impulse to bestow a favour (acquittal or pardon do not count as a service or *hupourgia*). So too, the *Rhetoric to Alexander* advises that 'people are grateful [*kharin d'ekhousi*] to those thanks to whom or to whose friends they believe that they or those they care for have experienced or are experiencing or will experience some good beyond what is due [*para to prosêkon*]' (34.2–3), whereas affection is stimulated by receiving what is in accord with desert.

Returning to Aristotle:

It is clear too on what basis it is possible to diminish the *kharis* and render people *akharistoi*. Either [argue] that the one party is rendering or rendered the service for their own sake (this was said not to be a *kharis*), or that the service happened by chance or they were constrained to do it, or that they paid back rather than gave, whether knowingly or not: for either way, it is 'in return for something,' and so would not thus be a *kharis*.

The three uses of *kharis* here clearly signify a favour or benefaction, since (among other things) the stipulation that it must be altruistic refers back to Aristotle's definition of the term. The point, then, is that showing that an act does not meet the conditions for being a *kharis* in this sense renders people *akharistoi*. The question is what this latter term implies. Roberts translates: 'We can also see how to eliminate the idea of kindness and make our opponents appear unkind,' taking *akharistoi* to mean refusal to perform a genuinely selfless act of kindness, and this is the standard interpretation. The difficulty is that *akharistos* does not mean 'unkind.' Rather, it means either 'miserable,' 'unpleasant,' or else 'ungrateful.'[18] The most telling instances are to be found in the works of Xenophon, where forms of the adjective and adverb occur twenty-three times, virtually always in the sense of 'ungrateful' (e.g. *Hellenica* 5.2.37: 'for he was known not to be *akharistos* to those who had done him a service'). Indeed, Xenophon is kind enough to provide us with a definition of the term. At *Memorabilia* 2.2.1, Socrates says: – 'Tell me, son, do you know that some people are said to be *akharistoi*?' – 'Indeed I do,' said the boy. – 'And have you learned what those whom people call by this name do?' – 'I have: when those who are well off and are able to repay a kindness [*kharin apodounai*] do not repay it, this is what people call them.' – 'Ought we, then, to list those who are *akharistoi* among unjust people?' – 'I think we ought.'[19] Aristotle's meaning, accordingly, is: 'It is clear too on what basis it is possible to disparage the favour that has been rendered and make the recipients ungrateful [*akharistoi*].'
Aristotle continues:

One must also consider all the categories. For it is a *kharis* either because it is this particular thing or of such a quantity or sort, or at such a time or place. An indication of this is if they did not do a lesser service [when it was needed], and if they did the same things or equal or greater for one's enemies: for it is then obvious that what they did for us was not for our sake. Or if they knowingly did an unworthy service: for no one will confess to have needed what is unworthy.

There is no question but that *kharis* here means a concrete favour or kindness rather than gratitude: Aristotle is showing how the description of a favour determines whether the response to it will be gratitude or not.[20]

The chapter on *kharis* concludes: 'We have now finished discussing *to kharizesthai* and *akharistein*.' I have already cited Roberts's version of this sentence: 'So much for kindness and unkindness.' Kennedy's (1991: 151) is similar: 'This finishes the discussion of being kindly and being unkindly.' For the first term, I prefer 'doing favours' to 'kindness' or 'being kindly,' inasmuch as the latter terms introduce an unwarranted reference to a psychological state.[21] As for *akharistein*, the meaning must, I think, be 'act ungratefully,' although it is just possible, I suppose, that it bears the sense of 'begrudge' or 'withhold.'[22]

Since gratitude is elicited by a service, it is no wonder that Aristotle's discussion of it focuses largely on what a service or *kharis* consists in. He is at pains as well to bring out the connection in Greek between the term for a favour and the expression meaning 'to be grateful,' that is, '*kharin ekhein*.' To do a favour (*kharizesthai*) puts the recipient in one's debt. So too, the English word 'oblige' means to both indulge and to put someone under obligation; in return for a service, we say 'much obliged' (cf. Portuguese 'obrigado' = 'thank you'). This accounts for why Aristotle summarizes the content of his chapter on gratitude by referring both to the act of generosity (*kharizesthai*) and the response of gratitude, or rather, in light of his concluding remarks on how to belittle favours, ingratitude.

Performing a kindness is not an emotion; neither is kindliness, for that matter. If a favour were to be prompted by an emotion, the relevant *pathos* would be love or *philia* (see chapter 8). The *pathē* in Aristotle are typically responses to the behaviour of others, and more particularly to words or deeds that have consequences for the relative social standing or *doxa* of the parties involved. Gratitude involves just such a relative positioning, since it derives from the prior need of the recipient in relation to the generosity of the benefactor, and the continued state of inferiority until the debt can be repaid (in this, it resembles anger as Aristotle conceives it).

That gratitude should figure among the basic emotions analysed by Aristotle is no cause for surprise, then, although it is very rarely encountered in modern lists.[23] For the ancients, gratitude was a powerful and innate sentiment. Cicero remarks of children, whom he takes to be a mirror of mankind (*On Ends* 5.22.61): 'What a memory they have for those who have deserved well of them, what a passion to pay back a favour!' (*quae memoria est in iis bene merentium, quae referendae gratiae cupiditas*; cf. C.A. Barton 2001: 11). It was also vital to a society predicated on competition and reciprocity, where maintaining one's status in the forum of public esteem required continual effort and wariness.

We must, then, revise the standard list of basic emotions that Aristotle treats in the *Rhetoric*, expelling benevolence or kindness, which never did sound much like an emotion (how is it different from *eunoia* or good will?) and inserting gratitude in its place – an emotion that would otherwise have been conspicuously lacking in a treatise devoted to rhetoric. But this is not the only consequence of understanding gratitude as the *pathos* Aristotle discusses in the *Rhetoric*. For gratitude has been interpreted by many scholars as pertaining to an obligatory system of reciprocal exchange, in which a service imposes upon the person who has benefited from it a quid pro quo responsibility to render compensation. Is gratitude, then, a duty or at best a virtue rather than an emotion?

Aafke Komter (2004: 196), for example, argues that gratitude is not just a matter of 'moral coercion' but is also 'a moral virtue.' She sees gratitude as 'part of a chain of reciprocity; it is universal and has survival value' (208–9); gratitude may be 'a response to a voluntary gift but is itself imperative,' and it 'derives its social importance and effectiveness from the moral obligation implied in it.' So too, Alan Gewirth (1978: 329) states: 'As for gratitude, it should first be noted that the duty is not one of feeling grateful, since this may not be within the power of the person benefited (though he can try), but rather one of expressing gratitude in words

or deeds or both for some favor one has received from another'
(quoted in McConnell 1993: 83).[24] Aristotle's own view of *kharis*
in the *Nicomachean Ethics*, according to Filippo Mignini (1994:
36), is that 'only actual restitution and not the sentiment of
acknowledging it satisfies the political requirement of equaliz-
ing the social balance sheet' ('Solo la restituzione fattuale e non
il sentimento della riconoscenza soddisfa l'esigenza politica di
pareggiare il conto sociale'). Indeed, Aristotle affirms that 'this is
the nature of *kharis*: one must do a service in return for the person
who did the favour' (*NE* 1133a4–5; cf. 1164b26–33).

Now, a social obligation may be mediated by, or take the form
of, an emotional reaction comparable to the anger evoked by an
insult, the fear at an impending threat of harm, or the shame
deriving from an act that betrays a fault of character. As the
sociologist Georg Simmel has put it (1996: 45), '[G]ratitude emerges
as the motive which, for inner reasons, effects the return of a
benefit where there is no external necessity for it.' Nevertheless,
its status as an emotion seems particularly equivocal. Thus,
Terrance McConnell, who has written the first extended philosophical treatment of gratitude, states (1993: 112) that 'the absence of feelings of gratitude is sometimes indicative of moral
failure,' but adds that 'experiencing specified emotions and feelings is not morally required of an agent. As a consequence ..., to
discharge a debt of gratitude one need not feel grateful.' He goes
on to insist, however, that 'there is more to ethics than overt
actions, more to being a morally good person than doing what one
ought to.' The additional element is precisely emotion. So too,
Hans van Wees (1998: 26) speaks in the same breath of the 'law of
gratitude' and a 'feeling of obligation.'

That the Greeks themselves could think of gratitude as a *pathos*
is evident from a variety of sources besides Aristotle's *Rhetoric*.
A particularly clear illustration may be found in another philosophical text, this one by the first-century BC Epicurean writer
Philodemus, many of whose works have been recovered in mutilated condition from a private library that was incinerated in the
eruption of Mount Vesuvius in AD 79. In his treatise on anger,
Philodemus draws a contrast between anger and gratitude: the
one is a response to deliberately inflicted harm, the other to a

voluntary service (*On Anger* col. 46.18–41). The passage reads (translation based on Sanders, unpublished):

If the sage will feel gratitude [*eukharistein*] toward people who have treated him well, he will also get angry at those who intentionally harm him. And he if doesn't get angry with the latter, then he won't feel gratitude toward the former. For the one passion in each case is the contrary of the other, and the voluntariness moves us to anger just as it does to gratitude. For just as we do not feel gratitude toward inanimate objects that produce some effect, nor to those animate ones that provide us something by no choice of their own, neither are we angry at them. And they assert that we are naturally moved to anger just as we are to gratitude by the contrary cause.[25]

Philodemus's contrast differs from that of Aristotle, who treats satisfaction as anger's opposite (see chapter 3), since Aristotle restricts the cause of anger to a slight, whereas Philodemus understands anger as a reaction to deliberate harm in general (this is in line with the Epicureans' relative indifference to public opinion and their focus on the well-being of the individual).[26] But his argument makes especially clear the parallel between anger and gratitude as emotions.[27] That the emotion depends on a judgment of intention, and is not a mere irrational or spontaneous feeling, accords perfectly with the cognitive conception of the *pathê* endorsed by Aristotle. So too, forensic orators tended to contrast gratitude with anger,[28] and to pair it in turn with such generous sentiments as pity.[29]

Nevertheless, there are any number of passages in which the emphasis falls rather on the obligation to make restitution. One 'demands back' (*apaiteô*) *kharis* for services performed;[30] in turn, one 'repays' (*apodidômi*) *kharis* (Lysias 18.27)[31] or 'owes' it (*opheilô*), and the one who performed the benefaction 'receives *kharis* back' (*apolambanô*: Lysias 20.31). *Kharis* may thus be paired with *timê* or 'payment' (Lysias 25.6). These locutions are too common to require further illustration.

Does Greek usage, then, simply reflect the confusion inherent in the idea of gratitude, which simultaneously signifies the moral acknowledgment of a debt and the emotion elicited by a gratuitous act of generosity?[32] It does not, but to see why it is necessary to attend not just to the word *kharis* itself but to its social and grammatical syntax as well. *Kharis* is one of the richer terms in classical Greek (cf. Chirassi Colombo 1994; Parker 1998: 108–14; and Harrison 2003: 40–3, 50–2, 75–7, and 174–8). It may mean simply 'charm' or 'pleasure.' It may also signify a favour, as in the definition that Aristotle offers in the *Rhetoric*, and again the return for a service, as in the examples cited above. Finally, it denotes gratitude. Now, when *kharis* bears the concrete sense of due return for a benefaction, it occurs in locutions that specifically refer to payment that is owed, above all involving verbs with the prefix *apo-* (roughly equivalent to the 're-' in 'return'; e.g., *apodidômi, apolambanô, apaiteô*). When *kharis* refers to gratitude, however, it occurs invariably in the expressions *kharin ekhein* (literally, 'have *kharis*') or *kharin eidenai* (literally, 'know or acknowledge *kharis*').[33] Ingratitude is *akharistia*, but there is no single term in classical Greek for the positive sentiment of gratitude apart from *kharis* itself.[34]

Whereas Greeks of the classical period demanded and repaid *kharis* (or a *kharis*) in the sense of the good turn deserved by another (cf. Sophocles, *Ajax* 522: '*kharis* always gives birth to *kharis*),' the terms for asking or paying back are never found in connection with *kharin ekhein* or *eidenai*. The emotion of gratitude is distinct from the act of reciprocation: it is felt, not due as compensation.[35] Thus Socrates, in Plato's *Apology* (20A), asserts that the disciples of the sophists 'give them money and are grateful besides [*khrêmata didontas kai kharin proseidenai*],' that is, over and above the payment that is required. The sentiment of course sustains the social system of reciprocity, but has its own grammar and role. Gratitude is never owed.[36]

It is natural that Aristotle should have concentrated on the emotion of gratitude in his treatise on rhetoric, since it is this sensibility, rather than repayment of an actual debt, that the orator would normally seek to elicit from his audience. His concern was different in his ethical works. The emotion itself, as we have seen, depends on an awareness of relative social positions, but being grateful was not 'regarded as a duty' (Westermarck 1908: 154). It was a response to the receipt of a benefit that had been bestowed precisely with no ulterior intention of gain on the benefactor's part, as Aristotle insists in his definition of *kharis*.[37] Recognizing the distinct character of the emotion of gratitude, as opposed to the social obligation to repay a service, may contribute to a new understanding of the subjective dynamics of classical Greek reciprocity.

CHAPTER EIGHT

Love

[We cannot speak] as if the history of courtly love, Romanticism, not to mention Christianity, makes no difference to a modern reader's approach to such a term.

Goldhill 1990: 101

It is worth repeating that feelings are very difficult to reconstruct historically.

Dixon 1992: 90

Classical Greek is rich in words signifying love or affection. Passionate sexual attraction is denoted by the term *erôs* (verb *eran*, whence 'erotic'), the love of parents for children by *storgê* (verb *stergein*). *Agapan* means 'to like or be fond of,' although the noun *agapê*, sometimes rendered 'brotherly love,' first occurs in the New Testament. But the most general and widely used term for 'love' is *philia*, with the associated verb *philein* (cf. 'philhellene,' 'anglophile'). This idea, together with its opposite, hatred or enmity (which we shall treat in the following chapter), is the subject of section 4 of book 2 of Aristotle's *Rhetoric*.

One might have imagined that love would pose relatively fewer problems of interpretation than other emotional concepts, and yet here too there are difficulties and disagreements, including over matters of terminology. *Philia*, for example, is not simply 'love,' but is often better translated as 'friendship,' and the cognate term *philos*, which as an adjective means 'dear' or (less often) 'loving,' commonly signifies 'friend.' Many scholars believe, however, that ancient friendship, both Greek and Roman, had little or no affective character, but was wholly a matter of duty. Thus, Malcolm Heath (1987: 73–4) writes that *philia* in classical Greece 'is not, at root, a subjective bond of affection and emotional warmth, but the entirely objective bond of reciprocal obligation; one's *philos* is the man one is obliged to help, and on whom one can (or ought to be able to) rely for help when oneself is in need.' Simon Goldhill (1986: 82) agrees: 'The appellation or categorization *philos* is used to mark not just affection but overridingly a series of complex obligations, duties and claims.'[1] *Philia*, then, would seem a poor candidate for a basic emotion, and hardly to correspond to the modern conception of love.

But that is not all. Some scholars hold that the words *philia* and *philos* do not in fact refer to friendship as we understand the term but rather to family ties. Thus, Elizabeth Belfiore (2000: 20) writes that 'the noun *philos* surely has the same range as *philia*, and both refer primarily, if not exclusively, to relationships among close blood kin.' Worst of all, Aristotle himself seems to have doubts about how to classify *philia*. At the beginning of his extended analysis of *philia* in books 8 and 9 of the *Nicomachean Ethics* (8.1, 1155a3–4), he affirms that *philia* 'either is a virtue or is accompanied by virtue,'[2] and earlier, in his discussion of virtues as a mean, Aristotle treats *philia* as a disposition (*hexis* or *diathesis*) rather than a *pathos*, and locates it between the extremes of ingratiation or flattery, on the high end, and generalized grumpiness, on the low (110826–30; but note 1226b22–3, where Aristotle says that this mean is 'most like *philia* ..., but differs from *philia* in that it is without *pathos*').

In my book *Friendship in the Classical World* (1997a), I argued at length that friendship was fundamentally an affective bond in ancient Greece and Rome, just as it is today, and that *philos* as a noun means precisely 'friend.' Scholarly opinion, nevertheless, remains sharply divided. Thus, Michael Peachin, the editor of a recent collection of essays entitled *Aspects of Friendship in the Graeco-Roman World* (2001: 135 n. 2), describes 'the standard modern view of Roman friendship' as one 'that tends to reduce significantly the emotional aspect of the relationship among the

Romans, and to make of it a rather pragmatic business' (and the same for Greek *philia*). Peachin notes that 'D. Konstan has recently argued against the majority opinion and has tried to inject more (modern-style?) emotion into ancient *amicitia*,' but the majority of the articles that follow, as Peachin says (7), 'point us back to a heavily formalized, even legalized, bond between friends.'[3]

These controversies show no sign of diminishing. It is not my purpose in this chapter, however, to rehearse the arguments concerning friendship yet again. Discussions of Aristotle's view of friendship tend to concentrate, reasonably enough, on his very full treatment of *philia* in the *Nicomachean Ethics*. But it is in the *Rhetoric* that Aristotle unequivocally includes *philia* among the *pathê*, and this, accordingly, is our point of departure in the present investigation.

Aristotle introduces his inquiry into the emotions of love and hatred (as we shall provisionally call them) as follows (2.4, 1380b35–6): 'Let us speak of those whom people *philousi* [third-person plural of the verb *philein*] and whom they hate, and why, by first defining *philia* and *to philein*.' The latter expression, *to philein*, is a nominalized infinitive, produced by prefixing the definite article (*to* = 'the') to the infinitive *philein* (we have encountered a similar construction in the case of 'being indignant' or *to nemesan*; cf. chapter 5, p. 112). I have for the moment transliterated rather than translated the key words involving the root *phil-*, since it is just the meaning of these terms that is in question. As it happens, however, there is, oddly enough, relatively less disagreement about the sense of the verb *philein* than about its congeners *philia* and *philos*. *Philein* is commonly translated as 'love,' 'regard with affection,' 'cherish,' or 'like' (it sometimes carries the more concrete sense of 'treat affectionately' or 'welcome,' but this usage is chiefly poetic). The nominalized or articular infinitive, in turn, is most naturally rendered as 'loving' (similarly, its opposite, according to Aristotle, is *to misein* or 'hating'). Now, if we understand *to philein* in this sense, and if, furthermore, we take Aristotle's phrase '*philia* and *to philein*' as simply a rhetorical way of expressing a single idea – or, perhaps, as Aristotle's notice that *philia* is here equivalent to *to philein* – then we may endorse the translation of the final bit given by Cope in his great commentary on the

Rhetoric (1877, vol. 2: 42): 'after having first defined love and loving.' Love, then, is the topic in the *Rhetoric*, and if *philia* has the same meaning in all the contexts in which it occurs, including the *Nicomachean Ethics*, then we will have simultaneously verified the connection between friendship and affection, at least so far as Aristotle is concerned. Thus, it is important to determine just why Aristotle resorts to the compound expression here.

Aristotle continues (1380b36–81a1): 'Let *to philein* be wishing for someone the things that he deems good,[4] for the sake of that person and not oneself, and the accomplishment of these things to the best of one's ability.' What Aristotle proceeds to define, then, is not *philia* but *to philein*, the verbal form that is generally agreed to signify 'love' or 'loving.' What is more, in contrast to his usage in the ethical treatises, Aristotle continues to employ the verb, in various inflections, throughout this section of the *Rhetoric*, returning to the term *philia* only at the end, and, as we shall see, in a special context. Aristotle is, I believe, being very careful in his choice of language here, deliberately restricting the scope of the definition to the verbal phrase rather than the noun. In order to see why, we must read a little further, and then compare what Aristotle says here with his discussion in the *Nicomachean Ethics*.

Rather than proceed immediately to illustrate the conditions under which love arises, Aristotle pauses to offer an ancillary definition (2.4, 1381a1–2): 'A *philos* is one who loves [*ho philôn*: present participle] and is loved in return [*antiphiloumenos*],'[5] and he adds: 'Those who believe that they are so disposed towards one another believe that they are *philoi* [plural of *philos*].'[6] *Philoi*, then, constitute a subset of those who love, namely, just those who both love and know or believe that their love is reciprocated. Such mutual affection is characteristic of friends, or those kin who are so disposed towards one another (it is by no means the case that all are). In the *Nicomachean Ethics*, Aristotle notes (8.2, 1155b27–34) that

in the case of affection [*philêsis*] for inanimate things, one does not speak of *philia*: for there is no reciprocal affection [*antiphilêsis*] nor the wish for their good ... But they say that one must wish good things for a friend [*philos*] for his sake. They call those who wish good things in this way 'well-disposed' [*eunous*], if the same [wish] does not occur on the other person's part as well. For [they say] that goodwill in people who experience it mutually [*en antipeponthosi*] is *philia*.

Aristotle then adds the further condition that each must know that the other is so disposed.

It is easy to see what is happening here. In the *Ethics* Aristotle elects to reserve the term *philia*, at least in the present context, for the reciprocal benevolence that is characteristic of friends or *philoi*. Accordingly, the term is not appropriately applied either to affection for inanimate objects, such as wine, or for people who do not like us in return. To be sure, we may like them. For the first kind of fondness, Aristotle coined the word *philêsis* (it is confined to the *Nicomachean Ethics*). In the case of a one-way fondness for another human being, Aristotle adopts the term *eunous*, 'well-disposed' or 'bearing goodwill.' It differs from our liking for wine in that we do wish good things for the other's sake, even if our sentiment is not reciprocated; but it is still not full-fledged *philia*, just because it is not mutual. As such, it corresponds precisely to *to philein* or 'loving' as Aristotle defines it in the *Rhetoric*: 'Let *to philein* be wishing for someone the things that he deems good, for the sake of that person and not oneself.'

Eunous or 'well-disposed,' then, is a stop-gap term, designed to distinguish unilateral from mutual love, for which, as we have said, Aristotle saves the word *philia*. Aristotle could just as well have employed the participle *ho philôn* (or rather the plural, *hoi philountes*), as he did in the *Rhetoric* (thus: 'they call those who wish good things in this way "ones who love"').[7] In fact, it would have been a better choice, since later in the *Nicomachean Ethics* (9.5, 1166b30–67a21), Aristotle explicitly contrasts *eunoia* with both *philia* and *philêsis* as rather a dispassionate form of affection (cf. *Eudemian Ethics* 7, 1241a3–14).[8] Here, however, in his definition of *philia*, Aristotle has not yet introduced this technical distinction, and he reaches for a convenient term to denote the unrequited sentiment.

But why does Aristotle go to such trouble to invent or press into service words and expressions (including *to philein*) to signify a unidirectional affection, while limiting *philia* to the mutual relationship that obtains between friends? For *philia*, as the noun corresponding to *philein*, can perfectly well designate love that is not reciprocal (Aristotle himself speaks of 'love for' someone [*philia pros*], *Nicomachean Ethics* 1161a22, etc.; cf. Isocrates 19.41, etc.). The answer, I believe, is that classical Greek lacked an ordinary noun corresponding to the English 'friendship' (or to the Latin *amicitia*, for that matter), which uniquely designates mutual affection as opposed to the individual sentiment (cf. Konstan 1997a: 53–6). Hence, he presses *philia* into serving as the name of the former, and finds other terms to do duty for the simple emotion, whether the nonce words *philêsis* and *antiphilêsis*, or *eunoia* (temporarily), or the verbal noun *to philein*. In proposing to define '*philia* and *to philein*,' Aristotle really is indicating two distinct notions.[9] It is *to philein*, or 'love,' that is the focus of the discussion in the *Rhetoric*; but he has no wish to exclude situations in which affection is mutual, and so he briefly stipulates what it is that constitutes two people as *philoi* or friends: the name of this two-way bond, though he does not say so explicitly, is just *philia*.[10]

Given the premises (*ta hupokeimena*) implicit in the preceding definitions, Aristotle draws the conclusion that a friend (*philos*) must share the other's pleasure and pain 'for no other reason than the other's sake' (2.4, 1381a5–6): this is so because people always delight in the realization of what they desire and are grieved by its failure (1381a3–7).[11] So too, friends will regard the same things as good and bad, and have the same friends and enemies. Contrariwise, a person who wishes the same things for another as he does for himself appears to be the other's friend. People also feel affection (*philousi*) for those who have treated them well for their own sakes, or who, they believe, wish to do so, or who care about the same things they do. Aristotle here seems to lump together the case of friends, which presupposes mutual love, and one-sided affection, which is but half of friendship. He then adds that people like 'those who are friends [*philoi*] of their friends and who like [*philein*] people whom they themselves like, and those who are liked by people liked by them; and also those who are enemies [*ekhthroi*] of the same people and hate [*misein*] whom they hate, and those who are hated by people hated by them' (1381a13–17).

For all these seem to regard the same things as good, and that is the sign of a friend.[12] Now, why these cumbersome and apparently redundant formulations? Aristotle is, I think, carefully taking into account three possible situations: first, he mentions those who have the same friends or enemies (in these cases, the feelings are mutual), and then he adds those who either like or are liked by the same people – instances of *to philein* and *to phileisthai* (the passive of *philein*) – without the further condition of reciprocality.[13]

Aristotle goes on to list the character traits that inspire affection in others: we like people who are generous, courageous, just, moderate, and unintrusive, and also, he adds, those who are not economically dependent on others: this latter is evidently a condition for liberality. Such people, he notes, do not seek their own advantage unfairly, and hence are likely to wish good things for us; if we ourselves are just, we will in turn be similarly disposed towards them. We also like those with whom we wish to be friends: virtuous and reputable or impressive people. In general, Aristotle adds, we are inclined to like those who are agreeable and not quarrelsome, as well as those whom we admire and by whom we wish to be admired. Clearly, we may in these cases like or love another without the feeling being reciprocated, though we may desire that it be so; only if it is, however, will there be friendship.

At the end of the passage in the *Rhetoric* devoted to love, Aristotle appends a short list of the varieties of *philia* – here he again uses the term itself – which include 'comradeship [*hetaireia*], familiarity [*oikeiotês*], kinship [*sungeneia*], and all such things' (1381b34), and he adds that *philia* is produced by a service or favour (*kharis*), especially when it is not demanded and when one does not publicize it, since in this way it seems to be performed for the other and not for some auxiliary motive. The affection between comrades (for example, members of the same club) and relatives usually is mutual, though it need not be.[14] But a favour engenders love in the beneficiary, and unless Aristotle is thinking of his argument in the *Nicomachean Ethics* (1167b17–18) to the effect that benefactors love those they have helped more than the reverse, he is using *philia* here loosely to signify love per se.

Returning to the definition of loving or *to philein*, it is clear that it represents an altruistic or generous sentiment in regard to another (wishing the good for that person's sake) that includes the desire or intention to provide the other with what she or he values.[15] No other conditions for loving are specified: nothing is said, for example, about duty or obligation. As far as the performance of services is concerned, loving just consists in the uncoerced wish to provide them. Here, then, there is no tension between the sentiment of love and the requirement or even the demand that one help others in achieving the goods to which they aspire. For if loving (to philein) as an emotion just is the wish to provide such assistance, then the failure to aid another convicts one of a want of love itself.[16] Friendship, in turn, is mutual love of this sort.

In Aristophanes' *Clouds*, Strepsiades, who is eager to enrol his son Phidippides in Socrates' 'thinkshop,' says: 'Kiss me and give me your right hand.' Phidippides responds: 'Here. What is it?' Strepsiades then inquires: 'Tell me, do you love [*philein*] me?' Assured that the boy does, he continues: 'If you truly love me from the heart, obey me, son' (81–2, 86–7). It is not that love is reducible to filial obedience; Strepsiades means that if his son loves him, he will oblige him – that is, desire his father's good. Xenophon, in his *Memorabilia* (2.9.8), has Socrates recommend friendships in which one 'receives services from worthy men and performs services in return.' This is practical advice, but not incompatible with an ideal of generosity among friends: decent people deserve our goodwill. In a Latin comedy based on a Greek model (Plautus, *Epidicus* 113), a character declares: 'A friend is one who helps out in difficult circumstances, when there is need of cash.' It may sound as though friendship is being treated here as a matter of obligatory gifts or prestations (cf. Raccanelli 1998: 164–6), but in fact there is no discrepancy with Aristotle's altruistic formula. Love is put to the test in situations of need, just because it consists in the desire for another's well-being.[17]

That love and friendship reside in an active wish to provide good things for another gives a special cast to these concepts in Greek (assuming that Aristotle's account is representative of popular attitudes). The second edition of *Webster's New International Dictionary* (1959) defines 'love' as 'a feeling of strong personal attachment' and 'ardent affection.' So too, in a recent handbook on emotion, Elaine Hatfield and Richard Rapson (2000: 654–5) write: 'Most scientists distinguish between two forms of love – "passionate love" and "companionate love." Passionate love ... is an intense emotion ... Companionate love ... is a far less intense emotion. It combines feelings of deep attachment, commitment, and intimacy.'[18] Aristotle says nothing about feelings or attachment; he mentions only a benevolent intent or concern for the well-being of another, which manifests itself in actions.[19] Rather than focus on interior states, and the possibility of recognizing them through involuntary signs such as facial expressions, Aristotle typically attends, as we have seen, to the social motives and consequences of the emotions.

So too, Aristotle carefully notes the personal qualities in others that elicit our love and benevolence. *Pathê* for Aristotle, as the word suggests, are characteristically reactions to the merits and intentions of others (see chapter 1, p. 27): this is as true of love as it is for anger, indignation, or gratitude. The recognition of virtue in others moves us to desire their good – for their sake. If it were only in the hope of a fair return, the sentiment would not be love as Aristotle defines it, nor as the Greeks in general conceived of it.

We may wonder, however, whether *philia* in the sense of friendship counts as a *pathos*. For *philia* does not depend solely on one person's affection, but involves the emotions of two. Thus, O.H. Green writes: 'In order to understand love or friendship, we must consider the attitude of friend toward friend or lover toward lover. The attitude, of course, may be found without the relationship, where it is not reciprocated; but the reciprocation of the attitude is what makes up the relationship of love or friendship' (1997: 215). Green goes on to say: 'It is in this vein that Aristotle, in Books VIII and IX of the *Nicomachean Ethics*, considers *philia*, which is translated both as "friendship" and as "love" or "liking."'[20]

So too, Martha Nussbaum, who describes love as 'an intense response to perceptions of the particularity, and the particular high value, of another person's body and mind' (2001: 465; cf. Smith 1982: 28), writes:

[L]ove, while an emotion, is also a *relationship*. I may feel love for someone, or be in love with someone, and that love is itself an emotion in the sense described here; but there is another sense in which love is present only if there is a mutual relationship ... Aristotle ... holds that love – or at least *philia* – is not merely an emotion. Although it involves emotion, it also has requirements that go beyond the emotional ... In other words, the term 'love' is used equivocally, to name both an emotion and a more complex form of life. (2001: 473–4)

We must not imagine, Nussbaum adds, 'that the emotions involved in love are unaffected by the presence or absence of a reciprocal relationship of the sort Aristotle depicts.' The knowledge that another loves me may affect the quality of my feeling for him or her (we recall that, in the *Nicomachean Ethics*, Aristotle insists that *philoi* must be cognizant of one another's sentiment). Beyond this, Nussbaum continues, 'lovers will have emotions toward their relationship itself, and the activities it involves. Thus we cannot even understand the emotional aspects of love fully without seeing how it is frequently related to interactions and exchanges of the sort Aristotle is thinking about' (474). There is a way, then, in which the nature of love itself might be nuanced by the mutuality condition attaching to *philia* between friends.

Aristotle does not raise these subtleties, although he is fully aware that confidence in love or friendship takes considerable time to develop (cf. *Nicomachean Ethics* 9.5, 1166b34). *Philia* does not, I think, have the abstract status of a relationship, in the sense of a bond distinct from each friend's love. It is not the kind of entity of which it is possible to say that friends 'will have emotions toward their relationship itself,' any more than it can impose obligations on those who love each other. The mutual love that obtains between *philoi* is better described, I believe, as a state of affairs, consisting simply in the fact that each loves the other. As a name for simple love, that is, the altruistic wish for the good of another, *philia*, like *to philein*, is a *pathos*; as a state of affairs obtaining between friends, it consists of two *pathê*, one for each *philos*.[21] If either fails to have the appropriate wish or to provide good things for the other to the extent possible, the state of affairs that depends on the twin *pathê* is dissolved.

At the end of his discussion of loving in the *Rhetoric*, we recall, Aristotle provides a brief list of the various kinds or species (*eidê*) of *philia*, among which he includes comradeship, familiarity, and kinship. This group differs from the way Aristotle subdivides *philia* in the *Nicomachean Ethics*, where he relates the different types to the kinds of things that are lovable (*philêton*). Here he explains (8.2, 1155b18–19): 'Not everything is loved, but only what is lovable, and this is the good or the pleasing or the useful' (since a thing is useful, Aristotle says, because it leads to what is good or pleasing, the three categories of 'lovables' are reducible to two). Scholars debate whether all three sorts are altruistic, or only that based on recognition of the other's virtue, which Aristotle calls the best or complete type. I myself maintain that all are, and that they differ not in regard to the wish for the other's well-being but in the qualities that elicit this desire (so J.M. Cooper 1997a, 1997b; contra Pakaluk 1998: 62–3). Love or friendship inspired by another's virtue is more durable than that inspired by an entertaining personality, perhaps, but both are love only insofar as they involve a selfless desire for the other's good. One reason why *philia* based on virtue is complete (*teleia*), according to Aristotle (8.3, 1156b7–11), is that people are good in themselves (*kath'hautous*), whereas they are useful or pleasant only incidentally (*kata sumbebêkos*). But this is something of a sleight of hand: for even if goodness is a more stable trait of character than wittiness, say, it does not follow that one likes a witty person only incidentally.[22]

In this controversy, however, there is a tendency to overlook other forms of *philia*, and most especially those involved in kinship and marriage. In the *Nicomachean Ethics*, Aristotle offers several explanations of these kinds of love. For example, fathers love their children because they are part of themselves: they are somehow, Aristotle says, one, even though they are separate individuals (8.12, 1161b16–33). The love between siblings and other blood relatives has a similar foundation, derived from the bond with the father. There are, however, additional causes of fraternal love, such as the fact that brothers are reared together and are of the same age: in this, their affection resembles that among comrades (8.12, 1161b33–5). The *philia* between husband and wife is in accord with nature, Aristotle says, since human beings are naturally given to forming couples (8.12, 1162a16–19; cf. *Politics* 1.1, 1252a26–30). In addition, children bind parents together, which is why childless marriages more readily dissolve. These loves, which correspond to the kinds of *philia* that Aristotle identifies in the *Rhetoric* ('familiarity' may well refer to the marriage relation), are surely altruistic as well.

Aristotle states in the *Poetics* (1453b19–22) that the plot of tragedy arouses more pity when the conflict occurs 'within loves' (*en philiais*), that is, as he specifies, between siblings or children and parents. The evidence at our disposal confirms Aristotle's judgment. In her book *Murder among Friends: Violation of Philia in Greek Tragedy* (2000: xv), Elizabeth Belfiore calculates that offences against blood ties are 'central to more than half' the extant tragedies. So too, among fragmentary plays whose plots can be reconstructed with some confidence, nearly half involve harm or the threat of harm to blood relatives, and a dozen more harm to spouses, together amounting to nearly three-fifths of the total number.[23] And yet, despite the title of Belfiore's book, violence between friends, as opposed to kin, is virtually non-existent in Greek tragedy, so far as the evidence permits us to judge.[24]

In Euripides' *Hercules*, the hero, in an episode of madness, murders his wife and children; in the end it is his friend Theseus who draws him out of his suicidal depression and brings him to live in Athens. The friendship between Orestes and Pylades was legendary, and in his tragedy *Orestes*, Euripides contrasts the loyalty of the friend with the lukewarm support of Orestes' uncle, Menelaus. As Orestes says: 'The saying is true: "Have comrades [*hetairoi*], not just kin!" For a man, though an outsider, who is conjoined by character is a better *philos* for a man to have than ten thousand of his own blood' (804–6). In Aristotle's terms, solidarity on account of virtue is more secure than that based only on biology.

Poulheria Kyriakou has argued (1998: 283) that Menelaus's fault in the *Orestes* is not a want of altruistic affection but of reciprocity: as 'Agamemnon's only surviving male relative,' he is obliged to 'succour his relatives, or *philoi*, in distress, thus returning the many favors, or *kharites* [plural of *kharis*], his dead brother had generously granted him.' Kyriakou affirms (283–4) that *philia* and *kharis* are closely related ideas: 'It should be noted that Menelaus is not expected to help his nephew because of the natural affection

kin might feel for each other ... Irrespective of emotions or principles Menelaus is supposed to assist Orestes because his debt to
Agamemnon obliges him to.'[25] She points out that Orestes and
Electra continually refer to Menelaus as *philos*, and yet 'nothing
like affection or love governs their relationship.' Rather, they are
bound by 'a very strictly organized system of mutual obligations,'
on which Menelaus reneges. Kyriakou agrees that *philos* normally distinguishes friend from relative in Greek literature, and
that, even among kin, the word usually suggests friendly feelings:
'But this does not mean that the term cannot be used irrespective
of emotions and that it does not imply a system of reciprocal
obligations, in some contexts at least.'

Now, on Aristotle's view, Menelaus's failure to assist his nephew
exposes the limits of his benevolence, not merely of his sense of
duty. Orestes indeed reminds Menelaus of the *kharis* or good turn
he owes in return for Agamemnon's support in recovering Helen
from Troy, but he also appeals to the *philia* implicit in kinship:
'Give your dear ones [*philois*], who are faring miserably, a share in
your own well-being, and do not keep for yourself what is good;
partake rather in our struggles in turn, and pay back the debt of
gratitude to my father, to whom you ought. For they are friends
[*philoi*] in name, not deed, who are not friends in misfortune'
(450–5; cf. 665–7). There are, I think, two demands here: the first is
that Menelaus share with his nephew and niece, who should be
dear to him, something of his own prosperity, just as Agamemnon
had done for him, without regard to repayment; the second is a
claim on Menelaus's debt to Agamemnon. The concluding generalization recapitulates the first point: all *philoi* are entitled to
expect spontaneous help from one another in times of trouble,
irrespective of prior favours.

Menelaus acknowledges the claims of kinship: 'I respect you
and wish to struggle along with you in your plight' (682–3), he
says, and adds that it is right to participate in the difficulties of
blood relations (*homaimones*, 684), when possible, both by dying
oneself and by slaying enemies (*enantioi*, 685). But he protests
that he has not the forces to assist Orestes in this way, and
recommends persuasion instead. Pylades is willing to gamble all
to save Orestes; Menelaus is not. As Orestes sees it (he sets a high

standard for loyalty), Menelaus is not sufficiently desirous of his good. It is thus true, as Kyriakou says, that Menelaus feels little love for Orestes and Electra – and that is the point. For the concern characteristic of a true *philos*, Orestes must await the arrival of Pylades.

Isocrates, in a speech (the 'Aegineticus') composed for the defendant in an inheritance trial before a court in Aegina, provides a vivid depiction of a friendship. A certain Thrasylochus bequeathed his property to the defendant, but the will is being contested by the testator's sister. The fathers of the two men had been intimate friends and connected by marriage, and the sons were closer than brothers: they shared everything, held similar political views, and had the same friends and enemies. When Thrasylochus fell ill, the defendant put his own health at risk and tended him assiduously, although the former was bedridden for six months and so cranky that no relative or even slave could abide him. On the point of death, indeed, Thrasylochus adopted the defendant (24–9; cf. Sternberg 2000). Now his sister, who did nothing for him when he was living, has come to claim the legacy, as though she were a relative of his money and not of the deceased himself (30–1). If there had been enmity (*ekhthra*) between her and her brother, then it is no wonder, the defendant avers, that he left her nothing, and if not, then all the more should she lose the inheritance, given her callous indifference to him (32). It is not those who 'claim to be kin by blood, but in their deeds behaved like enemies,' who should be vindicated, 'but much rather those who have not the name of kin but in misfortune showed themselves to be closer than the relatives' (33).

As Aristotle affirms, affection and friendship reside in a selfless concern to provide goods for the other to the best of one's ability; failure to assist in time of need, whether on the part of friends or relatives, proves the absence of the wish and hence the love itself. Sentiment and succor go hand in hand, for the sentiment consists precisely in the desire to promote the other's welfare. The speaker in Isocrates' discourse is not arguing that the deceased was obligated to make him his heir, but that he wanted to, in response to the kindness he had been shown (Thrasylochus himself, we are told, felt a debt of gratitude or *kharis*, 11). To see his behaviour as motivated by interest is to miss the benevolence that is the essence of *philia*. Thrasylochus's sister, who should have held him dear, lacked this selflessness, and lost her place in Thrasylochus's affections.

Isocrates' discourse, like Euripides' *Orestes*, affirms the solidarity of friends as against relatives. In fact, betrayal of friends is rarely if ever a subject of litigation in surviving forensic oratory (see Cox 1998: 194–202), and comedy too seems to have eschewed the theme, while delighting in the representation of quarrels between fathers and sons and husbands and wives (Konstan 2000a; 2006a). What is the explanation for this apparent reticence in respect to conflict among friends in the courts and on the stage of classical Athens, in contrast to its conspicuousness among kin?

Blood ties had a sacred character, and no doubt their violation was particularly shocking and pitiable, as Aristotle says. To see a mother slay her children, moreover, was wrenching because it defied an attachment that was presumed to be natural; for a child to kill a parent was to disregard the unrepayable debt owed for the gift of life itself (*Nicomachean Ethics* 8.14, 1163b19–28). So too, a wife who defied her husband threatened to invert the social order. But it may also be that the affection between friends was itself idealized, and was thus protected from negative representation. Alfons Fürst, in his study of classical accounts of strife among friends (1996: 119), cites Aristotle's *Eudemian Ethics* (7.5, 1239b15–16) for the maxim 'a friendship that is not stable is not a friendship.' Fürst concludes (228) that 'ancient reflections on friendship were in the last analysis shot through with an unshakable optimism.' If the only friendships are enduring friendships, then betraying a friend is logically impossible. A dramatic plot might expose the consequences of a shallow confidence in a fair-weather friend, but such people are merely contemptible. As Socrates puts it in Xenophon's *Memorabilia* (2.5.4): 'I neither see good slaves being sold nor good friends being betrayed.'

Whereas various obligations and forms of deference regulated relations in the Greek family and city alike, friendship may have emerged as a privileged zone of disinterested affection.[26] In the larger community, moreover, one was always defending one's status against insult, intimidation, or disapproval (the motives behind anger, fear, and shame), resenting the unfair advantage of others (envy, indignation), or being conscious of one's debt to them (gratitude). In this fraught arena of public life, friendship appeared as the locus of a selfless desire for another person's welfare that went beyond the demands of reciprocity or duty.[27] It was still marked, of course, by a concern with want and security, as opposed to being an etherealized feeling of attachment (as modern definitions would have it), and it was thus, like the other *pathê* Aristotle discusses, embedded in the world of social exchange, whether material or in the coin of reputation or status. But the love between friends nevertheless looked beyond the self, and in this resembles, for all the differences, the idea of love we have today.[28]

CHAPTER NINE

Hatred

I have ever hated all nations, professions and communities, and all my love is towards individuals. For instance, I hate the tribe of lawyers, but I love Councellor such a one, Judge such a one. For so with physicians (I will not speak of my own trade), soldiers, English, Scotch, French, and the rest. But principally I hate and detest that animal called man, although I heartily love John, Peter, Thomas and so forth.

Jonathan Swift to Alexander Pope, 29 September 1725[1]

To foster the conviction that God supports the murder of innocents requires a tightknit group and a settled hatred of the Other: in these circles, whites hate blacks and Jews; Jews and Christians hate Muslims and vice versa; anti-abortion crusaders hate gynecologists. All of them seem to have it in for homosexuals and most, even the Americans, hate contemporary America.

Hinton 2003: 50

Aristotle draws a sharp distinction, as we have observed (chapter 2, p. 47), between anger, which is provoked uniquely by a slight, and enmity or hatred, which is a response to something bad or harmful (*kakon*, as in 'cacophony'). Since Aristotle's account of hatred is relatively brief, we may quote it almost in full (*Rhetoric* 2.4, 1382a1–14):

Concerning enmity [*ekhthra*] and hating [*to misein*], one can understand them on the basis of their opposites. Anger, spite, and slander are productive of enmity. Anger, however, derives from what happens to oneself, whereas enmity arises also without [the offence] being directed at oneself. For if we believe that someone is a certain kind of person, we hate him. Also, anger is always about individuals, for example Callias or Socrates, whereas hatred [*misos*] is also felt towards types: for everyone hates a thief and an informer. Moreover, the one is healed by time, while the other is incurable. Also, the one is a desire to inflict pain, while the other is a desire to inflict harm: for a person who is angry wishes to perceive [his revenge], but to the one who hates this is a matter of indifference ... Besides this, the one is accompanied by pain, while the other occurs unaccompanied by pain: for someone who is angry feels pain, but someone who hates does not. Also, the one might feel pity if enough [misfortunes befall the other], but the other in no case: for the one wishes that the person with whom he is angry should suffer in return, but the other wishes that he should cease to exist.

Let me highlight some of Aristotle's claims in this passage. First, he maintains that the object of anger is to cause pain to the other, while the object of hatred is to inflict harm (2.4, 1382a8). We may wish that people whom we hate should die, but when we are angry, what we desire is that the other person feel hurt in return. In addition, we do not necessarily respond with hatred only to those who have harmed us in particular, but may experience it for wrongs directed to others as well. Finally, Aristotle affirms that we do not feel anger, in contrast with hatred, towards groups or classes. It is one of the fundamental differences between anger and hatred that while the object of anger must be an individual – it is strictly a one-on-one passion (cf. 2.2, 1378a34–5) – we can hate thieves or informers in general, whether or not they have injured us personally: it is enough that 'we believe that someone is a certain kind of person.' We may add that, according to Aristotle, hatred is a more durable emotion than anger.

Aristotle is right, as we might have expected, about Greek usage in respect to the generality of hatred. In practice, the verb *misein*, unlike anger, often expresses loathing for a category or class of people rather than a particular individual. For example, Phaedra, in Euripides' *Hippolytus*, declares: 'I hate women who are chaste in words but secretly engage in ugly escapades' (313–

14). Hippolytus, in turn, announces that he hates a wise woman (640), and, a little later, all women indiscriminately (664–5; cf. 93; Plato, *Republic* 334C4–5). In the *Prometheus Bound* attributed to Aeschylus, Prometheus says to Hermes: 'I have learned to hate traitors' (1068; cf. Pindar, *Pythian* 4.284–6: 'I have learned to hate an arrogant man'), while Lysias (16.18) speaks of hatred of people with long hair, an aristocratic affectation in imitation of the Spartans (at 14.39, Lysias contrasts hatred for the Spartans with anger towards the thirty tyrants, who unjustly usurped power in Athens; cf. 25.18).[2] The frequency with which first-person expressions of antagonism towards women and other groups turn up suggests that it was something of a formula. Since hatred is aroused by what is harmful or prejudicial to one's well-being, it embraces a wide range of hostile relations, including class conflict, foreign enemies, and partisan competition.

In his commentary on the *Rhetoric*, George Kennedy (1991: 137) writes that 'Aristotle regards hostile emotions as awakened by the perception that someone belongs to a detested class of individuals, such as thieves or sycophants. The negative feeling toward the class is a permanent one, but the identification of an individual with the class may be established or disproved in a speech.' One can, of course, detest an instantiation of a type: thus, a character in a fragmentary play of Euripides declares: 'I hate womankind, but of all of them, you, who speak well but do wicked things' (*Meleager*, fr. 528.1–2; cf. Menander, *Sicyonius* 160–1). I agree too that hatred is not simply a reflex of revulsion, but a considered antagonism or animosity based on an ethical judgment. In Euripides' *Electra*, Clytemnestra affirms, 'When people understand a matter, then if it is right to hate it, it is just to feel disgust [*stugein*] at it' (1015–17).[3] However, Aristotle does not deny that hatred may be directed at an individual, nor does he interpret all personal hatred as motivated by an association between the individual and a group. In this, moreover, he is consistent with ordinary Greek usage. Thus, Medea, in Euripides' tragedy, indicates that she bears no ill will towards Creon, since he, owing her nothing, did not wrong her; it is her husband she hates (309–11; cf. *Hippolytus* 962). In Sophocles' *Electra*, the heroine recalls how her mother abused her, calling her a 'hateful creature [*misêma*] loathesome to the gods' (289). In turn, Electra accuses her sister Chrysothemis of cowardice for failing to make manifest in action her hatred (*misos*) for her mother (347–8), and reproaches her (357–8): 'For me, you are a hater who hates in words, but in fact you live with our father's assassins.' Isaeus writes (9.16): 'I will prove to you that Astyphilus was the worst enemy [*ekhthiston*] of Cleon [not the Cleon to whom Aristotle refers], and hated him so thoroughly and justly that he was far more disposed that no member of his household should talk to Cleon than to adopt Cleon's son as his own' (cf. 9.31). In Aristophanes' *Knights* (225–6) a character affirms: 'There are a thousand knights, good men, who hate him' – that is, the Paphlagonian, who is a thinly veiled stand-in for Cleon, this time the very man Aristotle cites to illustrate that one can be angry only at an individual, not a type (cf. 400). Examples of this usage abound.[4]

Kennedy's view corresponds better to the modern idea of hatred, at least as it has evolved in the past few decades. In a recent book on hate crimes, Jack Levin (2002: 1) remarks:

Until recently, the term 'hate' referred to any intense dislike or hostility, whatever its object ... Beginning in the mid-1980s, the term 'hate' became used in a much more restricted sense to characterize an individual's negative beliefs and feelings about the members of some other group of people because of their race, religious identity, ethnic origin, gender, sexual orientation, age, or disability status.

Levin notes that, like 'hate,' 'prejudice' too has 'undergone a major shift in meaning ... from "any pre-judgment" to "a hostile attitude directed specifically toward members of an outgroup"' (he might have added that the same is true for the term 'discrimination').[5]

When such negative beliefs are intensified to the point that the other is perceived as less than human, they may enable people to undertake the deliberate eradication of an entire group or nation. Omer Bartov, writing of German action on the eastern front in the Second World War, observes (2001: 83): 'During the war in Russia the process of dehumanisation of the enemy was probably more successful than in any other war in modern history – the Russians, Slavs, Jews, Mongols, all had lost any relationship to the human race, and were nothing more than satanic monsters trying to appear human, imposters whose identity had to be exposed and whose existence endangered everything which civilised men held dear.' So too, Aaron Beck (1999: 16) observes: 'First, the members of the opposition are *homogenized*; they lose their identities as unique individuals. Each victim is interchangeable, and all are disposable. In the next stage the victims are *dehumanized* ... Finally, they are *demonized* as the embodiment of Evil' (cf. 170–96).[6] It is not acts, on this view, but identities (as determined by beliefs or other traits) that induce and excuse hostility.

Is this what Aristotle means when he says that hatred arises 'if we believe that someone is a certain kind of person'? Aristotle does not provide a definition of hatred, although the Stoics did: 'Hatred is a desire for something bad to happen to another, progressively and continually' (Diogenes Laertius, *Lives of the Philosophers* 7.113).[7] The Stoic definition looks only to the impulse, however, and does not include a reference to the motive for hatred, although we would expect such an account of Aristotle.[8] Since Aristotle treats hatred as the opposite of love, we may reasonably seek to infer the causes of it from his analysis of the latter emotion. Indeed, Aristotle invites us to do just this, since he introduces his account of hatred with the words: 'concerning enmity [*ekhthra*] and hating [*to misein*] one can understand them on the basis of their opposites.'

As we saw in the previous chapter, Aristotle defines love or loving (*to philein*) as wishing good things for another for that person's sake, and seeking actively to bring them about (2.4, 1380b36–81a1). One might, on this basis, conclude that hatred is a disinterested desire that harm accrue to another, together with a disposition to make it happen. This looks rather like the Stoic formula, and perhaps gave rise to it. Aristotle is aware, however, that a given term may have more than one opposite (*Topics* 2.7, 113a14–15, quoted in chapter 3, p. 83), and one must be cautious in making such transpositions. In any case, Aristotle does not include the causes of affection in the definition, as he does, for example, in the case of anger, and so for this we must look to the more detailed description that follows.

190 / The Emotions of the Ancient Greeks

Aristotle observes that we generally find genial people likeable, and it is plausible to suppose that we are inclined to dislike those who are contentious. So too, he says, we feel affection towards those people whom we admire. Now, the traits that are most admirable in themselves are the virtues, and Aristotle duly lists among the principal qualities that inspire affection liberality, courage, justice, and moderation. In the *Nicomachean Ethics*, moreover, Aristotle observes that things are lovable (*philêton*) either because they are good or because they are pleasing (8.2, 1155b18–19; he subsumes the third category, the useful, under the preceding two, since things are useful because they bring about the good or the pleasant). The best and most permanent kind of love, he concludes, is that on account of goodness or virtue, since virtue pertains to one's character (as opposed to a personality trait like affability). Aristotle, as we have seen, links the special role of character with the stipulation, in the definition of love, that the desire for the other's good be for his or her sake, since, he argues, our character is who we are (see chapter 8, pp. 177–9).

Aristotle mentions spite and slander as causes of hostility, and these may be taken as the contrary of amiability. In turn, an odious person – the kind we hate – is plausibly the opposite of one who is lovable because virtuous. If this is so, then the type of people we hate, according to Aristotle, are those with vicious characters, that is, marked by vices instead of virtues. Hatred, then, involves a moral evaluation as much as loving does.[9]

Aristotle's view clearly does not entirely conform to Jack Levin's account of modern hatred as characterized by 'an individual's negative beliefs and feelings about the members of some other group of people because of their race, religious identity, ethnic origin, gender, sexual orientation, age, or disability status.' Aristotle does regard non-Greeks and women as naturally inferior to adult male Greeks (*Politics* 1252a31–b12, 1254b13–24), but these groups are nevertheless capable of virtue in accord with their natures (as all creatures are). There is thus no motive in Aristotle for hostility towards a given natural class as such. What one dislikes are groups made up of morally corrupt individuals, such as thieves and informers, to cite Aristotle's own examples (an anonymous Byzantine commentator remarks on this passage: 'I am not said to hate Callias [i.e., an individual] but rather the whole race of Persians or informers' [99.15–16 Rabe]; but the example of the Persians is not Aristotle's). One hates each member of these groups for his or her own moral flaws, and the entire class since it is defined by the vice in question.[10]

The case is different for anger, since anger is provoked by an intentional slight, which is necessarily addressed by one individual to another. It is true, as we saw in chapter 2 (pp. 70–2), that acts of treachery could arouse anger against a city as a whole, to the point at which the conqueror was prepared to obliterate the entire population. In these cases, however, the anger results from a devious or unprincipled action – a particular offence that is perceived as undeserved – to which the people are understood to have given their consent: it is, as it were, a collective slight, for which each citizen must take responsibility. Such behaviour may, of course, be read as the sign of an endemic vice, but the Greeks did not tend to wage wars of extermination on the grounds of the inveterate depravity (not to say sheer otherness) of the enemy, as though it were constitutive of their identity. In this respect, mass killing in antiquity was different in kind from modern genocide: it was motivated by anger at an unjust act, not hatred of 'satanic monsters trying to appear human.'[11]

Modern writers almost invariably classify the hostile emotions as 'negative,' as opposed to ostensibly positive emotions such as love and sympathy. A not untypical judgment by a psychologist has it that 'hostility is an abnormal, destructive affect' (Kalogerakis 2004; cf. Emde 1980 and the essays collected in Iganski 2003).[12] Even physiological studies of aggressive violence may conclude that 'negative affect can precipitate and accentuate aggressive behavior' (Davidson, Putnam, and Larson 2000: 591). Anger occasionally gets a better press (e.g. Milhaven 1989), but hatred is almost universally condemned. Where it is defended, it is in the tough-guy language of survival of the fittest. Thus Melvin Konner (2003), reviewing Willard Gaylin's *Hatred: The Psychological Descent into Violence* (2003), writes: 'I harbor real hatred and I don't see it as pathological. Indeed, contra Gaylin, hatred can be adaptive, especially in a creature with long memory; in hunter-gatherer life, it may have been essential.'[13] Aristotle's analysis is a salutary reminder that there may be people deserving of our antagonism – even if absurd or fanatical figures, like Hippolytus, can in a fit of passion declare their hatred for women in general. As Isocrates (15.142) says, hatred towards good people is the sign of a bad character.

There is a conundrum connected with Aristotle's insistence that hatred, as opposed to anger, is not accompanied by pain (2.4, 1382a12–13), for this would appear to exclude hatred from the category of the emotions, as defined by Aristotle: it will be recalled that emotions are said to be accompanied by pleasure and pain.[14] Perhaps Aristotle believed that hatred, like anger, involves an element of pleasure deriving from the expectation of revenge (or rather, in the case of hatred, the elimination of one's opponent), and thus meets the definition of a *pathos*. Just as loving, moreover, causes one to share in the pain and pleasure of a dear one (2.4, 1381a5–6; cf. chapter 8, p. 174), so too hating may induce a reverse kind of sympathy, and in this way fulfil the condition for being an emotion. Aristotle says that it is in the nature of emotions that they cause people to differ in their judgments, and loving and hating in particular, he notes, have the effect that jurors and assemblymen 'can no longer see the truth well enough, but their own pleasure or pain clouds their judgment' (1354b10–11).[15] But hatred of a class of people, such as thieves, no doubt lacks the acute sense of injury that results from an intentional slight, and this, I imagine, is why Aristotle describes it – by contrast with anger – as a painless emotion.[16]

Aristotle lists anger, spite, and slander as particularly productive of hatred (2.4, 1382a2–3). Spite was also included among the causes of anger, as we have seen, since obstructing another's wishes for the sheer pleasure of it bespeaks a good measure of contempt. Slander too, one supposes, could elicit anger, if it took the form of a slight, but it may also be a sign of bad character and hence the object of hatred: sycophants who habitually denounce their peers presumably are guilty of this offence. Anger seems more difficult to understand as a stimulus to hating. Aristotle would seem to mean that it is the anger of another (like the spite or slander of another), not our own, that elicits our hostility, and hence that of someone whom we ourselves have demeaned. His reasoning, I imagine, is that an angry person is by definition seeking revenge, and hence out to do us harm. Similarly, the giving of satisfaction would, I presume, generate a friendly feeling.

So far, we have limited our discussion to the emotion of hatred or, more precisely, hating: *to misein* is a verbal noun, preceded by the definite article *to*, like *to philein* and *to nemesan* (cf. chapters 5, p. 112, and 8, p. 171). Aristotle introduces the topic, however, with the words 'Concerning enmity and hating, one can understand them on the basis of their opposites.' Is enmity (*ekhthra*) a mere synonym of *to misein*, or do the connotations of the two terms differ in some important respect?

The word *ekhthra* is related to the verb *ekhthairô*, meaning 'to hate,' and also to the concrete noun *ekhthros*, or 'enemy.' Like Latin, classical Greek had two words for 'enemy.' One of them, *polemios*, derives from *polemos* or 'war' and signifies a military enemy (compare the Latin *hostis*). *Ekhthros*, by contrast, usually denotes a personal enemy (like the Latin *inimicus*), although it is occasionally applied to foreign opponents, especially when the hostility is felt as particularly charged (e.g., Lysias 14.30, Demosthenes, *Philippics* 3.53).[17] Isocrates, who sought to unite Greece and Macedon by means of their common antagonism to the Persians, speaks of a long-term hostility (*ekhthra*) towards barbarians, imagined as inherited from the time of the Trojan War (*Panathenaïcus* 42; cf. 189; also Thucydides 2.11.2 on the *ekhthos* or 'hatred' of subject cities towards Athens). In English, we do not typically distinguish the two kinds of enemy lexically, although the term 'foe,' now pretty much obsolete in the United States except in certain expressions, such as 'friend or foe,' refers chiefly to enemy armies.

The Greeks tended to see their social world as divided between friends and enemies (that is, *philoi* and *ekhthroi*), and to assume that one was likely to have at least as many of the latter as of the former (cf. Chilon 3.14 Mullach). The well-known formula 'help friends and harm enemies' takes it for granted that neither category is vacant.[18] Enmities might even be defended as socially useful: Aeschines (*Against Timarchus* 2) notes that personal enmities (*ekhthrai idiai*), such as his own quarrel with Timarchus, can promote the public welfare, since they move people to prosecute fellow citizens who violate the ethical standards of the community.[19] In these contexts, the term used is invariably *ekhthros* (cf., for instance, Polybius 1.14.4 on hating the enemies of one's friend).

To the best of my knowledge, no Greek text states that personal enmity must be reciprocal, and that each party must be cognizant of the hostility of the other, in the way that Aristotle stipulates for friendship or *philia*. But Aristotle seems clearly to treat *ekhthra* as the counterpart to *philia*, just as *to misein* or hating answers to *to philein*. Hating is the simple emotion, whereas enmity represents the state of affairs that obtains when people regard each other with mutual hatred.[20] As with friendship, this is likely to be a lasting situation, not least because it is self-reinforcing, each side giving the other cause for continued antipathy, accompanied, no doubt, by the belief that the other possesses the detestable traits of character typical of the 'certain kind of person' who merits hatred.[21]

At the beginning of Euripides' tragedy *The Children of Hercules*, Hercules' sons and daughters, together with Hercules' mother Alcmene and his now aged comrade-in-arms Iolaus, have taken refuge in the temple of Zeus in Marathon, in the outskirts of Attica, to escape persecution by Eurystheus, the king of Argos. It was Eurystheus who had obliged Hercules to undertake his famous labours; now, after Hercules' death, Eurystheus is intent upon killing his surviving kin, and especially his children, so as to eliminate the potential threat they pose to his throne (cf. 465–70). A herald, sent by Eurystheus to dissuade the Athenians and their king Demopho (the son of Theseus) from harbouring the suppliants, asserts that Argos has a right to punish its own (139–43) and warns against provoking war with a mighty foe for the sake of a few helpless strangers. Iolaus protests that, having been expelled, they are no longer under Eurystheus's jurisdiction (184–9), and Demopho decides to protect the refugees. At this point, in one of those abrupt twists that are characteristic of Euripides, it is announced that, according to a series of prophecies, the Athenians can only emerge victorious from battle with the Argives if the virgin daughter of a noble family is sacrificed (408). Demopho refuses to immolate a daughter of his own or compel another

Athenian family to do so (411–13), but Hercules' eldest daughter offers herself on behalf of her relatives and the city that has sheltered them (501–2).[22] As she is led off to die, news arrives that Hyllus, the eldest of Hercules's sons, has returned to Athens with a company of soldiers, and old Iolaus girds himself for battle. The Athenians are victorious (784–7), and Iolaus, who has been magically rejuvenated (796, 857–8), succeeds in capturing Eurystheus alive (859–63).

Here again the action takes a surprising turn, apparently without precedent in the myth.[23] Alcmene protests that Iolaus should have killed Eurystheus (879–82) on the battlefield rather than spare his life, but the messenger who has brought her the news of the victory explains that Iolaus wished precisely to put Eurystheus in her power (883–4). Iolaus's squire leads Eurystheus in, bound and humbled, and Alcmene gives vent to her hostility towards him, declaring that he must be killed: indeed he ought, she says, to die many times over for what he has done (958–60). The squire objects that it is not permitted to slay him, but Alcmene is adamant: 'In vain, then, have we taken him captive' (962). If Athenian tradition (nomos) prohibits killing a prisoner of war (963–72), then she will execute him herself, for however much she loves the city of Athens, Eurystheus must not live, now that he has fallen into her hands (973–80).[24]

Here, then, the Athenians' defence of suppliants in a just cause and their triumph over an arrogant enemy give way to a mood of bitter retribution, in which the former victims turn against their enemies with a violence and loathing that seem no less extreme than what they had previously suffered. How is one to understand the vehement hatred on the part of the foreign (that is, non-Athenian) characters in the finale of the play, which appears to contrast so sharply with the moderation and respect for law and custom that characterize Athens's intervention in their behalf?[25]

It was, of course, Eurystheus who initiated hostilities against the Athenians, but his goal was limited to reclaiming the Argive refugees. The Athenians, in turn, are content to defeat his forces and protect the suppliants from being violated. Alcmene, by contrast, is moved by a fierce personal antagonism towards Eurystheus, going back to the time when he imposed the twelve labours on

Hercules. Thus, two kinds of enmity are active in the play. Iolaus may refer to the Argives as *polemioi* insofar as he thinks of them as a hostile army (315–16); this is the term he employs, for example, in connection with news from the battlefield (382, 655), or again in reference to the enemy ranks (676; cf. 738). The squire speaks of his desire to return to battle and engage with the *polemioi* (678–9). But when Iolaus declares that his only concern about dying is the possibility that his death may bring joy to his enemies (443–4), the term is *ekhthroi* (cf. 449–50 on the shame involved in death at the hands of an *ekhthros*, that is, Eurystheus; also 458, 468). In battle, he prays to be rejuvenated so that he can exact the due penalty from his *ekhthroi* (849–53), here clearly thinking of the Argives as his personal enemies. Hercules' daughter, having volunteered to die, tells Iolaus that he need no longer fear the enemy's spear (*ekhthron doru*, 500; cf. 512, 530).[26] But it is Alcmene who is most conscious of the irreconcilable hatred that exists between herself and Eurystheus. She insists that it is unwise not to avenge oneself when one has one's *ekhthroi* in one's power (881–2). The squire, as he leads Eurystheus in, tells Alcmene that 'it is most pleasant to see an *ekhthros* suffer misfortune after he has prospered' (939–40). Face to face with Eurystheus, Alcmene calls him 'a hateful thing' (*ô misos*, 941; cf. 52, where Iolaus applies the same expression to the herald), and berates him for daring to look his enemies (*ekhthroi*) in the face (943). So too, she justifies her intention to kill Eurystheus with the words 'Don't the Athenians think it a fine thing to slay their *ekhthroi*?' (965), to which the squire replies, 'Not one who has been taken alive in battle,' pointing up the contrast between personal antagonisms and the protocols of war.[27]

If Alcmene's ferocious assault on Eurystheus comes as a surprise, no less so is Eurystheus's own response in the face of her hostility.[28] After refusing to confront Hyllus, the son of Hercules, on the battlefield in what, at least according to the report of the messenger, seemed to be an open display of cowardice, Eurystheus suddenly acquires an unanticipated dignity as he confesses his earlier crimes and accepts his death with calm assurance. He explains that he had previously lived in fear of his *ekhthroi*; nor will he deny that Hercules, though an *ekhthros*, was a noble man.

After Hercules' death, he knew that he was hated (*misoumenos*) by his children thanks to their inherited hostility towards him (*ekhthra patrôia*), and he tried to eliminate them as well; Alcmene would have done the same, he says, concerning the cubs of a hostile (*ekhthros*) lion. He concludes by reminding Alcmene that Athens has spared him, respecting the laws of the Greeks and honouring the god above enmity (*ekhthra*) towards him (994–1013).

Alcmene is unappeased, and Eurystheus, prepared to die, announces – in yet another unexpected twist of the plot – that, in accord with an ancient prophecy of Apollo, if he is buried in Attica he will prove a saviour of the city, although he will remain forever at war (*polemiôtatos*) with the descendants of Hercules (1032–4). The tragedy concludes as Alcmene orders her servants to kill Eurystheus, since he is an *ekhthros* and on top of that his death will aid Athens, and to throw his body to the dogs (1045–51). In their final comment, even the chorus of Athenians agrees that it is best for Eurystheus to die (1053–5), which would seem to put in question all that Athens stood for earlier.

I have dwelled on the distinction between *polemios* and *ekhthros* because it points the way to an interpretation of the action of *The Children of Hercules* that goes beyond the contrast, emphasized by many critics, between Alcmene's savagery and the civilized restraint of Athens and its king. *Ekhthroi* regard each other as irremediably vicious. As Aristotle explains, although anger may be eased by time, hatred is 'incurable.' Hatred seeks to inflict not just pain but harm, and is indifferent to whether the revenge is perceived: Alcmene would have preferred to learn that Eurystheus had been slain on the battlefield. So too, hatred, unlike anger, is pitiless, since it is not concerned with getting even (at which point it may be mollified), but desires that the other simply 'cease to exist.'

Nowhere in the play is Alcmene described as angry at Eurystheus; the prevailing passion is clearly personal hostility. At the time of the action, the enmity between them has become inveterate: in this sense, Alcmene's detestation of Eurystheus is not simply an immediate response to his vicious nature but has hardened into a long-term disposition. Just as friendship, or *philia*, as Aristotle explains in the *Nicomachean Ethics* (9.5, 1166b34), requires time for mutual confidence to develop, so too, we may infer, prolonged enmity congeals into an entrenched distrust. Alcmene is unmoved by Eurystheus's apparently generous appraisal of Hercules, which she may very well regard as self-serving under the circumstances, or the excuse that he feared for his throne, which is an ignoble motive in any case. As Aristotle says, the emotions are just those things that cause people to differ in their judgments, and it is the pain or pleasure resulting from loving and hating that clouds the minds of jurors and assemblymen (1354b10–11). *The Children of Hercules* is a study in hatred and enmity, but it does not, I think, simply condemn such sentiments as base or perverse. Just as Athens overcomes its political enemies or *polemioi* on the battlefield, so too Alcmene and her family triumph over their hated *ekhthros*. The finale of the tragedy makes it clear that Alcmene's determination to eliminate her enemy coincides with the security of Athens itself. Rather than contrast her hate with the honourable moderation of Athens's king, I would see their motives as complementary and suited to their respective situations. Alcmene's loathing is extreme, but it is neither groundless nor evil.[29]

According to Aristotle, as we have seen, it is not necessary that one suffer harm oneself in order to feel hatred. Demipho and the Athenians could detest Eurystheus, insofar as he exemplifies the type of the unjust tyrant. Euripides did not place such a generalization in the mouth of the Athenian king, despite his apparent predilection for the formula, perhaps because he wished to keep the focus on the highly personal enmity between Alcmene and Eurystheus. So too friendship, as a special case of loving, is typically represented as a reciprocal affection between two people, although others too may like and admire one or both friends for their virtues (on mutual hatred, cf. Sophocles, *Ajax* 1133–4; Plato, *Republic* 351D–E).

The Greek language had other words for loathing, among them the verb *bdeluttomai* and related terms such as *bdeluros* ('loathsome'), but here the core idea is that of being revolted by someone or something (the term is particularly frequent in the comic poets: cf. the name Bdelycleon, or 'Cleon-Loather,' in Aristophanes'

Wasps). In the Hippocratic writings, for example, it is used half a dozen times in connection with nausea, and Orestes employs *bdeluktropoi* ('disgusting') of the hideous Furies in Aeschylus's *Eumenides* (52). It may also, of course, be applied to repugnant behaviour (Andocides 122; cf. *bdeluriai* [abstract noun, plural] at Isaeus 8.42). Demosthenes had a fondness for the term (twenty-nine occurrences), but it tends to be concentrated in certain speeches (over half the uses are in orations 19 and 21); in speaking of his arch-enemy Meidias, he pairs *bdeluros* with *hubristês*, 'violently abusive' (21.143), with *thrasus*, 'reckless' (21.98), and with *anaidês*, 'shameless' (21.107):[30] Meidias, he intones (21.98), is 'wanton [*aselgês*] and *bdeluros*: this is the truth. One ought to hate such men, Athenians, rather than save them' (note that *misein* is, as often, associated with hostility to a type). So too, thirteen of the fourteen occurrences of the root *bdel-* in the orations of Aeschines are in his attack on the repellent comportment of Timarchus, whom he portrays as a male prostitute (Lysias eschews the word). There is a moral quality to Aeschines' reaction, but the sense is primarily one of revulsion or disgust.

More closely related to *misein* is the set of terms based, like *ekhthra*, on the stem *ekhth-*, including the verbs *ekhthairô* and *apekhthanomai* (later in the form *apekhthomai*) and the adjective *apekhthês*. In the *Iliad* (3.415), Aphrodite warns Helen to obey her, lest her love for her turn to hatred.[31] Pindar (*Nemean* 10.83) refers to 'hated old age.' In Sophocles' tragedy *Ajax* (457–8), Ajax concludes that he is abhorred (*ekhthairomai*) by the gods and that the Greek army also hates him (*misei*); Ajax in turn hates (*misein*) Hector, who is most inimical (*ekhthistos*) to him (815–18). Isocrates is particularly fond of the oxymoronic compound *philapekhthêmôn*, 'fond of hatred' (noun: *philapekhthêmosunê*, *Antidosis* 315; cf. Demosthenes 54.37), which he associates with savage cruelty and misanthropy. *Ekhthairô* and its cognates, however, are more frequently passive in construction than *misein*, and their objects are less often groups or types: like *ekhthros* itself, they tend chiefly to designate personal hostility.[32]

There are pathologies of hatred. If it is true that we sometimes hate an aspect of ourselves that we have projected onto another, then we remain attached to the abominated other, and do not really wish to eliminate him or her: '[H]ate transforms this or that other into an object whose expulsion or incorporation is needed, an expulsion or incorporation that requires the conservation of the object itself in order to be sustained' (Ahmed 2004: 51). It would not be difficult to produce an interpretation of Hippolytus's extreme loathing of women generally, and of his stepmother Phaedra in particular, in this key. Modern psychology has made great advances in understanding the dynamics of repression and displacement in emotional life, and furnishes powerful, often indispensable, techniques for analysing classical literature and behaviour generally. Not all hatred, however, need be explained as a symptom of trauma or some other unconscious mechanism. In this book, I am concerned to elicit the differences, where they exist, between modern conceptions of the emotions and those of the ancient Greeks, and to see whether and how an awareness of these differences may affect our appreciation of Greek culture. Recognizing that the hatred that underpins enmity was conceived as a moral emotion will, I hope, contribute something to this end.

CHAPTER TEN

Pity

[T]o ask, say, why we feel sympathy for Philoctetes is a pseudo-problem bred by a bogus historicism.

Eagleton 2003: xii–xiv

[T]he history of the meaning of pity in English should caution us not to assume that its modern English usage is necessarily a guide to pity in a foreign work of art like the *Iliad*.

Zanker 1994: 23

Although pity figures centrally in all ancient lists of the emotions, it is remarkably absent from modern inventories (e.g., Plutchik 1991: 117–18). In part, pity has been displaced by neighbouring ideas such as sympathy, empathy, and compassion, all of which bear some relationship to pity, no doubt, but also differ in important ways, and more especially from the classical Greek concept represented by the term *eleos* (from which the English words 'eleemosynary' and, by a more circuitous route, 'alms' are derived). For one thing, Greek pity was not an instinctive response to another person's pain, but depended on a judgment of whether the other's suffering was deserved or not.[1] Pity, like the *pathê* we have examined in previous chapters, was both cognitive and social in character, and involved moral appraisals that inevitably reflected norms and values specific to classical Greek culture. It is precisely the distance between the pitier and the pitied that allows for this ethical dimension: to experience pity one has to recognize a resemblance with the sufferer, but at the same time not find oneself in precisely the same circumstances. Where complete identification occurs, one shares the emotion of the other, and that is not pity as the Greeks conceived it (the relative detachment characteristic of pity even today has led some to condemn it as a form of contempt).

I have explored some of the implications of the Greek conception of pity in my book *Pity Transformed* (2001a), to which I refer occasionally in what follows. In this chapter, however, I take a fresh look at some aspects of *eleos* that distinguish it from modern views of pity, but which at the same time widen its sphere of operation, as it were, by modifying the strict requirement concerning desert. First, I consider the role of public norms that set implicit limits on what people might legitimately be made to suffer, irrespective of whether they brought their misfortune upon themselves. Recognition of the importance of upholding such conventions provided the link by which pity might influence deliberations concerning matters of state, where, as we shall see, emotion was shunted aside in favour of arguments that looked to the public interest. Then, I take another look at the difference between pity and sympathetic identification in the context of Aristotle's theory of the tragic emotions, and argue that there is a place in Aristotle's own scheme of the *pathê* for a kind of humane sensibility towards the suffering of even an undeserving individual.

At the beginning of the Peloponnesian War (431 BC), Plataea, a small town in Boeotia to the north-east of Attica that was sympathetic to the Athenian side, was penetrated by a contingent of Theban hoplites (Thucydides 2.2–5). The Plataeans overcame the attackers and took a substantial number of prisoners, whom they later put to death. Subsequently, the Spartans forced the last defenders of the city to surrender. These men then made their case for being spared before the Spartans, while the Thebans argued in favour of their execution. The Plataeans, according to the speech that Thucydides records, appealed chiefly to the Spartans' own advantage. In their peroration, however, they represented themselves as suppliants (3.59.2), appealed to the common laws of the Greeks (*ta koina tôn Hellênôn nomima*, 3.59.1), and entreated the Spartans to be moved by reasonable pity (*oiktôi sôphroni*, 3.59.1). To this the Thebans retorted that pity is due only to those who have suffered unjustly: 'Those people are worthy of pity who have suffered something unsuitable, whereas those who have suffered justly, like these men, on the contrary deserve to be gloated over' (3.67.4). The Plataeans' fate, they added, is precisely *ennoma*, that is, within the law (3.67.5). The Thebans' argument won the day.

Plataea was restored in 386, but was again destroyed by Thebes in 373 (it would be refounded once more, many years later, by the Macedonians). In the same year, the orator Isocrates wrote the tract called *Plataïcus*, in which the Plataeans are represented as speaking before the Athenian assembly, urging them to take vengeance on Thebes. In the course of their argument, the Plataeans adopt the posture of suppliants (1, 6, 52, 53, 54, 56). Towards the end of their speech, moreover, they once again make an appeal to pity, alleging that it is not reasonable (*eikos*) that individuals are pitied if they have suffered unjustly (*para to dikaion*) while an entire city that is being wrongfully destroyed (*anomôs diephtharmenên*) should fail to win any pity at all (52; cf. *oiktron*, 56).

In both speeches, the Plataeans reserve their appeal to pity for the peroration, a strategy that was characteristic of forensic oratory.[2] What is more, both times they link their claim to pity to the justice of their cause (cf. Hogan 1972: 244). This is in accord with the prevailing view of pity in classical Greece, which was that pity is due not to suffering as such but rather to unmerited or illegitimate suffering. In fact, the practice of placing the appeal to pity at the end of a discourse is not unrelated to the connection between pity and desert. For speakers must first demonstrate, or attempt to demonstrate, that their case is just; only then can they appeal to pity on the grounds that they do not deserve the penalty or punishment that is proposed for them (see Konstan 2001a: 34–43; cf. Lateiner 2005, Tzanetou 2005).

The Greeks in the classical period, accordingly, did not perceive the same tension between pity and justice that modern jurists do when they exclude appeals to the emotions in the verdict phase of a trial on the grounds that they impede a fair and impartial appraisal of the evidence (Konstan 2001a: 28–30). True, the Stoics rejected pity on the grounds (among others) that it corrupts judgment, and their view was anticipated by Aristotle in the first chapter of the *Rhetoric*, where he asserts that 'one ought not to warp a juror by leading him to anger or envy or pity' (1.1, 1354a24–5), for that, Aristotle says, is like bending the ruler with which one takes a measurement. But Aristotle immediately comes round to endorsing the utility of appeals to the emotions, including pity, and, as we know, devotes several chapters of the second book of the *Rhetoric* to ways of rousing and assuaging them. This shift of perspective has been seen as a glaring inconsistency in the treatise as we have it (e.g., Kennedy 1991: 28; Barnes 1995: 262; Frede 1996: 264–5; Wardy 1996: 115–16). But perhaps the understanding of the emotions, and pity in particular, as grounded in moral judgments enabled Aristotle to accept their relevance to judicial pleading. For the condition that pity is a response not to any misfortune, or to misfortune that one has brought upon oneself, but only to undeserved hardship, provides the link between pity and justice.

Aristotle defines pity as 'a kind of pain in the case of an apparent destructive or painful harm in one not deserving to encounter it,' and which, he adds, 'one might expect oneself, or one of one's own, to suffer, and this when it seems near' (*Rhetoric* 2.8, 1385b13–16; on the proximity condition, cf. p. 131). So too, the *Rhetoric to Alexander* (ascribed by some scholars to the pre-Aristotelian rhetorician Anaximenes) advises:

We shall be capable of rendering things pitiable whenever we wish if we are aware that all people pity those whom they suppose to be well-disposed towards themselves and whom they believe to be undeserving [*anaxioi*] of misfortune. One must show that those whom one wishes to render pitiable have these qualities, and demonstrate that they have suffered or are suffering or will suffer wrongly [*kakôs*], unless the hearers help them. If this is not possible, then you must show that those for whom you are speaking have been deprived <or are are being deprived or will be deprived> of goods that all or most others have a share in, or have never obtained or are not obtaining or will not obtain a good, unless those who are now listening pity them [*oikteirôsin*]. (34.4–6)

Far from being incompatible with a verdict based on the merits of a case, then, pity depends upon a belief in the petitioner's innocence.

In Thucydides' report of the debate over the fate of Mytilene, which rebelled against Athenian hegemony near the beginning of the Peloponnesian War, Cleon accuses his fellow Athenians of being naively disposed to pity in their treatment of allied states (3.37.2). Pity, he continues, is ruinous to empire, and is wasted on those who are one's natural enemies (3.40.2–3). What the Mytilenaeans deserve, Cleon maintains, is total annihilation. Diodotus, in reply to Cleon, urges that the decision of the assembly should be based, not on considerations of justice or sentiment but solely on advantage (see Konstan 2001a: 80–2); the Athenians are persuaded and vote to slay only a thousand of the insurgents.[3] In the *Rhetoric* (1.3, 1358b20–9), indeed, Aristotle stipulates that the object of deliberative oratory is precisely the consideration of 'advantage and harm' rather than justice, which is the province of forensic rhetoric – and hence, we may add, the arena in which appeals to pity have a place. So too, in Plato's *Greater Alcibiades* (114D), the title character observes that in public deliberations the Greeks 'look to which will be of advantage to their affairs.'[4] It is telling that this pragmatic attitude is represented by Thucydides as favouring the milder option in respect to the punishment of the Mytilenaeans. The connection between pity and desert was not necessarily conducive to the humane treatment of the defeated, since an enemy deemed to have been unjust or perfidious might instead have to endure the victor's righteous anger (see chapter 2, p. 70).

Aristotle does allow that such painful but ethically neutral conditions as death, old age, and disease are pitiable (*Rhetoric* 2.8, 1386a4–9), and in the *Poetics* he acknowledges that, even when the moral conditions for tragic pity are absent – for example, when a character slays an enemy who presumably deserves his fate – the sheer pain or *pathos* of the event may still be pitiable (13, 1453b17–18; cf. Gorgias, *Defence of Helen* 9, 32, but contrast 7; Thrasymachus fr. 6 Diels-Kranz). Perhaps certain kinds of catastrophe never seem truly to be deserved. We shall return below to the question of whether pity or compassion might be evoked by the suffering even of a vicious person, according to Aristotle. First, however, let us consider a case, drawn from a Greek tragedy, in which cruelty in violation of conventional standards of decency seems to furnish grounds for pity even though the characters were responsible for their own misfortune.

Euripides' *Suppliant Women* opens with a dramatic tableau. In the centre is Aethra, the mother of the Athenian king Theseus, praying for the welfare of her son and her city in front of the temple of Demeter at Eleusis. A group of Argive women kneels at her feet: they have come to Attica, along with their king, Adrastus, to plead for help in retrieving the unburied bodies of their sons, which lie at Thebes, after the Argives' unsuccessful attack upon that city. A second chorus made up of boys, the sons of the fallen Argive warriors, also sits on stage. The old women bear a suppliant bough, and have suffered, as Aethra declares, a dreadful misfortune (*pathos pathousai deinon*, 10–11).[5]

Now, supplication does not necessarily entail an appeal to pity: the gesture by itself was ritually significant, and besides this, suppliants might also promise compensation (*Iliad* 21.75–80), invoke former services (Euripides, *Hecuba* 271–8), or claim a personal bond with the beseeched (Euripides, *Orestes* 665–79).[6] But the prostrate posture of the suppliant, enhanced by rent garments and unkempt hair, was designed to seem pitiable as well as humble (cf. Gould 1974: 94), all the more so when the appeal came, as here, from powerless figures such as women, children, and the aged. Thus, Aethra 'pities [*oiktirousa*] these childless, grey-haired mothers of sons,' while at the same time she 'reveres [*sebousa*] their sacred garlands,' that is, the symbols of a ritual petition (34–6).

The misfortune that prompts Aethra's pity is a double one. On the one hand, she is sensitive to the women's childlessness as a result of the war (11–16; *polias apaidas* in 35 answers *apaides* in 13); on the other hand, she regards the refusal of the Theban rulers either to bury the corpses of the fallen or return them to their mothers as a violation of divine law (*nomim' atizontes theôn*, 19).[7] The Argive mothers are thus in the right.[8] Aethra is also conscious of the similarity between herself and them, which Aristotle lays down as a condition for pity (*Rhetoric* 2.8, 1386a25–

7; *Poetics* 13, 1453a2–6): the chorus remind her that she is aged, as they are (50), and that she too has a son (54–8; cf. Euripides, *Hecuba* 339–41). Aethra's initial prayer for the well-being of Theseus and Athens (1–7) may indeed suggest that the women's fate has reminded her of her own vulnerability as a mother.

As for the weeping figure of Adrastus, Aethra remarks coolly that it was he who launched the unfortunate expedition against Thebes (20–3), and hence he bears the responsibility for its failure (that women do not decide on war perhaps mitigates their culpability). Adrastus's plea that Athens take up his cause (24–8), she adds, is strictly a political matter and thus men's business (40–1); she can do no more than summon Theseus so that he may consider whether to expel the Argives from the land or else, by helping them, perform a holy action for the gods (36–40). Aethra clearly foresees the pragmatic character of Theseus's reaction. When he arrives on the scene, he bids Adrastus uncover his head and tell his story. Theseus recognizes the grief-stricken comportment of the suppliants, but he withholds judgment until he has inquired into the facts of the case.

Adrastus affirms his status as suppliant (114; cf. 130) and reports the Thebans' denial of proper burial to the fallen. Theseus acknowledges that Adrastus's demands are holy (*hosia*, 123), and asks about the circumstances leading up to the disastrous campaign: 'Did you approach any seers and watch the sacrificial flame?' he asks, to which Adrastus replies: 'Alas, you are pursuing me where I most tripped up.' 'You didn't march forth, it seems, with the favour of the gods.' 'Worse than that: I marched forth against Amphiareus's will' (155–8). Adrastus blames his action on the pressure of young hotheads in Argos, but Theseus is dismissive of this excuse (159–61). At this point, Adrastus grasps Theseus's knees in the traditional gesture of supplication (165), and begs for pity for himself and the aged mothers of the dead (168–9), reminding Theseus that those who are well off should look to the pitiable fortunes of others (179). Adrastus concludes his appeal by affirming that Athens is both strong and has regard for what is pitiable (188–90), and the chorus add their voice to his in beseeching Theseus's pity (*oiktos*, 194).

Theseus responds with a lecture on the gods' rational arrangement of the cosmos and the need for humility, together with a defence of the decisive importance of the middle class for the well-being of the polis. With that, he sends Adrastus packing (246–9). While his speech may seem to be a showpiece of Euripidean didacticism – a kind of tragic parabasis – it in fact bears directly on Adrastus's petition. Adrastus revealed his contempt for the gods by ignoring the omens when he marched into battle, and his failure as a civic leader by yielding to the pressure of the young, who hanker after war regardless of justice – Theseus compares their role to the influence of the mob or *plêthos* in a democratic state (232–7). Since the fault lies with Adrastus and his city, there is no reason why Athens should become implicated in their woes. Adrastus does not deserve to be helped or pitied, because he has brought his misfortune upon himself.

Adrastus sees nothing for it but to submit to Theseus's decision, but the chorus, weeping, throw themselves at the king's feet and again beg for pity (280–1). The women make no allusion to the wisdom or justice of the war against Thebes: their appeal is based wholly on their terrible plight. There is no reason to suppose that they will succeed in moving Theseus where Adrastus has failed, and they do not. But Theseus perceives that his mother is weeping and groaning (286–91), and hears her exclaim: 'O wretched women!' (292). With this, Aethra presents the case for supporting the Argives' cause, on the grounds that it is right to honour the gods (301–2) and that it will bring honour (*timê*, 306) to Theseus if he prevents violent men from confounding the laws of all Greece (*nomima pasês Hellados*, 311). Besides, she observes, if Theseus does not undertake to right this wrong, he will gain a reputation for cowardice (314–19). Aethra affirms that she herself is unafraid, since Theseus will set out with justice on his side (328). Theseus replies that he stands by his former opinion concerning Adrastus's fault, but he nevertheless sees the force of his mother's arguments: it is not in his nature to avoid difficulties; rather, he is ever the chastiser of evils (338–41). He will, nevertheless, present the case first to the people for a vote, bringing Adrastus with him to support his arguments (350, 354–5).

There are no references to pity in this exchange, and in fact it is not mentioned again in the play. Nor is there any hint that

Theseus's change of heart has been inspired by pity (on his dismissal of pity, cf. Bernek 2004: 273). He has been convinced to help the Argives on the grounds that doing so will enhance his reputation and that of Athens, and will also vindicate a divinely sanctioned custom of the Greeks. This is a politically sober, if high-minded, motive, and Theseus is sure that the people will endorse it. That Adrastus foolishly went to war and brought disaster upon his city, however, sinks his claim to pity.

Aethra was moved to pity the women, at least, and hence tries to persuade Theseus to take up their cause (emotion, as Aristotle says, is that on account of which people differ in their judgments). She does so, however, not by referring to the women's misery but by appealing to Theseus's reputation for valour. It is a sensible tactic, insofar as political decisions are based on interest, not sentiment and justice. But if pity drops out of the argument, Aethra at least opens a space for considerations of right and wrong in deliberative discourse by casting the unjust sufferings of the women as a matter of Athenian interest.

I have suggested that Aethra's pity has an oblique relation to the question of the Argives' desert. If no one may be justly prevented from burying kin, then it is not right that the Argives suffer this misfortune, irrespective of their responsibility for initiating the war. This is not quite the same as the view Aristotle advances in his definition of pity: he focuses on the responsibility of the sufferer for her or his misery, not its relation to a universal standard of right. This latter conception is akin to the modern doctrine of human rights, which today too has served as a motive for intervention in disputes between foreign powers. Although the emotion of pity does not enter into the political discussion, it nevertheless finds common ground with the argument based on norms, and thus provides the link between Aethra's private sentiment and her advice to Theseus. The connection between interest, the common beliefs of mankind, and a capacity for pity will emerge clearly some three centuries later in the history of Diodorus Siculus (13.20–7; see Konstan 2001a: 75–95). But the problem was in the air when Euripides' *Suppliant Women* was staged, probably around the year 423 and thus shortly after the debate over the fate of Mytilinene in 427, and the tragedy may be read in part as a commentary on the role of pity, interest, and justice in international politics.

In a paper on the role of emotion in international politics, Neta Crawford (2000: 154) points out that 'recently, several scholars have argued that actors follow normative prescriptions for emotional reasons.' On the one hand, human attachment to social norms is emotional in character; on the other hand, 'sympathy is an important element of decisionmaking' (154 n. 126, referring to Sen 1990), even in the political sphere. The Athenians recognized the influence of emotion, and of pity in particular, on judgment; pity, moreover, was conceived of as based on desert, and hence involving justice. In the political climate of the 420s, however, when Euripides most probably produced the *Suppliant Women*, it appears that the Athenians were beginning to separate out the canons governing forensic discourse, to which the question of justice was central, from those of political deliberation, which was now seen as being properly restricted to the issue of advantage versus harm. Appeals to pity might still be made, of course, and citizens were not so callous as to be insensible to them, but they were likely to be dismissed as irrelevant to the hard realities of international relations. However, where the claim to pity could be linked to a violation of *nomoi*, or widely accepted principles of right or holy behaviour, then the argument from pity might be given a special twist. For the petitioner could then appeal to the practical need and religious duty to uphold such laws, and thus shift the grounds of the argument to a form of self-interest – and hence a theme proper to deliberative rhetoric. The Athenian theatre thus showed how pity might indeed have an effect on politics: even if it was not itself acknowledged as a basis for setting policy, it might nevertheless help to condition attitudes in a way that was favourable to the unfortunate.[9]

Let us consider now some further implications of Aristotle's conception of pity. Aristotle stipulates, as we have seen, that pity is elicited by an undeserved evil of the sort that 'one might expect oneself, or one of one's own, to suffer.' Because we must be able to anticipate the possibility of experiencing a misfortune like that afflicting the pitied, pity requires that we ourselves be vulnerable. Thus, Aristotle goes on to say that those who have lost everything are incapable of feeling pity, because they do not expect that anything worse will befall them.[10] For the same reason, those who are well off and confident that they will continue to prosper are immune to pity.[11] Aristotle also states that there must be a certain distance between the pitier and the pitied. We pity acquaintances when they suffer a catastrophe, but when it befalls someone who is closely related, for example one's own child, the result is not pity but rather what Aristotle calls *to deinon*, or 'horror.' And horror, Aristotle observes, tends to drive out pity (cf. Halliwell 2002: 215–16).

We can see from Aristotle's definition why he would distinguish between people we know and those who are kin or loved ones in regard to pity, for he specifies that pity is elicited by the kinds of evils that might afflict us or our own. Those nearest to us are as it were an extension of ourselves, whose misfortune affects us just as our own does. Our kin are part of the same substance as we, as Aristotle puts it in the *Nicomachean Ethics* (8.12, 1161b17–19), and friends, in Aristotle's famous expression, are another self. If, as Aristotle argues, 'in general, one must presume that people pity just those things, when they happen to others, that they fear when they happen to themselves' (*Rhetoric* 2.8, 1386a27–9), then fear rather than pity will result when such things happen, or rather, threaten to happen, to those closest to us.

Aristotle notes too that we pity those who are similar (*homoioi*) to ourselves, whether in age, character, family, or some other respect. If friends are indeed other selves, then we are not just similar but the same as they, in the strong sense of having a shared identity. In speaking of such intimate relationships, including that with our own selves in the case of self-love, Aristotle avoids the term *eleos* or pity. Rather, he prefers such expressions as *sullupeisthai*, *sunalgein*, and *sunakhthesthai*, meaning to 'condole' or 'feel pain together' with another. Correspondingly, for what we might call positive sympathy, Aristotle employs words such as *sunkhairein*, *sunêdesthai*, and analogous compounds with the prefix *sun-*, which signify that we feel the same pleasure as the other, or feel it as our own. In the case of pity, we do not experience the pain of the other directly. Rather, the pain entailed in pity, according to Aristotle, derives from the awareness that we might ourselves suffer a like misfortune. This looks very much like the pain involved in fear, which Aristotle defines as 'a kind of pain or disturbance deriving from an impression [*phantasia*] of a future evil that is destructive or painful' (*Rhetoric* 2.5, 1382a21–3; see chapter 6, p. 130).

The problem with treating pity as emotional identification becomes clear when we consider the condition of the pitied and the pitier. The title character in Sophocles' *Philoctetes* has been abandoned on a deserted island, and suffers from an agonizing and disabling infection in his foot. He has done nothing to deserve this affliction, and is thus a prime subject for pity. Yet just because he has lost everything, he is, on Aristotle's analysis, least likely to be able to feel pity for another. What Philoctetes experiences is not pity but pain, both physical and psychological; but pain is not, on Aristotle's definition, a *pathos* at all, but rather a sensation or *aisthêsis* (pain and pleasure are, we recall, components of *pathê*: *Rhetoric* 2.1, 1378a20–3). In any case, a pitier would only feel the same *pathos* as the pitied in the rather strange circumstance in which what elicited pity was an excess of pity – surely not the kind of situation Aristotle imagined to be characteristic of tragedy.

We can perhaps gauge something of what the original audience of Sophocles' *Philoctetes* might have experienced upon observing Philoctetes' suffering from the reactions of Neoptolemus and the chorus in the play.[12] At the sight of Philoctetes' miserable cave the chorus exclaim: 'I pity him: no human being to care for him, with no companion in sight, wretched, forever alone, he is afflicted by a savage disease and wanders at the mercy of every need that arises' (169–75).[13] Later in the play, Neoptolemus is provoked by Philoctetes' stubborn refusal to go to Troy, even though his wound can be cured only if he does so: 'It is not just to pardon or to pity those who are involved in self-willed harm, like you' (1318–20), he asserts. As Aristotle says, pity is aroused by undeserved suffering, and someone who suffers willingly fails to qualify. For a Greek, then, the mere spectacle of pain was not enough to elicit pity – something one might have inferred, I should think, from a consideration of such practices as the judicial torture of slaves. Pity was certainly among the chief emotions that tragedy was expected to arouse, as Aristotle and other writers make clear (Aristotle, *Poetics* 1452a2–3, 1452b32–3, etc.; Gorgias, *Defence of*

Helen 9; Plato, *Republic* 10, 606B–C; Isocrates, *Panegyricus* 112, 168). But Greek pity is not the sympathy of which Terry Eagleton speaks (see epigraph to this chapter), when he suggests that to ask why we respond as we do to Philoctetes' pain implies a 'bogus historicism.'

Between Greek pity and modern English sympathy there is a deep cultural divide, extending to basic conceptions of the self.[14] Sympathy involves putting oneself in the position of another so as to feel what the other person feels. Thus, Edmund Burke (1990: 41) writes that 'sympathy must be considered as a sort of substitution, by which we are put into the place of another man, and affected in many respects as he is affected.' David Hume, in turn, supposes that the thought of another's passion may acquire 'such a degree of force and vivacity, as to become the very passion itself' (*A Treatise of Human Nature* [1906; orig. 1739–40]: 317). Such a description of sympathy has little to do with the ancient Greek notion of *eleos*, and its roots lie elsewhere.[15] The spectators of Philoctetes' suffering, whether on stage or in the audience, did not expect to be affected as he was affected, or that his passion would become theirs. As a distinct emotion in its own right, pity did not mean identifying with the experience of another; rather, it was just insofar as one did not share another's misfortune that one was in a position to pity it. Eagleton's facile assimilation of ancient pity to modern sympathy fails to perform the work of translation that understanding the ancient emotions requires.

We have seen that pity, according to Aristotle's analysis in the *Rhetoric*, presupposes that there is a likeness between the pitier and the pitied, and that the suffering of the pitied is undeserved.[16] In his discussion of pity and fear in the *Poetics*, however, Aristotle modifies this position. The change occurs in his discussion of the kinds of reversal characteristic of tragedy. Here, Aristotle states that pity and fear are not excited when one sees thoroughly bad men brought to ruin, and he goes on to explain: 'for such a plot may involve *to philanthrôpon*, but neither pity nor fear, for the one concerns a person who is undeservedly unfortunate, while the other concerns a person who is similar [*homoios*]: pity concerns the undeserving person, fear concerns the one who is similar' (13, 1453a2–6).

In the *Poetics*, then, Aristotle splits up the factors of desert and similarity, dividing them between the two emotions of pity and fear. Pity, he continues to maintain, depends on the perception that the other person is suffering undeservedly. But Aristotle now exploits the idea of similarity in order to explain why tragedy also induces fear. If the characters in a tragedy are like ourselves in some relevant respect, then their misfortune will induce in the spectators 'an impression of a future evil that is destructive or painful' to themselves (cf. Halliwell 1998: 176, cited in chapter 6, p. 155). But how is this fear different from the fear that Aristotle has already associated with the emotion of pity, which is aroused precisely insofar as we ourselves may expect to suffer something like what the pitied is currently experiencing? The answer, as I suggested in chapter 6 (p. 155), is that the misfortunes that occur in tragedy may inspire fear, as opposed to pity, even if they seem to be merited, insofar as we are vulnerable to such calamities. It is, we may say, the non-moral side of our response to tragedy.

In separating out fear from pity, might Aristotle also have had in mind an other-regarding kind of fear that we might call 'fear for another'? Such an emotion would be distinct from feeling pain together with another person, which Aristotle denominates, as we have seen, by expressions such as *sullupeisthai* and *sunalgein*. We recall that, according to Aristotle, this sensibility arises in relation to those who are nearest and dearest to ourselves. It will not be an emotional response to tragedy for two reasons. First, by making *eleos* or pity one of the two tragic emotions, Aristotle makes it clear that we regard tragic characters not as kin or close friends but rather as individuals at a certain distance from ourselves: they are of the class of *gnôrimoi* or 'acquaintances,' as he puts it in the *Rhetoric* (1386a18), not *philoi* or intimates. Second, as we have remarked, feeling the same pain or pleasure as another does not mean experiencing the same emotion, since pain and pleasure are not themselves *pathê* but rather constituent parts of *pathê*. If my son is afraid of a monster, I may share something of his anguish, but I do not share his fear, because I do not believe in monsters.

The fear that tragedy inspires differs from pity, on Aristotle's view, in that it takes no account of desert. But the ruin of a thoroughly bad individual elicits neither pity nor fear, according to Aristotle: for the first, because the misfortune is deserved; for the second, however, it is because the spectators do not perceive a relevant similarity between such a person and themselves. They are not great malefactors, as for example a tyrant such as Lycus in Euripides' *Hercules*, and hence they do not fear vengeance from those whom they have oppressed. Yet Aristotle states, as we have seen, that such a story may elicit the mysterious response he calls *to philanthrôpon*. What is the status of this curious concept? Is it a third tragic emotion – one that tragedy does better not to evoke, perhaps, but which is nevertheless part of the possible range of emotional responses to the genre? Is it a reaction that is somehow other than an emotion? Could it have something to do with the modern idea of sympathy?

There are some who maintain that *to philanthrôpon* in fact signifies something quite different from sympathy or a philanthropic sentiment (see Konstan 2001a: 46–7). These scholars take Aristotle to mean rather that the sight of a bad person's fall into misfortune is morally satisfying: it is just and decent to be pleased at such a turn of events.[17] This interpretation has begun to enter into translations of the *Poetics*, and it clearly requires serious consideration. On this view, the audience is imagined as taking a positive pleasure in witnessing the destruction of a bad person; on the other, more traditional interpretation, however, the audience is presumed to feel at least some pain at the suffering even of those who deserve their fate. Thus Gerald Else, in his magisterial commentary on the *Poetics* (1967: 95 n. 88 ad 53a1), remarks of *to philanthrôpon* that 'the least forced interpretation of this much discussed term is that it denotes a rudimentary grade of pity which is accorded to all human beings (*anthrôpoi*) regardless of their deserts, whereas pity (*eleos*) depends on a judgment that the sufferer does not deserve his misfortune.' It is like pity but does not involve a judgment of desert: how, then, does *to philanthrôpon* differ from fear? Might Aristotle be imagining a non-moral response to the misfortune of another that is independent of considerations of our own vulnerability and results simply from the perception of another's suffering?

In later Greek, the word *philanthrôpia* and its relatives came to signify something very close to the Latin *humanitas*, that is, a humane generosity towards others; it was closely associated with the term *epieikeia* or 'kindness,' and might serve also as a near synonym for *eleos* or 'pity,' as it often does in the first-century BC historian Diodorus Siculus (e.g., 13.19–24; cf. Dover 1994: 201–3; and Cavallero 2000–1). To determine its meaning in usage of the fourth century BC, I have taken occurrences in Demosthenes as a test case. On the one hand, Demosthenes sometimes associates *philanthrôpia* with the idea of justice, as at *Philippics* 2.12, where he speaks of 'just and philanthropic arguments' (*logous dikaious kai philanthrôpous;* cf. 7.31, 20.109, 36.55, 44.8). This connection might seem to favour the view that Aristotle, in the *Poetics*, means by *to philanthrôpon* the just satisfaction one takes in seeing evil duly chastised. Elsewhere in Demosthenes, however, *philanthrôpia* means something more like 'kind' or 'gentle.' It is frequently paired with *praos*, for example, which in Aristotle's *Rhetoric* represents the state or emotion opposite to anger (cf. Demosthenes 8.31, 24.51, 24.196, 41.2, *Eroticus* 13), as well as with *hêmeros* or 'tame' (21.49); it is contrasted, in turn, with the quality of being frightening (*phoberos*, 13.17), with savagery (*ômotês*, 18.231), and with envy (*phthonos*, 20.165). *Philanthrôpia* is also associated with *eusebeia* or 'piety' (21.12), *eunoia* or 'goodwill' (18.5), and *epieikeia* (36.59); it is the quality that restrains a free man from behaving hubristically – that is, with arrogant abuse – towards his own slaves (21.48). Finally, *philanthrôpia* also occurs in connection with pity (25.76, 25.81; cf. 21.185, 24.196). In all, then, the evidence of Demosthenes favours the traditional view of *to philanthrôpon* as a sentiment analogous to sympathy or humane concern.

In Aristotle's own writings, *philanthrôpia* may be applied to animals in the literal sense of friendliness towards human beings (*History of Animals* 617b26, 630a9); when used of humans, it is connected, in the *Constitution of the Athenians* 16.2, with gentleness and a disposition to forgive those who err (*praos, sungnômikos*). *Philanthrôpia* is associated with pity in particular in the Aristotelian treatise *On Virtues and Vices* 5, 1250b32–5 (cited in Apicella Ricciardelli 1971–2: 391–2), though this work, like the *Constitution*, is probably not by Aristotle himself but a product of his school. We may also note that in the *Poetics* itself

(1452b36–8), Aristotle claims that the sight of 'bad men going from bad fortune to good is the least tragic of all, since it has none of the elements it ought, whether the *philanthrôpon* or the pitiable or the frightening.' But the decisive passage, in my view, is in the *Rhetoric* (1390a18–20), where Aristotle observes that, like the young, old men too are given to feeling pity (*eleêtikoi*), but not for the same reasons: for the young are so disposed on account of *philanthrôpia*, while the aged are so because of weakness, that is, decrepitude. *Philanthrôpia* evidently represents an instinctive sensitivity to the suffering of others, not one that grows, as pity does, with experience and the consciousness it produces of one's own vulnerability to misfortune. It is relevant too that elsewhere in the *Poetics*, as we have noted above, Aristotle recognizes that pity may be excited by the sheer emotionality or *pathos* of the events portrayed (*ouden eleeinon ... plên kat'auto to pathos*, 13, 1453b18).

There is, I think, one additional bit of evidence concerning the nature of *to philanthrôpon* in Aristotle that has not, to my knowledge, been adduced in this connection. In the *Rhetoric*, as we have seen (chapter 5, p. 112), Aristotle defines indignation (*to nemesan*) as 'feeling pain at someone who appears to be succeeding undeservedly' (2.9, 1837a8–9), and adds that it is the opposite of pity, *to nemesan* being pain at undeserved good fortune, while pity is pain at undeserved misfortune (2.9, 1386b9–12). Both emotions, Aristotle specifies, are characteristic of decent (*epiêkeis*) individuals, since it is wrong that people should do either well or ill if they do not deserve it.

Nevertheless, as we remarked in the chapter on envy and indignation, Aristotle is aware that, according to some, it is not *to nemesan* or 'indignation' that is the opposite of pity but rather *phthonos* or 'envy' (indeed, they hold that envy 'is related to and is in fact the same thing as indignation,' 2.9, 1386b16–17). Aristotle, however, insists on the distinction between the two emotions, since even though *phthonos* too is 'a disturbing pain arising from the well-being' of another (2.9, 1386b18–19; cf. 2.10, 1387b22–4), it takes no account of desert, but arises solely because the other is our equal or similar to us (2.9, 1386b19–20; cf. 2.10, 1387b23–5, where Aristotle specifies that *phthonos* arises just because others have a thing, irrespective of whether we ourselves need it or not).

It is this indifference both to desert and to one's own need that renders envy an emotion unsuited to a decent (*epieikês*) person.

In ruling out envy as the opposite of pity, however, and treating it rather as the contrary of indignation, Aristotle has implicitly opened up a further question: what is the opposite of *phthonos* itself? Since what disqualifies envy from being pity's opposite is just the fact that it fails to take desert into account, the opposite to *phthonos* should in turn be a 'a disturbing pain' that arises not, this time, 'from the well-being' of another, as is the case with envy, but rather from another's misfortune, in a way that is equally indifferent to desert and due simply to the fact of the other's distress. The missing fourth term would seem to correspond precisely to the idea of *to philanthrôpon* as a sympathetic response to another's suffering irrespective of merit or of fear for oneself.[18]

A vivid awareness of another's present suffering may generate in us a fear of a like misfortune occurring at some future time to ourselves. But suppose that we are not vulnerable to such a mischance. We should in that case be able to experience neither pity nor fear, according to Aristotle. We mortals, perhaps, are never wholly free of anxiety at the prospect of adversity, even if we have prospered or suffered inordinately, but a god is, certainly on Aristotle's conception of divinity. Yet a god can be *philanthrôpos*, in the sense of being concerned for human beings, as Prometheus is said to be in the tragedy ascribed to Aeschylus (11, 28). Ordinary people too, perhaps, do not experience pity or fear at the spectacle of a very bad man falling from good fortune to bad, because they do not normally conceive of themselves as 'terribly bad' (*sphodra ponêroi*), and hence do not recognize their likeness to the figure on the stage. Aristotle seems to have invested the notion of similarity here with a particular ethical charge, thereby moralizing tragic fear along with tragic pity. But one can experience the sentiment that moves a young person to pity, according to Aristotle, and which has nothing to do with weakness or vulnerability. This sentiment, which responds directly to the suffering of another person, irrespective of desert or fear for oneself, is, as Else and others have maintained, what Aristotle means by *to philanthrôpon*.

CHAPTER ELEVEN

Jealousy

Jealousy per se is the same everywhere.

Baumgart 1990: 26

Jealousy in the twentieth century neither continues unaltered – a human or Western constant – nor neatly shifts from common to rare as part of a tidy then-now contrast.

Stearns 1989: 176

The cross-cultural study of the emotions requires a special kind of self-awareness on the part of the scholar. For we tend to think of our own emotional repertoire as natural and to assume, consequently, that it is universal. Pity, which, as we have seen, was included among the basic emotions in classical antiquity, today often signifies something more like charity or a dutiful disposition to help another person in distress, a sense that *eleos* was already acquiring in ancient Christian texts; so conceived, pity seems out of place in the company of such visceral passions as anger, love, and fear (see Konstan 2001a: 3–4, 120–2). It is still more difficult to imagine that an emotion that we consider basic might be entirely absent in another culture. Linda Wood (1986: 194) has argued that loneliness today has the status of an emotion, though it is of recent vintage even in English: before the twentieth century, she observes, 'the term "loneliness" appears to refer most frequently to the physical absence of persons,' whereas 'by the 1970s, loneliness was treated as a feeling quite separate from isolation.'[1] Certainly, there is no corresponding term in classical Greek.

Jealousy is a still more elementary emotion in the modern lexicon than loneliness, and enjoys a far longer pedigree. Yet I argue in this chapter that no term in classical Greek or Latin quite answers to the English 'jealousy' and its equivalents in other languages, for example the Italian *gelosia*, French *jalousie*, and Spanish *celos*. What is more, I go so far as to suggest that ancient Greeks in the classical period may not have known jealousy at all in the modern, romantic sense of the word, and that what we call 'jealousy' may rather have been distributed among a variety of other sentiments. The very concept, that is, may have been lacking. Finally, I propose to identify the moment at which a notion resembling romantic jealousy entered classical literature – not Greek literature, in this case, but Latin, during the reign of the first Roman emperor, Augustus. If this is right, then we may be able to witness the birth of an emotion that had hitherto gone unrecognized in the Graeco-Roman world.

Perhaps one ought not to be entirely surprised if jealousy is parcelled out among different emotions in cultures other than our own. Many scholars and scientists have remarked upon the composite nature of jealousy as an aggregate or alloy of other, more fundamental sentiments. Lily B. Campbell (1960: 148) observes that '[j]ealousy was, in the thinking of the Renaissance, not one of the simple or elementary passions but a derivative or compounded passion. It is a species of envy, which is in turn a species of hatred ... It is this curious mingling of love and hatred with grief or fear that we see in jealousy' (cited in Friday 1997 [1985]: 39). Paul Ekman, in the 'Afterword' to his edition of Darwin's *The Expression of the Emotions in Man and Animals* (1998: 391), comments: 'Jealousy seems to have no distinctive expression, perhaps because it is an emotion where the person feels a number of other emotions: angry with the one whose attention is lost or with the rival; sadness at the loss; fear in anticipation of further loss; or disgust at himself or herself for feeling jealous. Envy, a term often confused with jealousy, also does not have a unique expression.' So too Sally Planalp (1999: 174) remarks that '[j]ealousy ... is a complex emotion blended primarily from anger-, sadness-, and fear-like feelings.'[2] What reason is there for supposing that so tangled and synthetic an emotion or emotional concept must be universal?[3]

Jealousy, or, more precisely, romantic jealousy, is also odd among the emotions in that it 'pertains to a triangular relationship' (Segal 1973: 40, cited in R. Lloyd 1995: 3; Baumgart 1990: 25). The *Oxford English Dictionary*, for example, defines jealousy (s.v., definition 4) as 'the state of mind arising from the suspicion, apprehension, or knowledge of rivalry.' This general description is divided into two parts. The first pertains to amatory relations, with which the present discussion is exclusively concerned. Here, jealousy is defined as 'fear of being supplanted in the affection, or distrust of the fidelity, of a beloved person, esp. a wife, husband, or lover' (the first citation dates to 1303). The second part of the entry treats jealousy 'in respect of success or advantage,' and offers 'envy' and 'grudge' as synonyms.[4] True, Jon Elster (1999a: 144) maintains that '[m]any emotions ... are triadic,' in the sense that they 'are triggered by beliefs that make reference to two other persons,' but he acknowledges that 'jealousy is the only example known to me of a triadic emotion that is named in ordinary language' – more specifically, in English. In particular, as Aaron Ben-Ze'ev (2000: 289) remarks, this quality of jealousy as 'a three-party relation' distinguishes it from envy. So too Ruth Caston observes that in definitions of jealousy, 'it is common to use envy as a comparandum,' and adds: 'Jealousy tends to involve three people, while envy involves two.'[5] Once again, it is plausible that not every language evolves a special term to express a sentiment at once so complex and specific.

A further distinction between jealousy and envy is that '[t]he wish in envy is for something one does not have, while in jealousy it is something one fears losing.'[6] Since jealousy is a three-party emotion, I would say rather that it concerns some*one* we fear losing.[7] More precisely, what we fear in jealousy is not losing the person so much as the alienation of that person's affection.[8] Death may deprive us of a loved one, but the emotion it produces is grief, not jealousy. Even where a third party is involved, as in kidnapping, anger or hostility rather than jealousy is the characteristic reaction.[9]

Complex as jealousy may be, some theorists have defended its universality on functional grounds. Thus, Sally Planalp (1999: 174) holds that jealousy 'mobilizes us to protect our attachments with people whom we value.' In the new discipline of evolutionary psychology (heir to the earlier 'sociobiology'), jealousy is sometimes elevated to the status of a biological necessity (cf. Ben-Ze'ev 2000: 262; Buss 1994: 2, 16; Buss 2000; cf. chapter 1, p. 12).[10] But such an account will only be persuasive if jealousy is in fact common to all cultures; an evolutionary argument cannot be invoked to demonstrate the innateness of jealousy.

When in doubt about an ancient Greek concept, turn to Aristotle. Aristotle, however, does not include jealousy among the emotions he discusses in the *Rhetoric*, although he treats such competitive sentiments as envy, emulousness, and indignation. Perhaps this is not surprising, given that his primary interest is in political and forensic oratory, where there was presumably less occasion to manipulate feelings of jealousy in the audience. But neither does Aristotle discuss jealousy as such anywhere else. In fact, the Greek word that is commonly translated as jealousy – *zêlotupia* – appears only once, I believe, in the Aristotelian corpus, in the late compilation *On Marvellous Tales* (846a28–31).

The term *zêlotupia* is a somewhat odd formation, compounded of *zêlos*, or emulousness, and the root *tup-* meaning to strike (as in 'type'). As Elaine Fantham observes (1986: 46–7), the latter stem may be interpreted as passive – 'struck by envy' – or active – 'striking out of envy.' The earliest occurrence of the term appears to be in Aristophanes' *Wealth* (388 BC), in which an old woman complains that, now that riches are plentiful, the young man who courted her has made himself scarce. Once upon a time, she says, 'At the Great Mysteries, by Zeus, when someone kept looking at me as I rode in a carriage, I was beaten [*etuptomên*] for it the whole day – that's how violently *zêlotupos* the boy was' (1013–16). The apparent pun on *tuptô* and *zêlotupos* leads Fantham to wonder whether Aristophanes might not have coined the term himself (47); I am inclined to think that it is a sign rather that the term was already current, and that the humour consisted in bringing out the implicit force of the termination *-tupos*. But more fundamentally, can we be certain that the meaning of *zêlotupos* here is in fact 'jealous'? In the context, a significance such as 'niggardly' or 'grudging' – that is, in regard to sharing her favours – would be as appropriate, particularly since the young man's motive must have been to keep at bay other gigolos interested in her money – a nuance the audience would have been prepared to pick up. Indeed, Chremylus, the protagonist of the comedy, mutters to himself, 'It seems he liked eating alone' (1017), the point being that the youth did not want any other men sharing in the bounty.[11]

It may seem supererogatory to seek an alternative sense for *zêlotupos*, when 'jealous' is perfectly apt. That is how Liddell and Scott render the term, while for the noun *zêlotupia* they give 'jealousy, rivalry, envy.' So too, Arndt and Gingrich's lexicon of New Testament Greek (1957) defines *zêlotupia* simply as 'jealousy.' Our confidence in the equation may be shaken, however, if, in the absence of an analysis by Aristotle, we consult the Stoics, whose minute classifications of the passions go back at least to Chrysippus in the third century BC and thus furnish the earliest definition of *zêlotupia* that survives from Greek antiquity. The Stoics, as we have mentioned previously, subsumed the emotions under four general headings: pleasure, pain, desire or attraction, and fear or repulsion. The doxographer Diogenes Laertius reports their list of emotions involving an element of pain as follows: 'Pity is a pain arising when someone suffers undeservedly; envy [*phthonos*] is a pain at other people's goods; emulousness [*zêlos*] is a pain at someone else having what one desires oneself; *zêlotupia* is a pain at another's having what one also has oneself,' and so forth (D.L. 7.111 = fr. 412 *SVF*). So too John Stobaeus, who compiled an anthology of quotations in the fifth century AD, follows the Stoics in defining *zêlos* as 'pain at someone else getting what one wanted, when one does not get it oneself' (he also provides a couple of alternative meanings), and *zêlotupia* as 'pain at another getting what one wanted,' irrespective, that is, of whether one ultimately gets it oneself (*Ecl.* 2.92.7 W = fr. 414.14 *SVF*).[12]

The Stoics' conception of *zêlotupia* seems more like malice or spite than jealousy, nastier even than envy. Envy arises when another is better off than ourselves, whereas *zêlotupia*, as the Stoics define it, occurs because another person has what we ourselves already possess: we want to be the only one who has it.

There is no reference here to the role of a third party, to the alienation of affection, or to losing what is one's own. Stoic *zêlotupia* is rather a variant in the series of competitive emotions that includes envy, rivalrousness, and even pity.

Although Aristotle, as we have seen, does not discuss *zêlotupia*, the Stoic account is modelled on his analysis of related emotions. Aristotle defines *zêlos* as 'a kind of pain at the perceived presence of good and honourable things that are possible to acquire for oneself, belonging to those who are similar in nature [to ourselves], not because the other has it but because one does not oneself' (2.11, 1388a30–3). This comes close to the Stoic description of *zêlos* as rivalrous emulation. In a similar vein, Descartes defines emulation as 'a warmth that disposes the soul to undertake things that it hopes [or expects] it can attain because it sees others attaining them' (1988: 257 art. 172).[13] Being indignant (*nemesan*), according to Aristotle, consists in pain at the undeserved success of another (2.9, 1386b9–12); here, the emphasis is on the element of merit or desert, as in the case of pity (see chapter 5, p. 112). Finally, *phthonos*, or 'envy,' is 'a disturbing pain resulting from the well-being of another' (2.9, 1386b18–19), not, however, out of a desire to have something oneself but simply that the other not have it (2.10, 1387b23–4).[14] This last qualification distinguishes envy from *zêlos*, which, Aristotle explains, is a decent emotion, whereas envy is base; for emulousness stimulates one to obtain good things for oneself, whereas envy merely aims to deprive one's neighbour of them (2.11, 1388a33–6). Aristotle's conception of *phthonos* thus comes close to the Stoic definition of *zêlotupia*.

The distinctions by which Aristotle classifies the rivalrous emotions relate to the reason why one resents another's goods: because one wants them oneself, because they have been unjustly acquired, or out of simple malice in the case of envy.[15] What of the situation in which one has been deprived of something that is one's own? The response, according to Aristotle, is either anger, if the other's motive was contempt, or hostility for the damage suffered. Conceivably, indignation will be aroused if the appropriation is deemed illegitimate, although I believe this sentiment operates only where one's own interests are not directly at stake (in this, it is like its opposite, pity). Like the Stoics, Aristotle does not separate out the special case in which one has lost another's affection to a rival. Perhaps, to a Greek of his time, it did not merit a name of its own.

There are, in fact, numerous passages in Greek literature in which *zêlotupia* signifies the kind of covetous resentment of another's goods that the Stoic definition implies. In his speech *Against Ctesiphon* (211), Aeschines accuses Demosthenes of saying the kind of thing wastrels do when 'they feel *zêlotupia* of virtue.' Aeschines means that Demosthenes begrudges the virtue of better men without aspiring to it himself. Plutarch, writing centuries later, asks rhetorically (*Life of Pericles* 10.6): 'How can one believe Idomeneus when he accuses Pericles of having treacherously slain the popular leader Ephialtes out of *zêlotupia* and envy of his reputation, when he was a friend of his and shared his preference in type of government?'

The historian Polybius, writing in the second century BC, connects *zêlotupia* particularly with the behaviour of courtiers: 'For a new method of slander was discovered, doing harm not by finding fault but by praising one's neighbours. Such mischief [*kakentrekheia*], denigration [*baskania*], and treachery were first encountered among those who frequent the court, and result from their *zêlotupia* and ambitious strife [*pleonexia*] towards one another' (*History* 4.87.1–5). *Zêlotupia* here means something like 'invidious contention,' which is the more dangerous for the veneer of politeness. So too, Polybius characterizes those who disparaged Scipio's accomplishments as motivated by intense *zêlotupia* (*diazêlotupoumenoi*, 36.8.2; cf. 16.22.5–8, 29.7.1–4). Diodorus Siculus (first century BC) observes that, once one of Alexander's generals declared himself king, the rest followed suit out of *zêlotupia* (20.53.4; cf. 19.87.2–3), and he distinguishes such grudging contention from honest rivalry: 'Among the Romans, one can see the most distinguished men competing [*hamillômenous*] for fame ...; in other states they feel *zêlotupia* for one another, but the Romans praise one another' (31.6.1 [fragment, cited in Photius, *Library* p. 381 B]).[16] While the Romans struggle to advance the common good, the malicious strife represented by *zêlotupia* harms the nation.[17]

In the first century BC, Dionysius of Halicarnassus writes in an essay on literary criticism (*Letter to Pompeius* 1.13): 'Plato had, it is true, a streak of ambitiousness [*to philotimon*] in his nature, despite his virtues; he manifested it above all in his *zêlotupia* towards Homer, whom he banished from his ideal city, albeit garlanded and annointed with myrrh.' Athenaeus, in turn, speaks of Plato's *zêlotupia* towards Xenophon, who also wrote Socratic dialogues (*Deipnosophistae* (11.112). Plato evidently had a reputation for wanting to be top dog. Philostratus, however, comes to Plato's defence by distinguishing between envy (*phthonos*) and *philotimia*: 'He [Plato] was as far from maligning [the sophists] as *philotimia* is from *phthonos*. For *phthonos* nurses wicked natures, while *philotimia* rouses brilliant ones; one maligns what one cannot achieve, but has *philotimia* for what one will be better or at least not worse at.'[18]

That *zêlotupia* has a wider application than erotic jealousy does not exclude it from designating erotic jealousy as well. We have already remarked that, according to the *Oxford English Dictionary*, jealousy is 'the state of mind arising from the suspicion, apprehension, or knowledge of rivalry,' and that, in addition to the romantic sense, it may also signify envy of another person's success, although today the latter sense pertains more to the adjective, 'jealous,' than to the abstract noun (cf. Friday 1997 [1985]: 36). Correspondingly, some ancient definitions of *zêlotupia*, dating from a later epoch than the Stoic classification, point to a specific connection of the term with love. For example, the grammarian Ptolemaeus of Ascalon (2nd century BC to 2nd century AD), in his treatise *On the Differences between Words* (ed. Heylbut 1887: 395.32–4), writes that '*zêlos* is an imitation of a fine person, as when a boy feels *zêlos* towards his teacher, whereas *zêlotupia* is being immersed in hatred [*to en misei huparkhein*], as when this man feels *zêlotupia* in regard to this woman.' Pollux, in his thesaurus composed between 166 and 176 AD, includes *zêlotupia* in a catalogue of erotic terminology that features *erôs*, *himeros* (yearning), *pothos* (longing), and *epithumia* (desire), and specifies that '*zêlotupein* is used in connection with young boys, women, and anything we like [*pantôn de tôn agapômenôn*]' (3.68–72). The last phrase shows that Pollux knows the wider application of the term, and thinks it worth mentioning in this context (for the non-erotic sense of *agapaô*, see LSJ s.v.). While Pollux illustrates *zêlotupia* by reference to male desire, the *Etymologicum Gudianum* ascribes it to women: 'such-and-such a woman feels *zêlotupia* in regard to such-and-such a man' (*zêlotupoi de hê deina ton deina*). The fullest definition of the erotic sense of the term, however, is to be found in the Byzantine lexicon known as the Suda (tenth century AD), where *zêlotupia* is glossed as 'suspicion on the part of a husband of his own wife in regard to a man who is licentious' (ζ 58). The Suda, like the sixth-century lexicographer Hesychius, from whom this definition seems to have been derived (ζ 38 = Latte 1966: 261; the text is garbled), mentions other meanings of *zêlotupia* as well, equating it for example with hatred (ζ 59; cf. the scholia to Aeschines 3.211) and envy.[19] But the amatory sense is clearly distinct and well defined.

There is good reason to believe that the definition in the Suda derives, by way of Hesychius, from a Christian compilation known as the *Cyrillian Glosses*, which may have been composed by a disciple of St Cyril to assist less-educated readers of the holy man's works.[20] If so, in defining *zêlotupia* the author had in mind Cyril's *De adoratione et cultu in spiritu et veritate* (Migne, *Patrologia Graeca* 68: 132–1125), where the word occurs four times (909.17, 26, and 48 and 912.16), all in reference to the biblical book of Numbers. Indeed, in the Greek translation of the Hebrew Bible known as the Septuagint (third century BC), *zêlotupia* occurs only in Numbers (four times at 5:18.3, 5:25.2, and 5:29.1), where it refers to a man's ritual responsibilities in testing and responding to his wife's possible infidelity. We can, I think, safely set aside the definitions that depend on the *Cyrillian Glosses* as being of Christian or biblical inspiration.[21]

Ptolemaeus and Pollux do, of course, testify to the currency of *zêlotupia* in amatory contexts outside of Christian literature, a fact that can be illustrated from a variety of classical Greek texts. Since they offer not so much definitions as uses of *zêlotupia*, however, the question remains open as to what it means. Let us, then, examine some specific cases, beginning with the second earliest mention, after Aristophanes' *Wealth*, of *zêlotupia* in Greek literature.

In Plato's *Symposium* (213C8–D4; cf. Fantham 1986: 47–50), Socrates complains to Agathon about how Alcibiades harasses him: 'From the time I became his lover, I can no longer look at or talk with a single pretty fellow, or else he feels *zêlotupia* and envy [*phthonôn*], does outlandish things, insults me, and barely keeps his hands off me.' Clearly, Alcibiades wants Socrates entirely for himself; but the charge is not that Alcibiades fears rejection, as jealousy in the modern sense might suggest, but rather that he is unwilling to share Socrates' company with others. Once again, the meaning of *zêlotupia* seems to be an unwarranted insistence on exclusive possession, even where nothing is gained by hoarding. The situation conforms nicely to the Stoic definition of *zêlotupia* as 'a pain at another's having what one also has oneself.'

In his oration *Antidosis* (245), Isocrates compares grouchiness (*duskolôs ekhein*), *zêlotupia* (verbal form), and being out of sorts (*tetaragmenôs diakeisthai*) to what people experience when they are in love; the dominant idea would appear to be surliness. Again, Aeschines, in his speech *Against Timarchus* (58), claims that 'when he [Timarchus] deserted Pittalacus and was picked up by Hegesander, Pittalacus was hurt, I believe, since he had spent so much money in vain, and he felt *zêlotupia* over what happened [*ezêlotupei ta gignomena*].' What emotion is being indicated? I expect that Pittalacus expected exclusive possession of the boy in return for his investment, and is resentful that another man is profiting from it. Alienation of affection is beside the point, just as it was for the young man in Aristophanes' *Wealth*. Even in modern times, Descartes held the view that a jealous man does not love his wife so much as 'the good that he thinks consists in having sole possession of her' (1988: 256 art. 168).

Perhaps the personality most consistently characterized by *zêlotupia* is Hera, for her peevish reaction to the philandering of her husband, Zeus, and here, at least, it would seem to correspond to jealousy in the modern sense (cf. Baumgart 1990: 94: 'Hera, on the other hand, is jealous'). The word itself is not found in archaic poetry, but a scholium on Apollonius of Rhodes' *Argonautica* (1.761) reports that, according to Pherecydes of Syros (ca. sixth century BC), 'Zeus had sex with Elara of Orchomenus and then thrust her into the earth when she was pregnant, in fear of Hera's *zêlotupia*. When she died, the earth sent forth Tityos.' We may doubt whether Pherecydes himself used the word *zêlotupia*, but the description of Hera's behaviour is familiar from early Greek literature, for example the Homeric *Hymn to Apollo*, where Hera prolongs Leto's birth pangs out of *zêlosunê* (3.100: the word occurs only here). The cause of this sentiment is that Leto will bear a mighty son; Hera resents (*kholoomai*, 3.305) Zeus's splendid off-spring, in particular Athena, whom Zeus bore from his own head, whereas Hera's own child Hephaestus is lame (3.317). Since Zeus had no partner in the procreation of Athena (*oios*, 3.323), Hera's irritation is not over sexual infidelity. Her revenge is to produce the monster Typho by parthenogenesis, so that she too may have a brilliant child (326–30).

The epic poet Rhianus (third century BC), who is said to have recounted the full story concerning Hera's jealousy of Alcmene (in his *Heraclea*, fr. 9 Powell [*Collectanea Alexandrina* p. 11]; cited in Scholia A, B on Homer, *Iliad*. 19.119), explains in turn that 'Hera, who was constitutionally given to *zêlotupia* [*zêlotupôs diatetheisa*], repressed the birth pangs of Alcmene, and made Antibia (whom some call Nicippe), the wife of Sthenelus, who was pregnant, give birth to Eurystheus at seven months,' so that Eurystheus would have priority over Hercules. Diodorus Siculus too recounts Hera's jealousy over Alcmene (4.9.4), as well as her revenge against Semele, the mother of Dionysus (3.64.3), and the geographer Strabo cites Hera's *zêlotupia* in connection with her efforts to thwart Leto's delivery of Apollo and Artemis (*Geography* 14.1.20). So too Rhea, traditionally the wife of Cronus but in one variant, which Diodorus Siculus (3.68) found in the mythographer Dionysius Scytobrachion (second century BC), the wife of Ammon, king of Lydia, reacts with *zêlotupia* when Ammon takes an erotic inter-est in Amalthea, who in this version gives birth secretly to Dio-nysus. This is clearly a take-off on the pattern usually associated with Hera, Rhea's daughter.[22]

Is Hera jealous? Her principal preoccupation is with the status of her children rather than with Zeus's philandering as such. The definition of *zêlotupia* recorded by John Stobaeus – 'pain at an-other getting what one wanted' – seems to fit the case of Hera as well as jealousy in the modern or romantic sense. In a famous scene in the *Iliad*, Hera, with the help of a magic girdle borrowed from Aphrodite, entices Zeus to sleep with her in order to distract him from the battle raging below. The stratagem works. Zeus exclaims to Hera: 'Never before has passion for a goddess or mortal woman so overcome the heart in my breast' (14.315–16), and he proceeds to list seven of his earlier conquests to confirm the point. The episode is undoubtedly comic, but it is nevertheless revealing of ancient attitudes towards sexual jealousy.[23]

Among mortals, the paradigm of *zêlotupia* seems to be Medea. Again the report comes from Diodorus Siculus (4.54.7), who tells us that 'so far had she progressed in anger, along with *zêlotupia* and indeed savagery [*ômotês*], that when he [Jason] had escaped the danger that accompanied his bride [i.e., Creon's daughter, incinerated by Medea's potions], she catapulted him into the ultimate disaster by the slaughter of their own children.' Sandwiched as it is between rage and barbaric cruelty, *zêlotupia* might be better rendered as 'resentment' than 'jealousy.' There is also an odd story told by Myrsilus (cited in a scholium to Apollonius of Rhodes 1.615) in the first book of his *Lesbiaca*, according to which the Lemnian women acquired the foul odour that drove away their husbands when Medea 'cast a drug at Lemnos out of *zêlotupia*' as she was sailing by the island on the Argo's return from Colchis. Medea's motive was presumably Jason's earlier affair with Hypsipyle, the queen of the Lemnians. I imagine that Medea's *zêlotupia* was by Myrsilus's time (third century BC) a commonplace (the Stoic Chrysippus wrote a treatise about her), and this made it possible to invoke it in a deviant aetiology of the Lemnian women's stench. Since the business between Jason and Hypsipyle was by now over and done with, however, 'jealousy' may not be the best equivalent for *zêlotupia*; again, 'pain at another getting what one wanted,' irrespective of whether one has acquired it oneself, may come closer.[24]

It is noteworthy that the archetypes of *zêlotupia* in conjugal contexts are mainly women, and in fact it was considered to be particularly vicious in wives.[25] Theano, a woman to whom several neo-Pythagorean epistles are attributed, counsels a fellow disciple to mend her ways (Hercher p. 604, Nr. 5): 'Theano greets Nicostrate. I have heard of your insanity [*paranoia*] concerning your husband, because he has a courtesan and you feel *zêlotupia* concerning him.' Theano concludes with an allusion to Medea (200): 'Hasn't tragedy taught you to control *zêlotupia*, my dear – the one with the plot in which Medea transgressed the law?' Perictione (ca. second century AD), in a pamphlet on 'Women's Concord,' advises that women yield to their husbands in everything, and pardon them if they stray: 'For this kind of error is permitted to men, but never to women ... Thus, one must heed custom and not feel *zêlotupia*, but one must bear his anger, stinginess, fault-finding, *zêlotupia*, calumny, and whatever else is in his nature; in this way a wise woman will dispose all things in a manner that is agreeable to him' (cited by Stobaeus 4.28.19, p. 688 Herscher [Mullach vol. 2, p. 34]). Plutarch, in his *Life of Lycurgus* (15.6), reports that when the lawgiver had properly regulated marriage, he further 'expelled vain and effeminate *zêlotupia*' by making it honourable both to defend one's marriage against insolent assault (*hubris*) and 'to share in the creation of children with other worthy men.'[26] *Zêlotupia* in men was regarded as a barbarian trait; thus, in the *Life of Themistocles* (26.4–5), Plutarch comments: 'The Persian race is by nature savage and harsh in regard to *zêlotupia* concerning women. For not only do they strenuously guard their wedded wives but also women whom they have purchased and keep as concubines.'[27]

We have seen that in the public or political sphere, *zêlotupia* signified a selfish contentiousness, by which men sought to block the success of others either for their own ends or out of malicious spite. In domestic contexts, however, *zêlotupia*, while equally a vice, was more frequently associated with women. The gender-weighted distribution of the term in different spheres is ideologically significant,[28] but it does not necessarily mean that *zêlotupia* had two distinct senses, one applicable to political rivalries and the other to amatory possessiveness, like the double definition of 'jealousy' as 'fear of being supplanted in the affection ... of a beloved person' and envy 'in respect of success or advantage.' If the emotion designated by *zêlotupia* was more uniform than that, then its public use may tell us something about its significance in amorous or matrimonial contexts as well. More precisely, in ascribing *zêlotupia* to women, and above all wedded women, including Hera who was exceptional in the Olympian pantheon for being married, Greek writers were not, I think, signalling anxiety over loss of affection, such as we associate with the term 'jealousy,' but rather a kind of selfish spleen that begrudges the husband the pleasures that custom itself permits him – a licence not regarded as reciprocal, as Perictione makes clear.[29] Hera's *zêlotupia* is not the jealousy of a scorned spouse, but an unseemly ambition to control her husband's behaviour even when she stands to gain nothing from it, and it brands her as a truculent spoilsport. This is why Hera is invariably an unsympathetic character in the mythological tradition, and her behaviour is treated as comical or perverse.[30]

I have been approaching the idea of jealousy in classical Greece by analysing the semantics of *zêlotupia*, the term most commonly rendered as 'jealousy' in English. The results are informative for how Greeks later than the fifth century BC, when *zêlotupia* and cognate terms first appear, viewed the motives of Hera or Medea, though of course the word itself is foreign to Euripides' tragedy and contemporary literature. If I am right, one ought perhaps to modify the entries in modern Greek-English dictionaries. Of course, there might be other words in Greek for jealousy, such as the simple form *zêlos*. Even in the absence of a specific term, it does not follow that the idea of jealousy was lacking. Some concepts current in a society have no name. Aristotle provides several examples in the *Nicomachean Ethics*, such as the trait of being too fearless or too little prone to anger (2.7, 1107b7–8, 1108a5; 3.7, 1115b25–6; cf. Ortony, Clore, and Collins 1988: 8). Ruth Caston, in her study of jealousy in the Roman elegists, observes: 'In the majority of cases, it is not a word or even a cluster of words which announces the presence of jealousy. Instead, we must rely on references to other emotions like fear and anger, which are a crucial part of the jealousy complex, the poetic context, and characters' behavior' (Caston 2000: 3; cf. 10–11).[31]

It would be a lengthy and elusive business to review all the scenes in which jealousy might occur and seek to determine whether one is right to identify it there. In general, it is safe to say that jealousy in the modern sense is foreign to archaic epic. Achilles in the *Iliad* wishes that Artemis had slain Briseis before she could be the cause of the deadly quarrel between himself and Agamemnon (19.55–62): she is not an object of jealousy, but rather a pawn in a struggle over honour between two men – the kind of rivalrous interaction among males that Eve Sedgwick (1985) has called a 'homosocial' relationship. How different is Ovid's treatment in the *Heroides*, where Briseis imagines that Achilles in fact loves her, and cannot understand how he could have refused the rich ransom that Agamemnon offered him – he ought rather to have taken her back even without a reward (for a comparison of the two versions, see Lindheim 2003: 51–62). Similarly, nothing suggests that Menelaus is jealous of Paris in the *Iliad*, although his wife has abandoned him for a handsome lover (the domestic scene with the reunited couple in *Odyssey* book 4 gives no hint of such a passion). Nor has anyone, to my knowledge, ever imagined that Odysseus feels jealousy in respect to the suitors in the *Odyssey*; on the contrary, he is proud of Penelope for prolonging their courtship in order to eke out gifts from them (18.282). It would be absurd to allege jealousy as the motive for his bloody revenge.[32]

Jealousy is equally absent in archaic lyric poetry (I consider below the apparent exception of a famous poem by Sappho). Nor does it play a significant role in tragedy: no Othello ever stalked the ancient Greek stage. Neither are women portrayed as jealous in this genre. The motive of Euripides' Medea – she is, as we have seen, the other outstanding *exemplum* (along with Hera) of *zēlotupia* in the later tradition – is not so much jealousy as anger at Jason's violation of his oaths and his want of gratitude for her services.[33] Although Jason complains that Medea and women generally are fixated on the bed (555–6, 568–75), and Medea herself acknowledges its importance in a marriage (1367–8), Jason believes it is a trivial matter and fails to see why Medea makes such a fuss about it. Had he the word, he might have accused her of *zēlotupia*. But the charge only serves to divert attention from his abandonment of Medea, which is the real issue. Aegeus, the king of Athens who hears Medea's tale of woe, provides a clue to how an ordinary man might respond to Jason's actions. That Jason prefers another woman as mistress of his household Aegeus regards as shameful; if he has done it out of passionate love (*erôs*), his advice to Medea is to let him go (695, 699). When Medea reveals that Jason's ambition is to ally himself to the royal house of Corinth, Aegeus recognizes that her pain is legitimate; finally, when he learns that Jason has consented to her banishment from Corinth, he expresses open disapproval (703, 707). Medea carefully escalates the charges against Jason from a love affair that puts at risk her status in the household to outright exile, but Aegeus's concern, like Medea's own, is focused throughout on the threat to her welfare, not on her amorous sensibilities.[34]

But surely men and women were hurt when their loved ones betrayed them. In Lysias's defence speech on the murder of Eratosthenes (1.32–3), the defendant remarks that a law inscribed in the Areopagus 'judged that men who commit rape [tous biazomenous] deserve a lesser penalty than seducers [tous peithontas],' on the grounds that rapists are hated by their victims, whereas seducers 'corrupt the soul in such a way as to make other men's wives care more for them than for their own husbands.' The anxiety over the alienation of affection is reminiscent of the modern conception of jealousy. However, the consequence of this estrangement, according to Lysias, is that 'it is uncertain whether the children are those of the husband or of the adulterer.' It is not so much his wife's love that the speaker is concerned for as the integrity of his home and the legitimacy of his children.[35]

Modern jealousy, as we have seen, involves three parties: a lover, a beloved, and a rival who has alienated or is believed to have alienated the beloved's affections.[36] The definition thus furnishes both a cast of characters and a scenario, and it is reasonable to expect that jealousy, even if it is not named, would find expression – if anywhere – in genres that are characterized by a narrative structure in which the relevant conditions are met.[37] The Greek genre most hospitable to such a configuration is without a doubt New Comedy, and the most vivid representation of a jilted lover in all Greek literature is to be found, I believe, in Menander's Perikeiromenê or 'Shorn Girl' (late fourth century BC).[38] The soldier Polemo, having learned that his concubine Glycera has kissed the young man next door (it is possible that he witnessed the scene personally), becomes enraged at her behaviour and cuts off her hair. Glycera takes refuge with the people living next door, and Polemo moves out of the house he shared with her and gives himself over to grief. He then returns to the stage with the intention of recovering Glycera by force, but he yields to reason when his friend Pataecus points out that even though Polemo may have thought of her as his legal wife, Glycera is in fact her own mistress (*heautês est' ekeinê kuria*, 497). Thus, Polemo's only recourse as lover (*erônti*, 499), rather than husband, is persuasion – apart, perhaps, from lodging a legal complaint (*enklêma*, 503) against the young man at some future time for having seduced or corrupted Glycera (*diephtharkôs autên*, 499–500) in his absence. Polemo is desolate, and cries out pathetically: 'I don't know what to say, by Demeter, except that I'll hang myself. Glycera has left me, Glycera, she's left me, Pataecus!' (504–7). Here are all the elements of the jealousy archetype: the alienation of the beloved's affections by a rival (a licentious rival, in the Suda's genteel formulation), desperate grief, and, we may add, the desire to return to favour with the beloved rather than retrieve her violently from the rival. Later, however, when he realizes that the man Glycera had kissed was her brother and not a *moikhos* (adulterer or paramour), Polemo laments: 'But I, fiend that I am and *zêlotupos* creature ..., immediately went crazy' (986–98; there is a small lacuna in the papyrus). Here, *zêlotupos* seems to indicate not jealousy so much as an unwarranted or excessive reaction to perfectly legitimate behaviour.

It is no accident that Glycera is a courtesan: only in this way could she be 'her own mistress' rather than dependent on a *kurios* or legal guardian in Attic comedy; as such, she is an autonomous desiring subject.[39] Because she is free to grant or withdraw her love, as Pataecus remarks (491), Polemo must reckon with the 'fear of being supplanted in [her] affection,' as the *Oxford English Dictionary* puts it. This would not be the case with a marriageable citizen girl, who in New Comedy is never the subject of erotic desire. It was social constraints of this sort, I expect, that retarded the representation of romantic jealousy in archaic and classical literature – even in pederastic poetry.[40] New Comedy itself, indeed, was sparing with the formula. Where the rival is the lover's comrade, for example, the theme of the false friend rather than the faithless courtesan predominates, and the response is not so much jealousy as anger and disappointment. Thus, Charinus in Terence's

Andria, believing that his friend has chosen deliberately to marry the girl with whom he himself is in love, exclaims in language that recalls Aristotle's definition of *phthonos*: 'Is it believable or heard of that a person should have such innate lunacy [*vecordia*] as to rejoice in another's adversity and derive his pleasure from the other's displeasure?' (625–8). Charinus's role in the comedy may be Terence's own contribution, but there is a model for his reaction in Plautus and Menander (cf. Plautus, *Bacchides*, 467–572, with Menander *Dis exapatôn* 102–12). Jealousy as such is absent.

In the opening scene of Terence's *Eunuch*, Phaedria is indignant that Thais has banished him in favour of a rich officer, whom she is ingratiating, as she later explains, in order to acquire a girl who is in his possession. When Phaedria protests that the story is a lie and Thais really loves the soldier, she agrees to oblige Phaedria rather than have him as an enemy. At this point Phaedria exclaims: 'If only you said that from the heart and honestly [*utinam istuc verbum ex animo ac vere diceres*], "rather than have you as an enemy"! If I could believe that was sincerely said [*sincere dici*], I could endure anything' (175–7). Phaedria at last consents to her spending time with the soldier, but he begs 'that when you are with that soldier of yours, you not be with him; that day and night you love me, miss me, dream of me, wait for me, think of me, hope for me, rejoice in me, be totally with me – to sum it up, become my soul [*animus*], since I am yours' (191–6). The situation contains all the conditions for jealousy: an enamoured youth, a rival, and the desire for reciprocated love, more sentimentally expressed here than in any other passage of ancient comedy. Phaedria's response, however, is not quite jealousy but rather what we may call an interiorization of passion: if Thais loves him sincerely and from the heart, then he can accept her spending three days with the soldier. His reaction at the beginning of the play prepares for the conclusion, in which Phaedria agrees to share Thais with the soldier on a permanent basis, since he will pay the bills and, being a buffoon, will pose no threat to Thais's affection for Phaedria. We see here how New Comedy neglects to thematize jealousy even where the scenario clearly favours it (see Konstan 1995: 131–40).

The heir to Roman comedy was elegiac poetry, which converted the comic courtesan, who by convention was of foreign rather than Attic birth, into a citizen woman of undisclosed lineage. No fathers or brothers encumber the liberty of such women as Propertius's Cynthia, Tibullus's Delia and Nemesis, Lygdamus's Neaera, or Ovid's Corinna – or, we may suppose, of Gallus's Lycoris, who may have been the model for these later elegiac mistresses – although the poets do not scruple to mention mothers or sisters (Konstan 1994: 153–5; cf. Griffin 1985: 204–8). The women of elegy, like the cortesans of New Comedy, have no male guardians. This convention permitted the elegiac mistress to consort freely with lovers, even when she was imagined as married or at least attached to a man (*vir*), and it provided fertile ground for jealousy. But if jealousy was a felt motive in this genre, as Ruth Caston has argued (2000), it nevertheless had antecedents in Roman lyric poetry of the first century BC.[41] Just how these earlier elements coalesced in a remarkable poem by Horace to yield the image of a passion very like modern jealousy is the subject of the balance of this chapter.

Catullus (approximately 84–54 BC) wrote just prior to the development of elegy as a distinct poetic form, with its characteristically subjective sensibility. But he too drew inspiration from New Comedy, taking as a model Phaedria's plea in Terence's *Eunuch* for a sincere and heartfelt commitment by which he might endure the soldier's power over Thais. Catullus adapts this outcry to his own hope for a lasting relationship with a woman who was formally the spouse of another man:

> Iucundum, mea vita, mihi proponis amorem
> hunc nostrum inter nos perpetuumque fore.
> di magni, facite *ut vere* promittere possit,
> atque id *sincere dicat et ex animo*,
> ut liceat nobis tota perducere vita
> aeternum hoc sanctae foedus amicitiae.[42]

> You, my life, promise me this pleasant love –
> this love of ours – will last forever between us.
> Great gods, make her able to promise it truly
> and say it sincerely and from the heart,
> so that we may prolong for our whole life
> this eternal bond of sacred friendship.

Catullus does not insist that Lesbia be his and his only (cf. 68.135–40, and esp. 145–8), which the circumstances render impossible in any case, since she is married. What appals him is rather her random promiscuity, and he expresses his consternation in a way that recalls Polemo's anguished outburst in the Menander's *Shorn Girl* (my emphasis):

> *Caeli, Lesbia nostra, Lesbia illa,*
> *illa Lesbia,* quam Catullus unam
> plus quam se atque suos amavit omnes,
> nunc in quadriviis et angiportis
> glubit magnanimos Remi nepotes.[43]

> Caelius, my Lesbia, that Lesbia,
> Yes that Lesbia, the only one whom Catullus
> loved more than himself and all his dearest,
> now on street corners and in alleys
> is screwing the great-hearted sons of Remus.

The feeling is intense, but the emotion is evidently disgust rather than jealousy. I am not convinced that Catullus ever expresses the latter sentiment in relation to Lesbia.

Catullus's image of a life-long bond of affection in the final couplet of poem 109 had a considerable influence on later Latin poetry, and it is conceivable that Horace had it in mind when he wrote the concluding verses of *Ode* 1.13:[44]

> Cum tu, Lydia, Telephi
>   cervicem roseam, cerea Telephi
> laudas bracchia, vae meum
>   fervens difficili bile tumet iecur.
> tum nec mens mihi nec color
>   certa sede manet, umor et in genas
> furtim labitur, arguens
>   quam lentis penitus macerer ignibus.
> uror, seu tibi candidos
>   turparunt umeros inmodicae mero
> rixae, sive puer furens
>   inpressit memorem dente labris notam.

non, si me satis audias,
 speres perpetuum dulcia barbare
laedentem oscula, quae Venus
 quinta parte sui nectaris imbuit.
felices ter et amplius
 quos inrupta tenet copula nec malis
divolsus querimoniis
 suprema citius solvet amor die.

When you, Lydia, laud Telephus's rosy
 shoulder, Telephus's waxen
arms, ayy! my boiling liver
 swells with harsh bile,
neither my mind nor my complexion
 stays put, tears secretly slide
down my cheeks, proving with what
 slow fires I'm tortured inside.
I'm seared, whether what bruised
 your white arms were wild fights
begot by wine, or the passionate boy's teeth
 impressed a lasting mark upon your lips.
If you heed me well, you won't
 hope for a man who cruelly wounds
those lips which Venus has imbued
 with the quintessence of her nectar.
Thrice happy and more are those
  whom an unbroken bond unites, and whom love,
unsundered by evil quarrels,
 will not set loose ere death itself.

More obvious, however, is Horace's allusion to the depiction of emotional symptoms in Catullus 51:

Ille mi par esse deo videtur,
ille, si fas est, superare divos,
qui sedens adversus identidem te
 spectat et audit
dulce ridentem, misero quod omnes
eripit sensus mihi: nam simul te,

Lesbia, aspexi, nihil est super mi
   <vocis in ore,>
lingua sed torpet, tenuis sub artus
flamma demanat, sonitu suopte
tintinant aures geminae, teguntur
   lumina nocte.
otium, Catulle, tibi molestumst:
otio exsultas nimiumque gestis,
otium et reges prius et beatas
   perdidit urbes.

He seems equal to a god to me,
he seems, if piety permit, greater than the gods,
who sits opposite you and again and again
   sees and hears you
laughing sweetly, though it rips up
all my senses in my misery: for as soon as
I've seen you, Lesbia, I've no more
   voice in my throat,
but my tongue is stiff, a thin flame flows
beneath my bones, my ears ring
with their own buzz, my eyes are
   covered in night.
Leisure, Catullus, is bad for you:
You delight and perform too much in leisure,
Leisure has ruined kings ere now, has ruined
   glorious cities.

Catullus's poem is, of course, a translation of Sappho 31, apart (perhaps) from the final stanza. Although Sappho's and Catullus's poems (like Horace's) both involve three individuals – the speaker; the addressee, in each case a woman who is the cause of the speaker's condition; and a man who sits calmly facing her – neither, I would argue, portrays the effects of jealousy, in spite of the consensus to the contrary of the great majority of scholars today.[45] The poems rather describe the symptoms of passionate love. The function of the third party, who sits opposite the beloved, is to highlight the extraordinary reaction of the lover: that man *must* be a god if he can sit so close to the loved one, engage in intimate conversation and laughter with her, and yet remain immune to her influence, which produces such a devastating effect upon the lover. The point is, of course, that that man is not in love. After Sappho, the symptoms she describes become the conventional signs of love or lovesickness.[46]

In Horace's ode, the third person, Telephus, is not present; rather, the poet's persona listens as the addressee, called Lydia, praises the other man's charms. The persona, and through him the reader, overhear her words, unlike the situation in Sappho's and Catullus's poems, where the sight of the beloved blocks up the speaker's ears (*sonitu suopte tintinant aures geminae*), and the conversation opposite goes unrecorded.[47] It is what Lydia says that induces a physical reaction in the speaker (*cum ... tum*, 1–5). Lydia, we see, is infatuated with Telephus, a circumstance we have no reason to believe is paralleled in the poems by Sappho and Catullus. What, then, is the speaker in Horace's ode feeling? Quinn, in his commentary (1984: 149), takes it for granted that he is jealous, but Nisbet and Hubbard (1970: 174 ad v. 9), with exemplary caution, leave open the possibility that Horace's speaker, like Sappho's and Catullus's, is in the grip of erotic passion, or for that matter of anger, rather than jealousy.[48] Here we see the complexity of jealousy as an emotion: unless he is enamoured of Lydia and simultaneously upset or indignant at her relationship with Telephus, Horace's speaker will not be jealous. The set of symptoms on its own cannot answer whether these conditions obtain. But even if Horace's persona is or has been in love with Lydia, he may nevertheless be experiencing at this moment either anger, or envy, or a sudden recrudescence of erotic passion, any one of which is sufficient to account for his reaction. The question thus remains whether Horace identified jealousy as an individual emotion in its own right, or rather perceived an array of distinct sentiments – 'anger-, sadness-, and fear-like feelings,' in Planalp's words – where we see just one.

Although the symptoms described by Horace resemble the conventional syndrome of lovesickness in classical literature, a modern reader, like Quinn, has no difficulty in understanding them as signs of jealousy. The psychologist Leila Tov-Ruach reports that 'jealousy can, when it is experienced as a feeling, involve intense vertigo, like that of fainting or a loss of consciousness, or a sense of strong disorientation and disassociation' (1980: 470; cf. 471), and the actress Jeanne Moreau reports that jealousy 'is more than a feeling, it is a horrible sensation, so violent as to shake you from head to foot, your entire body begins to tremble, you're on the point of losing consciousness' (quoted in Chapsal 1977: 16). For us, jealousy is a familiar emotion with characteristic causes and forms of expression (cf. Marguerite de Navarre, *Heptaméron* 1999: 377: 'Je sçay bien que la jalousie est une passion aussi veritable comme l'amour'). Although Quinn is surely right (1984: 149 ad vv. 9–12) that what inflames Horace 'is not Lydia's beauty but the evidence of her new young lover's ardor,' just because he assumes that jealousy is a well-defined passion in classical erotic literature, Quinn fails to notice that Horace's originality lies precisely in having transferred the symptoms normally associated with enamourment to this new context involving the beloved's infatuation with another person. While preserving the three-person structure of Sappho's and Catullus's poems, Horace has in fact constructed a wholly new scenario.[49]

Comparing Lydia's role in other odes of Horace (1.8, 1.25, and 3.9), Quinn imagines that Lydia was formerly Horace's mistress and that, by taking him into her confidence about her new lover, she is 'thereby subjecting H[orace] to an exquisite torture' while he tries manfully to maintain his detachment.[50] Quinn's story is of course consistent with jealousy: if there had never been a relationship between Horace's persona and Lydia, then one ought rather to identify his emotion as envy – a possibility that cannot be excluded. But since the speaker announces his torment at the very beginning, it is hard to believe that he is here adopting 'the role of the middle-aged observer of the human comedy.' Rather than concoct fanciful narratives where the poet deliberately leaves matters unclear, we may turn to the contrast Horace introduces in the final verses of the ode between Lydia's intense but transient passion for Telephus and a life-long bond of love.

Horace's speaker does not openly propose himself as Lydia's permanent partner, although his acute reaction to her current enamourment suggests that he may be doing so implicitly. In

Catullus poem 109, two alternative types of relationship – a brief affair (*amorem*) and an eternal bond of *amicitia* – are conceived of as available to the poet's persona (cf. *mihi, nobis*). Lesbia offers him the one, while he himself desires the other. By representing Lydia as amorously interested in a third party, however, Horace establishes a double opposition in his poem: on the one hand, there is the tension between himself and Telephus as objects of Lydia's affection; and, on the other, there is the contrast between two kinds of love, the one enduring, the other passionate but transient. Horace's persona suffers not only because Lydia is not his, but because she prefers the kind of affair of which he disapproves to the type of love that he himself, we may suppose, has to offer.[51] By grafting the contrast between two types of love in Catullus poem 109 onto the three-party scenario borrowed from Catullus poem 51, Horace converts Lydia's preference for a rival into a rejection not only of himself as a lover but also of his very way of loving.

Tov-Ruach (1980: 471) explains that jealous fear occurs 'when the sense of danger to an aspect of one's identity generates a set of obsessive scenario-constructing thoughts,' which 'generally involve the construction of vivid stories, with the jealous person as a voyeur of an endless series of vignettes that cause him pain.' We do not have to accept Tov-Ruach's psychoanalytic framework to recognize the cogency of her description of modern romantic jealousy.[52] Yet jealousy of this sort is not a natural or universal emotion, but one that emerges under determinate conditions and in specific forms. Horace's own social world was favourable to such a development: among the upper classes, at least, an ideal of reciprocal love as the basis for marriage was slowly gaining ground (cf. Veyne 1978). But the paradigm of jealousy required a condensed and exemplary expression, a scenario that united what had been disparate sentiments into a single archetype. I suggest that, by combining elements in two poems of Catullus, which themselves allude in turn both to Sappho and to a remarkable scene in Terence's *Eunuch* (a comedy that Horace knew well: cf. *Satires* 2.3.259–71), Horace created a model case of a three-party passion that comes very close to what a later epoch would come to think of as erotic jealousy.[53] We might even credit him with being its inventor.

CHAPTER TWELVE

Grief

Unlike mourning, in which the past is declared resolved, finished, and dead, in melancholia the past remains steadfastly alive in the present.

Eng and Kazanjian 2003b: 3–4[1]

One may think of grief as a human universal ..., but the reality is that grief is quite different from culture to culture.

Rosenblatt 1997: 41

In the previous chapter, I argued that the Greeks of the classical period had no term signifying romantic jealousy as it is understood today. In this, the final chapter, I take up another sentiment that poses a classificatory problem, namely grief. I do not propose to make the case that grief too was unknown to the Greeks, of course. It was known, and named by a variety of terms, such as *lupê* and *penthos*; still other words denoted various manifestations of grief and mourning, including lamentation in various forms, from sobs and ululation to ritualized actions such as the tearing out of hair and the beating of one's breast. An entire genre, the so-called consolation, was developed to help people recover from sorrow over the loss of a loved one (I examine this literary form in more detail below). The question remains, however, whether grief was conceived of as an emotion. Although it might seem to be among the most basic emotions of all – it is taken as paradigmatic in Martha Nussbaum's recent (2001) investigation of the emotions, for example – I shall suggest that it may not typically have been grouped with the other *pathê* we have examined so far.

My point of departure for these reflections is the absence of grief from Aristotle's treatment of the passions in the second book of the *Rhetoric*. One explanation that suggests itself is that Aristotle's inventory of emotions in this treatise is governed by their relevance to or usefulness in persuasion, and it may not have seemed to Aristotle and his contemporaries that grief was as salient in this context as, say, anger, pity, gratitude, fear, shame, and hatred, which are regularly appealed to in forensic and deliberative speeches. Yet surely grief too could influence the opinion of a juror or member of the assembly, whether over private or public losses. If the purpose of exciting the emotions is to alter people's judgments – and the emotions are, according to Aristotle, precisely 'all those things on account of which people change and differ in regard to their judgments,' with the proviso that they are attended by pain and pleasure (2.1, 1378a20–2) – then grief would on the surface seem to be as eligible an emotion as any of the rest in Aristotle's catalogue.

One reason why Aristotle may not have thought to devote a special treatment to grief turns, perhaps, on a point of Greek vocabulary. As I have indicated above, one of the Greek words for 'grief' – indeed, by far the most common in ordinary language – is *lupê*. But *lupê*, we have seen, is just Aristotle's word for 'pain'; it is the opposite of pleasure, and constitutes one of the two sensations or *aisthêseis* that, according to Aristotle, are consituent elements of those *pathê* that qualify as emotions (the term *pathos*, as we noted in chapter 1, has a wide range of meanings in Greek, apart from its use in the sense of 'emotion'). As William Harris (2001: 343) observes, 'The meaning of *lup-* words is from a modern point of view ambiguous: they can refer to physical pain or to psychological distress.' Harris concludes (340) that 'the archaic and classical Greeks did not construct any definite barrier between physical suffering and intense emotional suffering.'[2] This is perhaps not entirely the case. Words based on the root *alg-*, such as *algos* and *algêdôn* (cf. English 'analgesic'), refer principally to physical pain, and indeed the Epicureans and Stoics, in the generation after

Aristotle, adopted *algêdôn* rather than *lupê* as the term for the strictly corporeal sensation.[3] However this may be, since pain for Aristotle is a sensation, and along with pleasure is a component of emotion rather than an emotion proper, he may have found it awkward to treat *lupê*, even in its significance as 'grief,' as a phenomenon on the same level as other *pathê*.

But the absence of grief from Aristotle's account of the emotions may have been motivated by something more than a lexical accident; or rather, the coincidence of grief and pain in a single term may itself be informative about the Greek view of sorrow as a sentiment.[4] We may consider, first, that pain is not simply a physical phenomenon: we may feel pain as occurring in our leg or arm, but the sensation itself is not necessarily localized there. Pain is registered in the mind, or what the Greeks would have called the psyche. Second, and more important, in affirming that the emotions or *pathê* are accompanied by pleasure and pain, Aristotle is manifestly thinking not of pain resulting from bodily harm but of what we might call psychological suffering. The pain that forms part of the definition of such emotions as anger, pity, or indignation, for example, is not a physical ache like that of a damaged tooth. It consists rather in a sense of injury or injustice, like hurt feelings. Thus, the pain that is an ingredient of *pathê* already resembles grief more than it does physical pain.[5]

The question remains whether grief is something more than, or different from, the kind of pain that, according to Aristotle, accompanies the *pathê*. It would seem that we could invent an Aristotelian account of grief in which pain was an element, for example: Let grief be a pain resulting from the death or loss of one who is dear (cf. the definition of envy as 'a disturbing pain resulting from the well-being of another,' *Rhetoric* 2.9, 1386b18–19). In specifying the cause of the pain peculiar to grief, we endow grief with a cognitive component that would appear to differentiate it from the mere sensation of pain.[6] Is there something about the nature of the motivating stimulus in the case of grief – that is, the fact of loss – that distinguishes it from the fact of another person's well-being, which is what excites the acknowledged *pathos* of envy?

It may be that the loss of a loved one involves relatively little in the way of appraisal, in comparison with other emotions. Anger is provoked by a slight, which requires, according to Aristotle, an evaluation of the intentions of the author of the insult, that person's status relative to our own, our own capacity to exact revenge, and various other factors. Pity and indignation depend on an estimation of desert, gratitude on the disinterested nature of the benefaction. Fear requires a sense of whether another individual or group is hostile, and a judgment concerning their relative strength in comparison with one's own. Even envy entails more complex intellectual operations in the fuller version of Aristotle's definition (2.10, 1387b23–5), where he stipulates that it is 'a kind of pain, in respect to one's equals, for their apparent success in things called good, not so as to have the thing oneself but [solely] on their account': the provision concerning equals implicitly suggests, if not an appraisal of desert, at least a sense of equivalent entitlement.

Grief seems different in this respect: it involves no judgment of intentions, no reckoning of relative power, no reference to desert or to social status. We are aware, of course, of our degree of closeness with the departed – we do not mourn for just anyone – but we do not normally calculate it along an axis of intimacy. The loss of a loved one strikes us with greater immediacy, as if the fact itself were painful, irrespective of anyone's intentions or the consequences for our social position. In this sense, the grieving is like physical pain.

Grief is unlike other emotions too in that it does not involve, or only minimally involves, what is sometimes called 'action readiness,' that is, the enhanced disposition to respond to whatever aroused the passion (on 'action tendencies' associated with emotion, cf. Parkinson 1995: 70–82). Anger, according to Aristotle, is by definition a desire for revenge; love is the wish that good things accrue to another, and a willingness to bring those things about (hatred involves the reverse). Envy and competitive rivalry (zêlos) look to equality with one's peers; we seek to avoid those circumstances that are productive of shame or fear. While Aristotle does not write into the definition of pity an impulse to ameliorate the condition of the pitied, it is implicit in his idea that pity, like indignation, depends on a judgment of desert. Grief, however, invites no compensatory act, no attempt to redress a wrong or a disequilibrium in one's social world. There is no agent who bears responsibility for one's grief, no one to get even with. Of course, loss can be the consequence of an action, as when someone, through deliberate aggression or culpable negligence, brings about the death of another (along with damage to one's public self or reputation). In that case, however, we hate or are angry with the author of the deed, but the sense of bereavement has as its object not the one who caused the loss but the loved one who has passed away. Nothing will bring that person back, as the consolation literature constantly reminds those who are in mourning. There is simply nothing to do but wait until the pain diminishes. Time alone heals such a wound.

The emotions that Aristotle identifies and analyses are social, in the strong sense that they are responses to behaviour by conscious agents. They are not typically elicited by inaminate objects (see chapter 1, p. 39). What is more, they are deeply enmeshed in a world of competitive honour and esteem (doxa), in which people are intensely aware of their status relative to their peers, their inferiors, and their betters, and of the effects on their public standing of other people's attitudes and actions. Rather than a mere reaction to an impinging event or circumstance, a pathos is part of a social transaction. The natural fact of death stands outside this system.[7]

In Sophocles' tragedy Electra, the heroine has been living under the watchful eyes of her mother Clytemnestra, who, together with her lover Aegisthus, murdered Agamemnon, her husband and Electra's father, upon his return from Troy and seized control of the throne in Argos. In the initial scene, Electra's brother Orestes has entered Argos secretly for the first time since Electra arranged to have him spirited away as an infant from his native land.

Electra's first words – 'Oh wretched me!' (ô moi moi dustênos, 77) – are uttered from inside her house. When he hears Electra's cry, the old tutor who has accompanied Orestes mistakes it for the groaning of a slave, but Orestes divines that it may indeed be his unhappy sister. When the men withdraw, Electra, unaware that her brother is nearby, emerges from the house, and sings: 'Oh holy light of the sun, and sky coextensive with the earth, how many odes of mourning, how many answering blows upon my bloodied breast have you heard, each time dark night has been overtaken by you? The hated bed in my miserable house knows the sorrows of my wakeful nights as I bewail my wretched father' (86–95). Electra's soliloquy and her subsequent duet with the chorus of Argive young women are among the most poignant passages in Greek tragedy. What is it that Electra is feeling?

Given that she is lamenting her deceased father, we might well suppose that it is grief. But Electra continues: 'my father, whom bloody Ares [the god of war] did not seize in a barbarian land' – that is, in Troy, which the Greek army besieged for ten years – 'but my own mother and her bed-partner Aegisthus split his head with a murderous axe like woodcutters splitting an oak' (95–9). Electra is not simply in mourning; had her father died while fighting in Troy, she would of course have grieved for him, but the cause of her present distress is that he was assassinated by his own wife and her paramour, dying not a hero's death but by treachery. 'And there has been no pity [or lamentation: *oiktos*] for these things from anyone but me, although you, my father, died so shamefully and pitiably [*aikôs oiktrôs te*]' (100–2). It is the nature of her father's death that galls Electra, and it is anger, not sorrow, that she is feeling (for a catalogue of her motives, see her almost legalistic brief to her mother at 558–609).

Electra calls upon the gods of the underworld and above all the Erinyes, or Furies, whose province is unlawful death and violated marriage beds, to avenge the death of her father and bring Orestes back, since she can no longer bear her anguish (*lupê*) alone (110–20). When the women of the chorus enter, they try to pacify Electra, although they are aware of the nature of Agamemnon's death: 'Electra, child of a dreadful mother, what is this insatiable complaint that is wasting you away for Agamemnon, who was godlessly ensnared long ago by your treacherous mother's wiles and betrayed by her evil hand? May the one who did it die, if it is right for me to say so!' (121–7). Agamemnon's death belongs to the distant past: why, the chorus wonder, must she still belabour it?

By pointing to the remoteness of Agamemnon's death, the Argive maidens are exploiting, as we shall see, a commonplace in the literature of consolation. This genre did not deny the propriety of timely grief, but advised the bereaved to give over sorrowing after a decent interval of time (cf. Konstan 2001a: 63–4; Euripides, *Alcestis* 1077, 1079: 'What will you gain by desiring to grieve forever?'). As the chorus later put it, 'Time is a comforting god' (179; cf. 1085: 'Time will soften the pain, which is now still young').[8] In a similar vein, they remind Electra of the futility of lamentation: 'You will not resurrect your father from Hades' communal lake either with wailing or with prayers' (137–9; cf. Archilochus fr. 13; *Alcestis* 875: 'You are not helping her who died'; and 985–6: 'Endure! You will not raise up the dead from below by weeping'), and they offer the hoary solace that she is not the only mortal to have endured such a loss, instancing Electra's sisters and Orestes himself as examples (153–63). They mean to say that death touches everyone (cf. *Alcestis* 892–4: 'Endure! You are not the first to have lost a wife; one or another tragedy oppresses all mortals'; and 931–2: 'Death has undone the wives of many ere this'), but they cannot help recognizing that only Electra's siblings have suffered this particular outrage – the slaughter of their father at the hands of their own mother – along with her.[9]

The trouble with these consolatory commonplaces is that they do not apply to Electra's case, since Electra is distraught not over Agamemnon's death but over his murder: 'Only a fool,' she says, 'forgets parents who have died pitiably [*oiktrôs*]' (145–6).[10] Electra offers as her own examples of perpetual mourning Niobe and the nightingale (148–52), apparently forgetting that the nightingale murdered the very child for which it grieved (cf. 'child-slayer,' 107). Finally, the women of the chorus counsel Electra to moderate not just her grief but her resentment as well: 'Entrust your all too painful anger [*kholos*] to Zeus, and don't suffer overmuch [*huperakhthesthai*] because of your enemies, nor yet forget them' (176–7), and they return obsessively to the moment of the murder, which was inspired by erotic passion and accomplished by deceit (193–200). In so doing, they move Electra to focus once again on her desire for revenge (*poinima pathea*, 210).

At this point, the chorus alter their approach and advise Electra to temper her rage and stubborn outspokenness: 'You are hurling yourself ignominiously to your own destruction' (215–16). But Electra terminates the discussion with an unanswerable statement of principle: 'If the dead man is to lie there wretchedly, mere earth and nothingness, and they do not pay the murderous penalty, there go reverence and piety among all human beings' (245–50). With this, the chorus yield, and Electra goes on to expound, in the metre of ordinary dialogue, the on-going humiliations that feed her wrath.

There are, then, elements both of mourning and of anger in the lyric exchange between Electra and the chorus, but the passion that drives the heroine is less grief than rage and a corresponding desire for vengeance. There is a good dramatic reason for this latter motive. Bereavement is healed, if at all, by time; it would be a static play that took for its theme a woman unable to accept the irreversible loss of her father.[11] Electra's wrath sets her actively in conflict with her mother and Aegisthus; it is not merely the psychic residue of a past event but has implications for the present and the future. It is thus a factor in the opposition of wills on which drama depends. To put it differently, the cause of Electra's passion is not just an incident – the passing away of her father – but an action, instigated by agents whom she holds responsible. This social dimension is what distinguishes Electra's emotional response of anger from the passive grief elicited by a morally neutral event.[12] The opening scene of Sophocles' *Electra* can be read as a subtle examination and confrontation of two distinct kinds of sentiment.[13]

Modern interpretations of Electra, including dramatic adaptations such as the *Elektra* of Hugo von Hofsmannsthal (and the operatic version by Richard Strauss) or Eugene O'Neill's *Mourning Becomes Electra*, tend to treat Electra's fixation on the death of her father as pathological, a symptom of her inability to liberate herself from grief at the loss of her father. In Freud's terms (1957), she is suffering from melancholia, an irrational attachment to the past, as opposed to normal mourning, from which one is expected to recover after a decent interval of time has elapsed. While it is often productive to interpret ancient works of literature according to modern psychological theories, it is important also to appreciate the terms in which they present themselves. Sophocles' Electra is obsessed with the past not because she has suffered a traumatic separation from her father, but because he was slain in cold blood. The deed demands vengeance, as does the loss of status for Agamemnon's children, and it is this that consumes Electra, not just grief. The dynamic interaction between the two motives is what gives the opening of Sophocles' play its dramatic tension.

The time allowed for grief has historically been subject to regulation. The imposition of limitations regarding the period of mourning, attire, and other facets reflects an understanding of grief as a social function, not merely a private sentiment. Mourning is a condition as much as a feeling: one speaks in English of being 'in mourning,' just as, in Greek, one is said to be *en penthei* (cf. Plato, *Republic* 395E12: 'in misfortune and mourning and lamentation' [*en sumphorais te kai penthesin kai thrênois*]; *Republic* 605C12; *Laws* 958E7; Sophocles, *Electra* 846; Euripides, *Helen* 166).[14] Here too one sees a difference between grief and other emotions. Grief, understood as mourning, has a ritualized aspect, and hence falls under the jurisdiction of public authority and custom.

A funerary law from ancient Rome stipulates that 'parents and children over six years of age can be mourned for a year, children under six for a month. A husband can be mourned for ten months, close blood relations for eight months. Whoever acts contrary to these restrictions is placed in public disgrace.'[15] Plutarch writes to his wife concerning the death of their young daughter (612A) that, according to custom, people

neither bring libations to those of their children who died while still infants nor do they perform any other acts concerning them, such as it is usual to perform on behalf of the dead, for they have no share of the earth or the things of the earth. Nor do they frequent their graves, monuments, and the layings out of corpses here, or sit by their bodies: for the laws do not permit it for those of such an age.

These restrictions may seem heartless, but we must be on guard against projecting our sentiments onto civilizations different from our own. As Paul Rosenblatt (1997: 41) observes: 'A mother in the slums of Cairo, Egypt, locked for seven years in the depths of a

deep depression over the death of a child is not behaving patho-
logically by the standards of her community. A bereaved Balinese
who seemingly laughs off a death is also behaving appropriately
by the standards of her culture' (references suppressed).[16] There is
also, of course, the opposite danger of attributing to ostensibly
simpler societies a diminished capacity for humane feeling. Up
until the 1970s in Australia, Aboriginal children were forcefully
separated from their families and raised in foster homes or state
institutions as a way of integrating them into modern society; as
for the deprived Aboriginal parents, it was assumed that their grief
was short-lived and that, in the words of one inspector, 'they soon
forget their offspring' (quoted in Bryson 2000: 353) – a view that
reflects intercultural insensitivity rather than an awareness of
socially conditioned differences in the experience of grief.

There are social norms that control the expression of emotions
such as anger and fear as well, but the time limits on mourning
suggest that the proper duration of grief is in fact arbitrary, in the
sense that its termination does not depend on altering or rectify-
ing a determinate state of affairs. The gestures associated with
grief, such as covering one's own body with ashes, have symbolic
significance, for example that of assimilating the living to the
condition of the dead, but unlike the *pathê* examined by Aristotle
they are not governed by considerations of competitive standing.
Mourning is a painful state for which time is the only salve. How
much time is established by convention, which both acknowledges the necessity of grief and sets limits to its extent.

There existed in classical antiquity a hard line on grieving for
the dead, according to which death is not an evil and hence not a
reason for sorrow. Anaxagoras famously replied to the news that
his son had died, 'I knew he was mortal when I fathered him'
(Diogenes Laertius 2.31); since death is a natural phenomenon it
should be accepted with equanimity.[17] So too Phaedo, in Plato's
dialogue by that name, recalls the death of Socrates (58E–59A):

Indeed, I experienced something amazing when I was with him. No pity
overcame me, as if I were present at the death of someone dear to me: for
the man himself seemed happy, Echecrates, both in his demeanour and in
what he said ... Thus no sense of pity overcame me, as would seem

natural in the presence of grief, nor again pleasure as when we were philosophizing together as usual – for in fact there was such a discussion – but rather I felt some entirely strange emotion, an unusual mixture compounded of pleasure and pain at once.

Socrates' own tranquillity in the face of death communicates itself to his friends, without however entirely erasing the habitual response of sadness. These philosophical responses to grief are analogous to the treatment of the emotions, or *pathê*, in that they redescribe the event that elicits the sentiment in such a way as to change its valence: if death is not an evil, then it is not to be lamented any more than it is to be feared. To the extent that grief is motivated by the idea that the deceased are unhappy, the strategy is reasonable, although such sorrow is more like pity for another (as Phaedo suggests) than a sense of one's own loss.

Consolation literature availed itself of this kind of argument, especially when it was addressed to people with pretentions to philosophy, but it typically acknowledged the necessity of grief in the immediate aftermath of bereavement. Servius Sulpicius Rufus wrote to Cicero on the occasion of the death of his daughter Tullia (*To His Friends* 4.5; translation in Shelton 1998: 93):

Even if she had not died at this time, she must nevertheless have died a few years from now because she was born a mortal ... Consider, for example, that she lived as long as it was necessary ...; she enjoyed almost all of life's blessings. And she departed from life when the republic died ... There is no grief which the passage of time does not lessen or soften; but it is unworthy of you to wait for the time to pass rather than anticipating this result with your own good sense.

Sulpicius urges upon Cicero, in consideration of his reputation for wisdom, a dispassionate response to his loss, in the manner of Anaxagoras, although he tempers this argument with the re- minder that Tullia had enjoyed a rich life and that circumstances in Rome were such that she might be better off having died when she did.[18] In the ordinary course of events, Servius acknowledges, time of its own relieves the pain. Similarly, the consolation ascribed to Plutarch, in which the author seeks to comfort a certain Apollonius on the death of his child, begins: 'For a long while now, Apollonius, I have suffered and condoled with you [*sunalgein, sunakhthesthai*]' (101F). So long as the disease was ravaging the boy, the writer states, it would have been inappropriate to encourage the father to bear his lot as a mortal; rather, it was necessary to share Apollonius's emotion (*sumpathein*, 102A). But when time enough has passed, friends should help one overcome grief and vain anguish (102B). Menander the rhetorician, in his handbook on oratory, recommends that in composing a consolation one begin by dwelling on the grief and only afterwards look to comfort it (413.6, 21–3 Spengel). Menander goes on to observe (2.11 = 419.3–10):

If a funeral speech is delivered not very long after the death, but rather after only some seven or eight months have gone by, then one should pronounce an encomium, although there is nothing against using consolatory topics towards the end – unless a close relative of the deceased happens to be giving the speech. For the latter, memory does not grant release from the emotion even after a year, which is why, even after a year, he will retain the style of an emotional speech.

These writers take it for granted that the initial response to the loss of a loved one is grief, even as they recommend ways to overcome it (cf. Plato *Republic* 10, 603E7–8).

The Roman poet Statius (first century AD) composed several poems known as *epicedia*, which were imagined as being pronounced at the funeral itself. In one, on the death of the foster-child of Atedius Melior (*Silvae* 2.1), Statius acknowledges that he should be offering healing words, but he concedes that this would be cruel, since Atedius is racked with grief (5–6). Accordingly, Statius encourages him to give rein to lamentation and the 'joy of weeping' – work it through, we might say today – until he is ready to heed 'friendly entreaties' (15–16). He himself, Statius says, is equally riven by grief (25, 28–30). Only at the end of his poem does he turn to the consolation proper (208–34). Statius's 'Consolation to Flavius Ursus on the Loss of His Beloved Boy' begins (*Silvae* 2.6.1–18, excerpted): 'You are too cruel, who would assign gradations to tears and limits to grieving. It is pitiable for a parent to light the pyre for infants and – horrible! – growing children ... Do not repress your tears, do not be ashamed: let your grief break its bonds ... Who will disapprove of mourning given free rein for this funeral?' Again, in *Silvae* 3.3, the 'Consolation for Claudius Etruscus,' Statius asks: 'For who, when they see someone beating his breast in unexhausted lament and embracing the pyre and falling upon the cinders, would not suppose that the funeral of a young wife is being bewailed or the adolescent image of a child is being seized by the flames? It is a father who is weeping' (8–12). In the epicedion for the death of his own foster-child (5.3), Statius exclaims: 'Perhaps people will say I am too eager for grief and have exceeded due modesty in my tears; but who are you to weigh out my groans and lamentations?' (56–8). So too, Pliny (*Epistles* 5.16), a younger contemporary of Statius, describes his pain at the death of his friend Fundanus's daughter, and remarks that although Fundanus is a learned man, all his wisdom is for naught; but this, he adds, is because the wound is still fresh – when time has worked its healing, he will be ready to accept words of solace.

Grief, then, was reasonable and necessary in its proper place, or rather, in its proper moment. It is persistent, unrelenting grief that the ancients are unanimous in discouraging. Consolations are necessary because there is a powerful desire to hold on to the past and people do sometimes persist in grief beyond its season. In his 'Consolation to Marcia' (6.1.6–7), Seneca asks: 'What then will be the end of it ...? The third year has now passed.' So too, in the 'Consolation to Polybius,' Seneca offers the usual commonplaces about mortality: not even the universe is eternal (11.1.2), all who have lived so far have died (11.1.4), grief serves no purpose (11.2.1), our tears cannot alter fate (11.4.1), life itself is a vale of tears (11.4.2–3), your own deceased brother would wish you to give over mourning (11.5.2), excessive displays of grief are servile and womanish (11.6.2) and inconsistent with high station (11.6.4), proximity to Caesar (to whom Polybius owes all) is itself a cure for grief (11.8.1), and your brother is better off where he is now (11.9.7–8). And yet Seneca also affirms (11.18.5–6):

Never will I demand of you that you not grieve at all. I know that there are to be found certain men, whose wisdom is more harsh than courageous, who deny that a wise man should mourn. I don't believe that these men have ever experienced such a misfortune, for otherwise fortune would have knocked such arrogant wisdom out of them and forced them, all unwilling, to confess the truth. Reason will manifest itself sufficiently if one simply eliminates from one's grief whatever is excessive and disproportionate: no one should hope or desire to feel that it is wholly non-existent ... Let the tears flow, but let them also cease; let the groans be drawn from one's deepest bosom, but let them also come to an end.

When mourning takes the form of an inveterate and unending dedication to the dead, it becomes an obsession – melancholia, in Freud's terminology. Such is the warning that Plutarch gives his own wife in connection with the death of their two-year-old daughter (609F–10A):

Each person invites his own grief to stay with him. When, in the course of time, it is established and becomes his companion and housemate, it does not leave even when people really want it to. This is why one must struggle with it at the doorway and not abandon one's guard through funereal dress or cutting one's hair or any of those things which, by confronting and shaming us daily, make our minds small, narrow, closed, harsh, and timid, so that they no longer take part in laughter or light or a generous table, since our minds are clad and practised in such things on account of grief. Neglect of the body follows upon this evil, and disparagement of unguents, baths, and any other of life's comforts.

The genre of the consolation was intended not so much to cut grief off at the root as to prevent it from settling in as a permanent habit.

The Greeks and Romans recognized the power of grief, and devised ways of assuaging it, from philosophical advice to official limits on the period of mourning. After a certain amount of time, it was necessary to forget the dead and to cease dwelling on the past (forgetting is not necessarily easier than remembering).[19] But grief was one thing, defence of one's dignity and an angry antagonism to injustice another.[20] A photograph in the Spanish daily *El País* (Aznárez 2002: 7), which accompanies an article on the crisis in Venezuela over the coup d'état that briefly removed Hugo

Chávez from power on 11 April 2002, shows a man holding up two posters with the motto: *PROHIBIDO OLVIDAR ... ¡JUSTICIA YA!* ('It is forbidden to forget ... Justice now!'). The occasion is a demonstration in Caracas protesting the shooting of several participants in an earlier march against Chávez' regime. Injustice inspires anger, and anger endures until such time as one is in a position to avenge the initial wrong or insult. Forgetting anger, or love, gratitude, and shame, for that matter, takes on the character of a moral failure.[21]

As the consolation tradition insists, there is no way to redress the loss of one who has died. One can only wait until time does its work of healing, and in the meanwhile be careful not to indulge in mourning to the point at which it becomes, as Plutarch puts it, a guest in our home that is impossible to expel. Whereas in politics one may insist, with the Venezuelan protester, that forgetting is prohibited, the Roman law regarding mourning enjoined just the opposite, that grief must, after a due period of time, come to an end.

Today, when emotions are commonly understood as feelings or internal phenomena, without a necessary component of evaluation and reference to the outside world, it seems natural to think of controlling or eliminating painful affects as such, whether grief or rage. That anger is grounded in a perceived injustice, whereas grief is rooted in loss, is of less consequence, on this modern view, than the perturbation of the psyche that both sentiments engender. On the classical conception of the emotions, however, which looked more to agency and effect on social standing than to one's inner state, grief and anger look radically different, even to the point that grief might not qualify as a *pathos* at all. Recognizing the distinction between the two kinds of sentiment may not only help illuminate classical literature and psychology, but may also contribute something to our understanding of grief today.[22]

Conclusion

The world that Aristotle evokes in his account of the emotions is highly competitive. It would appear that the Greeks were constantly jockeying to maintain or improve their social position or that of dear ones, and were deeply conscious of their standing in the eyes of others. When ordinary people stepped out of the house and into the streets of Athens, they must, on the basis of the picture Aristotle draws, have been intensely aware of relative degrees of power and their own vulnerability to insult and injury. The emotions of the ancient Greeks, in turn, were attuned to these demands.[1]

It was understood that people naturally strive to have the goods that others – or at least, their equals – have; emulation or rivalrousness (*zêlos*) is an emotion characteristic of decent people, according to Aristotle, for it motivates them to obtain things appropriate to their position. Envy is the mark of poor character or *êthos*, since it aims merely to deprive one's neighbour of such goods, without advantage to oneself (2.11, 1388a33–6).[2] But emulation too has a negative side: for its opposite, Aristotle says, is contempt (*kataphronêsis*), and those who are disposed to emulate others or be emulated by them tend to be contemptuous of people who do not have the goods that are vied for (*zêlôta*, 2.11, 1388b23–7). We may recall, although Aristotle does not mention it in this context, that contempt was among the three causes of anger, which is the impulse to avenge a slight. Like emulation, anger too works to maintain an equilibrium of goods or honour in a society where everyone is trying to get ahead of the rest.

Fear depends on an evaluation of the relative strength of one's enemies (2.5, 1382b15–19), just as confidence, fear's opposite, derives from the knowledge that our competitors – if we have any – are either weak or well disposed towards us (2.5, 1383a22–5). We feel shame for our vices, such as cowardice, injustice, and the servility that is manifested in begging or flattering others for the sake of some advantage, and also for not having the fine things our equals have (2.6, 1384a9–11): like emulation, shame is a goad to maintaining one's level in society. We feel shame particularly before those who are of some account, for example people who admire us or whom we admire – or those with whom we compete. Like anger, shame is symptomatic of a society in which one's reputation in the eyes of others is crucial: one must not be seen to sink beneath the level of one's peers.

Some passions respond to the relative success or failure of others, without primary reference to oneself: pity is elicited by undeserved misfortune, indignation by undeserved good fortune. But both are predicated on norms of well-being, which are correlated with social station. There are generous sentiments, such as love, by which we wish others well without advantage to ourselves; gratitude is the emotional response to a benefit that has been altruistically bestowed. But love and gratitude mark out smaller circles of intimacy and alliance within the larger, rough-and-tumble context of Aristotle's Athens, where there was always the threat of loss of station.

The attitudes that entered into the ideological construction of the emotions in ancient Greece are not the same as ours.[3] The change in perspective is no doubt in part associated with the relative neglect of the categories of honour and insult in modern social life, at least in the United States. In part, too, it reflects an altered sense of self, in which the emotions are perceived as interior states of feeling rather than responses to social interactions.

I do not wish to deny that there are broad similarities between the ancient *pathê* we have discussed in the course of this book and modern emotions, as represented by the basic emotion terms in English. Perhaps there exist, at a more general level than emotions proper, something like what Silvan Tomkins (1995) calls affects, which have a universal extension. We might imagine, for example, that the cross-cultural constants in emotions are like the four elementary tastes of bitter, sweet, sour, and salty. If we rely on taste buds alone, shutting our eyes and holding our nose, then apples and onions, which have similar textures, are indistinguishable (this was an experiment that delighted children once upon a time). Add smell, and the difference between the two is evident. Knowledge is also a factor: we recognize a taste better when we know and can name the food in question. We may think of emotions, too, as constructed on the basis of some elementary human responses, but profoundly conditioned by other sensibilities and cognitive distinctions.

The Greek emotions are specific to Greek society and to societies similar to that of the Greeks. But cultures have blind spots: we can doubtless perceive better than Aristotle himself the ways in which the *pathê* he describes form a coherent group. In turn, attention to classical Greek ideas of the emotions may illuminate some unclear aspects of our own emotional concepts. As we have seen (chapter 1, pp. 34, 39), it is only recently that psychologists have begun to investigate the emotions as responses to intentional acts, as well as the effects of emotion on belief, which was central to Aristotle's definition of a *pathos*. Finally, we may note that in no society are the emotions, either severally or as a whole, understood in a uniform way across time and place or class and gender. The views that I have been attributing to the Greeks will resonate with some people today more than others; in turn, no doubt, the Greeks themselves thought of the *pathê* variously, if indeed they all understood the term *pathos* itself to signify an emotion in Aristotle's sense of the word. It is impossible, for want of sources, to recover the nuances that corresponded to differences of social condition in classical antiquity. But I do not doubt that if we knew the whole story, there would be areas in which their conception of the emotions would come closer to our own, and others, perhaps, in which the distance would be still greater than we have so far perceived.

Notes

Preface

1 For example, I have placed the chapter on shame immediately after that on satisfaction, since both involve a discussion of a positive sentiment analogous to 'pride.' I have also postponed the chapters on love and hatred, since they both have a somewhat problematic status as emotions on Aristotle's definition.

2 But see J.M. Jones 1995, who takes the view that emotions are a function of human cognitive capacities, which is what differentiates them from the feelings that animals have; with the acquisition of language, human feelings, Jones argues, changed fundamentally.

Chapter One

1 Interestingly, English seems to owe the importance of indigo as a basic colour to Isaac Newton, although Newton himself vacillated over whether the spectrum should be divided into six or seven zones; in the end, he opted for seven because of the mystical value of that numeral (Gage 1995). For a comparison between emotion and colour, see Reddy 2001: 3–8.

2 Longinus, *On the Sublime* 22.1 speaks of 'innumerable emotions'; the Stoics provided long lists of them (Diogenes Laertius 7.111; Andronicus, *On Emotions* (*Peri pathôn*). More recently, Cohen 2003 has created a taxonomy of no fewer than 412 discrete human emotions.

3 My thanks to Hugh Mason for this reference.

4 Liddell, Scott, and Jones 1940, s.v.; E. Irwin (1974: 5–7) notes that the difficulty in interpreting Greek colour terms according to spectral values led some scholars, including Goethe and William Gladstone, to conclude that the Greeks were colour-blind.

5 Cf. Pastoureau 2001: 13–48 on the absence of a coherent category of 'blue' in classical antiquity; and Ball 2001: 233–8 on the difficulty of producing blue pigments. In English, the only basic colour terms, besides black, white, and grey, that are non-spectral in nature are brown and pink. So too, in the time of Goethe the German word 'braun' signified not only what we call 'brown' in English, which is more or less what Germans mean by 'Braun' today, but also tones in the region of violet or purple, which, unlike modern brown, are grouped with the spectral colours of the rainbow.

6 To someone who can aurally distinguish phonemes not present in English, e.g., Arabic stops, poetry in that language will yield richer aesthetic effects than to one whose ear is deaf to them.

7 Yvor Winters once analysed the verse by Robert Browning 'So wore night; the East was gray' (from 'A Serenade at the Villa') by explaining: 'The verb *wore* means literally that the night passed, but it carries with it connotations of exhaustion and attrition which belong to the condition of the protagonist; and grayness is a color which we associate with such a condition' (cited in Brooks 1970: 200). To this, Cleanth Brooks responded (201): 'But the word *wore* does not mean *literally* "that the night passed," it means literally "that the night *wore*" – whatever *wore* may mean, and as Winters' own admirable analysis indicates, *wore* "means" ... a great deal.' I would add that 'gray' too means a great deal, and that its meanings will not necessarily be the same as ostensible synonyms of 'gray' in other languages.

8 It has found an unlikely exponent, however, in the Marxist critic Terry Eagleton, who cites (2003: xii–xiv) the distinguished Italian philologist, Sebastiano Timpanaro (1975: 52) for the view that '[c]ultural continuities ... "have been rendered possible by the fact that man as a biological being has remained essentially unchanged from the beginnings of civilization to the present; and those sentiments and representations which are closest to the biological facts of human existence have changed little."' Eagleton is undeterred by the possibility that 'culturalists may wince at this cheek-by-jowl

consorting of "sentiments and representations" with "biological facts."'

9 Though the collocation of non-Europeans, children, imbeciles, and the insane may suggest a racist view, it is worth stating that this was not Darwin's intention. Rather, by demonstrating that 'the chief expressions exhibited by man are the same throughout the world,' Darwin thought to show as well that 'the several races [are] de-scended from a single parent-stock' (1998: 355). That all human beings have a common range of emotions was an argument, in Darwin's view, against innate racial differences.

10 Because the character of the response seems not to be determined by the function as such – presumably other signalling behaviours could have served as well – Darwin implicitly appeals to one of his three basic explanatory principles for emotive expression, namely, anti-thesis. According to this principle, once a certain state of mind is associated with particular habits, then, 'when a directly opposite state of mind is induced, there is a strong and involuntary tendency to the performance of movements of a directly opposite nature, though these are of no use' (1998: 34).

11 Buss notes that 'only 5 percent of the male elephant seals do 85 per-cent of the mating' (1994: 9); a colleague has pointed out to me that in this respect, the analogy with human beings obtains principally in high school.

12 Buss writes: 'Since all an ancestral man needed to do to reproduce was to impregnate a woman, casual sex without commitment would have sufficed for him' (1994: 49). Sufficed for what? Unless he was going to tend his progeny, what need had he to be sure that they were his? Buss further explains (2000: 52) that by being faithful, 'men risk wasting all the mating effort they expended, including the time, energy, and gifts they have invested while courting a woman. The man also incurs what economists call "opportunity costs," the missed opportunties with other women as a result of devoting all their effort to one woman.' The image of primitive men diversifying their sexual portfolio is anachronistic, and arbitrarily projects onto them a proprietary interest in their offspring.

13 Even neuro-scientists tend to produce quixotic explanations of be-haviour when they seek evolutionary explanations. Thus, Edmund Rolls (1999: 229) suggests that masturbation effects the removal

from the vagina or the testes of old sperm; thus the male at the time of intercourse 'will have many young sperm especially of the killer and fertilizing type' (cf. Baker and Bellis 1995), and be better prepared to engage in 'sperm warfare' (230; the term is taken from Baker 1996). More immediate reasons for the practice suggest themselves.

14 Descartes recognized that there are innumerable subspecies of the basic types, which he defines in the third part of his essay.

15 We may add that the Cartesian emphasis on expression coincided with a view of the self or soul as a distinct internal domain, which one was obliged to read or interpret by means of surface manifestations in the face and body.

16 Christopher Wright (1984: 94) appears to take an opposite view, for example in his comment on Poussin's *Judgment of Solomon*, painted in the late 1640s: 'All the figures are seen in exaggerated gestures of anger, accusation, fear, embarrassment and violence. Poussin was expressing, through the means of this composition, his whole theory of emotion. Each figure must be made to typify the specific emotions concerned.' So too he remarks of the *Lamentation over the Dead Christ*: 'Each figure is taken to an extreme of exaggeration, saturated with grief, almost over-acting' (114–15); compare too the vivid expressions on the faces of Poussin's early *The Martyrdom of St Erasmus*, or his late *St Peter Healing a Sick Man*. Still, the individual figures seem poised in a choreographed arrangement, bound up with the events of which they are part. The representation of a personal emotion does not stand free of the context so as to claim the viewer's exclusive attention.

17 So too, Grinker (1998: 78–9) writes of the Korean concept of *han*: 'Although *han* is loosely and simply defined as "resentment," it requires an elaborate discourse to explicate it more fully. *Han* refers to a consciousness of ongoing trauma and a lack of resolution and reconciliation. Paradoxically, however, *han* also provides a means of resolution ... *Han* is a distinctive psychological concept ..., a complex of suppressed emotion.' My thanks to Stephen Epstein for this reference. Ayumi Nagai informs me that there are no precise English equivalents for the Japanese expressions 'natsukashii,' denoting the 'feeling we have when we think about (or see or hear or smell) something we haven't seen for a while'; 'sabishii' (or 'samishii'), the

'feeling that we're "missing" something'; and 'setsunai,' the 'feeling we get when we want something, but can't get it' (though not used of material things). Cf. Metcalf and Huntington 1991: 60: 'Cultural differences work on human emotional reactions, just as they do on supposedly universal modes of reasoning or requirements of institutional arrangement'; and Reddy 2001: 34–62.

18 Cf. Ekman 1984; and Oatley 2003: 169. LeDoux (1996: 112–14) provides a summary of the various theories; see also Hillman 1992: 40–1.

19 In an undergraduate class to which I had assigned the second book of Aristotle's *Rhetoric* (in translation), I asked the students each to draw up a list of ten emotions. It was remarkable how small an overlap there was between their inventories and the passions analysed by Aristotle. Anger was prominent in both sets, but beyond that, there was little agreement. Among the emotions suggested by the students which do not figure in Aristotle's discussion were grief, sorrow, sadness, happiness, jealousy, missing someone, and loneliness. By contrast, none of the students mentioned pity, envy, indignation, shame, gentleness or satisfaction, confidence, rivalry, or gratitude. Cf. Barbalet 1998: 82: 'Confidence is conventionally not thought of as an emotion' – though it figures in Aristotle's inventory. Planalp (1999: 176) cites Schoeck 1966 for the view that 'envy is particularly unmentionable in the United States because Americans do not want to admit that they are not all equals.'

20 For example, the pre-Aristotelian *Rhetoric to Alexander* (1428a36–b5) includes under *pathos* sensations such as pleasure and pain, as well as desires.

21 Cf. the Spanish translation of Christa Wolf's *Kassandra* (1986: 14–15): 'De cómo el asalto de sentimientos irreconciliables – asombro, emoción, admiración, horror, desconcierto y, sí, incluso una infame hilaridad – desembocó en un ataque de risa' ('How the attack of contradictory emotions [*sentimientos*] – shock, suspense [*emoción*], wonder, fear, confusion, and yes, even a shameful hilarity – ended in uncontrollable laughter'); and Moliner 1990: 1079, s.v. 'emoción': 'Alteración afectiva intensa que acompaña o sigue inmediatamente a la experiencia de un suceso feliz o desgraciado o que significa un cambio profundo en la vida sentimental ... Puede consistir también en interés expectante o ansioso con que el sujeto participa en algo

que está ocurriendo' ('An intense change of feeling that accompanies or follows immediately upon the experience of a happy or unfortunate event, or that indicates a deep alternation in one's affective life ... It can also consist in an eager or anticipatory interest that one feels at something occurring at the moment').

22 Cf. Harris 2001: 36: 'The study of classical emotions has been seriously impeded by our failure to realize, with a few noteworthy exceptions, that the relevant Greek and Latin terminology is very unlikely to correspond neatly to modern English usage.'

23 Cf. Russell and Fernández-Dols 1997b: 4: 'Linking faces to emotions may be common sense, but it has turned out to be the single most important idea in the psychology of emotion. It is central to a research program that claims Darwin as its originator.' On the small number of basic, innate emotions presupposed by this program, see p. 11; on the universality hypothesis, pp. 14–17; and for an excellent summary of the debate over facial expression as a sign of emotion, see Parkinson 1995: 121–38.

24 This argument was anticipated by Landis (1934; cited by Fernández-Dols and Ruiz-Belda 1997: 258–9), but the results of his experiments met with incredulity.

25 In a further study, Fernández-Dols and Carroll (1997: 275) ask what 'are the figure-ground interactions between facial expression and context? The answer implicit in the mainstream view of facial expression is very simple: There are none.'

26 Of course, it continues to be part of popular attitudes towards the emotions, as reflected, for example, in modern fiction and popular thought; cf. Eloy Martínez 2002: 56: 'The emotions are always irrational and possess human beings in the same irrevocable and unavoidable manner as diseases' ('Las pasiones son siempre insensatas y se apoderan de los seres humanos del mismo modo fatal e inevitable que las enfermedades'); or Lt Colonel Bryan McCoy, commander of the Third Battalion in the U.S.-led invasion of Iraq: '"I'm not allowed to have the luxury of emotions to guide my decisions," he said. "It'll cloud my decisions, and I'll make a bad one if I submit to that. I have to look at everything very clinically"' (quoted in Maass 2003: 35). The view of the emotions as irrational was implicit in the 'mentalités' school of cultural history (see Rosenwein 2003: 434); it was also a commonplace view in classical antiquity: cf.

Euripides, *Medea* 446–50, and Antiphon, *On the Murder of Herodes* 71–2, with Harris 2001: 169–73 and 178: 'Herodotus was one of the first surviving writers to create an opposition between anger and rational decision making.' For the contrary view, cf. Shakespeare, *A Midsummer Night's Dream* 1.1.234: 'Love looks not with the eyes, but with the mind' – this for love's power to make the vilest object appear attractive.

27 Cf. also Lazarus, Kanner, and Folkman 1980: 198; and Solomon 1984: 249: 'an understanding of the conceptual and learned appetitive functions of emotion is all that there is in identifying and distinguishing them from each other and from non-emotions'; also Frijda 1993; there is a survey of cognitivist views in LeDoux 1996: 22–72; see also Buck 2000; Gainotti 2000; and Konstan 2001a: 8–10.

28 Fortenbaugh (2002: 111 n. 1) rightly challenges Martha Nussbaum's view (2001: 64) that Aristotle 'views pain itself as an intentional state with cognitive content'; rather, Aristotle 'distinguishes between the cognition and the pain involved in emotions like fear, anger and pity. The former is intentional; the latter is so only in a derivative way.' On pain and pleasure as sensations, see Fortenbaugh p. 17.

29 Aristotle, however, holds that emotions, or at least some emotions, involve both pain and pleasure; see below, pp. 33–4).

30 Fortenbaugh notes (2002: 100) that for Aristotle, 'believing (*doxazein* 427b21) is not idly entertaining a thought; it is thinking that something actually is the case. And when the belief concerns things terrible or encouraging, then emotional response follows: one feels frightened or emboldened, seeks safety or acts aggressively' (I wonder whether this sequence of belief followed by an emotional feeling quite captures Aristotle's view). However, the mere image or *phantasia* of a thing, independently of belief, 'does not have the same effect. Much as we view a painting or drawing of something threatening without becoming afraid, – we do not confuse an artistic representation with reality – so we may imagine a threatening situation without being frightened, for we do not believe the danger real.'

31 Aristotle holds that animals possess 'similarities to intelligent understanding' (*tês peri tên dianoian suneseôs homoiotêtes*, *History of Animals* 588a23–4; cf. *Politics* 1332b5–6 for human beings alone

possessing reason (*logos*). Compare also *Nicomachean Ethics* 1098a3–4, *Eudemian Ethics* 1224a26–7, *Metaphysics* 980b26–8; *History of Animals* 641b8–9; and Sorabji 1993: 13. Hence, only man can feel happiness (*Parts of Animals* 656a5). So too, animals are incapable of *philia* or love in the full sense of the term (*Eudemian Ethics* 7.2, 1236b6). The elder Pliny (*Natural History* 7, proem 5) affirms that only man can experience grief, fear of death, and hostility. Fear, according to Aristotle, makes people more delibera-tive (*Rhetoric* 2.5, 1385a5; cf. chapter 5, p. 135); but only human beings can deliberate (*History of Animals* 488b24–5). For the ex-treme position of the Stoics, who held that the difference between human beings and other creatures ruled out the possibility of justice between them, see Diogenes Laertius 7.129; cf. Cicero, *De officiis* 1.50 and, for a similar view, Epicurus, *Principal Doctrine* 32. Con-trast Plutarch, *On the Cleverness of Animals*, e.g. 960–2, where the claim is made that animals do have a share both in reason and *pathê* (966B); cf. Scully 2002: 227–8; also Newmyer 2006. On an-cient attitudes toward animals, see also the survey in Franco 2000–1.

32 The emotions for Aristotle (and for the Stoics: cf. Seneca, *On Anger* 1.3.3–4) pertain to a world fully symbolized in language. Even if they have their origin in animal responses, human emotions and the judgments they involve are possible only in human society. Evolu-tionary explanations of the emotions fail, among other reasons, be-cause the reactions favoured by natural selection at the pre-human level are categorically distinct from human emotions.

33 Cf. Oliker (1998: 20): 'The cultural ethos of individualism encour-aged people to view themselves as distinct, complex, and interesting – to develop identities that could not be specified by their social roles'; as a result, people tended toward introspection and the cultiv-ation of 'individual selves and inner lives.' A sense of inwardness, personal uniqueness, and separation from others may generate a view of the self as wholly autonomous and sealed off from the outside world – a monad within which the emotions circulate in an endless loop, feeding on themselves.

34 It is worth noting the absence in this list of feeling tone, or what is called the 'quale' in philosophical literature on the emotions. There is no reliable way of measuring such states of consciousness, or of determining whether a given state corresponds to a specific emo-

tion. On the physiological basis of 'feelings,' see Damasio 1994: 160–4; Kim 1996: 69–70, following Hilary Putnam, argues that mental states cannot be reduced to states of the brain (or the body generally) if a sense of pain (for example) is the same for creatures with different physiological systems (the 'multiple realization' argument). Of course, there are typical descriptions of feelings, and these vary from one culture to another; for some vivid Greek metaphors, see Padel 1992: 81–98.

35 Action is relevant to ancient ideas of the emotions, but does not play the central role it does in modern models that stress the function of emotion in producing motivation; cf. the *Encyclopedia Britannica* entry on 'Human Emotion and Motivation,' cited above, or the volume *Socioemotional Development* (Thompson 1990) in the *Nebraska Symposium on Motivation*. Robert Gordon (1987: 84) explains emotions as 'wish-frustrations,' consisting of a belief and a desire, and affirms that emotions 'motivate' us to act in regard to things we 'care about.'

36 Modern action movies, with their chase scenes, explosions, suspense, and sudden violence, produce intense sensations in the audience, but these are not emotions in the Aristotelian sense of *pathê*.

37 Thus, I do not mean simply to contrast modern individualism with the social rivalry characteristic of Athens's face-to-face culture.

38 Harris (2001: 78) notes the 'change which occurred in the practice of Greek artists in the fourth century B.C. ... Sculptors and painters began to represent emotional states for their own sake.' Harris quotes Pliny, *Natural History* 35.98 on Aristeides: 'He, first of all, depicted the mind and attitudes [*animus et sensus*] of man – what the Greeks call *ethos* – and also emotions [*perturbationes*].' See also Zanker 2004: 152–61.

39 Brilliant (2000: 16) notes Cicero's Stoic approval of mastering pain (*Tusculan Disputations* 2.23.55), 'thereby translating an *exemplum doloris*, such as the *Laocoön*, into an *exemplum virtutis*.' Contrast Winckelmann's view (1968 [orig. 1764]: 4.10.1.6; cited by Brilliant p. 17) of the statue as 'representing a man in extreme suffering ... While the muscles are swelling and the nerves are straining with torture, the determined spirit is visible in the turgid forehead ... The expression of the face is complaining, but not screaming; the eyes are turned for help to a higher power. The mouth is full of sorrow,

and the sunken under lip is heavy with the same feeling; but in the
upper lip, which is drawn upwards, this expression is mingled with
one of pain.'

40 On expressiveness in art, cf. Cicero *Orator* 70–4; Cicero describes
the sadness visible in the portraits of several figures present at the
immolation of Agamemnon's daughter, Iphigeneia, but adds that
Agamemnon is represented covering himself with his garment,
because 'that extreme of grief cannot be reproduced with a paint-
brush' (translation is that of Perry 2002: 154).

41 It is worth noting too that in the theatre in Aristotle's time, the
faces of actors were concealed by masks, which necessarily preserved a uniform expression throughout the drama.

42 Mackay (2002: 62) shows how the complex use of allusion in black-
figured vase painting works to 'bring to the forefront additional
contexts in order to heighten the potential emotional content of the
picture.' Mackay emphasizes the use of contrastive references, e.g.
to a happy moment such as a wedding that precedes the tragic
episode that is the principal scene on the vase, but her examples
also reveal how vase painters systematically evoked the causes and
context of an emotional representation.

43 Corbeill notes further (2004: 159) how, according to Tacitus *Annals*
1, the aristocracy under Tiberius 'arranged their expressions (*vultu …
composito*) so as not to seem too happy at Augustus' death or too
upset at the new beginning … The Republican model of truth in
appearances has been subverted; the faces of the elite have become
texts that are deliberately misinterpreted by Tiberius, a perverse
reader' (159).

I do not mean to suggest that Greeks of the classical period did
not imagine that the face could reveal emotion, although more
often they looked not so much for signs of passion, which could be
inferred from the situation, as signs of character, which could not.
This is also the case for the physiognomic treatises, the earliest
of which go back to the time of Aristotle; cf. pseudo-Aristotle
Physiognomonica 805a.18–31 and 805a.33–b.9 on *êthos*; 806a.12–18
and 806b.28–34 on how facial expressions of *pathê* (e.g. anger) may
reveal temperament (irascibility); and 808b.27–34 on the expression
of *pathê* in animals. Cf. Xenophon, *Memorabilia* 3.10.1–5 for the
mimetic representation of character (the *êthos* of the soul, e.g. the

difference between a proud and servile nature), which Socrates
argues is revealed through the eyes. Socrates then questions the
sculptor Cleiton on his technique for the life-like representation
of athletes (3.10.8): 'Does not representing the *pathê* of bodies in
action give pleasure to the viewers ...? And shouldn't one represent
the threatening look in the eyes of men who are fighting, and
imitate the glance of the happy victors ...? It is necessary, then,
that a sculptor represent the deeds [*erga*] of the soul in the physical
appearance [*eidos*].' Xenophon clearly expects that sculpture will
capture something of the emotions of the subject, above all in the
eyes.

Ann Mackay has pointed out to me in a personal communication
that the Exekias 'Ajax' (Boulogne-sur-mer 558 = *ABV* [= Beazley
1956] 145.18, para. 60, Add.[2] 40) reveals furrows on the brow and
cheek of the hero that are, quite exceptionally, indicative of strong
emotion (for general dicussion of this image, see Mackay 2002: 66–8;
cf. Toohey 2004: 171–2). Peter Toohey (2004: 15–20) argues that
classical vase paintings in fact give evidence of certain emotional
states, in particular melancholy, that are not described in literature
until much later, when the literary tradition was able to '"catch up"
with the insights exemplified by the Eumenides Painter's Orestes'
(p. 20; the reference is to the Apulian red-figure vase painting ascribed to the so-called Eumenides Painter and labelled 'The Purifica-
tion of Orestes,' dating to the first quarter of the fourth century BC;
the vase is number CP 710 in the Louvre Museum). Toohey observes
that 'the picture itself provides no explanation, no etiology for
Orestes' state of mind ... It aims not at explanation but at the con-
veying of affect ... It presents to us a vision of sorrow without cause'
(25) – not an emotion in the Aristotelian sense, I would add. Toohey
considers that, in modern terms, Orestes (along with Ajax, Hercules,
Bellerophon, and even Jason) would be classified as manic-depressives
(34). John J. Herrmann Jr, curator of classical art at the Museum of
Fine Arts in Boston, has pointed out to me that Apulian vases,
which derive from Greek towns in South Italy, are more given to
indicating differences in facial expression than are contemporary
vases produced in Greece. The conventions of Apulian vases are
indeed quite different in various respects, including painterly
technique.

274 / Notes to pages 31–3

44 Jakob Wisse (1989: 292–4) has drawn attention to a difference
between Aristotle's treatment of pity in the *Rhetoric* and Cicero's in
De oratore (2.211; cf. *De inventione* 1.108), where Cicero places a
new emphasis on the personal experience of the pitier as a factor
that enables pity. In the words of Antonius, a character in Cicero's
dialogue, 'Pity is aroused when he who listens can be brought to
refer to his own circumstances [*ad suas res revocat*] – the bitter
things that he has endured or fears – that which he is lamenting in
the case of the other, so that he may, while contemplating the other,
frequently turn back to himself [*ad se ipsum revertatur*].' So too
Virgil's Dido tells Aeneas: 'not unacquainted with misfortune, I have
learned to help those who are suffering' (*Aeneid* 1.630: *non ignara
mali miseris succurrere disco*).

45 Reddy (2001: 171–2) writes of eighteenth-century France: 'The court,
its manners, and its fashions became the epitome of immorality
and corruption ... Doubts about sincerity had to arise, when open
emotionality no longer gave an unambiguous message.'

46 Compare too the Stoic analogy between emotions and a person who
is running and cannot stop when he chooses to; the emotions, once
aroused, continue independently of the original impulse. In Ovid's
series of elegies *The Loves*, Cupid's arrow inspires in the poet an
erotic passion before there is any object for it; his mistress Corinna
first makes her appearance in the third elegy (1.3.1–2); see Cahoon
1985: 29; and Greene 1998: 72. Toohey (2004: 4–5, 81–7, etc.)
identifies a change in the representation of the emotions with the
emergence of boredom, melancholy, depression, and lovesickness as
well-defined emotional states. Contrast Harris 2001: 16: 'Aristotle
and all the other classical authors who defined anger agreed, in
effect, that it was an emotion with a specific object, which is precisely what a mood is *not*.' On anxiety in particular, note Philodemus's distinction in *On Anger* between *orgê* (anger) as a rational
emotion that the sage too may experience and *thumos* (temper), an
irrational passion based on empty belief.

47 For other lists of emotions, see Aristotle, *Rhetoric* 3.19, 1419b24–6,
where, in speaking of the epilogue to a speech as the place to rouse
emotion, he mentions *eleos* (pity), *deinôsis* (perhaps = shock or
outrage), *orgê* (anger), *misos* (hatred), *phthonos* (envy), *zêlos* (emulation), and *eris* (i.e., bad competitiveness). Cicero, *de Oratore* 2.206,

says that the most important emotions to arouse are *amor, odium, iracundia, invidia, misericordia, spes, laetitia, timor, molestia,* which May and Wisse render 'affection, hate, anger, envy, pity, hope, joy, fear, and grief'; this is Aristotle, plus *spes, laetitia,* and *molestia.* In *Brutus* 188, Cicero says that a crowd listening to a good speaker *gaudet, dolet, ridet, plorat, favet, odit, contemnit, invidet, ad misericordiam inducitur, ad pudendum, ad pigendum; irascitur, mitigatur, sperat, timet* ('feels joy and pain, laughs and cries, lauds and hates, scorns, envies, is moved to pity, shame, and disgust, grows angry, calms down, hopes, and fears'; cf. Marincola 2003). Cicero has clearly added representatives of the Stoic fourfold classification of emotions, namely, pleasure, pain, desire or anticipation, and fear or avoidance, rendered in the first passage as *spes, laetitia, timor, molestia,* and less distinctly in the second as *gaudet, dolet, ridet, plorat. Irascitur* and *mitigatur* = Aristotle's *orgê* and *praünsis.* See also Dionysius of Halicarnassus *Demosthenes* 22 (1.322, Usher 1974–85), who says that when he reads Demosthenes' speeches, he is led to feel one emotion after another (*enthousiô te kai deuro kakeise agomai, pathos heteron ex heterou metalambanôn, apistôn, agôniôn, dediôs, kataphronôn, misôn, eleôn, eunoôn, orgizomenos, phthonôn, hapanta ta pathê metalambanôn, hosa kratein pephuken anthrôpinês gnômês,* which Usher translates: 'I am transported: I am led hither and thither, feeling one emotion after another – disbelief, anguish, terror, contempt, hatred, pity, goodwill, anger, envy – every emotion in turn that can sway the human mind.' Of this list, the first two items are odd as emotions – disbelief and anguish – and are better taken as responses; anguish perhaps = *lupê,* while *apistôn* suggests amazement or wonder (*thauma*), which was considered an emotion in various contexts. Cf. Horstmanshoff 1999: 261 on the list in the medical writer Caelius Aurelianus, who 'caractérise les émotions: *appetere, desiderare, timor, maestitudo* et *iracundia* comme des *passiones animae,* des affections de l'âme, distinctes des *passiones corporis,* des maladies du corps'; Galen, *On Diagnosing and Curing Ailments of the Soul* 3.5.7 K., who cites as *pathê psukhês: thumos kai orgê, kai phobos kai lupê, kai phthonos, kai epithumia sphodra philein ê misein hotioun pragma* ('temper and anger, fear and pain, envy, and an intense desire to love or hate anything'); and Gregory of Nyssa, *On the Beatitudes* 44.1228.21–33. See

Lada 1993: 99–100 on the importance of arousing emotions in the audience, and on the requirement that the orator himself feel them in order to induce them the better, Quintilian 6.2.26–36 with Bons and Lane 2003: 141–4.

48 Frede 1996 argues that the mixture of pleasure and pain in the emotions as described in the *Rhetoric* betrays the still lively influence upon Aristotle of Plato's account in the *Philebus*; by the time he wrote the *Nicomachean Ethics*, Aristotle had moved away from the Platonic notion of 'process-pleasures' to his own mature view of 'activity-pleasures' (p. 278). Striker 1996 draws the line rather between the brief account of the emotions in *Rhetoric* 1.10–11, where Plato's influence is still palpable, and the more detailed description of the individual emotions in *Rhetoric* 2.2–11; here, even if painful emotions may be associated with pleasures, pleasure is not a necessary ingredient in them (291). Striker argues that in this part Aristotle is clearly moving towards a dichotomized class-ification of emotions according to pleasure vs. pain (292), which anticipates the later elaboration of this opposition by the Stoics (294). Aspasius, in his digression on the emotions in his commen-tary on Aristotle's *Nicomachean Ethics* (42.27–47.2, Heylbut 1889), affirms that the emotions are grouped generically according to pleasure (*hêdonê*) and pain (*lupê*); Sorabji 1999 argues that desire or appetite is also essential to the Aristotelian classification.

49 Cf. Spinoza 1989: 223; the translation by Shirley (1982: 151) reads: 'The emotion called a passive experience is a confused idea whereby the mind affirms a greater or less force of existence of its body, or part of its body, than was previously the case, and by the occurrence of which the mind is determined to think of one thing rather than another.'

50 Cf. Ortega y Gasset 1976 (orig. 1924): 54: 'Perhaps the vision of someone in love is more acute than that of a lukewarm individual; perhaps in every object there are qualities and values that only reveal themselves to the excited gaze ... Typically, the case is that someone in love with another person or thing has a more precise image of them than one who is indifferent ... No, love neither lies, nor is blind, nor deludes: what it does is situate the beloved in a light so favorable that the most hidden charms become apparent.'

See also Reddy 2001: 94–5 for a definition of emotion as sets of thoughts that tend to be activated together.

51 Parkinson (1995: 285) states: 'I would argue that anger does not depend on concluding that someone else is to blame, as appraisal theory has implied, but rather is an interpersonal tactic for blaming someone else'; I would rather say the two processes are interdependent.

52 Value terms typically have a range of meanings that are not always reducible to a single core sense; see Rademaker 2005: 14–35.

Chapter Two

1 Solomon goes on the indicate how risky this assumption is. Cf. also Rosaldo 1984: 144–5.

2 The mention of pain and pleasure may be a succinct way of distinguishing emotional responses from those based exclusively on reason or *enthymemes*, a topic that Aristotle treated with particular pride in the first book of the *Rhetoric*. The same criterion is invoked, however, at *Nicomachean Ethics* 2.5, 1105b21–3.

3 The relationship between *phantasia* and *aisthêsis* in Aristotle is controversial; the most relevant evidence is *On the Soul* 3.3 and *On Dreams* 2, 459a15–19, where *phantasia* is said to be a motion that arises from (or as a result of) the activity of perception. Nussbaum (1996: 307) suggests that *phantasia* here is not so much a technical term as the abstract noun corresponding to the verb *phainomai*. Aristotle does not make clear just what the nature is of the pain that accompanies anger, but it seems reasonable to suppose that it results from direct perception of something harmful or unpleasant, rather than from memory or anticipation; contrast the case of fear, which Aristotle defines as 'arising from the *phantasia* of a future evil that is fatal or harmful' (*ek phantasias mellontos kakou phthartikou ê lupêrou*, 2.5, 1382a21–2).

4 Aristotle adds that by dwelling on revenge in our minds (*dianoia*), the *phantasia* that thereby arises instils pleasure, analogous to that we feel in dreams (2.2, 1378b1–9). I cannot agree with Grimaldi (1988: 25 ad 1378b1–2) that '[t]he feeling dominant in the emotion anger is *hêdonê*.' Compare *Nicomachean Ethics* 4.5, 1126a21–2,

where Aristotle says that 'revenge ends one's anger, instilling pleasure in place of pain.'

5 Cf. Aristotle's definition of pity as a painful feeling in response to 'a perceived evil that is either fatal or painful' (*epi phainomenôi kakôi phthartikôi ê lupêrôi*) that has befallen another person who has not deserved it (2.8, 1385b13–14). There is no need to take *phainomenos* in the sense of 'manifest' or 'conspicuous' (e.g. Roberts 1984: 2195; cf. Grimaldi 1988: 21 ad 1378a31–3), still less to delete *phainomenês* before *timôrias* (Spengel, Ross).

6 At *Topics* 4.5, 125b28–34, Aristotle states that pain cannot be equated with anger, since pain is prior to anger and not vice versa; I take it that the painful thing upon which anger follows is just the slight. At 4.6, 127b26–32, Aristotle argues that pain involved in anger and the suspicion (*hupolêpsis*) of a slight are two distinct aspects of anger. Finally, at 6.13, 151a14–19, Aristotle states that being caused by pain is not the same as being accompanied by pain.

7 Spite (*epêreasmos*), which is listed as one of the three types of slight in Aristotle's treatment of anger (2.2, 1378b14), is also cited as one of the causes of hatred or enmity (2.4, 1382a2); it would appear that, in certain circumstances, spite can generate a hostile response that is not accompanied by pain, and is therefore distinct from anger.

8 Cf. Solomon 1984: 250: 'Anger ... is essentially a *judgmental* emotion, a perception of an offense (as Aristotle argued in *Rhetoric*). It consists of a series of concepts and judgments that among other ingredients, involve the concept of blame.'

9 Lazarus, Kanner, and Folkman (1980: 198), for example, define emotion as 'consisting of cognitive appraisals, action impulses, and patterned somatic reactions,' and assert: 'Emotions and cognitions are thus inseparable.' Solomon (1984: 249) states (and endorses) a strong version of 'a cognitive theory of the emotions' which holds that 'an understanding of the conceptual and learned appetitive functions of emotion is all that there is in identifying and distinguishing them from each other and from non-emotions' (the weak version is that these are sufficient conditions). For a survey of modern studies of cognitive aspects of the emotions, together with a critique of definitions of the emotions based exclusively on cognitive properties, see Griffiths 1997: 21–43; see further chapter 1, pp. 20–4.

10 Cf. also, e.g., Damasio 1994: xi: 'I had been advised early in life that sound decisions came from a cool head, that emotions and reason did not mix any more than oil and water'; and cf. Hillman 1992: 188; and Bailey 1983: 24: 'The dichotomy between reason and emotion is part of our overt culture; that is, part of the shield of falsification by which we make life comprehensible'; see also Barbalet 1998: 29–61. The view has a long pedigree: Plutarch, e.g., in his *Comparison of Theseus and Romulus* (3.1), speaks of the 'irrational temper' (*thumos alogistos*) and 'anger's unreasoning haste' (*orgê ekhousa takhos aboulon*) that drove Theseus to slay his son and Romulus his brother; cf. Alexiou 1999: 104.

11 Introductions to this approach may be found in Zahn-Waxler, Cummings, and Iannotti 1986, and Barkow, Cosmides, and Tooby 1992. In a popular vein are Buss 1994 and 2000, and Lewis, Amini, and Lannon 2000. Anger has been defended from a phenomenological perspective, e.g. by Milhaven 1989; for an accessible and sensible survey of views on anger, see Tavris 1989.

12 She may simply be startled. On the difference between fear and being startled, cf. Oatley 1992: 19; and Nussbaum 1996: 306.

13 Compare Strawson 1974: 5: 'If someone treads on my hand accidentally, while trying to help me, the pain may be no less acute than if he treads on it in contemptuous disregard of my existence or with a malevolent wish to injure me. But I shall generally feel in the second case a kind and degree of resentment that I shall not feel in the first.' One's feelings change as new knowledge of another's motives is acquired.

14 On the theory that stimuli resulting in emotional responses may travel by two distinct pathways in the brain, the shove, indicating danger, might be imagined as travelling directly from the thalamus to the amygdala, triggering the relevant reaction, while the thalamus also transmits information to the sensory cortex, which processes it and sends it in turn to the amygdala, permitting a second, more reflective response (the shove was likely to be accidental, etc.). See LeDoux 1996: 168–78; and Elster 1999b: 31–5.

15 Cf. Oatley (1992: 19): 'I may suddenly feel frightened if the vehicle in which I am traveling seems to be heading for an accident. I evaluate a perception in relation to my concerns for safety, though not necessarily consciously. This may be the common experience in

such situations. But a person confident that an accident would not occur, perhaps the one who is driving, or the one who is unconcerned about personal safety at that moment, may not feel fear.' If the woman in my story were to persist in feeling angry, perhaps as a result of heightened physiological tension, she would undoubtedly produce a narrative that justified it.

16 Modern English speakers are inclined to identify a wider range of causes or anger (or irritation), including frustration, noise, and crowds; see Tavris 1989: 164–77. Plutarch continues to see mockery and other insults as chief causes of anger, although he, like others of his time, believes that a wise person should rise above such provocations; cf. *On Controlling Anger* 454D, 460D–E, Alexiou 1999: 105.

17 On the idea of superiority in connection with anger, see Viano 2003.

18 One might suppose that Aristotle excludes revenge or retribution as a cause of anger on the grounds that the victim is aware that he has earned it, and, as Aristotle says, we do not get angry when we perceive that we are suffering justly (cf. *NE* 5.8, 1135b25–9, where Aristotle remarks that 'anger resides in a perceived injustice [*adikia*]'). But what of harm inflicted for the sake of personal advantage? Aristotle's reasoning is clearly the same in both cases: getting even with another, or doing harm for the sake of gain, do not in themselves betray a belief that the target of such behaviour is of no importance, and hence do not count as slights, which are the only grounds for anger. For fuller discussion, see Konstan 2004.

19 Yet the difference is not, perhaps, as extreme as it may seem. André and Lelord (2002: 45) report that 'an Australian researcher asked 158 employees to describe an event at the workplace that provoked their anger'; the result was that 44% identified being treated in an unjust manner; 23% being witness to incorrect behaviour; and 15% being witness to incompetence on the job; while 11% pointed to being an object of contempt or disrespect, and 7% to enduring a public humiliation (45–6, citing Fitness 2000). To treat another unjustly, if there is no advantage to be gained, is a sign of disrespect.

20 For the near equation of anger and hatred, cf., e.g., Baird and Rosenbaum 1999: 10. Bishop Butler (1896: 139–44) distinguishes between deliberate anger (or resentment) as a necessarily moral emotion and what he calls 'sudden anger,' an instinctive response to pain or harm that does not necessarily entail a judgment of injury or

injustice on the part of another (I am grateful to Charles Griswold for calling my attention to this passage).

21 Stocker (1996: 266–7) rightly distinguishes the causes of enmity from those of anger in Aristotle.

22 In *Topics* 8.1, 156a27–b3, Aristotle confronts the objection that anger towards parents does not entail a desire for revenge: in fact it does, he argues, although the pain to be inflicted is limited to remorse.

23 If hatred does not involve pain, does it qualify as a *pathos* on Aristotle's definition, which stipulates that emotions must be attended by pleasure and pain (2.1, 1378a21–2; cf. J.M. Cooper 1996: 243; and Fortenbaugh 2002: 114, cited in chapter 1, p. 34)? In the *Nicomachean Ethics*, Aristotle states that *philia* resembles a settled state of character or *hexis*, since it is accompanied by deliberate choice (*proairesis*), and he coins the term *philêsis* – a 'feeling of love' – to denote the *pathos* (8.5, 1157b28–32). But there he is concerned principally with *philia* in the sense of friendship (that is, between *philoi*). In the *Rhetoric*, however, *philia* and hatred (*misos*) are treated as *pathê* (as also at *NE* 1105b21–3). Aristotle perhaps supposed that the wish (*boulesthai*) that good things accrue to a friend (or bad to an enemy) is accompanied by a *phantasia* of its fulfilment, just as the desire (*orexis*) for revenge is in the case of anger. If so, both love and hatred would be accompanied by pleasure (J.M. Cooper [1996: 248] notes that hatred ought not to be a pleasurable emotion; but Aristotle, as we have seen, does not divide the emotions on the axis of pleasure vs. pain). See further chapter 9, p. 192.

24 Muellner (1996: 31) understands *mênis* as 'the irrevocable cosmic sanction that prohibits some characters from taking their superiors for equals and others from taking their equals for inferiors,' a definition that suits the resentment that Achilles feels towards Agamemnon.

25 So too, Harris (2001: 131) observes that 'the hero's rage, first against Agamemnon, later against the Trojan prince Hector, gives the poem its principal structure' (cf. 143: 'The second of Achilles' great angers'); and Lateiner 2004: 27: 'Achilleus' rage at Hektor replaces and surpasses his rage at Agamemnon.' George Robertson (1999: 5) comments that '[t]he Achilleus whom we see towards the end of the poem is motivated by emotional forces similar to those that prompt

his desire to kill Agamemnon in Book 1,' forces that are indicated by
his blazing eyes. I grant that the intensity of Achilles' passion in the
two contexts is comparable, as Robertson argues, but stop short at
characterizing the emotions as being entirely the same. Robertson
has kindly informed me that he finds the above account cogent.

26 After Achilles and Agamemnon are reconciled, Agamemnon
prepares to deliver the gifts he had promised him if he would return
to battle (19.184–97). Achilles, however, prefers to put off the
exchange and go immediately into battle for the sake of the men
whom Hector cut down while Zeus granted him glory (*kudos*,
19.204), and to dine only at nightfall, when 'we may avenge the
outrage' (*teisaimetha lôbên*, 19.208). Does the term *lôbê* here
suggest that Achilles regards Hector's rampage as an insult? Achilles
uses the verbal form (*lôbaomai*) of Agamemnon's behaviour in
book 1 (232, repeated by Thersites at 2.242), and later refuses Agamemnon's gifts until such time as he shall compensate for the
'heart-rending *lôbê*' (9.387). Clearly, then, the word can pertain to
the kind of affront or insolence that has led Achilles to withdraw
from battle. The noun *lôbêtêr*, which is applied to Thersites (2.275)
by the Greek army, by Diomedes to Paris for employing the bow
rather than the spear (11.385), and by Priam to his remaining sons
now that Hector is dead (24.239), seems a more general term of
abuse. Hector in turn reproaches Paris for being a *lôbê* in the eyes of
others (3.42), and when Hector challenges one of the Achaeans to an
individual duel, Menelaus declares that it would be a *lôbê* if no one
volunteered to confront him (7.97); here, 'scandal' or 'disgrace'
seems the relevant meaning (at 24.531, Achilles says that he on
whom Zeus bestows only evils is *lôbêtos*, 'subject to outrage').

In Book 11, Peisander and Hippolochus, two sons of Antimachus,
plead for their life with Agamemnon. Antimachus had been bribed
by Paris to oppose the return of Helen, and when Menelaus and
Odysseus came to Troy to claim her back, proposed killing them.
Now, says Agememnon, 'you will pay for [*tisete*] the foul *lôbê* of
your father' (11.142). *Lôbê* here clearly signifies outrageous action:
slaying unarmed ambassadors and defending the unjust seizure of
Helen – for base motives, at that – are signs of contempt for the
Achaeans, which inspire Agamemnon's anger and the desire for
revenge. So too in book 13, Menelaus slays another Peisander (the

repetition of the name is not, I think, mere coincidence) and denounces the *lôbê* and shameful deeds (*aiskhos*) of the arrogant Trojans, who stole his wife and much wealth besides; Menelaus implores Zeus to punish them for their violent contempt (*hubristês*) and insatiable passion for war (13.620–39). Finally, when the goddess Iris descends from Olympus to inform Achilles of the battle round the body of Patroclus, she says that it would be a *lôbê* for Achilles if Patroclus's corpse were mutilated (18.180). What, then, is the *lôbê* that Achilles hopes that he and his men (or the Achaeans in general) will avenge in book 19? I suspect that it refers to the Trojans' arrogance in fighting for an unjust cause, in the course of which they have harmed so many Achaeans and now Patroclus as well. This is what demands requital, not just the personal loss that Achilles has suffered.

27 *Kholos* in this part of the epic is used in reference to women's quarrels (20.251–5; Aeneas speaking); to Zeus's possible anger should Achilles slay Aeneas before his time is up (20.300–2; Poseidon is the speaker); to the river Scamander's anger at Achilles' vengefulness, which is appropriate for a god in respect to a mortal's pride (21.136–8; cf. 21.146–7, where Xanthus is enraged at Achilles' lack of pity); to Hera's anger at Artemis for daring to oppose her in battle (21.478–82); and to a snake's *kholos*, or venom, in a simile illustrating Hector's determination to face Achilles' onslaught (22.93–7); this is the sum total for books 20 to 22. The first occurrence in book 23 is indeed applied to Achilles' rage over the death of Patroclus as the motive for his maltreatment of Hector's body and the sacrifice of twelve Trojan youths (23.21–3). A little later, the term is used in reference to Patroclus's anger, which caused him to slay a young companion in a quarrel over a game of knucklebones (23.88); several subsequent occurrences in book 23 have to do with bickering among contestants in the funeral games (23.482, 543, and 567). The final book of the epic mentions the anger of Hera (24.55) and of Zeus (24.114 = 135); there is also the reference to Achilles' anger at Agamemnon, noted above (24.395), while the last occurrence in the entire poem (24.586) is in reference to Achilles' command to cover Hector's corpse for fear that Priam may become angry upon seeing it. Some of these passages are discussed below; for an exhaustive discussion of *kholos* in the Homeric epics, and the difference between *kholos* and *kotos*,

which signifies the long-term hostility associated with the feud, see T.R. Walsh 2005.

28 We recognize too that one purpose of the simile is to underscore Achilles' sense of paternal responsibility for his comrade – conceivably there is an allusion here as well to his feelings concerning Briseis, whom Agamemnon stole from him.

29 Other heroes become angry when they feel slighted or cheated in the course of the funeral games (book 23); see n. 26 above.

30 The Latin term *ira* also carries both senses; contrast Virgil, *Aeneid* 12.108 with 12.946, and cf. Braund and Gilbert 2004.

31 The confrontation between a ruler and his greatest warrior, and the pattern of insult leading to the warrior's seething rage, are common to many epics, e.g. *El Cid*, *Le chanson de Roland*, the Persian *Shâh-nâma*; see D.A. Miller 2000: 178–87 for examples, and esp. 183 on Irish tales that 'depict a mortal tension between a king and his "man," as when a champion's loyalty to his chief is broken because of a woman'; also pp. 201–3, and Jackson 1982. This pattern is often accompanied by the hero's demonstration of his prowess in slaying a great antagonist, whom he may pity or else abuse in defeat (D.A. Miller 2000: 222–5); Achilles' reaction is violent at first, but finally compassionate when he returns Hector's body to Priam. The ambition to avenge the death of a dear friend is a separate motif, and has its source not in the arrogance of the king but in the identification between warrior and squire or friend; the hero's motive here is not anger at a slight but an almost transcendental or existential grief over the loss of one so intimate as to constitute a part of his very self. The intersection of these two motives – mistreatment by a superior and the death of a friend – can lead in real life to the kind of unbounded rage that Achilles experiences; see Shay 1994. I understand the *Iliad* as an exploration of the warrior's psychology under extreme stress, rather than as 'a lesson against uncontrolled and unassuaged wrath' for the danger that it poses to the civil community (Harris 2002: 153). See also Hammer 2001: 213: 'The pain that Achilles experiences from the loss of Patroklos recasts his earlier understanding of pain that caused him to withdreaw from battle. Achilles saw himself as "suffering-from" the dishonor brought about by Agamemnon. Achilles' response is one of anger: he seeks to restore his esteem. ... With the death of Patroklos, though, Achilles

experiences a "suffering-with," in which his own pain is connected to the suffering of another.'

32 To be fair to Wilson's subtle argument, I quote at some length her summary of it: 'Achilleus' aggressive appropriation of a conflated Chryses/Apollo model brought him the embassy and Agamemnon's *apoina*. His strategy has failed, however, to produce a culturally acceptable offer of *poinê* or to cast Agamemnon in a dependent position in relation to himself. Achilleus is, as I have already suggested, determined that Agamemnon's superiority, unlike Zeus' own superiority, is not unassailable. He will therefore deploy his strategy of *tisis* to the limit, and beyond, in the struggle for dominance. Moreover, he does so not by rejecting heroic tradition, but by appropriating and aggressively exploiting its ambiguities ...; he is set on taking *poinê* and, after that, *apoina*' (107).

33 The scholia remark too (ad 9.651–2) on Achilles' use of the epithet 'divine' (*dios*) in regard to Hector, which, they point out, Homer does not employ in his own voice. They explain it as Achilles' way of irritating (*lupôn*) the Achaeans (they compare 9.356, Achilles speaking to Odysseus), but it is worth noting that his attitude towards a military enemy is very different from the wrath he bears towards Agamemnon.

34 This is not to say that slaves really were unresentful at abuse, even if it was prudent for them to swallow their pride; see Barton 2001: 11: '[E]motionally the slave was every bit as sensitive to insult as his or her master.' Barton cites (12) Horace, *Satires* 1.6.23–4, 'sed fulgente trahit constrictos gloria curru / non minus ignotos generosis' ('but glory draws, in its shining chariot, the humble no less than the noble') and (13) Cato the Elder, as quoted by Aulus Gellius (10.3.7): 'servi iniurias nimis aegre ferunt' ('slaves bear insults very badly'); cf. Seneca, *On Constancy* 5.1, etc. Aristotle's class analysis does not reveal the entire truth about ancient sensibilities. Cf. also Abu-Lughod 1999 (orig. 1986): 111, a propos Bedouin society: '[D]ependents, including women, strive for honor in the traditional sense. They share with their providers the same ideals for self-image and social reputation, which they try to follow in their everyday lives. Yet the situations in which they can realize these ideals, in particular those of independence and assertiveness, are circumscribed.'

35 Harris (2001: 139) observes: 'Showing anger was a prerogative of the gods and of princes'; but it may be that even feeling anger was such a prerogative; as Harris notes, in the *Odyssey*, 'Telemachus has to learn anger' (140). For the association of anger with dishonour, see also Sophocles, *Oedipus the King* 339–40 (quoted in chapter 1, p. 38).

36 Richardson Lear (2004: 19) notes that, for Aristotle, 'without a final resting point, "our desire (*orexis*) would be empty and vain" (1094a20–1)'; for 'no one would try to do anything if he were not going to come to a limit' (*peras, Metaphysics* a2, 994b13–14). Compare *Iliad* 22.15–20, where Achilles, who has been distracted from the battle before the walls of Troy by Apollo, declares that he would make the god pay for the harm that he has done him – if he could. But vengeance is not possible, and neither is anger against a god. Reginster (1997: 297) observes that 'the purpose of revenge is not the punishment of a deed of which one disapproves. Rather, if I have been defeated, my revenge essentially aims to restore my challenged superiority.' For Nietzsche, the abiding desire for revenge, coupled with the certainty that it is unattainable, produces the characteristic psychological state of *ressentiment*. The slave, on the contrary, is one who 'never even forms the expectation to live the life his masters value' (ibid., 287).

37 Cf. Harris 2001: 139: 'Showing anger was a prerogative of the gods and of princes'; Creon, in Sophocles' *Antigone*, and Oedipus, in *Oedipus Tyrannus*, are both quick to become angry.

38 For *Medea* as a revenge play, see Mastronarde 2002: 8–15, and on Medea's anger, 17–18, 312–13; for a different reading of anger in *Medea*, see Harris 2001: 169–71, 277–8.

39 The same tension is apparent in the classical Greek conception of erotic love, which casts men as the subject of passion – men are lovers, women are loved – but at the same time represents the lover as feminized because he is dominated by desire; see Konstan 2002b for discussion.

40 Compare the topos of women's excessive and violent anger towards servants in modern literature, for example in the second act of George Bernard Shaw's *Widowers' Houses*; by such representations, strong-willed women are shown to be unfit to exercise authority and thus safely reduced to a subordinate role.

41 Though the phrasing is difficult, editors agree that the anger must be that of Hyllus, not Dejanira.

42 Wohl (1998: 8) remarks that the robe Dejanira gives to Hercules 'evokes the robe in which Clytemnestra kills Agamemnon in Aeschylus' *Agamemnon,*' and notes further that weaving is the characteristic activity of women (25). Like Medea, Clytemnestra is sufficiently powerful to exact revenge, and hence to experience anger at Agamemnon's treatment of her. On women and weaving, see also Ferrari 2002: 12, and D. Lyons 2003: 122–3, who describes the poisoned garment sent by Dejanira as 'a feminine delivery system'; Foley (2004: 78) describes a production in 2002 of *Bad Women*, by Tina Shepherd, Sidney Goldfarb, and the Talking Band, which had 'Medea and Deianeira simultaneously rubbing poisons on different ends of the same huge strip of cloth, followed by Clytemnestra with her ... deadly tapestry and net.'

43 Cf. 543, on Dejanira's inability to 'grow wroth' (*thumousthai*) with Hercules for his behaviour; Harris 2001: 266. It is possible to suppose that Dejanira's error in regard to the potion was an unconscious act of aggression; cf. Scott 1995. Carawan (2000) argues that Dejanira would have been perceived as guilty by the Athenian audience because her act, even if not intentional, was nevertheless reckless and resulted in her husband's death; be that as it may, she does not act in anger. In the Senecan version (attribution of the *Hercules Oetaeus* to Seneca is disputed), Dejanira initially reacts with fury to the news concerning Iole, and determines to seek vengeance: 'I shall not go unavenged. Though you bear up heaven and the whole world owes its peace to you, there is something worse than the Hydra: the pain of an angry wife' (282–5; cf. 296–8, 308, 436–2). But her nurse counsels fear (442; cf. 476), and Dejanira decides to employ a love potion instead (473–534; cf. Carawan 2000: 207 n. 45).

44 For what the statistic is worth, in Virgil's *Aeneid* women are represented as angry twelve times, but ten of these cases pertain to goddesses, whereas men's anger is indicated thirty-eight times, with only two instances pertaining to deities: the winds at 1.57 and Cupid at 4.532 (Dion 1993: 68–9).

45 Cf. Mossman 1995: 208: 'A certain unity, then, is to be found within the character of Hecuba.'

46 Harris (2001: 58) observes, in connection with Aristotle's insistence

that one must be in a position to retaliate in order to experience anger: 'It would be absurd to suppose that Aristotle's definition of *orgê* was seriously mistaken. This was what *orgê* was.' Harris accordingly emphasizes the quality of *orgê* as 'a propensity for action' rather than a feeling. Be that as it may, Aristotle's definition of *orgê* seems too restricted even in Greek terms.

47 Cf. Stobaeus, *Anthologia* 3.19.12 Hense = 526.4, Fortenbaugh et al. 1992; Seneca, *On Anger* 1.12.3 = 446.1, Fortenbaugh et al. 1992.

48 Lewis and Short and the Loeb edition translate *exsequar* here as 'take revenge' or 'avenge him'; the *Oxford Latin Dictionary* (ed. Glare, 1982) does not cite this passage s.v.

49 *SVF* 3.395 = Stobaeus 2.91.10; cf. Diogenes Laertius 7.113; also Posidonius fr. 155, Edelstein-Kidd 1972 = Lactantius, *On the Anger of God* 17.13.

50 It may be doubted, however, whether this change represents 'a certain shift from shame culture to guilt culture,' as Harris (2001) suggests; on the question of shame culture, see chapter 4, p. 91.

51 Cf. Aristophanes, *Wasps* 572–4; also Virgil, *Aeneid* for the contrast between *ira*, 12.946, and *misericordia*, 12.933–6.

52 Cf. also Andocides 1.8, 1.24, 1.30; Lysias 10.26, 10.29, 11.10, 12.20, 12.58, 12.96, 14.8, 14.13, 16.17, 20.1, 25.16, 27.15, 28.2, 29.9, 29.12, 30.23, 31.11; and Demosthenes 16.19, 18.18, 18.20, 19.7, 19.302, 20.8, 21.34, 24.215, 40.5. It is wrong to conclude from this usage, however, that *orgê* and *orgizesthai* 'came to mean, for a time, not only "anger" and "to be angry" but also sometimes "punishment" and "to punish"' (Harris 2001: 62). Harris himself attributes to Demosthenes a frank desire to stimulate the anger of his public (188–90).

53 For the role of anger in judicial verdicts, see also D. Allen 2000: 18–24; and on anger as the counterpart to pity, Konstan 2001a: 41–3. Even the resentment at long-term domination by another power might be described as *orgê* rather than as hatred or hostility; thus, Thucydides (2.8.5) observes that both cities that wished to be free of Athenian rule and those that feared being subjugated to it regarded the Athenians with *orgê* (the attitude can also be described as *ekhthos* or 'hatred,' 2.11.2). Tomkins (1995: 139) sees contempt for the other as characteristic of hierarchical societies, which depend on aloofness from the other, whereas democracies more typically resort

to shaming, which may be accompanied by 'anger in which the critic seeks redress for the wrongs committed by the other.'

54 For the apparent contradiction between this admonition and Aristotle's advice in the second book on how to arouse emotion, see Konstan 2001a: 44–5; also below, chapter 10, p. 204.

55 For the contrast between anger and judgment (gnômê), cf. Thucydides 2.23.1, 2.59.3; 8.2.2 on anger motivating a decision (cf. 3.43.5); and, for anger paired with haste, 4.122.5, 8.27.6.

56 Compare also NE 7.6, 1149a24–32, where Aristotle compares thumos (analogous to anger) to a slave who carries out an order precipitously, before having listened to all his master (i.e., reason) has to say.

57 Contrast NE 5.8, 1135b19–29, where Aristotle explains that an unpremeditated act, such as those due to anger, is indeed a wrong (adikêma), but the injury does not arise out of wickedness (mokhthêria): 'For it is not he who acts in a passion who initiates [the conflict], but he who angered him ... For the anger depends on a perceived injustice.' So too Aristotle regards lack of self-control in respect to anger (thumos, which is here equivalent to orgê) as more venial than carnal appetites, insofar as it is more human and natural (NE 7.6, 1149b27–9).

58 Cf. Pritchett 1991: 312; Konstan 2001a: 76–7; Konstan 2006c; and, on Rome, Lintott 1968: 42–4. The entire population, or at least adult males, was held responsible for the actions of the state, and hence could be punished for them.

59 Attitudes towards anger, especially among the intellectual elite, changed to a certain extent after the classical period (conventionally marked by the death of Alexander the Great in 323 BC); for details, see Harris 2001. Already in the fifth and fourth centuries BC, there was a tendency to distinguish judicial cases, where justice was at stake, from public deliberation over international affairs, where policy, some held, should be decided on the basis of interest alone (cf. Aristotle Rhetoric 1.3, 1358b20–9; further discussion in Konstan 2001: 82–3; and Konstan 2005c; and see chapter 10, p. 210).

60 On slighting and timê, cf. Grimaldi 1988: 22 ad 1373b28.

61 See Herman 1995 on timê in the Attic orators; contra, e.g., Cohen 1991.

62 Aristotle notes at De anima 1.1, 403a19–22 that when we are tense, we are more vulnerable to emotions in general.

63 Kassell (1976) excises the words in 2.2, 1379a15–18 that point to this line of reasoning.

64 Cf. Elster 1999a: 54. On analogous differences between kinds of pleasures, cf. *NE* 10.5, 1175a19–30 and Leighton 1996: 219.

65 See Seneca, *On Anger*; Plutarch, *On Controlling Anger*; and a comprehensive survey of the sources in Harris 2001. Anderson (1964: 173 and passim) argues that even Juvenal came to doubt the propriety of anger, and abandoned the severe indignation of his persona in the later satires.

66 The condemnation of royal anger continued into the Middle Ages; cf. Bührer-Thierry 1998: 75: 'If anger was reprehensible for all mankind, it was still more so for kings.' There was also, however, an alternative tradition of just anger, which was not only the prerogative but the duty of monarchs. Althoff (1998: 59) writes: 'Royal anger thus appears as a part of his [the king's] "rulership practice," that is, as part of a personally grounded system of rulership based on a range of unwritten laws'; cf. S.D. White 1998: 139: 'Public displays of anger are almost always made by kings or other males whose noble status entitles them to express anger'; and R.E. Barton 1998: 154: '[A]nger was frequently justified as necessary and righteous, especially when exercised by those with rightful authority.' The model for royal anger was the just wrath of God (cf. Lactantius's essay *On the Anger of God*).

67 Partially cited in chapter 1, p. 23. Elster concludes that 'being ashamed of one's anger was not a typical Greek reaction.' This is true, but only because anger was not necessarily a vice or the sign of a vicious character (cf. *NE* 2.7, 1108a4–6); being ashamed of spite or envy, which are reprehensible in themselves (2.6, 1107a8–11), is entirely consistent with Aristotle's view of the emotions.

68 This description applies, of course, only to adult male citizens; where there were real status differences, e.g. between free man and slave, the anger of the subjugated had to be repressed or concealed.

Chapter Three

1 The contrast between pain and pleasure cannot be the basis of these oppositions, as the case of pity and indignation shows, since both of these emotions, which Aristotle insists are opposites, are said to be

accompanied by pain; see chapter 1, p. 33, for discussion; also chapter 10, p. 217.

2 See, e.g., G.E.R. Lloyd 1966.

3 Grimaldi adds: 'There would be no reason to question this save that St. Thomas Aquinas in his extended study of the emotions ... remarks, *Summa Theologiae* Ia IIae, q. 23, art. 3, q. 46, art. 1, that anger alone of the emotions has no contrary.' Grimaldi goes on to concede Thomas's point, insofar as 'In the other emotions the contrary is usually a possibility toward which a person can move ... But this is not true of anger. In anger the move toward the contrary is effectively blocked since the evil which causes the anger is actually present in the individual ... The only alternatives open to him are to accept this evil and so experience the concomitant pain and distress, or to reject the evil and so become angry' (1988: 49–50). If I understand Grimaldi's argument here (and I am not certain that I do), then the opposite of anger proves not to be an emotion after all.

4 An anonymous Byzantine commentator, or rather scholiast, notes that we become *praoi* in respect to one who, we learn, intended the opposite of a slight because 'he did it not for contempt but for my esteem [*dia doxan emên*]' (93.32–3 Rabe).

5 Kassell (1976), for no very good reason, marks this comment as a later addition by Aristotle.

6 Compare Heath (2001), who offers an Aristotelian explanation of why the painful emotions of tragedy yield pleasure, although he concedes that it may not be Aristotle's own.

Chapter Four

1 Cf. Tangney and Dearing 2002: 11: 'In everyday conversations, people typically avoid the term "shame"'; Barton 2001: 235: 'At the time I am writing, the idea is popular in the United States that no one should ever be shamed. We forget that teasing and mild shaming are among the most important socializing mechanisms of society – *provided that trust is there and that the teaser is prepared to exchange roles with the teased.*' Correspondingly, the study of shame has been largely neglected; cf. Gilbert and Andrews 1998: v: 'Shame has been recognized since antiquity. A strong theme of shame exists in the early stories of Adam and Eve. However, it has only been in

the last 20 years or so that shame has been subject to systematic research and theory development'; Kaster 2005: 28–9. For a good survey of recent theories, see Gilbert and Andrews 1998.

2 Cf. Wurmser 1981: 17, though Wurmser maintains that one can 'be ashamed in front of oneself and feel guilty in front of someone else'; Kant 1981: 62; Sartre 1996: 302: 'I am ashamed of myself *as I appear* to the Other ... I recognize that I *am* as the Other sees me'; Creighton 1990: 296: 'Shame, with its corresponding fear of rejection, is not a very effective sanction in American society, where individuals are *encouraged* to become independent.' For a critique of the idea that shame requires an audience, see Taylor 1985: 57–68; Cairns 1993: 16–18; Morrison 1996: 16: 'To feel shame, therefore, we do not need the presence of an actual *shamer* or even a viewing *audience*; we need only these internalized figures who have become a part of what we are'; and Tangney and Dearing 2002: 14, who report that in their empirical studies '"solitary" shame was about as prevalent as "solitary" guilt.' Cf. Kaster 1997: 4–7 on Roman *pudor* as 'generated from within' (5). Seidler (2000: 3) discusses the phenomenology of the self-visualization involved in shame.

3 Cf. Pattison 2000: 43–4; for criticism of the idea of a shame culture, see Lloyd-Jones 1987: 2; Creighton 1990; Cairns (1993: 27–47) affirms that criticism has left the antithesis 'in tatters' (42); Wissmann: 1997: 17. But the idea persists in modern scholarship, e.g. Margalit 1996: 248–9.

4 Creighton 1990: 286: 'Shame feelings precede the development of the superego, although they may later be integrated into the superego formation. Guilt develops later during the oedipal phase and requires the presence of a superego'; Scheff 1997: 210; Scheff 2000: 86. Jacoby (1991: 53) observes that '[i]n [Erik] Erikson's view, shame is connected with being seen by others, and is therefore prior to a sense of guilt, in which one is alone with the voice of the superego or the internalized "other"' (referring to Erikson 1950).

5 Nathanson 1992: 19: 'Whereas shame is about the *quality* of our person or self, guilt is the painful emotion triggered when we become aware that we have acted in a way to bring harm to another person or to violate some important code. Guilt is about *action* and laws. Whenever we feel guilty, we can pay for the damage inflicted'; Jacoby 1991: 1: 'Feelings of guilt make me feel like a bad person

because I have done something – or perhaps only thought about doing something – that I should not have done ... Feelings of guilt have to do with ethical or moral principles called "should-laws" in philosophical ethics ... At a certain intensity, shame has the power to make us feel completely worthless, degraded from head to foot, sometimes without our having done anything bad at all'; M. Lewis 1992: 10; Lansky 1992: 105–6; Williams 1993: 89–90; Sedgwick 1995: 212; Morrison, 1996: 12: 'We feel guilt about our wrongdoing; we feel shame about the very essence of our selves'; Denham 1998: 40–1: in shame, 'the offensive behavior is seen as a reflection of an equally offensive self ...; guilt motivates corrective action rather than motivating avoidance'; M. Lewis 2000: 629: 'The emotional state of guilt or regret is produced when individuals evaluate their behavior as failure but focus on the specific features or actions of the self that led to the failure ... In fact, the emotion of guilt always has associated with it a corrective action that the individual can take (but does not necessarily take) to repair the failure ... As such, the emotion is less intense and more capable of dissipation ... The emotion of guilt lacks the negative intensity of shame'; Ben-Ze'ev 2000: 498; Tangney and Dearing 2002: 24: 'Shame involves fairly global negative evaluations of the self (i.e., "Who I am"). Guilt involves a more articulated condemnation of a specific behavior (i.e., "What I did"),' although surveys show that the two terms are often used 'inconsistently or interchangeably' (11).

But contrast Solomon 1993: 259, 301: 'What distinguishes guilt [from shame] ... is its ability to encompass the sense of worth of the whole person'; shame 'is more specific than guilt ... and not generally self-demeaning'; Cairns 1993: 23–4: 'I doubt very much whether shame must involve the ... complete denigration of the self'; also 25: '[E]ven if a distinction between self-evaluations which focus on what we are and those which focus on what we do is tenable in the abstract, this distinction will not furnish an absolute criterion for the separation of shame and guilt in ordinary usage.'

6 Plutarch (*On Bashfulness* 528D) discusses an exaggerated shyness or sensitivity to shame (*dusôpia*), but this is a disposition (in Aristotle's terms, a *hexis*) rather than a generalized emotional state; Plutarch refers, however, to the intense shame itself as a harmful *pathos* (529E); cf. Aristotle, *Nicomachean Ethics* 1108a33–4.

7 Cf. Ohly: 1992; H. Lewis (1987a: 11) remarks that in modern
theories, 'shame is an even less prestigious emotion than guilt.'

8 Barkan (2000: xxviii) remarks on what he sees as a new sensitivity
on the part of entire nations to guilt: 'One new measure of this
public morality is the growing political willingness, and at times
eagerness, to admit one's historical guilt.'

9 The Greeks could, nevertheless, describe something very like our
sense of guilt; thus Thucydides (7.75.2–5) reports that when the
Athenians, having been defeated at Syracuse, could not rescue their
wounded comrades, they experienced 'censure of their own selves'
(katamempsis sphôn autôn); for discussion, see Sternberg 1999:
196–7.

10 It is claimed that shame exists in all human cultures (Casimire and
Schnegg 2003), but this begs the question of possible differences in
the meaning of the terms used. For shame in China, with a bibliography on shame in other cultures including those of Indonesia,
India, Japan, and the Middle East, see Li, Wang, and Fischer 2003.

11 The noun aiskhunê first occurs in the sixth-century poet Theognis
(verse 1272), in the sense of being a 'disgrace,' and becomes common
towards the middle of the fifth century BC.

12 Shipp endorses Dodds's hypothesis of a development from shame
culture to guilt culture in Greece, which he sees reflected in the
shift from aidôs to aiskhunê. I ignore here the different nuances of
the noun aidôs and the verb aideomai, although as Cairns (1993: 2)
observes, they 'do have different senses.' In Euripides' Hippolytus
verse 244, Phaedra exclaims: 'I feel aidôs [verbal form aidoumetha]
at what has been said,' which indicates that the verb can assume the
sense of remorseful shame; for a similar use of the noun, cf. Euripides,
Hecuba 968–72, where it is equivalent to aiskhunê. See also
Gauthier and Jolif 1970: 320, who affirm that aidôs in the classical
period 'n'est plus seulement l'appréhension d'un déshonneur futur,
mais aussi la honte d'un déshonneur présent ... et le regret d'une
faute passée' ('is no longer only the apprehension of a future dishonour, but also shame at a present dishonour ... and regret over a
past error').

13 Hooker (1987) argues that aidôs and related terms only acquired the
sense of 'shame' in post-Homeric literature. An illustrative case is
Odyssey 8.83–9, where Odysseus covers his head with a cloth to

conceal his tears from the Phaeacians, who have been enjoying a poetic recital of his quarrel with Achilles during the war at Troy: 'for he felt *aidôs* [verb: *aideto*] before the Phaeacians as he let tears drop from beneath his eyelids' (8.86). Odysseus is not ashamed at having been seen to weep, since it is to avoid just this that he conceals himself. Nor is it likely that he feels shame at the thought that he might be seen ('prospective' shame, though clearly not inhibitory in this instance). Rather, he is motivated by respect for the Phaeacians, who are his hosts, and hesitates to interrupt their pleasure in the song by a display of his own grief.

14 Compare W.I. Miller 2000: 70: 'Shame bears a close connection with courageous motivation; it might in fact be its chief motivator'; cf. Wissman 1997: 13–18. In Euripides' tragedy *Children of Hercules*, the girl Macaria consents to be sacrificed for the good of Athens, since she would be ashamed (516) not to die on behalf of the city that gave them refuge (cf. 541–2); the Athenian king Demipho recognizes her gesture as a sign of courage (*eupsukhia*, 569).

15 In Euripides' *Ion* 934, cited by Shipp, Creousa exclaims: 'I feel *aiskhunê* [verbal form, *aiskhunomai*] before you, aged sir'; cf. also verses 341, 367, 395, 1074. It is the 'restrictive' sense of *aiskhunê* that is chiefly at play in Plato's *Gorgias*, where it inhibits Socrates' interlocutors from confessing openly to opinions that are at odds with conventional values; cf. 482E, 487B–E, 492A, 494C–E, 508B–C, etc., and, for discussion of individual passages, Chichi 2002, with references to earlier studies. Cf. also Euripides, *Electra* 45–6, in which a humble farmer who has been given Electra as wife affirms: 'I feel *aiskhunê* [*aiskhunomai*] at treating arrogantly the offspring of upper-class men whom I, who am not worthy, have received.' In the previous verse (44) he affirms that he has not 'shamed her in the marriage bed,' but rather she remains a virgin; the point is that it would be shameful for the princess Electra to submit to a humble peasant.

16 Gauthier and Jolif (1970: 321) specify that Aristotle does not distinguish *aidôs* from *aiskhunê* in the *Rhetoric*.

17 Cairns (1993: 13) distinguishes two senses of *aidôs*, namely, 'I feel shame before ...' and 'I respect,' but he adds that the two are related: '[T]o feel inhibitory shame ... is to picture oneself as losing honour, while to show respect is to recognize the honour of another. The

combination of the two in one concept, however, is unfamiliar,'
though it is also, Cairns affirms, quite logical. For the rich meta-
phorical texture surrounding the idea of *aidôs*, which includes the
image of a protecting mantle, see Ferrari 2002: 74–81, and cf. Kaster
1997: 3: 'Sensitivity to the emotion [the Latin *pudor*] is ... often
spoken of metaphorically as a garment, a cloak that conceals the
ethically naked self and provides an acceptable social identity.'

18 The verbal form *aiskhunomai*, like that of *aidôs*, is used in the
sense of 'feel shame before ...'; cf. Aeschines (fourth century BC),
Against Timarchus 24, also 180: 'One of the old men before whom
they feel shame [*aiskhunontai*] and whom they fear stepped forward.' Aeschines uses the negative expressions *anaides, anaideia* =
'shameless' (e.g. 1.189), but not *aidos*, which was, as I have said,
obsolete by this time. In contrast, Kaster (1997: 12) observes of the
Roman idea of *pudor* that 'it is vastly more often a source of remorse
or reproof than of counsel and prevention.'

19 W.I. Miller (1997: 34) observes that shame that inhibits 'is not the
emotion shame, but the sense of shame, the sense of modesty
and propriety that keeps us from being shamed.' The adjective
aiskhuntêlos denotes shyness or bashful modesty as a character
trait, and stands to *aiskhunê* in the way that *aidêmôn* does to *aidôs*
(or, in Latin, as *verecundus* and *pudicus* stand to *verecundia* and
pudor). Plato, in the *Charmides* (158C), remarks that 'Charmides
blushed and seemed even more handsome; for his modesty [*to
aiskhuntêlon*] was suitable to his age.' Cf. 160E: 'It seems to me, he
said, that modesty [*sôphrosunê*] makes a man feel *aiskhunê* and
renders a man *aiskhuntêlos*, and that modesty [*sôphrosunê*] is
basically *aidôs*'; Aristotle, *Eudemian Ethics* 1220b17, 1128b10–35,
Physiognomonica 812a30–1; and, for the contrast between
aiskhuntêlos and *anaiskhuntos* ('shameless'), *Rhetoric* 1390a1–2.
Cf. also Menander's *Misoumenos* ('The Hated Man') 208–10, in
which a young would-be seducer blushes with shame when he is
exposed. The reaction indicates both his base intention and, at the
same time, a saving sense of modesty in his character, which
prepares for the denouement of the comedy, in which the boy will
be recognized as the brother of the protagonist who is his rival; see
the discussion in Lape 2004: 222–31.

20 *Questiones naturales et morales* book 1, problem 21 ('On *Aidôs*'), in

Commentaria in Aristotelem Graeca, suppl. 2.2, ed. I. Bruns; the treatise is generally supposed to be wrongly attributed to Alexander. Once again, I cannot enter into this question exhaustively here, and limit myself to observing that Aristotle tends to treat *aidôs* in the ethical works as an emotional temperament or *dunamis,* and speaks in these contexts of *ho aidêmôn* or 'a man given to feeling *aidôs.*' In popular parlance, *aidôs* and many other affects, such as *erôs* or passionate love, could of course be described as *pathê*; cf. Heraclitus the Allegorist (first century AD) 28.7, describing Helen in the *Iliad* as torn between two *pathê,* '*erôs* for Paris and *aidôs* towards Menelaus.'

21 *Stoicorum veterum fragmenta* (*SVF* = Arnim 1921–4) 3.264.9–10, from Stobaeus 2.60.9; cf. Kamtekar 1998: 137–8. The sense of *aidôs* as 'chastity' comes particularly close to that of *sôphrosunê* in erotic contexts.

22 Cf. *SVF* 432 = Andronicus, *On Emotions* 6, p. 20 Kreuttner; *SVF* 439.1–3 = Plutarch, *On Moral Virtue* 449A; *SVF* 440 = Galen, *On the Opinions of Hippocrates and Plato* 4.4 [140] p. 354 M. 21, etc.; see Kamtekar 1998: 138–43 on the problems that this classification entails. Kamtekar argues (144–60) that Epictetus reclassifies *aidôs* as a self-evaluative cognitive capacity, akin to the modern idea of conscience (147, 160).

23 The definition is Zeno's, recorded in Diogenes Laertius 7.112; cf. *Definitions* 416A9 (ascribed to Plato but almost certainly a later product of his Academy). Cf. Aulus Gellius 19.6.3: 'One might still inquire why shame [*pudor*] diffuses the blood, while fear reduces it, given that *pudor* is a species of fear and is defined as follows: 'fear of just reproach.' For so the philosophers [surely the Stoics] define it: "*aiskhunê* is fear of just blame."' Cicero (*Republic* 5.6) offers a similar definition of *verecundia* as 'a kind of fear of not unjust censure.' On *pudor* and *verecundia,* see Kaster 2005: 13–65.

24 In common parlance, both *aidôs* and *aiskhunê* might be associated with fear; cf. (e.g.) Xenophon, *Memorabilia* 3.7.5.

25 There are various other indications in this passage that Aristotle considers *aidôs* to be different from *aiskhunê,* as Alexander of Aphrodisias too observed (in the text cited above), for example, that *aidôs* is particularly appropriate to young people; cf. Aristotle, *Nicomachean Ethics* 4.9, 1128b15.

26 *SVF* 3.416.17–22 = Nemesius, *On the Nature of Man* chap. 20;
   Kamtekar (1998: 140–1) suggests that Nemesius may be responding
   to Epictetus's innovative conception of *aidôs*.

27 Rusten (1990: 169), commenting on Thucydides 2.43.1, remarks that
   '*aiskhunê* and *aiskhunomai* denote properly the guilty shame for an
   act committed, *aidôs* and *aidoumai* the inhibitory emotion which
   prevents such acts; but the distinction between them becomes
   blurred by the late fifth century, so that *aiskhunomai* may be used
   positively here'; but the evidence does not, I think, support this
   story of progressive confusion between the two terms.

28 '*Aidos* est pudor profectus ex verecundia. *Aischyne* est pudor
   profectus ex turpitudine.' Riezler adds: 'The origin of *Aischyne* is
   dishonor, of *Aidos*, awe,' and affirms that the former pertains to
   'man-made codes,' while the latter responds to a sense of how things
   naturally are.

29 So too Cope (1877: 71–2), commenting on Aristotle's *Rhetoric*,
   distinguishes between '*aidôs, verecundia*, a subjective feeling of
   honor which precedes and prevents a shameful act' and '*aiskhunê*,
   pudor, an objective aspect which reflects upon the consequences of
   the act and the shame it brings with it' (as summarized in Grimaldi
   1988: 107).

30 Cf. Scheff 1995: 1053: '[W]hen we compare the concept in other
   languages, the definition of shame in English is narrow and extreme'; Scheff adds (1053–4) that French *honte* is equivalent to
   English shame, *pudeur* to a 'sense of shame.' Spinoza (1992: 147)
   affirms: 'Shame is the pain that follows on a deed of which we are
   ashamed. Bashfulness is the fear or apprehension of shame, whereby
   a man is restrained from some disgraceful act.' On *Scham* and
   Schande, cf. Parker 2000: 559–63.

31 For a similar inclusiveness in the Chinese conception of shame, see
   Li, Wang, and Fischer 2004.

32 For the close connection between *aiskhunê* and disgrace or *adoxia*,
   see (e.g.) Demosthenes, Oration 19.41, 83, 146. On the basis of 'a
   survey of some two thousand places in classical Latin where *pudor*
   and its cognates occur,' Kaster (1997: 4) offers a definition of the
   Roman emotion that comes close to Aristotle's view of *aiskhunê*:
   '[P]udor primarily denotes a displeasure with oneself caused by
   vulnerability to just criticism of a socially diminishing sort.'

33 Some researchers have argued that memory itself is 'forward-acting, generating predictions and intentions, rather than being a contemplative and retrospective faculty,' and that 'a recollection ought to be called an anticipatory image' (McCrone 2004: 4, referring to the work of U. Neisser; cf. Neisser 1988, 2000).

34 Cf. Scheff (1997: 206): 'We propose that pride is the emotional correlate of a secure social bond; and shame, the emotional correlate of a threatened bond'; also Cooley 1983: 183; W.I. Miller 1997: 24; M. Lewis 2000; Ben-Ze'ev 2000: 491, 512; and Manstead and Fischer 2001: 231; Jacoby 1991 is entitled *Shame and the Origins of Self-Esteem*, and devotes a chapter (pp. 24–45) to self-esteem and the related notion of personal dignity. Spinoza's *gloria*, or 'honour,' is something like pride; Spinoza (1992: 147) defines it as 'pleasure accompanied by the idea of some action of ours which we think that others praise,' whereas '[s]hame is a pain accompanied by the idea of some action of ours that we think that others censure'; cf. also Descartes 1988: part 3, art. 204. Contrast Seidler 2000: 103: 'The postulation of shame and pride as polar opposites is frankly unconvincing. Only if we decide to limit "shame" to the affective expression of the impairment of self-esteem can we conceivably regard "pride" as the opposite pole, and even then it would appear more appropriate to regard the capacity for realistic self-evaluation to be the more convincing alternative.'

35 Scheff (1997: 208) notes that in the Hebrew Bible, '[v]irtually every reference places pride in a disparaging light,' and speaks of the need for a notion of 'justified pride.' Cf. M. Lewis 1992: 78: 'Hubris can be defined as an exaggerated pride or self-confidence ... It is an example of pridefulness, something dislikeable and to be avoided ... The emotion I label pride is the consequence of a specific action.' On the complex meaning of self-esteem or pride in English, see also Scheff, unpublished.

36 Cf. Kaster 1997: 11: 'To a person with an active sense of *pudor*, all those who constitute his social world are constantly visible, as he is visible to them.' From another point of view, the opposite of shame might be seen as envy: both reflect an underevaluation of the self, manifested in the case of shame as a pain at one's own disgrace, and in the case of envy as the overevaluation of another's reputation or achievement; see Lansky 1997. A given term may have several

opposites, as Aristotle himself observes (*Topics* 2.7, 113a14–15; quoted in chapter 3, p. 83).

37 A character in Aristophanes' *Clouds* (1220) declares that he will not put his country to shame by failing to collect on a debt – that is, not living up to the standard that his countrymen set. Those of an inferior social class will not necessarily feel shame at shortcomings relative to their superiors: the humble farmer to whom Electra has been wedded in Euripides' *Electra* (357–432) does not hesitate to invite two well-born guests into his modest home, though Electra herself is mortified at the idea. A special case is that of persons whose status has changed abruptly, for example, those who have been recently enslaved and cannot accept the deference required of them in their new role (as Kaster [1997: 9] observes, elite Romans supposed that '[s]laves had no sense of *pudor* at all'); Euripides' *Hecuba* and *Trojan Women* provide poignant illustrations of this situation. A similar tension arises when a despised group achieves a new sense of equality, and begins to experience shame at treatment formerly regarded as natural or inevitable; thus, Lewis (1987a: 4) observes that 'our sexist intellectual heritage contains an explicit devaluation of women and an implicit, insoluble demand that they accept their inferior place without shame.'

38 Izard 1977: 423–4: 'Guilt results from wrong-doing'; H.B. Lewis 1971: 81: 'Guilt ... is evoked by ... the acceptance or acknowledgment of moral transgression' (both cited in Frijda 1993: 364).

39 Cf. Gilbert and Andrews 1998: 11; H.B. Lewis 1987a: 18.

40 If Aristotle had the word, he might perhaps recognize such events as productive of embarrassment. But cf. the Hippocratic treatise *On the Sacred Disease* 15, where it is observed that people on the point of an epileptic attack hide 'because of shame at the condition and not out of fear of a demon, as most people suppose ... But children allow themselves to fall anywhere at first, and later run to their mothers or other people whom they know, out of terror and fear of the condition; for they do not yet know what it is to be ashamed [*to gar aiskhunesthai oupô gignôskousin*].' Plutarch, however, writing in the first century AD, argues that Homer 'scorns those who cast shame [*aiskhunomenôn*] upon lameness or blindness, since he does not consider blameworthy [*psekton*] what is not shameful [or ugly: *aiskhron*] nor shameful what occurs not through ourselves but by

chance [*tukhê*]' (*On How a Young Man Should Listen to Poetry* 35C).

41 Cf. p. 89: 'The most primitive experiences of shame are connected with sight and being seen, but it has been interestingly suggested that guilt is rooted in hearing'; H.B. Lewis 1987a: 1, 'Shame makes us want to hide.' Pindar, *Pythian* 8.81–7 describes how young men who have been defeated in athletic contests skulk in shame upon returning to their home cities. Jacoby (1991: 13–14), after surveying attitudes towards nakedness in various cultures, concludes that 'nudity has taken on various unusual meanings that can be mutually contradictory,' and is 'related on the one hand to the humiliation of being stripped, but on the other to the will to power and dominance.' He observes further that 'it is clear that the potential for sexual attraction in physical nakedness is one of the most important causes of shame. For any society, it is important to keep unbridled instinctuality in check and to redirect sexuality into civilized channels,' and Jacoby expresses the hope that his 'comments have sufficed to establish the association of the archetypal feeling of shame with the unveiling of physical nakedness.' If this is meant as an account of how and why a sense of shame evolved, it seems dubious to me.

42 There is some debate about the original meaning of the proverb; Grimaldi (1988: 117) argues that it refers to the look of the guilty person (cf. Ferrari 2002: 54–6 on the visibility of maidenly *aidôs*), but Kennedy (1991: 146 n. 57) defends the possibility that it pertains, as Aristotle evidently takes it, to the disapproving look of others.

43 Jacoby (1991: 11–13) plays down the significance of this and related customs, concluding that 'the practice of nudity hardly implies an absence of shame' (12–13). The preoccupation with sexuality and the body characteristic of Christian asceticism and Victorian prudishness can lead to intense sensitivity to shame connected with the body, particularly the sexually mature or maturing body. Simone de Beauvoir (1974: 344–55) describes with particular vividness the shame experienced by pubescent girls in respect to their emerging breasts and the onset of menstruation, but she concludes that '[i]n a sexually equalitarian society, woman would regard menstruation simply as her special way of reaching adult life …; the menses

inspire horror in the adolescent girl because they throw her into an inferior and defective category' (354), and hence are experienced as a sign of inadequacy. It may be worth noting that in Greek medicine of the classical period, menstruation was regarded as a natural way of releasing bad blood, which in men had to be achieved by the artificial means of blood-letting (see Dean-Jones 1994: 64, 123–4).

Modern psychoanalytic theory relates shame to narcissism, or more precisely to the narcissistic stage in infantile development, at which point the child begins to project an ego ideal; this precedes the Oedipal stage, when the superego is formed (H.B. Lewis [1987b: 31–2] challenges this distinction). It is sometimes suggested that shame is a reaction to the fear of separation from the parent, typically the mother, whereas guilt is a response to the fear of punishment by the father (cf. Morris on 1989: 60–1). Freud himself wrote little about shame, and mostly in the early years, before he had arrived at the idea of the superego (Morrison 1989: 22–9), but the Freudian focus on sexuality has led other writers in the psycho-analytic tradition to identify infantile sexual abuse as a major source of pathological shame. H.B. Lewis (1987a: 5) observes that '[i]n turning his attention away from actual seductions to guilt over fantasies, Freud turned away from shame.' For subsequent contribu-tions in the Freudian tradition, see Morrison 1989: 31–66. Jacoby (1991: 21) is unusual in the psychoanalytic tradition in acknowledg-ing a positive function for shame: 'Shame reinforces interpersonal distinctness and a sense of one's own individual identity. On the other hand, an excessive tendency toward reactions of shame may lead to disturbances of contact and social isolation ... Shame's function is thus highly complex, serving the interests of both individuality and conformity'; and again (46): 'Shame ... sets bound-aries on interpersonal contact, thus protecting individuality and identity.' Jacoby concludes (60) that '[s]hame stands in close rela-tionship to the persona. When the persona has holes in it, letting what is beneath "show through," there is a feeling of nakedness, and thus a reaction of shame.'

44 Let me note here again that the shame and honour complex identi-fied by so-called Mediterranean anthropology (see, e.g., Cohen 1991) is not particularly evident in the Greek world of this period. Aristotle observes that we may feel shame over the deeds of ances-

tors or near kin, but he does not single out sexual misconduct of female relatives as a cause of such shame; see Herman 1995. On honour as a traditional value, see Bourdieu 1966; for a powerful critique of the notion of 'tradition' in this context, see Narayan 1997: 43–80.

45 The idea of a divided self was perfectly familiar to Aristotle and his contemporaries; see Aristotle's discussion of self-love in *Nicomachean Ethics* 9.4, and cf. Cicero, *Tusculan Disputations* 2.20.47. Euripides' *Electra* 900–5 offers an interesting case in point. Electra wishes to gloat over the corpse of her arch enemy, Aegisthus, whom her brother Orestes has just slain, but she simultaneously feels shame at the idea: she understands triumphing over the dead to represent a vice. Orestes reminds her that they now have nothing to fear, but she is concerned that someone may react with disapproval (the term here is *phthonos*); her sense of shame is not independent of what others may think. Orestes assures his sister that no one will blame her, but she remains wary of a town given to censuring them. Finally, Orestes dispels her doubts by reminding her that their hostility towards Aegisthus is implacable, and hence (we infer) not even death exempts him from the ill treatment due to enemies. Electra's inner conflict is thus resolved by a new description of the act.

46 Corbeill (2002) argues that the Roman public speaker had a positive duty to maintain a 'desirable fear of shame' (198), and in the service of this moral goal made vigorous use of vituperation and personal insult.

47 See especially Gill 1993, 1996; Foucault 1985; and the essays in Larmour, Miller, and Platter 1998.

48 On shame as the motive for Ajax's suicide, cf. Williams 1993: 85. Of course, if shame is understood to affect the essence of the self and to induce a desire for concealment, it is natural to take it as the cause of self-destructive violence. Shame is also taken to be the motive by Elise Garrison, in her catalogue of male suicides (on the web); but the ancient sources she cites do not mention shame (in her dissertation [1987: 56], Garrison describes Ajax's suicide as 'egoistic,' in the terminology of Durkheim 1996; cf. Garrison 1995: 46–53). Nelli (2002) argues persuasively that 'el suicidio de Áyax se vuelve heroico a través de la re-significación que le otorga la puesta en práctica de

un ritual' ('the suicide of Ajax becomes heroic via the resignification that the establishment of a ritual bestows upon it'). Van Hooff (1990: 85) produces a chart in which 32 per cent of motives for attested suicides in antiquity are ascribed to *pudor* or shame, but the analyses of individual cases (107–20) leave some doubt as to the actual motive; thus, van Hooff notes that a captive 'could be disfigured by torture, which especially in ancient eyes meant a fatal loss of dignity. Therefore in most cases of suicide of people confronted with captivity it was not anguish or despair that were regarded as the main motives, but shame' (110). The argument is not wholly compelling.

49 *Aiskhunê* occurs elsewhere in the play in contexts unrelated to Ajax's sentiments. In the debate over the burial, Menelaus insists that fear (*deos, phobos*) and shame (*aidôs* and *aiskhunê*) are necessary to the well-being of a city, since they prevent the kind of outrage that Ajax sought to commit (1073–86). Later, Teucer declares he feels no shame before Agamemnon and Menelaus with respect to their ostensibly nobler birth (1304–5). The first is an instance of prospective, the latter of retrospective shame. Of course, it is possible that Ajax's shame is implicit in the play, unrecognized by himself or anyone else but present as a latent force. Lansky (2001: 1015), writing of Shakespeare's *Tempest*, observes that '[m]anifest shame never appears in the play at all, but the defenses deployed are defenses specifically against shame.'

50 Unless perhaps he perceives his madness as contributing to a loss of standing; but this motive is not emphasized in the drama.

51 Thus, for Aristotle, *hubris*, which he defines as speaking or acting in ways that cause shame to another for the sheer pleasure of it (*Rhetoric* 2.2, 1378b23–5), is one of the causes of anger (see chapter 2, p. 46). Modern psychology tends rather to associate humiliation with shame (cf. Jacoby 1991: 69–72). H.B. Lewis (1987a) comes close to equating shame with what she calls 'humiliated fury' (12–13; cf. H.B. Lewis 1987b: 32–5), which entails among other things that one 'try to get even or turn the tables on the "other"' (12, cf. 19; 1987b: 35); I find the collapse of a distinction between shame and anger to be one of the confusing elements in her treatment of shame. Toohey (2004: 40–1) argues that Ajax was in fact melancholic, or in modern terms manic-depressive, and that after his attack of madness, he exhibits the signs 'of someone who has fallen victim to such a

manic attack' (41; cf. 172: 'Ajax was probably mentally ill'). According to Toohey, 'People do not kill themselves because they are
depressed or lovesick or bored or in pain ... They kill themselves
because they are ill' (161). Toohey recogizes that suicide as a literary
motif has its own logic or mythic structure (189).

52 After Neoptolemus returns the bow, Philoctetes persists in his
intention to return home rather than proceed to Troy, where he can
both be healed and assist in the conquest of the city; he only changes
his mind when the ghost of Hercules himself appears and bids him
fulfil his own destiny and that of the bow. In an intriguing paper, so
far unpublished, on *Philoctetes*, Melvin Lansky analyses Philoctetes'
reaction as a function of hidden shame.

53 Shweder and Haidt explain that 'to be full of *lajja* is to be in possession of the virtue of behaving in a civilized manner and in such a
way that the social order and its norms are upheld' (408), and they
add (409): 'In a cultural world based on an ethics of community,
emotions may exist that are not fully felt by those whose morality is
based on an ethics of autonomy. *Lajja* is a clear example.' Cf. Abu-
Lughod 1999: 105: 'In the leading dictionary of modern standard
Arabic, various words formed from the triliteral root ḥashama are
translated by a cluster of words including modesty, shame, and
shyness. In its broadest sense, it means propriety.'

54 Scheff (2000 and elsewhere) describes the social utility of shame as
creating a bond within a community; but shame can also serve to
exclude those who are shamed. These two functions are evident also
in ridicule or joking (cf. O'Higgins 2003: 4).

55 This does not mean, of course, that it is illegitimate to interpret
Ajax's behaviour as shame in the modern sense, or to detect 'hidden
shame' in his behaviour. I am grateful to Melvin Lansky for comments on this and other aspects of the present chapter.

Chapter Five

1 Cf. Lucian, *Prometheus* 18, who defines *phthonos* as 'preventing
people from sharing in things they need although it costs you
nothing'; Rawls 1971: 532, on envy as 'the propensity to view with
hostility the greater good of others even though their being more
fortunate than we does not detract from our advantages.'

2 Planalp (1999: 176) cites Schoeck (1966) for the view that 'envy is particularly unmentionable in the United States because Americans do not want to admit that they are not all equals'; cf. Hochschild 1975: 292: 'Envy without a social movement is a particularly private, unlegitimated feeling'; and Elster 1999a: 164, 167–9, 183. The ideology of equality in classical Athens does not appear to have had the same repressive effect on the concept of *phthonos*, but see Plutarch (1st–2nd century AD), *On Envy* 537E; and Dickie 1981 on Roman satire.

3 There are exceptions, of course; Pseudo-Plutarch, *On Homer* 132 follows Aristotle. Cicero, *To Atticus* 5.19.3 distinguishes two senses of the Latin *invidia* with reference to the difference between *to nemesan* and *to phthonein*; Kaster (2003, 2005) shows that the former sense predominates in Roman literature, and is invoked to elicit shame or *pudor* in another.

4 Aspasius, a second-century AD commentator on Aristotle's *Ethics* (p. 55.12–27 Heylbut 1889), confesses his confusion at Aristotle's classification here. In his dense analysis of the laughable, Plato describes *phthonos* as pleasure at the misfortunes of others, which is legitimate (and therefore not *phthoneron* or malicious) in the case of enemies and illegitimate (and hence strictly speaking malicious) in the case of misfortunes suffered by friends (*Philebus* 48B, 49C–D). Plato's *phthonos* thus comes close to Aristotle's *epikhairekakia*, or 'Schadenfreude,' and is translated as 'malice' by Dorothea Frede (1997: 437–4). Plato specifies that in itself *phthonos* is painful, and hence the pleasure associated with it is mixed (50A). The reference to friends versus enemies perhaps goes back to Socrates himself, since Xenophon (*Memorabilia* 3.9.8) ascribes to him the view that *phthonos* is 'pain ... not at the misfortunes of friends nor at the good fortune of enemies, but rather only those feel *phthonos* who are hurt by the well-being of friends.' Cf. also pseudo-Plato, *Definitions* 416, where *phthonos* is defined as 'pain at the goods, either present or past, of friends.' But the latter two characterizations are otherwise consistent with Aristotle's view. On pleasure in the misfortune of enemies, compare Euripides, *Children of Hercules* 939–40: 'For it is sweetest to see one's enemy [*ekhthros*] fall from good fortune and suffer misfortune.'

5 E.g., Theognis 1.660, 1182; Pindar, *Isthmian* 1.3–4; Euripides,

Orestes 1361–2; Sophocles, *Philoctetes* 518, 602; Herodotus 1.34; Plato, *Minos* 319A3–4; Plato Comicus, *Phaon* fr. 173.13–14 Kassel-Austin; Theocritus, *Idyll* 27.63; Theophrastus, *On Piety* fr. 3.1–2; Callimachus, *Aitia* fr. 96, *Hymn to Delos* 259; Polybius 27.8.4 (a speech).

6 Cf., e.g., Theognis 1.280; Plato, *Cratylus* 401A5, *Theaetetus* 175E2, *Laws* 684E4, 876C8; Aeschines, *Against Ctesias* 66.1–3; Callimachus, *Hymn to Artemis* 64, *Hymn to Delos* 107.

7 It is an 'emotionale Reaktion ... auf Handlungen anderer, die nicht den allg. moralischen Erwartungen entsprechen' ('emotional reaction to the behaviour of others who do not respond to general moral expectations'), Stenger 2000: 818.

8 Cf. also 8.198; Stenger (2000: 818) observes that the gods respond with *nemesis* 'wenn Menschen versuchen, die Grenze zu ihnen zu überschreiten' ('when human beings attempt to overstep their boundaries').

9 Cf. N.R.E. Fisher 1992: 193; Cairns 1993: 51–2; for the pairing of shame with negative judgments on the part of others in Chinese, see Li, Wang, and Fischer 2003.

10 E.g., *Odyssey* 1.263; cf. Redfield 1975: 117; and Cairns 1993: 85 n. 120. This is not the place to investigate in detail the Homeric idea of *aidôs* and *aideisthai*, but I should like to suggest that *aidôs* is not simply a response to social norms, but also a way of invoking their application: one adopts a posture of modesty (that is, one shows oneself to be *aidoios*) in order to elicit respect (*aidôs*) in the other. As Gloria Ferrari (2002: 55) argues, '*Aidos* ... is made visible by the chastely downcast glance and by the act of covering oneself.' *Aidôs* is thus something one performs as well as elicits: it is a reciprocal concept. A paradigmatic case is the plea of the young Trojan Lycaon, who, stripped of his armour, encounters a raging Achilles on the battlefield (*Iliad* 21.74–5) and assumes the position of supplication: 'I grasp your knees, Achilles; you, in turn, show me *aidôs* and pity me; I am in the position of an *aidoios* suppliant.' Had Achilles accepted the plea (in fact, he did not), he would have acknowledged a relationship between himself and Lycaon represented by the term *aidôs*. The double sense is inherent in the word *aidoios*, which means deserving of *aidôs* or regard (Liddell, Scott, and Jones 1940: s.v. *aidoios*), but also 'showing reverence or compassion' (ibid. = LSJ;

cf. Adrados et al. 1980–, s.v.). Both aspects are part of the exchange
in which an appeal to *aidôs* is enacted. For examples of the active
and passive senses of *aidoios*, cf. *Odyssey* 9.269–71; *Iliad* 3.172
(Helen addresses Priam as *aidoios*: he is worthy of her reverence but
also the only one who has shown regard for her); and 14.210 (Hera
declares that she will be an *aidoia* friend of Aphrodite; cf. 18.386,
394, of Thetis). Ferrari has called attention to the passage in
Pausanias (3.20.10), in which Penelope, after choosing Odysseus
as her husband, is pursued by her father Icarius, who wishes that she
and Odysseus remain with him in Lacedaemon. When Odysseus
demanded to know whether she will be a wife or a daughter,
Penelope said nothing, 'but covered her face with a veil in reply
to the question, so that Icarius, realizing that she wished to depart
with Odysseus, let her go, and dedicated an image of *Aidos*.' By her
gesture, Penelope both exhibits *aidôs* and demands due regard. She
cannot openly defy her father. Instead, she reminds him that she is
aidoia and entitled to *aidôs*. Brought up short, Icarius acknowledges
his daughter's simultaneous sign of her own decorum and her claim
to his respect, and he erects the statue to Aidôs.

11 Cairns (1993: 53) observes that '[t]he range of *nemesis* is very wide;
it is frequently employed in condemnation of violence or excess,
and also in a number of minor social contexts, where it censures
infringement of decorum. In some cases it seems to signify little
more than anger, although, as Redfield [1975: 117] points out, it
always connotes anger in which the subject feels himself justified.'
This last qualification is doubtless true, but it is equally so of *orgê*
or 'anger,' at least according to Aristotle's definition of *orgê* as 'a
desire, accompanied by pain, for a perceived revenge, on account of a
perceived slight *on the part of those who are not fit to slight one* or
one's own' (*Rhetoric* 2.2, 1378a31–3).

12 So Herrmann 2003; contra Most 2003; Bulman 1992: 1, 15–16 takes
it that Homeric usage is simply loose.

13 There is also a second occurrence of the root *phthon-* in the form
aphthonon, 'abundant' (118), a sense that perhaps points to an
original meaning of 'deny' or 'begrudge' for *phthoneô* (*phthoneô* is
the only form that appears in the Homeric Hymns: *To Aphrodite*
4.536; *To Earth Mother of All* 30.8, 16).

14 Aeschylus, *Seven against Thebes* 236; Euripides, *Medea* 63; Plato,

Gorgias 489A; Xenophon, *Symposium* 3.5; cf. ibid. 1.12: 'It is shameful to begrudge [*phthoneô*] someone the shelter of a roof: let him enter'; Isocrates, *Antidosis* 62 on people who 'will not go so far as to say "good"' (*to gar 'eu' phthonêsousin eipein*); Walcot 1978: 26.

15 Twenty-five occurrences, according to Bulman 1992: 1; four times in what remains of Bacchylides; once in Theognis, 1.770; for the different attitude towards *phthonos* in Pindar, where it inevitably accompanies success, and Bacchylides, where poetry can moderate it, see Most 2003.

16 Only three times in Pindar, as in Theognis; twice in Aeschylus as contrasted with seventeen times for *phthonos* and related terms, excluding *aphthonos* and the like, in the surviving plays.

17 Cf. Herodotus 3.52; Thales 108.10d17, Diels and Kranz 1951–2; Heliodorus, *Aethiopica* 6.10.2; and Arnold Schwarzenegger, governor of California, as quoted in LeDuff 2004: A12: 'You have to remember something. Everybody pities the weak. Jealousy you have to earn.'

18 Nicias hints that the *phthonos* of the gods may have been provoked by the Athenians' overreaching ambition; for the novelty of this concession on the part of an Athenian within Thucydides' history, and its relation to the theme of the other states' envy of Athens, see Tzifopoulos 1995: 100–1, and 1997: 501–4.

19 See Konstan 2001a: 34–43; cf. Euripides' *Suppliant Women* 168 with 186 and 194, 233 with 280, 304, and 328 (the words are *oiktos* and *oiktirein*); Ničev 1985.

20 Cf. *Plataïcus* 52.4; *Against Callimachus* 62; Plato, *Protagoras* 323D.

21 For the positive sense of *phthonos* in Attic prose, see Fisher 2003: 199–202; Saïd 2003: 225; and Cairns 2003: 246–8.

22 The scholia comment unhelpfully: '*phthonos* and pity are two most opposite things' (Dilts 1986: 247).

23 Cf. *Plataïcus* 47; *Peace* 124; *To Archidamus* 15, on unjust envy of people of greater ability; *Panegyricus* 47, of those with greater knowledge; *To Nicocles* 59, where Isocrates advises his disciples not to *phthonein* those who excel (*tois prôteuousin*), but rather compete (*hamillasthe*) so as to make themselves equal (*exisousthai*), the point being that *phthonos* towards those who have made progress is wrong, since it implies a desire to bring them down to one's own level rather than raise oneself to theirs (*phthonos* would have been

their due if they had advanced themselves illegitimately); on these
and other examples in Isocrates, see Saïd 2003.

24 LSJ s.v. I.3, citing Isocrates 8.124, 4.184, Demosthenes 28.18; cf.
Walcot 1978: 3: '[E]ven *phthonos* is not wholly bad'; and especially
Ranulf 1933: 106–11 for the 'moral' use of *phthonos* and cognate
terms.

25 On litigation against the rich, cf. Demosthenes 20.139–40; Isocrates
15.31, 141–2, and 159–60; Lysias 21.15; Walcot 1978: 67–73; Ober
1989: 217–19; and Cohen 1995: 82–3, 113–14; on service to the
dêmos, P. Wilson 2000: 172–84; Cairns 2003; N.R.E. Fisher 2003;
and Saïd 2003. Benefactions by the rich rather deserve gratitude:
Pindar, *Olympian* 7.89–91, *Nemean* 11.13–17; Demosthenes,
Epistles 3.28; cf. Walcot 1978: 73–4; and Kurke 1991: 209–14.

26 Cf. Euripides, *Electra* 30 (of Clytemnestra's decision not to kill
Electra): 'She feared she might be subject to *phthonos* [*phthonêtheiê*]
for the murder of her children'; ibid. 902, where Electra hesitates to
gloat over the corpse of Aegisthus, 'lest someone smite her with
phthonos.' Bulman (1992: 1) affirms that 'human φθόνος in Pindar is
a completely negative emotion' arising from 'ignorance of human
limitations' and a passion to transcend them (cf. p. 3: 'φθόνος is the
supreme negative emotion in Pindar'), but that 'the φθόνος of the
gods is better understood as equivalent to νέμεσις,' and should be
translated not as 'envy' but rather as 'retribution,' for example at
Isthmian 7.39–42 (31; survey of examples of human *phthonos* in
Pindar on pp. 17–31, and of divine *phthonos* on pp. 31–6). But
Bulman offers no explanation for why the word should have such
radically different meanings in the two contexts. As Cairns (1996:
20) remarks: 'There is no question of a total separation of meaning
between human and divine *phthonos*'; when the gods feel *phthonos*,
they, like human beings, believe that the emotion is justified (21).
Bulman is right, in my view, to reject the attempt of Steinlein (1941:
20) and others to salvage a positive sense for *phthonos* as 'a barom-
eter to measure the good fortune possessed by an individual' (5); cf.
Milobenski 1964); no self-respecting aristocrat wants to deserve
envy in the sense of being perceived to possess good things to which
he is not entitled or which he abuses. The *phthonos* that Pindar
singles out for blame is that directed against virtue (*Parth.* 1.8–9;
cf. *Pythian* 7.19–20, on *phthonos* provoked by *kala*; also *Pythian*

11.29) – that is, the misguided *phthonos* characteristic of the
phthoneroi, who harbour an illegitimate resentment against their
betters. This does not mean that *phthonos* is never deserved,
however; and it is just this justified sense of *phthonos* that the gods
presumably feel at human excess, and which human beings can feel
as well. While Pindar's usage certainly anticipates, as Bulman says
(7), the negative account of *phthonos* in Aristotle, as contrasted for
example with *zêlos*, it reveals less a 'thoroughly consistent concept
of φθόνος' (1) than the social source of the pejorative sense of the
term.

27 Stearns (1989: 12) suggests that envy may be characteristic of the
lower orders, since 'it involves coveting something or some attribute
that someone else has,' while jealousy, as the desire to retain what
one possesses, is typically 'the emotion of the upper classes.' For
phthonos on the part of the worse towards their betters, cf. Euripides,
Alcestis 306.

28 *Cypria* fr. 9, Bernabé 1987 = Athenaeus 8.334B; cf. Apollodorus
3.10.7; Hornum 1993: 1–9; Stafford 2000: 78–9; and Stenger 2000:
818.

29 Hornum 1993: 174 = no. 35 in his catalogue of inscriptions mentioning Nemesis or *nemesis* on pp. 153–317; also published in G. Mik-
hailov, *Inscriptiones graecae in Bulgaria repertae* I: 118 n. 220.

30 For the personification of *Phthonos*, cf. also Callimachus, *Hymn to
Apollo* 105–13.

31 Cf. Lucian, *Prometheus* 18: 'The gods ... should stand outside all
phthonos.'

32 E.g., Pindar, *Pythian* 10.21–2; cf. *Olympian* 13.25–6; Aeschylus,
Persians 362; Euripides, *Alcestis* 1135; *Iphigeneia at Aulis*, 1097;
Suppliant Women 348; cf. Dodds 1951: 28–63; and Dickie 1987.
Kirkwood (1984: 176) suggests that divine envy may be a topos of
praise in Pindar; cf. Cairns 2003: 250.

33 In Sophocles' *Electra*, Aegisthus, believing that Orestes lies dead
before him, exclaims (1466–7): 'O Zeus, I see an apparition that has
descended not without *phthonos*; whether *nemesis* too attends on it
I cannot say.' Aegisthus presumably means that Orestes had of-
fended the gods (hence their *phthonos*), but that perhaps there will
be no further vengeance. Ranulf (1933: 90–106) argues that the
Greeks of the classical period did not clearly discriminate between

cases in which the gods visited misfortune upon human beings because of their guilt (his Type I), randomly (Type II), or out of jealousy (Type III). He allows, however, that 'the expression "jealousy of the gods" may stand for "moral disapproval on the part of the gods" in Euripides' (110). Ranulf's erroneous assumption that the 'original sense' of *phthonos* was jealousy (111) leads him to assume that this meaning was progressively 'toned down,' thus acquiring a moral significance it did not originally possess; but the analogy between divine *phthonos* and divine *nemesis* undermines his theory.

34 E.g., Aeschines 2.22, 51, 54, 129, 3.81; Isocrates 12.15–16, 14.4, 8, 13, 163–4, 244–6; Lysias 3.9.

35 Cf. Plato, *Lysis* 215D; Milobenski 1964: 66–9, 72 nn. 41–2; Schoeck 1966: 39; Walcot 1978: 11, 63–5; Elster 1999a: 171; and Cairns 2003: 240: 'Envy thus aims at ideal equality, but thrives on perceived inequality.'

36 For Pindar's role, see n. 26 above. There is perhaps a hint of a wider contention over the class character of *phthonos* in the view expressed by the chorus of sailors in Sophocles' *Ajax*. Aware that Odysseus is accusing Ajax of having slaughtered the army's cattle, they remark: 'About you he is very persuasive, and everyone who hears him speak rejoices the more insolently over your troubles, since one never misses when casting at great spirits. If someone were to say such things against me, he would persuade no one, for *phthonos* stalks the one who has' (150–7). The object of envy here is not so much one who exceeds his station (the older view) as one whose station or character is above the ordinary: Odysseus is cast as a demagogue (often his role in tragedy, although he is not, in fact, in this one) who is stirring up resentment among the masses. The chorus members themselves defend a hierarchical order based on a mutually beneficial relationship between a great or noble individual and lesser men (158–61), a point that senseless people – an allusion to the rabble – are incapable of grasping (162–3).

37 There is an interesting analogy with the differentiation between the archaic *nemesis* and the more recent *phthonos* in the pair *homilos* (Homeric) and *okhlos*, meaning 'crowd.' As Karpyuk (2000: 81) observes, *okhlos* 'surfaces for the first time' in the 'first half of the

fifth century B.C.,' when there was considerable activity in the coining of new terms. 'Aeschylus, Sophocles, and Thucydides used the two words interchangeably,' but in the course of the fifth century *okhlos* assumed the pejorative connotation of 'mob.' For a model study of how the meaning of a Greek value term (*eleutheria* or 'freedom') might be modulated by class interests, see Raaflaub 2004.

38 Cf. Walcot 1978: 165; Fuentes 2001: 54: 'Envy is a powerless poison'; Farrell 1989: 254 on envy as 'something objectionable and, in its extreme forms, even sinful'; Lansky 1997: 327: 'Envy is especially malignant because the hate and destruction it engenders are directed at what is seen as good, not as bad'; Lansky argues that chronic envy 'is instigated by an experience of shame' (331), and simultaneously generates feelings of shame (332).

39 Cf. Ben-Ze'ev 2000: 262, 283; Farrell 1989: 262: '[E]nvy does not, in our culture, come in for anything like the abuse that jealousy tends to receive' (Farrell [1989: 253, 263] questions whether 'friendly envy' or admiration counts as envy at all); Smith 1991: 83: 'the person feeling envy (in its typically hostile form) will believe that the envied person's advantage is to some degree unfair' (cf. 89); Parrott (1991: 10) distinguishes between non-malicious envy ('I wish I had what you have') and malicious envy ('I wish you did not have what you do'). In a *New Yorker* cartoon (21 May 2001, p. 91) by Barbara Smaller, a man standing before his boss's desk says: 'O.K., if you can't see your way to giving me a pay raise, how about giving Parkerson a pay cut?'

40 Plutarch too associates 'the hostility of the masses toward eminence' with fifth-century Athenian democracy; cf. Wardman 1974: 73. It suits an elite class to assume that they are naturally immune to the envy of their inferiors; but see Aristotle, *Politics* 1280a23–5, 1301a28–35 on the poor seeking to equal the rich while the rich desire to preserve their privileges: the result is envy on the part of the poor: *tôn men phthonountôn tôn de kataphronountôn* (1295b21–3); cf. Walcot 1978: 64, Ober 1989: 202–8. Parrott (1991: 7) follows Aristotle in insisting that envy is principally directed towards equals: 'People do not necessarily envy the Rockefellers' wealth, because the discrepancy does not reflect badly on them.'

41 Rawls (1971: 533) distinguishes between envy, which is not a moral feeling, and resentment, which is; so too Emanuel Swedenborg wrote in 1768 that 'there is a just and an unjust jealousy' (English trans. in Swedenborg 1928; cited by Stearns 1989: 15).

Chapter Six

1 Scheff (2000: 97) observes more cautiously that '[t]he sources of fear and anger, unlike shame, are not uniquely social.'
2 Latin, we may remark in passing, distinguishes the two senses by varying the case of the object (accusative versus dative), where as Greek, like English, uses a preposition.
3 Contrast Delumeau 1978: 22: 'L'animal n'anticipe pas sa mort. L'homme au contraire sait – très tôt – qu'il mourra.'
4 As indicated in chapter 2 (p. 42), Aristotle treats the anticipation of pleasure (and presumably of pain as well) as a weak *phantasia*, or perception (*Rhetoric* 1.11, 1370a27–34); the mere expectation or presentiment of pain, then, is an *aisthêsis*, not a *pathos*. The emotion of fear entails a judgment about the harmful nature of a perceived thing or event.
5 Solomon (2000: 11–12) points out that cognition is variously equated by students of the emotions with beliefs, judgments, thoughts (e.g., Spinoza), and evaluations.
6 Aspasius adds rather that his claim is particularly evident in the case of desires, as in the desire for something beautiful (*Commentary on Nicomachean Ethics*, pp. 44–5 Heylbut). Whether desire constitutes an emotion for Aristotle is debatable; Sorabji 1999: 134–6) holds that it does, whereas my own view is that it is rather an appetite. Certainly, the Stoics added desire, along with fear, to Aristotle's simple pair of pleasure and pain, and classified all emotions under one or another of these four rubrics. Both anger and hatred, for example, fall under the genus desire in their system. This still does not mean that the Stoics considered desire itself to be an emotion, any more than Aristotle held pain and pleasure to be emotions; rather, they are a necessary component of any emotion (the Stoic categories may be conceived as 'approach' and 'avoidance' rather than 'desire' and 'fear' in their usual sense). We need not enter into the question of the Stoic genera here, as it involves some highly

technical issues; it seems clear, at all events, that Aspasius was prepared to denominate desire as an emotion, and on the basis of this description to argue that emotions may be aroused by simple perception, independently of belief or judgment.

7 William Miller, who approves an element of rashness in courage, writes (with Aristotle in mind) that '[t]he proponents of deliberate courage are rather uncharitable to the more passionately motivated' (Miller 2000: 160). In the *Rhetoric*, however, confidence (*tharros*) is an emotion, not a vice, and, precisely as an emotion, it involves a large measure of calculation. A rash person (*thrasus*) tends to have an excess of confidence (*Nicomachean Ethics* 2.7, 1107b2–3; 3.7, 1115b28–9). When courage is defined as a mean between fear and confidence (*Nicomachean Ethics* 3.6, 1115a6–7), the extremes stand for dispositions (fearfulness, boldness) rather than passions.

8 At *Nicomachean Ethics* 1116b31–3 Aristotle contrasts humans with animals, which are moved by pain or *thumos* but not by rational motives; cf. Polin 1953: 20 on Thomas Hobbes: 'La crainte, passion proprement humaine, est bien différente de la terreur qu'éprouvent aussi les animaux' ('Fear, properly a human emotion, is quite different from the terror that animals also experience'; cited in Romilly 1956: 124 n. 1).

9 Demetrius (*On Style* 159) notes the comic effect that results when someone is relieved from an empty (*diakenês*) fright, for example mistaking a strap for a snake. Scruton (1986: 34) observes that fear of snakes does not develop until children reach a certain age; if it is in some sense innate, it is nevertheless activated by training or education.

10 Cf. *Eudemian Ethics* 1228b4–30a34 (contrast *Topics* 4.5); Smoes 1995: 217–33. Plutarch, in his essay 'On How a Youth Should Listen to Poems' 29E, observes that the Trojan Dolon boasts that he can reach Agamemnon's own ship (*Iliad* 10.325–6); 'Diomedes, however, does not boast, but says that he is less afraid if he is sent out with another [*Iliad* 10.222–3]. Foresight is Greek and smart, boldness barbarian and ignoble.' Aristotle's view of the relationship between courage and fear is complicated by his belief that a continent or self-controlled person resists and conquers pains and pleasures, whereas a virtuous person is free of such internal conflict; thus, a truly courageous person should not experience the pain associated with

fear (see Leighton 1987: 81–2). Aristotle can call a person courageous who is fearless (*adeês*), for example, before the prospect of a noble death (*Nicomachean Ethics* 1115a33). As Leighton (85) observes, however, Aristotle's 'commitment to fearlessness in courage is not long lasting.' Cf. *Eudemian Ethics* 1228b24–37, where Aristotle distinguishes things that are frightening to a person qua human being, but not qua courageous. For further discussion of Aristotle's position on courage, see Pears 1978; Mills 1980; and Duff 1987.

11 Xenophon, *Memorabilia* 3.5.5–6; cf. Xenophon, *On Horsemanship* 7.7 (*phobos*); Isocrates *Areopagiticus* 6 (*dedienai*).

12 Andronicus, a scholar living in the time of Augustus who is frequently cited in the Homeric scholia, adopted the view of Aristarchus that in Homer the word *phobos* and the associated verb *phobeomai* just mean 'flight' or 'flee,' while 'what we call *phobos*, he [i.e., Homer] calls *deos*' (ad 11.71; cf. ad 2.767, 5.223 [followed by LSJ s.v. *phobeomai*], 5.252, 5.272, 6.97, 6.278, 8.159, 11.173, 11.402, 12.144, etc.). Andronicus is worried by 12.46, with good reason: *tarbei* is clearly equivalent here to *phobeitai*. Cf. also 9.2, where *phobos* is the companion of flight and is described as 'cold' (on coldness as a sign of fear, cf. Pseudo-Plutarch, *On Homer* 131 and Porphyry, *Homeric Questions* p. 64.5–12 Sodano 1970); also scholia ad 10.10: 'Homer usually calls *phobos* cowardly fear [*deiliasis*] accompanied by flight.' At *Odyssey* 22.299 (of the suitors), the term clearly indicates flight, being equivalent to *epessumenoi* at 307. Thus, a propos the present passage, Andronicus remarks that *phobêtheis* is used in place of *phugôn*, 'taking to flight.' While Andronicus overstates the case for synonymy, in my view, we need not belabour the issue: if *phobos* means 'flight,' it is flight induced by danger and no other kind. Hector runs in fear. But it is fear proportionate to the cause. After a careful review of passages, Harkemanne (1967: 61) concludes: 'chez Homère, φόβος signifie déjà "peur."'

13 Cf. Odysseus at *Iliad* 11.404–10; Trümpy 1950: 231: 'Die Flucht [sc. in Homer] ist eine taktische Massnahme, gilt also meist nicht als feige Handlung' ('Flight is a tactical measure, and so it does not usually count as cowardly behaviour'); Wissmann 1997: 29. As W.I. Miller 2000: 129–30 remarks, 'Fear was a tormenting omnipresence in the heroic world ... One paid homage to fear ... Homer insists

that the strong-hearted feel the grip of fear; no hero in the *Iliad* does not feel fear at one time or another.' See too the newly edited but still unpublished fragment of Archilochus (Oxyrhynchus papyrus 4708), available in partial form on-line at http:// www.papyrology.ox.ac.uk/monster/demo/Page1.html.

14 W.I. Miller (2000: 71) remarks: 'In the Western aggressive precedence-setting system the assumption is that only the few will not show themselves cowards some of the time. Even Hector must run, Ajax and Diomedes retreat.' This may be true of the later Western tradition, but it does not apply, I am arguing, to the Homeric code.

15 We might be inclined to distinguish between deliberate flight and a panic reaction, which is outside our power to control: '[O]f fleeing there be two sorts; the one proceeding of a sudden and unlooked for terror, which is least blameable; the other is voluntary, and, as it were, a determinate intention to give place unto the enemy – a fault exceeding foule and not excusable' (W.I. Miller 2000: 96, quoting William Winthrop's *Military Law and Precedents* [1920] under 'Running Away,' which in turn cites the late-sixteenth-century writer Robert Barker (1602: 1.16). But it is not clear that the distinction is germane to Hector's conduct here. I return to the Greek conception of panic below.

16 Cf. W.I. Miller 2000: 130: 'It is not until the nineteenth century that we first find soldiers admitting in letters home or in memoirs that they were afraid, but they still took all due precaution about voicing their fears to comrades.' Contrast the official ideology of fearlessness in the face of death that is expressed in the following citation for the Medal of Honor awarded to gunnery sergeant William Walsh (Second World War), who is said to have 'fearlessly charged ... against the Japanese entrenched on the ridge above him, utterly oblivious to the unrelenting fury of hostile automatic weapons fire' (U.S. Senate *Medal of Honor Recipients* 705, as quoted by W.I. Miller 2000: 68).

17 W.I. Miller (2000: 87) observes that 'so insistent are the beliefs engendered by a model of fearless warrior courage, a model [men] even know is not the only model of courage nor the only one they may subscribe to, that the experience of fear makes them, in their own eyes, a chicken.'

18 At the end of *Prometheus Bound*, Prometheus acknowledges that the thunderbolts and threats of Zeus arouse *phobos* in him (1089–90);

this fear, however, does not diminish his resolve. Griffith (1983: 279 ad loc.) comments: 'P. can feel fear (cf. 127, despite 933), but not to the point of "cowering" (174, 960) or surrendering his secret ... Like most of the great tragic heroes, he is subject to the same emotions and weaknesses that ordinary people experience ..., yet at the same time distinguished from ordinary people by peculiar characteristics ... which enable him to act in extraordinary ways. If P. felt no pain or fear, his plight would not move us.' I would say more simply that fear is inseparable from courage, and no one – not even a god – would be fearless in Prometheus's position.

19 Wissmann (1997: 75) concludes that avoiding the charge of cowardice was a crucial motivation in the warrior society represented by Homeric epic.

20 Today, by contrast, '[i]t is usually supposed that fear leads to flight' (W.I. Miller 1997: 25).

21 See C.A. Barton 2001: 2: 'What we, with our ideal of freedom from the befuddling fumes of passion, might ascribe to politics or economics, class or gender, the Romans would have attributed to fear, desire, shame, arrogance, ambition, envy, greed, love, or lust.'

22 Hostile states may be mutually wary of each other, especially if one is restless to get out from under the domination of the other, for then there is a permanent motive for attack, residing precisely in the fear that the other party may grow too strong. At Thucydides 3.11.2, the Mytilenaeans appeal to the Spartans to support them in their rebellion against Athens. Benjamin Jowett translates: 'Mutual fear [to antipalon deos] is the only solid basis of alliance: for he who would break faith is deterred from aggression by the consciousness of inferiority [tôi mê proukhôn].' But how can there be a mutual consciousness of inferiority? In fact, Thucydides says 'by virtue of not exceeding the other.' Now, the Mytilenaeans had already expressed their fear of Athens's growing power as they themselves were becoming more isolated (3.10.4–11.1). Before the rest of the allies had been reduced, the Mytilenaeans' naval power induced fear (phobos) in the Athenians that they might ally themselves with another state (3.11.6). During this stand-off, there was mutual anxiety, the Athenians fearing (dediotes, 3.12.1) what the Mytilenaeans might do in case of war, the Mytlinaeans fawning on the Athenians in peacetime. 'Whereas it is goodwill that most confirms

trust for others, for us it was fear [*phobos*] that made it strong, and
we were bound together as allies by dread [*deos*] rather than friendship, and to whichever side security furnished confidence [*tharsos*],
that was the side that was going to transgress' (3.12.1). If the Mytilenaeans made the first move, that too was reasonable, they claim;
'for if we were able to counter-plot and outwait them on an equal
basis, why on a similar basis did we have to be in their power? Since
it was in their power ever to attack, with us lay the necessity as well
to anticipate them by defending ourselves' (3.12.3). And they conclude: 'Having such motives and reasons, Lacedaemonians and
allies, we revolted, reasons clear enough for those who hear us to
know that we did what was natural, and sufficient for us to fear
and to turn to some safety' (3.13.1). For all their waffling, the
Mytilenaeans' fear is the same as that which drove the Spartans
to make war on Athens.

23 The Romans inclined to think that fear of the enemy (*metus
hostilis*) inspired courage; cf. C.A. Barton 2000: 51 with n. 93: '"Up
against the wall" was, for the Romans, the most stimulating and
indeed the strongest position' (51–2). W.I. Miller (2000: 133) observes
that Nicias exhorts his men in Sicily (Thucydides 6.68) 'not by
rousing rah-rah, but by cold reason's grimmest ҩssessments of the
present situation.' Cf. Romilly 1956: 122 (of Thucydides): 'Et l'on
arrive bientôt à ce paradoxe que la crainte devient une force et rend
le faible supérieur au fort' ('One soon arrives at the paradox that fear
becomes a force and renders the weak superior to the strong').

24 I say 'Thucydides' text,' because neither the Peloponnesian generals
nor Phormio is likely to have addressed their troops in this manner.
Apart from the characteristically compressed style that Thucydides
employs in all his speeches, which reveals his active hand in composing them, it is in practice impossible, Mogens Hansen has argued
(1993), to deliver such orations to an army with the unaided voice,
except under special conditions, though there is a case to be made
that the ancient historians were aware of the difficulties and recognized a difference between pre-deployment and post-deployment
harangues.

25 W.I. Miller (2000: 169–71) offers a remarkable analysis of the general
Demosthenes' speech to the Athenians defending Pylos against the
landing of a superior force of Spartans (4.10). Demosthenes begins by

cautioning his men not to be clever (*sunetos*) and calculate
(*eklogizomenos*) the risk, but to engage the enemy with uncritical
optimism (*aperiskeptôs euelpis*). Miller paraphrases (170): 'Don't
think, just charge. Thinking will only prompt despair.' But, as Miller
notes, Demosthenes proceeds to contradict his own advice and
demonstrate that the situation is in fact better than it seems: the
Athenians already control the beachhead, and there is no reason
greatly to fear (*agan phobeisthai*) the Spartans' superior numbers
since they will not be able to land their men simultaneously.
Demosthenes reminds his men that the Spartans too will face
obstacles. As Miller explains Demosthenes' strategy, he insinuates
that 'the Spartans must be scared stiff because ... we have been in
the exact situation the Spartans are in now and we were scared stiff
ourselves' (171) – though not as badly, since the Athenians are better
sailors. 'Thus I believe,' Demosthenes concludes, 'that their difficulties will counterbalance our numbers.' The Athenians, Thucydides
tells us (4.11), took heart (*etharsêsan*) from Demosthenes' exhortation. As Miller says, 'The speech is rhetorically and psychologically
masterful. Demosthenes' wits did not undo *his* courage, but he did
not need them to embolden himself. Rather his courage kept his
wits functioning so that he could use them to aid the cause of his
men's faltering courage, undone in part by their wits' (171). The
mutual interaction of judgment and emotion (for Miller's 'courage'
it is better to understand 'confidence') illustrates perfectly both the
cognitive basis of the emotions and their role as 'those things on
account of which people change their minds and differ in regard to
their judgments.' For modern discussions of this reciprocal influence, see Frijda, Manstead, and Bem, eds 2000. Walbank (1985: 242–
3) refers the inclusion of speeches by the ancient historians to 'the
concept that man is a rational being, whose actions are the result of
conscious decisions, and that these decisions are the outcome of
discourse.'

26 Thalmann (1978: 102) observes: 'The chorus are not just a group of
panic-stricken virgins ... they represent Thebes as a whole.'

27 Cf. Marina and López Penas 2001: 47: 'Los sentimientos producen
otros sentimientos. El desprecio provoca el rencor, el rencor la
venganza, la venganza el dolor y el odio y a veces la frustración, y
posiblemente la culpabilidad' ('Emotions generate other emotions.

Contempt induces resentment, resentment revenge, revenge pain
and hatred and sometimes frustration, and possibly guilt too');
Lansky 1991: 484 on 'the transformation of shame into fear' (cf. 488;
the idea of such transformation is central to psychoanaltyic theory);
Rendell 1981: 37 (quoted in chapter 1, p. 19). Ancient Greek writers
tended to think of contradictory emotions as coexisting rather than
displacing one another: cf. Diodorus Siculus 32.27.2 (Const. Excerpt
4, pp. 380–1); Fusillo 1999; Kytzler 2003. Longinus (*On the Sublime*
21.1), however, mentions how people jump from one emotion to the
next and back again.

28 Cf. Kövecses 2000: 17, 61–86 on the widespread image of emotion as
a force, and for discussion of the 'hydraulic' conception of emotions,
Rosenwein 2003; contrast the metaphor of entanglement or *fifir
nagnafa* among the Cheke Holo of the Solomon Islands, as described
in White 2000: 36–7.

29 Livy reports that during the debate over whether to rescind the Lex
Oppia, which put severe limits on women's right to conspicuous
luxury items such as jewellery, the Roman matrons took to the
streets to pressure the Senate and tribunes into endorsing the repeal
(34.1–8). Cato the Censor, defending the law, argued that the women's
riotous conduct shows just why they must be subject to restraint;
the tribune Lucius Valerius, however, replied that the women were
behaving just as other citizens do when wronged. The contrasting
interpretations of the women's behaviour, seen as a manifestation
of irrational passion by Cato and as a practical political gesture by
Valerius, correspond, I suggest, to the opposing views of the chorus
in the *Seven against Thebes* as hysterical or rationally fearful for
their city.

30 Cf. Gordon 1987: 22: '[I]t appears that no one is truly angry unless
he or she is angry about something.'

31 Cf. Wierzbicka 1999: 83, who explains the 'freefloating' character of
anxiety as the feeling that 'the bad events threatening me are un-
identified,' though she includes in this category uncertain outcomes,
as in the case of 'a student awaiting the results of examinations.'
James (1997: 102) points out that 'Descartes does not rule out the
possibility of passions whose objects are vague, even to the point
where it is difficult to make sense of the claim that they have
objects at all ...; the functioning of a passion does not depend on its

having an identifiable object, nor do all passions possess them.' So too, Hobbes (1991: 76) argued that in a state of intense anxiety 'we often invent a terrifying object of it' (cited in James 1997: 166). Cf. LeDoux 1996: 228: 'Anxiety is usually distinguished from fear by the lack of an external stimulus that elicits the reaction'; and Griffiths 1997: 28: 'States such as depression, elation, and anxiety are generally thought to be capable of clinical instances where they have no (intentional) object.'

32 Trans. Smith 1993: 385; the last word represents one possible restoration of the Greek text, which breaks off at this point.

33 Cf. Thucydides 6.53.3, on the mood in Athens after the desecration of the herms: 'The people were continually afraid and regarded everything with suspicion.' This mood of persistent mistrust is not precisely anxiety, but a worry that a real danger might come from any quarter (cf. 6.53.2, *panta hupoptôs apodekhomenoi*). The point is that people are nervous, edgy, skittish – but because they know that a precise kind of danger lurks.

34 Keith Oatley (1992: 65) lists among the 'psychopathological extensions' of fear 'phobias, panic attacks, generalized anxiety states, and obsessive-compulsive disorders. Phobias are intense fears of specific objects or circumstances. A panic attack is a strong autonomic disturbance with an irresistible urge to escape to safety. Anxiety states may have no apparent object.' Webster's *International Dictionary of English* (2nd ed.) defines panic as '[a] sudden, overpowering fright; esp. a sudden and groundless fright; terror inspired by a trifling cause or a misapprehension of danger, esp. when accompanied by unreasoning or frantic efforts to secure safety.' In colloquial usage, 'panic' may mean no more than intense fear; cf. the response of Connecticut State Representative Themis Klarides to a case of anthrax poisoning (Zielbauer 2001): 'We can't panic until we know where it came from.' On the neurophysiology of panic, and its treatment with the tricyclic antidepressant imipramine and other drugs, cf. Schneier 1999: 284; on the biochemical basis of anxiety, see Pujol Gebellí 2001.

35 Borgeaud (1988: 89–95) cites as examples of panic Josephus, *Jewish War* 5.7–9 (the collapse of a tower during the night); Pausanias 10.23.5–8, on the Gauls after their defeat at Delphi: 'They snatched up arms and killed one another or were killed, without recognizing

their own language or one another's faces or even the shape of their shields' (Loeb trans.); Cornutus, *Theology* 27: 'Panic alarms are sudden and irrational' (Cornutus compares them to the fright that sometimes seizes sheep and goats at a sudden sound); Aeneas Tacticus 4; Polybius 20.6.12; and Longus, *Daphnis and Chloe* 2.25.3–4, where Pan frightens off pirates with a horrible noise. Borgeaud notes (90) that one way to counteract panic is with pass-words or countersigns, which allow one to distinguish enemies from friends.

36 Cf. Thucydides 2.65.9 on Pericles' speeches; Critias fragment B 25.28, Diels and Kranz 1951–2; Gorgias, *Palamedes* 4; Plato, *Phaedrus* 261A8; Isocrates, *Evagoras* 9.10.

37 E.g., Plato, *Euthyphro* 12B9–11, where *aidôs* and *aiskhunê* are associated with *deos* and *phobos*; cf. *Laws* 646E3–47C6 on two kinds of *phobos*, one concerned with future evils, the other with one's reputation or *doxa*; the latter fear is again connected with both *aiskhunê* and *aidôs* (cf. also pseudo-Plato, *Definitions* 415E5–8; Sophocles, *Ajax* 1071–80; *Oedipus at Colonus* 1625: *phobôi deisantes*). At *Phaedo* 68D, Plato poses the paradox that courageous men face death for fear (*phobos*) of still greater evils; hence men (apart from philosophers) are courageous by virtue of fright (*deos*) and fearing. See Renehan 1971: 70–1 on the expression (quoted in the *Euthyphro*) 'where there is *deos*, there too there is *aidôs*'; the scholiast ad loc. in codex T. attributes it to Stasinus's *Cypria* = fr. 18, Bernabé 1987 (so too Stobaeus, *Anthology* 3.671.11); Renehan compares a similar formula in Epicharmus frag. 221 Kaibel (cf. Bernabé's apparatus ad loc.). The association was clearly traditional. For the connection between *phobos* and *sebas*, cf. Aeschylus, *Eumenides* 690–1.

38 At Sophocles, *Trachinian Women* 457, for example, *dedoika* is contrasted with *tarbeô*.

39 Cf. Smoes 1995: 51 on *tharsos*: 'Il s'oppose à la crainte, au *déos* (peur raisonée); il empêche de céder à la panique, au *phobos* (peur subite et instinctive).'

40 E.g. p. 121, citing 1.75.3, 6.83.4 (*deos*) vs. 1.77.6, 1.123.1 (*phobos*) in politics; 4.62.4 vs. 6.34.9 on preparations for war; cf. Müri 1947: 265: 'Fear before the unknown, fear that has no visible basis, is called 'the unsubstantiated (*atekmarton*) *deos* of the unseen' (4.63.1, 2.87.1).

41 Wartelle (1989: 54–6) notes that fear in relation to the sacred is usually *phobos* in earlier Christian literature (Septuagint, New Testament, apostolic fathers), whereas *deos* is rare.

42 Needless to say, the nature of tragic pity and fear has been much debated. For views different from mine, see Marušič 2000, esp. 120–4; Halliwell 2001: chap. 7, sec. 2.

43 As Halliwell (2002: 217) observes, Aristotle states in the *Rhetoric* that fear can drive out pity (2.8, 1386a31–2). Halliwell continues: 'That goes to show, first, that those who think fear in the *Poetics* is principally a self-regarding (as opposed to a vicarious) emotion have a serious exegetical problem, because Aristotle appears not to believe that pity and overtly self-regarding fear belong together; and, second, that not everything said about the emotions in the *Rhetoric* ... is necessarily or straightforwardly transferable to the interpretation of tragic pity and fear.' In a note (n. 32), Halliwell reaffirms his earlier interpretation of tragic fear as 'essentially other-regarding, felt not directly for oneself but vicariously "for" (*peri*, *Poet.* 13.1453a5–6) the tragic agents; it is therefore not so much a distinct impulse as an index, in the experience of mimetic art, of the intensity of the impulse to pity.' I am not convinced that this view can be extrapolated from Aristotle's statements, whether in the *Rhetoric* or the *Poetics*.

Chapter Seven

1 Christof Rapp and I arrived independently at the interpretation defended below, but he has the honour of priority in publication (as Rapp notes, Striker [1996: 301 n. 15] had already adumbrated the view). I first presented my arguments in a seminar at the University of Toronto, during the same week in which I gave the Robson Lectures on which this volume is based; I presented a revised version a year later (2002) at a conference at Rutgers University in honour of William Fortenbaugh. I wish to express my gratitude to David Mirhady and William Fortenbaugh for valuable comments on that occasion.

2 So too the Spanish linguist Antonio Tovar (1953: 115) renders the opening phrase: 'A quiénes se hace favor y sobre cuáles cosas, o en qué disposición, resultará claro una vez que hayamos definido el

favor.' Lane Cooper (1932: 117) titles the section 'Benevolence.' The
Penguin edition (trans. H.C. Lawson-Tancred, 1991: 111) begins: 'To
what people men show *favour*,' etc. The Budé version (trans. DuFour
1960: 80) runs: 'A l'égard de quelles personnes, en quelles occasions
et dans quelles habitus l'on est *obligeant*, c'est ce que sera évident
quand nous aurons défini cette passion.' Franz G. Sieveke (1980 [3rd.
ed. 1989]: 108) offers: 'Wem gegenüber man *Freundlichkeit (Wohlwollen, Gunst)* erweist und wofür bzw. in welcher Disposition, das
wird klar, wenn der Begriff "Freundlichkeit" definiert ist.' The Loeb
version (trans. Freese 1926) has 'benevolence'; the Spanish translation by Bernabé (1998: 166) offers 'Con quiénes tenemos generosi-
dad ...,' and the still more recent one by Ramírez Trejo (2002: 90)
gives 'Y a quienes hacer un favor ...' And so on.
3 What survives of the seventh-century Byzantine commentary by
Stephanus of Alexandria (ed. Rabe, 1896) does not treat this section
of the *Rhetoric*, nor do two fragmentary commentaries or periphra-
ses (also edited by Rabe). The anonymous Byzantine commentary, or
rather scholia, to the *Rhetoric* begin with the definition of *kharis*
(108.9, Rabe, 1896), thus skipping the crucial introductory sentence
in Aristotle; for the rest, the comments deal exclusively with *kharis*
rather than *kharin ekhein* or gratitude.
4 The full text reads: 'quibus hominibus, et quibus in rebus gratia fieri
videatur, et quo pacto affecti sint qui gratiam faciunt, ex definitione
eius rei aperte constabit. Gratia est res, qua is qui facit et collocat
gratiam, dicitur obsequi precibus, indigentiaeve alicuius, non
reddendae vicissitudinis causa, aut gratiae referendae, sed gratuito.'
5 The passage reads: 'aliud enim significat Gratia quae definitur, aliud
Gratia quae in definitione ponitur. nam prior absolute beneficium
non significat, ut posterior, sed beneficium quod gratia illius fit,
in quem confertur. reliqua sunt facilia' ('The *gratia* that is being
defined means one thing, that which is included in the definition
another. For the former does not, like the latter, mean an unquali-
fied benefit, but rather a benefit that is for the sake of the person
upon whom it is bestowed. The rest is easy').
6 So too Theodore Goulston, in his edition and translation of 1619
(p. 110), which was frequently reprinted (see K. Erickson 1975 for a
full catalogue), provides the chapter title 'De gratia seu Gratificandi
affectu,' and renders the first sentence: 'Quibus autem Gratiam

praebeant *homines,* et in Quibus *rebus,* et Quomodo ipsi *se* habentes, cum definiverimus gratiam, perspicuum fuerit: Sit igitur Gratia, per quam *is,* qui *rem* possidet, dicitur gratiam exhibere ei, qui indiget; non pro ulla *re accepta,* neque ut quicquam omnino *referatur* ipsi qui exhibet, se ut illi *soli, cui exhibetur, contingat* bonum.' The chapter concludes (p. 111): 'Ac de conferenda *quidem* Gratia, et non conferenda dictum est.' The sense of the phrases 'gratiam praebere' and 'gratiam conferre' is evident from 'gratificor' in the chapter rubric.

7 Nor again 'obligeance,' 'Freundlichkeit,' 'Wohlwollen,' 'beneficium,' or 'se obsequia' (in the Portuguese version of Fonseca 2000: 49, 53).

8 Here I supplement the rather more brief analysis in Rapp 2002.

9 It is otiose to cite examples, but simply for the record, cf. Herodas, *Mimiambi* 5.81: *kai ekhe tên kharin tautêi,* which plainly means, 'Be thankful to her'; also Plutarch, *De audiendis* 42C6.

10 As Jeffrey Rusten (1990: 157) – from whom I have borrowed the translation from 'with the result that ...' – explains, 'χάριν δοῦναι = "grant a *favour*"; χάριν ὀφείλειν = "owe *gratitude.*"'

11 Aristotle varies the formula in introducing the last three emotions he treats, namely, indignation, envy, and emulousness: for the first and last he employs the expression 'if, then, it is ... (ei gar esti, 1387a8–9, 1388a30), while for *phthonos* he uses the synonymous phrase *eiper estin* (1387b22).

12 Compare also the expression *aitian ekhein* in the sense of 'be accused,' as opposed to *aitian epipherein,* etc., 'impute a fault' (LSJ s.v. *aitia;* my thanks to Eckard Schütrumpf for this observation). Donald Russell suggests to me that *kath' hên* here may specify the sense of *kharis* according to which one who 'has' it is grateful, that is, a disinterested service as opposed to other senses of *kharis* such as 'grace' or 'charm.'

13 Why does Aristotle insist on the intensity of the need? According to Aristotle's definition of a *pathos (Rhetoric* 2.1, 1378a20–3), pain and pleasure are necessary components of an emotion, and the pain associated with gratitude might consist in a recollection of the disagreeable state that called for the favour. Being indebted to a benefactor, however, is in itself a condition of social diminishment, and enough to account for the unpleasantness of the emotion.

14 Roberts thus associates the perfect participle with the middle verb *kharizesthai*, which uniquely means 'do a favour,' 'please,' 'oblige'; examples in Aristotle, *Nicomachean Ethics* 1133a3–5, 1164b31–2 and *Politics* 1263b5–6.

15 It is true that *lambanein* or *apolambanein* would be the more natural verb (cf. Xenophon, *Memorabilia* 2.2.5, 2.2.14). I suspect that Aristotle may again be playing with the idea that 'receiving a benefaction' (*tên kharin ekhein*) gave rise to the expression 'feel gratitude' (*kharin ekhein*), and is here simply substituting *hupourgian* for *kharin*.

16 Cf. 2.1, 1378a23–4, where Aristotle sets out three aspects relevant to the discussion of any emotion: *pôs diakeimenoi [ekhousin]*, *tisin*, and *epi poiois*.

17 In the present passage, Roberts translates 'kindness is shown'; for the meaning 'gratitude' in Aristotle, cf., e.g., *Politics* 1334b40–2, on the *kharis* of children towards their elders.

18 For the sense 'miserable,' cf. Euripides' *Medea* (chorus) 659–60: 'May he die *akharistos* who does not honour his *philoi*'; so too, in Isocrates, *To Demonicus* 31.7–8 the adverb means something like 'ungraciously' ('nor did he do favours ungraciously, as most people do'; note the wordplay in *kharitas akharistôs kharizomenos*). In Euripides, *Ion* 879–80, however, it may well mean 'ungrateful': 'I shall not point out the *akharistoi* betrayers of the bed'; cf. *Hecuba* 137, 254. When Herodotus (5.91.15) speaks of the *akharistos dêmos*, the term clearly carries the sense of ungrateful (cf. Aristoph., *Wasps* 451).

19 For the noun *akharistia* and the verb *akharistein* cf. ibid. 2.2.2–3; also 2.2.13–14, 2.6.19, 4.4.24; *Anabasis* 1.9.18, 7.6.24; *Cyropaedia* 1.2.7; *Agesilaus* 11.3. For the sense 'unpleasant,' see *Oeconomicus* 7.37, *Anabasis* 2.1.13, 2.3.18; for *akharistein* in the sense, 'not to indulge,' cf. Eryximachus in Plato, *Symposium* 186C and *Republic* 411E2, where *akharistia* is paired with *arrhuthmia* and evidently means 'gracelessness.' On *kharin apodounai* = 'repay a favour,' cf. Isocrates 4.57; contrast *kharin prodounai* = 'betray a kindness,' Euripides, *Heraclidae* 1036.

20 When Roberts translates 'As evidence of the want of kindness, we may point out that a smaller service had been refused to the man in

need,' etc., he imports a reference to a disposition rather than an act, in accord with the supposition that *kharis* in this passage denotes a *pathos*.

21 Paul Gohlke's (1959) 'Über Dank und Undank is damit gehandelt' cannot be right in respect to *kharizesthai*; Gohlke's version is presumably indebted to Sieveke (1989: 109): 'Das sei nun über die Erweisung von Dank und über das Undankbar-Sein gesagt.'

22 Cf. Plato's *Symposium* 186C (quoted above), where too it is contrasted with *kharizesthai*. The Portuguese version of Fonseca (2000: 53) gets it right, in my view: 'Relativamente ao fato de prestar favor e de nâo retribuírlo, já tudo foi dito.'

23 See Solomon 2004: v: 'Gratitude is one of the most neglected emotions and one of the most underestimated of the virtues. In most accounts of the emotions, it receives nary a mention.' Cf. Mignini 1994: 17 on the 'inesistenza di una storia sistematica dell'idea di gratitudine nella letteratura filosofica o psicologica' ('absence of a systematic history of the idea of gratitude in philosophical or psychological scholarship'); Mignini provides a survey of the concept from Homer to Kant and beyond.

24 Cf. McConnell 1993: 3: 'Richard Price lists gratitude as one of his six "heads of virtue," and of it says, "The consideration that we have received benefits, lays us under *peculiar* obligations to the persons who have conferred them"' (quoting Price 1974 [orig. 1797]: 152); Gouldner 1996: 62: '[T]he *norm* of reciprocity holds that people should help those who help them and, therefore, those whom you have helped have an obligation to help you'; Bollnow 1992: 37: 'Die Dankbarkeit ist also eine Tugend' ('Gratitude is thus a virtue'). Note also Mignini 1994: 27: 'Il sostantivo *charis* indica più spesso favore, godimento e gradimento. Ma vi sono anche testi nei quali si allude al ricambio dei favori come a un mezzo di equilibrio economico e sociale, o nei quali la gratitudine nei confronti di un beneficio ricevuto è considerata come virtù e dovere' ('The noun *charis* most often indicates a favour, enjoyment, and gratitude. But there are also texts in which there is an allusion to an exchange of favours as a means of economic and social equilibrium, or in which gratitude in response to a benefit received is considered a virtue and a duty').

25 Cf. Epicurus, *Principal Sayings* 1; *Letter to Herodotus* 77.

26 Cf. R.C. Roberts 2004: 75: 'Like resentment and regret, envy is in some ways the reverse of gratitude, so that the disposition to gratitude tends to rule out the disposition to envy and thus to reduce episodes of envy.' In this contrast, gratitude is a positive attitude towards the relative prosperity of others, whereas envy and resentment are negative attitudes.

27 Philodemus employs the term *eukharisteô* for 'feel gratitude' (a Hellenistic or later usage, according to LSJ; cf. Harrison 2003: 74), in place of the classical *kharin ekhein*; see also Bremer 1998: 129.

28 E.g., Lysias 12.80 (*orgê*), 27.11 (*orgizesthai*); Isocrates, *Panegyricus* 157, *On the Peace* 14 (opposed to *duskolôs diatithesthai*), *Aegin.* 2 (contrasted with *khalepôs pherô*), *Busiris* 6 (contrasted with *aganaktein* and paired with *praos*); cf. Xenophon, *Memorabilia* 2.6.21, 2.7.9.

29 Cf. Lysias 6.3 (*katakharisasthai* paired with *kateleêsai*), 14.10; Isocrates 18.62, *Against Callimachus* on gratitude and pity owed to those who have earned it.

30 Lysias 18.23; cf. 18.27 (*exaiteomai*), 21.25.

31 Cf. *dounai kharin*, 21.17; also 30.27, 31.24; and Isaeus 7.41, 9.23.

32 On the paradox, see Derrida 1995: 81–115; Derrida 1997a: 18–19; and Derrida 1997b: 128: 'For there to be a gift, there must be no reciprocity, return, exchange, countergift, or debt. If the other *gives* me *back* or *owes* me or has to give me back what I give him or her, there will not have been a gift'; this is the ground of 'the impossibility or double bind of the gift' (131). Cf. Bourdieu 1977: 6; Bourdieu 1990: 105; and Bourdieu 1997: 231: 'The major characteristic of the experience of the gift is, without doubt, its ambiguity. On the one hand, it is experienced (or intended) as a refusal of self-interest and egoistic calculation, and an exaltation of generosity – a gratuitous, unrequited gift. On the other hand, it never entirely excludes awareness of the logic of exchange or even confession of the repressed impulses or, intermittently, the denunciation of another, denied, truth of generous exchange – its constraining and costly character.' For a response to Derrida's notion of the impossibility of the gift, see Bernasconi 1997. Guizzi 1998 sees a historical shift from Pericles' dictum in the funeral oration (Thucydides 2.40.4–5)

that the Athenians win loyalty by bestowing rather than receiving favors, to an aristocratic conception of disinterested generosity as defined by Aristotle; but the two aspects of *kharis* coexist in both periods.

33 In Bremer Papyrus 49, a certain Hermaeus writes to Aelius Apollonius, thanking him for his goodwill and friendship (*philia*) and explaining (7–8): 'Since I am small, I am grateful [*kharin soi eidenai*], but the gods will compensate you [*ameipsontai*]'; the feeling of gratitude is distinct from actual repayment. It is a weakness in James Harrison's fine study (2003) that he does not discriminate adequately the sense of *kharin ekhein* and *eidenai* from *kharin apodidonai*, etc.

34 As a disposition, ingratitude is also a vice or defect of character; thus, Hecuba (Euripides, *Hecuba* 245) brands the entire tribe of demagogues as ungrateful (*akhariston*, 254). It is worth remarking that in classical Greek there is no adjective meaning 'grateful.'

35 Harrison (2003: 48) observes that *kharis* 'captures the attitudinal aspects behind the reciprocity system, spotlighting not only the conventional return of favour but also the importance of a genuine and commensurate gratitude on the part of the beneficiary.'

36 In Latin, one must similarly distinguish between the expressions *gratiam habere* and *gratiam agere*, etc.; the former signifies gratitude as a sentiment, not a material return for a benefaction; it is gratitude, not compensation, that one offers the gods in Roman rituals of thanksgiving (cf. Hickson Hahn 2004a, 2004b).

37 Harrison (2003: 167–210) surveys the topics of benefaction and gratitude in the Greek and Roman philosophical traditions, particularly in relation to the 'ethos of reciprocity'; although he duly notes (174–5) that Aristotle and others stipulated that a true benefaction must be wholly altruistic, he emphasizes the contrast between the Graeco-Roman view of euergetism and St Paul's conception of divine grace, which 'up-ends the hellenistic ethics of beneficence' and is 'unilateral, not reciprocal' (288). Leaving aside the question of Pauline theology, I believe that a more nuanced distinction between generosity and gratitude, on the one side, and the repayment of a debt, on the other, mitigates the apparent conflict between pagan and Christian attitudes.

Chapter Eight

1 Cf. Walter Donlan (1980: 14): 'Homeric "friendship" appears as a system of calculated cooperation, not necessarily accompanied by any feelings of affection.'

2 Carlo Natali has suggested (oral communication) that the reference to virtue or *aretê* is in effect a transitional formula to connect the *philia* books with the main argument of the *Nicomachean Ethics*; but Aristotle's belief that virtue is an activity (*energeia*) and not just a capacity (*dunamis*) may also have motivated the association.

3 For a response, see Konstan 2002a. Some critics have sought a compromise between the two positions, according to which ancient friendship involved both an affective component and the expectation of practical services. Thus, Raccanelli (1998: 20) remarks: 'Certainly, Konstan is right to observe that the common model of true friendship must grant major importance to sentiment ... But it is nevertheless well not to ignore the role that notions of obligation, mutual exchange of gifts, and prestations also play within relations of friendship ... The element of concrete and obligatory exchange seems inseparably bound up with friendship, which can not be identified with the mere affective dimension of the relationship.' And yet, we too expect friends to assist us in times of crisis, without thereby denying the affective nature of the bond. The inference runs: 'If you loved me as a friend, you would assist me in my time of need; since you do not, you are not a true friend.'

4 Cope (1877, vol. 2: 42) translates 'whatever we think good,' but the singular *oietai* goes better with the antecedent *tini*; those who love, according to Aristotle, do not necessarily impose their own idea of what is good on their friends.

5 Kassell (1976) marks this sentence as a later addition to the text by Aristotle himself, on insufficient grounds, in my opinion. Grimaldi (1988: 67) defends it, rightly on my view, on the grounds that it is 'necessary to indicate the reciprocity of the feeling required if the word *philos* is to be employed as it is in the following sentence.' Cope (1877, vol. 2: 43) renders: 'And a friend is one that loves, and is beloved in return.'

6 This definition accords with that in *Nicomachean Ethics*, book 8;

however, when Aristotle treats *philia* as a virtue, that is, the mean
between the excess of flattery and the deficiency of enmity or
hostility (*ekhthra*), he takes it to be a quality of an individual, whom
he designates as a *philos* – that is, one who behaves as a *philos* ought
(*Magna Moralia* 1.31.1–2); cf. *MM* 2.11.6–7, where Aristotle argues
that *philia* is indeed used of our feelings towards god or inanimate
things such as wine, but that he is investigating not this type, but
rather 'that towards animate things, and moreover those capable of
feeling *philia* in return [*antiphilein*].'

7 Cf. *Eudemian Ethics* 7, 1236b3–5: *philon men gar to philoumenon
tôi philounti, philos de tôi philoumenôi kai antiphilôn* ('What is
loved is dear to the one who loves it, but a friend is dear to the one
who is loved and loves in return').

8 At *NE* 9.5, 1166b30–5, Aristotle asserts that *eunoia* has not the
'tension and longing' associated with *philêsis*.

9 *Philia* and *to philein* are paired on three occasions in the
Nicomachean Ethics. In one passage, Aristotle says that among
good men 'both *to philein* and *philia* are most present and are best
[*aristê*]' (1156b23–4); the last term ('best') is in the feminine singular,
thus strictly modifying only *philia*, which suggests perhaps that
Aristotle is here treating *philia* and *to philein* as effectively synonymous. A little later, Aristotle says that 'there is more of *philia* in
loving [*to philein*; sc. than in being loved, *to phileisthai*],' and adds
that '*to philein* seems to be the virtue of *philoi*' (1159a33–5).

10 Aristotle might have called friendship something like 'loving and
being loved' (*to philein kai antiphileisthai*), or else specified it as
philia between *philoi*. Neither he nor other Greeks, however, spoke
this way, and the mutuality of *philia* as friendship must be inferred
from the context. Although the focus of the two ethical treatises is
on reciprocal love, once he has clarified the nature of this bond,
Aristotle does not hesitate to employ the word *philia* in the sense
simply of 'love,' for example when he states that the most natural
kind of *philia* is that of a mother for her infant child (8.8, 1159a28–
33; this caused great perplexity for the ancient Greek commentator
Aspasius [179.28–80.5, Heylbut 1887], who with misplaced rigour
suggests that Aristotle ought to have labelled this affection *philêsis*;
see Konstan 1997: 68–9).

11 In his definition of a *pathos* (*Rhetoric* 2.1, 1378a20–3), Aristotle

stipulates, as we have seen, that it is accompanied by pain and pleasure. The pleasure associated with the impression (*phantasia*) or anticipation of a loved one's welfare (and pain at the reverse) would seem to meet this condition; at all events, it is not radically different from the pleasure of imagined revenge that Aristotle sees as intrinsic to anger (see chapter 2, p. 42; alternatively, the pleasure may lie in anticipating one's own success in imparting goods to the other). In Aeschylus's *Libation Bearers* (222–3), Electra, still suspecting that the stranger she has met may not be her brother, asks: 'Do you then wish to laugh at my adversity?'; to this Orestes replies: 'At mine too then, if yours.' Needless to say, love is also among those things 'on account of which people change and differ in regard to their judgments.'

12 That two people regard the same things as good does not guarantee that they will desire these things for each other. Presumably the awareness that others share our idea of what is good and bad disposes us to like them and hence to wish good things for their sakes.

13 I disagree with Cope (1877, vol. 2: 45), who takes *kai* as epexegetical: 'And friends' friends, that is (*kai*) the friends of those whom we love ourselves'; as Cope himself notes, 'If friendship is *mutual*, surely this is a "vain repetition."' Grimaldi (1988: 69) is right to state that '*kai* here introduces another group: namely, "and those who like the people whom they themselves like."' As Grimaldi observes, 'There is no reason to think from 81a 14–20 that mutuality (*philôn - antiphiloumenos*, 81a 2–3) is present in each of the topics mentioned.' There is, I think, a similar inclusiveness at *Nicomachean Ethics* 9.4, 1166a2–6, where Aristotle writes: 'They posit that a *philos* is one who wishes and performs good things, or what appear to be good things, for the other's sake, or else one who wishes that his *philos* exist and live for his [i.e., the other's] sake – which is what mothers feel towards their children, and, among *philoi*, those who have quarrelled.' The definition that Aristotle ascribes to unnamed others is similar to his own, save that it does not include the element of reciprocity, and adds the simple desire for the continued existence of the other. He illustrates this latter sentiment first with reference to maternal love, and then among *philoi* – or rather, former *philoi*, since even when they have parted ways, they still at least desire that the other survive. Christopher Rowe (2002) trans-

lates: 'so it is with mothers towards their children, and with friends who are angry with each other'; and Terence Irwin (1985) has, 'this is how mothers feel towards their children, and how friends who have been in conflict feel [toward each other].' Douglas Hutchinson (oral communication) suspects a lacuna before the phrase, 'and of *philoi* ...,' since the transition seems harsh; but if we take 'of *philoi*' as complementary to 'mothers,' the latter exemplifying a one-way *philia* (in accordance with the preceding definition), while the former adds the case of *philoi* proper, in Aristotle's sense, then the sentence may stand as is.

14 Cope (1877, vol. 2: 55) takes the three relationships specified by Aristotle as 'three degrees of association,' and adds: '*en koinôniâi pasa philia esti*' ('all *philia* resides in community': *Nicomachean Ethics* 8.14, 1161b11). Kinship, for Aristotle, is a source of love, and often of mutual love; but kin are not automatically *philoi*; see *Nicomachean Ethics* 8.12, 1161b11–16, and Konstan 1997a: 69–71.

15 On altruism in Greek thought, see Konstan 2000a. Schopenhauer (1995: 143–4) too affirms that there is altruism only 'when the ultimate motive for doing or omitting to do a thing is precisely and exclusively centered in the *weal and woe of someone else*,' but such a motive 'necessarily presupposes ... that I am in some way *identified with him*, in other words, that this entire *difference* between me and everyone else, which is the very basis of my egoism, is eliminated, to a certain extent at least.' For Aristotle, the other remains a distinct person.

16 Cf. Cope (1877, vol. 2: 43): 'Love is a feeling, a sort of appetite, the wish to do good.'

17 Numerous Greek aphorisms testify to the expectation that friends will provide help in a crisis (e.g., Democritus fragments 101 and 106 Diels-Kranz; Euripides, *Orestes* 454–5; Menander, *Sentences* 1.40, 143, 147, 263, 276), as well as to the reality that few prove true friends in the crunch.

18 O.H. Green (1997: 209) argues that love is not an emotion, which involves 'belief-based intentionality and rationality,' but rather a complex conative state, a set of desires' (cf. 216). Green sees his account as compatible with Aristotle's, save that Aristotle assigns primacy to 'the desire for the good of the friend' (216), whereas Green emphasizes 'the desire for association with one who is loved.'

Here again we see a sign of the modern preoccupation with intimacy. Aristotle recognizes that friends rejoice in each other's company and wish to live together (*suzein*), but he treats this desire as the active state or *energeia* of friendship, which permits the realization of the wish to provide good things to the other (*Nicomachean Ethics* 8.5, 1157b5–11).

19 In general, Aristotle pays little attention in the *Rhetoric* to 'qualia,' that is, the feeling states peculiar to the several emotions.

20 Strictly speaking, a one-way attitude also constitutes a relationship, namely, that between lover and beloved. Green does not define 'relationship,' but 'relation' customarily renders Aristotle's term *pros ti* ('towards something'), which he introduces in the *Categories*: the examples he offers are 'double, half, and larger' (1b29–30); as we have seen, Aristotle speaks of *philia pros* or 'love towards' someone in the *Nicomachean Ethics*. Perhaps we can define a relationship as a symmetrical relation (both parties are equally lover and beloved).

21 Contrast Grimaldi 1988: 65: 'Friendly feeling rather than friendship is perhaps a more accurate interpretation of *philia* since as an emotion it is a transitory, psycho-physical experience rather than what is implied in English by friendship, i.e., a more permanent disposition or state.'

22 A little later (8.4, 1157a14–16), Aristotle states that friends on account of the useful are *philoi* not of one another but rather of what is advantageous (*to lusiteles*), but strictly speaking there can be no *philia* for an object. In the *Magna Moralia* (2.11.14–17), Aristotle affirms that friendships based on pleasure or utility are related to that based on virtue in that they depend on the same thing, or are about and derived from the same things; he compares the way a scalpel and a physician may both be called 'medical.'

23 On the centrality of the filial bond to tragedy, see Alaux 1995.

24 Belfiore's 'friends' renders the Greek *philoi*, which she takes to have a wider application than the English term, though on my view the noun normally means 'friend' to the exclusion of kin; see Konstan 1996 and 1997a: 53–6.

25 Kyriakou (1998: 284 n. 5) directs her argument against my claim that *philia* 'denotes the affectionate feelings shared by family members and does not imply a set of reciprocal formal obligations.'

26 Cf. the elegant methodological statement by Citroni Marchetti

2000: viii: 'se l'amicizia è cambiata per il cambiamento di potere, possiamo chiederci se anche le formule non siano cambiate nel loro significato: se esse, pur essendo le stesse, non si applichino di fatto a qualcosa di diverso da ciò che originariamente e naturalmente significavano' ('if friendship is changed by a change in power, we may wonder whether the expressions too haven't changed in meaning – whether, even though they are the same, they are not in fact being applied to something different from what they originally and naturally signified').

27 Archaic Greek poets, for example Solon and Theognis, did caution against false friends, though generally in a sententious and impersonal vein. An Athenian drinking poem runs (number 908 Page): 'He who does not betray a man who is his friend [*andra philon*] has great honour among mortals and gods, in my judgment.' Such verses were recited in the aristocratic milieu of symposiastic clubs, where friendship to some extent served as a model for upper-class allegiance; it thus retained a political function, and was not, perhaps, conceived of as the manifestation of a wholly personal affection. Again, in the Hellenistic courts, where kings employed official councils of 'friends' as advisers, one sees a new concern with the need to distinguish between true and false friends (see Konstan 1996 and 1997a: 95–108).

28 Contrast the attitude towards friends in the following – first, a Latin epigram ascribed to Seneca but probably dating to the second or third century AD (403.3–12, Shackleton Bailey 1982 = 407.3–12, Riese 1926):

'Live and avoid all friendships': this is more true
　　Than just 'avoid friendships with kings.'
My fate bears witness: my high-ranking friend ruined me,
　　My humble one abandoned me. Shun the whole pack alike.
For those who had been my equals fled the crash
　　And abandoned the house even before it collapsed.
Go then and avoid only kings! If you know how to live,
　　Live for yourself only – for you'll die for yourself.

The second is from a Byzantine advice book (Wassiliewsky and Jernstedt 1984: 236): 'If you have a friend living in another place and he passes through the town in which you live, do not instal him in your house, but let him go elsewhere. For in your house, hear how many problems you will have: One is that your wife, your daughters, and your daughters-in-law will not be able to come forth from their chambers and therefore will not properly take care of your house. If it is necessary, however, that they appear, your friend will crane his neck to inspect them ... When he finds a chance, he will pursue your wife with amorous attentions and gaze at her with intemperate eyes, and, if he is able to, he will even seduce her. And when he departs, he will brag unworthily about what he did.'

Chapter Nine

1 My thanks to Andy Silber for this reference.
2 Cf. Euripides, *Electra* 645, where Orestes' old tutor declares: 'An impious woman is hated [sc. by all]'; *Archelaus* fr. 248.2–3, Kannicht 2004; *Erechtheus* fr. 360.30; *Melanippe* fr. 492.2–7, 498.1; *Chrysippus* fr. 886.1–3; also the uncertainly attributed fragments 905.1 and 1053.1–2. Conceivably, this usage was perceived as a tick of Euripides, since Aristophanes, in the *Frogs* (1427–8), puts in his mouth the sentence 'I hate a citizen who appears slow to aid his country, but quick to harm it greatly,' but the formula also occurs at *Acharnians* 509 (hatred of the Lacedaemonians), while in the *Birds*, Prometheus declares (1547): 'I hate all the gods' (cf. *Lysistrata* 1018, of women). Cf. also Isaeus (3.66): 'No one hates profit or values others more than himself'; Demosthenes, *Oration* 19.258.5–6, 268.8; 21.98.4–5; Menander, *Sentences* 1.332, 352, 360; Plato, *Republic* 2, 382A–C, 402A, on hating falsehood or lies (cf. Euripides fr. 410, Kannicht 2004, on hating what is shameful). Aristotle himself in *Nicomachean Ethics* 1172a23, 1179b26 uses the verb in this way. In Aeschylus's *Seven against Thebes*, Eteocles calls the hysterical women of the chorus 'hateful things [*misêmata*] to anyone with self-control' (186); cf. also Plato, *Republic* 334C, 382A4–402A2 and *Laws* 653B, 660A, 802C, 887C; Aeschines, *Against Timarchus* 188 (in 146, the object is an individual, but represents a type of vicious behaviour). In Homer, the verb *misein* occurs only once (*Iliad* 17.272), used with the infinitive; when Achilles expresses his disdain for the class of people who say one thing but mean another, he says rather: 'that man is an enemy [*ekhthros*] who ...' (*Iliad*

9.312–13). For the impossibility of hating people in certain categories, cf. Sophocles, *Electra* 770–1, where Clytemnestra responds to the news of Orestes' death: 'It is a terrible thing to bear children; for even when they treat you badly it is impossible to feel hatred for those you've borne'; also Euripides fr. 296 Kannicht 2004: 'A good man never hates a good man.'

3 On the basis of this passage, the standard Greek-English lexicon (LSJ s.v. *stugeô*) observes that *stugein* is 'stronger than *miseô*, for it means *to show hatred*, not merely to feel it'; however, the distinction might better be drawn between the evaluative character of *misein* and the reflex of loathing associated with the root *stug-* (mainly in poetry), as in the adjectives *stugeros* (used of Hades and a Fury in Homer, *Iliad* 8.368 and *Odyssey* 2.135, respectively) and *stugnos* (employed to describe a sullen expression in Aeschylus, *Agamemnon* 639), or the abstract form *stugnotês* (referring to the gloom of a frigid climate, Polybius 4.21.1; cf. 3.20.3).

4 At Sophocles, *Electra* 1309–11, Electra says that her inveterate hatred for her mother allows her to mask the joy she feels at Orestes' arrival, and thus not give away the game to Clytemnestra. See too Aeschylus's *Seven against Thebes*, where the chorus characterizes Clytemnestra as 'an object of hatred [*misos*] to the citizens' (and cf. *Agamemnon* 1411, 1413).

5 Cf. Ahmed 2004: 49: 'Hate may respond to the particular, but it tends to do so by aligning the particular with the general.' Bishop Butler (1896: 162–3) argues that with anger in the sense of hatred, 'the whole man appears monstrous, without any thing right or human in him: whereas the resentment should surely at least be confined to that particular part of the behaviour which gave offence: since the other parts of a man's life and character stand just the same as they did before' (Butler uses the term 'resentment' in the sense of moral anger).

6 See further the essays in Wistrich 1999; R. Rorty 1999: 263–5 doubts that an inclusive definition of the human species is by itself enough to avert extreme violence against other groups.

7 Or, more literally, 'accompanied by a certain maturation and duration [*meta prokopês tinos kai parataseôs*].' The Stoics, who divided emotions into four general classes under the headings of pain, pleasure, desire (*epithumia*), and fear, located both anger and

hatred (along with *erôs*) under desire: 'Anger is a desire for revenge against someone who, one believes, has wronged one inappropriately' (so too *thumos*, which is characterized as 'incipient anger'). Aristotle had already identified the desire (*orexis*) for revenge as essential to anger, as we have seen (chapter 2, pp. 41, 56). Cf. Cicero, *Tusculan Disputations* 4.21: 'Let anger [*ira*] be a desire to punish one who is believed to have harmed one undeservedly ..., hatred [*odium*] an inveterate anger, and enmity [*inimicitia*] anger that awaits the right time to take revenge' (Cicero's *excandescentia* corresponds to *thumos* or, as Cicero calls it, *thumôsis*).

8 Either Zeno or Chrysippus argued that the object of erotic desire is *philia* or love rather than sexual intercourse, citing in evidence Menander's *Misoumenos* or *Hated Man* (Diogenes Laertius 7.129). In this comedy, Thrasonides, a soldier, refrains from touching a girl he loves, even though she is his slave and in his power, because she hates him. Her hatred is based on the mistaken belief that Thrasonides has killed her brother, and in their more detailed analyses the Stoics would necessarily have cited the kinds of judgments that elicit hatred and other emotions.

9 Contrast España 2000: 22, who writes that 'often one need not know one's opponent in order to hate him. Strolling along the street, one runs into individuals whose face, expression, way of walking or dressing makes one want to hit them ... We find ourselves facing the purest of hatreds, the origin of which is entirely aesthetic and before which we are unable to adopt a rational attitude.'

10 Contrast Gordon 1987: 3: '[I]t is in the nature of anger that it arises from – is "provoked by" – certain specific types of situations (or "cognitions"), such as a "slight," whereas hatred is a long-term disposition that, once established, needs no provocation at all.' Bishop Butler (1896: 139–41) distinguishes between 'sudden anger,' which is sometimes 'mere instinct,' and 'settled anger,' which he calls 'resentment.' The latter is provoked by insult or injustice, and is directed 'against vice and wickedness.' As distinct from malice, this kind of resentment 'is one of the common bonds, by which society is held together; a fellow-feeling, which each individual has in behalf of the whole species, as well as of himself' (141).

11 On the role of anger, as opposed to hatred, in justifying mass exterminations, see chapter 2, pp. 70–3, and cf. Isaac 2004: 47, who

340 / Notes to pages 191–2

argues that despite 'a good deal of bloodshed, mass murder, and cruelty' in the ancient world, there was 'no racist society as such nor any systematic racist policy leading to mass murder as seen in the twentieth century'; also 222: 'There was no emotional need for the Romans to declare their victims animals or inferior humans. None of our sources express a need to justify such acts.' In the *Iliad*, the Greek leader Agamemnon cries out: '[L]et not one of them [i.e., the Trojans] go free of sudden death and our hands; not the young man child that the mother carries still in her body, not even he, but let all of Ilion's people perish, utterly blotted out and unmourned for' (*Iliad* 6.57–60, trans. Lattimore 1951; cf. Konstan 2006c). Achilles, in his anguish over the death of Patroclus, compares the antagonism between him and Hector to that between wolves and lambs (22.262), and wishes that he could eat Hector's raw flesh (22.346–8). Yet neither hero imagines that the Trojans are 'satanic monsters' or 'the embodiment of Evil.' Hate in this sense is absent from the *Iliad*. On later Greek attitudes to Persians, see Isaac 2004: 257–303.

12 España (2000: 9) remarks: 'es evidente que una canción que se hubiera titulado *Hate is in the air* no se habría encaramado precisamente a los primeros puestos de las listas de venta' ('It's obvious that a song called "Hate Is in the Air" would not exactly have risen to the top of the sales charts').

13 As the last clause indicates, Konner too sees hate as atavistic. España (2000: 13) is among the few who assert that 'hatred, as a human emotion, can on occasions be positive for those who know how to channel it,' but no consistent view of hatred emerges in this journalistic ensemble of pugnacious opinions.

14 Fortenbaugh (2002: 105) observes that in the *Politics*, 'Aristotle compares hate with anger and argues that hate makes greater use of calculation, "for anger is accompanied by pain, so that it is not easy to calculate, while hate is free of pain" (1312b32–34).' Fortenbaugh concludes (107) that, given the absence of pain, 'hate fails to qualify as an emotion.' He cites (109) *Eudemian Ethics* 1220b12–14: 'Emotions are such things as rage, fear, shame, appetite and gener-ally things that are in themselves accompanied for the most part by sensory pleasure and pain,' and suggests that the phrase *epi to polu* ('for the most part') may point to the exceptional nature of hate and love, but he wisely rejects this way out of the dilemma.

15 Cf. the plea to the jurors neither to love nor to hate in Lysias 16.19.

16 The Epicurean philosopher Philodemus (first century BC), in his treatise *On Anger* (col. 41.28–42.14), allows that the wise man will sometimes become angry, but he will not have a powerful desire (*epithumia*) to pursue offenders, even when the harm is great; rather, 'they are kept far removed, and he hates [*misein*] them – this follows – but he does not experience a great disturbance [*tarakhê*],' since external things are of small importance to the sage. Unlike anger, hatred, as a steady kind of hostility, is not incompatible with the imperturbability (ataraxy) of the wise.

17 The ancient grammarian Ammonius, writing on the distinctions between near synonyms in Greek (*On the Differences among Words* 208), states that '*ekhthros* differs from *polemios* ... For an *ekhthros* is a former friend, while a *polemios* is someone who advances towards one under arms'; his meaning is evidently that an *ekhthros* is in the category of those who might be a friend.

18 On this contrast, see Blundell 1989; and cf. *inter alia* Homer, *Odyssey* 6.184–5; Solon 13.5–6; Plato, *Philebus* 49D; Euripides, *Alcestis* 1037, where Dale's preference (1954: 124 ad v.) for *aiskhroisin* over *ekhthroisin*, on the grounds that an allusion here to enemies would be 'ungracious,' overlooks the Greek habit of treating *philoi* and *ekhthroi* as all-inclusive. On the possible derivations of *philos* and *ekhthros* from roots meaning 'close' (Indo-European *bhi*) and 'outside' (*eks*), see Schwartz 1982: 196.

19 For personal enmity in Athenian lawsuits, see Rhodes 1998: 160–1; and Kurihara 2003, who shows that the expectation was that 'public suits should not be motivated by private enmity' (466); and, in Athenian politics, Mitchell 1996 and Rhodes 1996, who show that political alliances do not always line up neatly with personal friendships. On political enmity at Rome, cf. Epstein 1987.

20 We can of course be hated by someone we love; cf. Plato, *Lysis* 212B–C.

21 The suggestion that one treat enemies as potential friends (thereby acknowledging the vicissitudes of time) was undercut by the parallel recommendation that one regard friends as potential enemies; cf. Demosthenes 23.122; Sophocles, *Ajax* 678–83.

22 Mendelsohn (2002: 88) argues that Demopho's refusal to allow the sacrifice of an Athenian maiden shows that, for him, 'the affairs of

the *polis* are a private, even family affair.' But this is not Athens's war; gestures of sacrifice are appropriate when one's own group is at risk. In general, Mendelsohn seems to me to place excessive emphasis on the contrast between loyalty to the values of the city and a more narrow commitment to the clan, represented above all by Iolaus (79; cf. 91, 97).

23 Mendelsohn 2002: 17–18; on the shocking character of the scene, cf. Seidensticker 1982: 99–100.

24 Mendelsohn (2002: 120) observes: 'Not surprisingly, this scene has been the object of especially harsh critical puzzlement and outrage'; like other critics, Mendelsohn notes that 'in pursuing her terrible revenge Alkmene becomes the double of her arch-enemy' (126). I am not convinced, however, by Mendelsohn's claim that Alcmene's 'mad scene' (120) is 'motivated by an extreme version of the *genos*-creed' (121; cf. 124–5), that is, loyalty to clan values as opposed to those of the city. A desire for vengeance is equally characteristic of civic hostilities.

25 For the positive representation of Athens in the play, with a bibliography of earlier views, see Grethlein 2003: 396–424.

26 The expression *ekhthron doru* is also used in 312–15, where Iolaus says that the Heraclids must forever regard the Athenians as *philoi*, that is, friends, and never raise a hostile spear against them. *Philos*, which may mean 'ally' as well as 'friend,' is usually paired with *ekhthros* as its opposite; cf. 19–20, 690–1 (on the order of the lines, see Wilkins 1993: 138).

27 When the messenger reports to Alcmene the Athenian victory, he says (786–7): 'We are victorious over our *ekhthroi* and a trophy has been set up bearing all the arms of your *polemioi*'; I presume that the trophy elicits the idea of a defeated army. At 410, however, Demopho announces that it is necessary to sacrifice a girl to be a trophy over their *ekhthroi*. Cf. Euripides, *Electra* 832–3 (Aegisthus speaking): 'The son of Agamemnon is the most hated [*ekhthistos*] of mortals and a foe [*polemios*] to my house.' On the contrast between *polemioi* and *ekhthroi*, see also Thucydides 3.54–9, where the Plataeans, defending themselves before the Spartans, 'carefully distinguish between *polemioi* (which is what they are) and *echthroi* (which is what they are not)' (Macleod 1977: 233 n. 11 = 1983: 109 n. 11).

28 I do not see that Eurystheus has 'become a double' of Macaria, however, as Mendelsohn (2002: 128) suggests, nor that there is an implicit feminization of his character.

29 For further discussion of violent antagonism in this play and in Euripides' *Suppliant Women*, see Konstan 2005c. The various mentions of Electra's hatred for her mother in Sophocles' *Electra* (289, 347–8, 357–8, and 1309–11, all cited above) also point to a justified antagonism on her part, whereas Clytemnestra, who is depicted in this play as clearly in the wrong, vacillates in her hostility to her children (770–1).

30 It is elsewhere associated also with *ponêros*, 'wicked' (35.46), and with *anaiskhuntos*, 'shameless' (43.39).

31 For the contrast between love and hatred, cf. *Iliad* 9.614; on being hateful to the gods, *Odyssey* 10.74–5; Lysias 6.53; cf. Demosthenes 22.59 for the compound *theoisekhthria*; and Plato, *Euthyphro* 8A–C for the contrast between *theophilês* and *theomisês*; and *Laws* 916E.

32 The noun *apekhtheia* is applied to hatred or antagonism towards the Thebans at Demosthenes, *On the Crown* 36; cf. pseudo-Andocides, *Against Alcibiades* 28. Verbal forms based on *ekhth-* are on the whole far less common than the nouns *ekhthros* and *ekhthra*.

Chapter Ten

1 For empathy as the vicarious sharing of another person's emotional or intentional state, see Bischof-Koehler 1988, 1989, 1991, 1994, and 2001; Bischof-Koehler distinguishes empathy from 'emotional contagion,' which involves an indistinct assimilation to another person's mood, without a full awareness that the shared state is that of another. Bischof-Koehler relates the capacity for empathy to mirror-recognition in young children. Unlike sympathy or compassion, moreover, Bischof-Koehler argues that empathy need not lead to prosocial emotions, but is compatible even with intentional cruelty.

2 Macleod (1977: 227, 234, 236–67) reads the entire speech as an example of forensic oratory (227); cf. 236: '59.1 explicitly evokes pity, and the whole speech aims to create it.' But he too recognizes that the Plataeans chiefly cast their argument in terms of the Spartans' interests (234).

344 / Notes to pages 205–10

3 Diodotus does not entirely ignore considerations of right; as Orwin (1984: 492) observes, 'From the depths of Diodotos' argument pipes the still, small voice of justice.'

4 Alcibiades continues: 'For I do not think that what is just and what is advantageous are the same; on the contrary, many who have committed great wrongs have profited from them, while others who have performed just deeds have reaped no advantage'; cf. Chrysothemis in Sophocles, *Electra* 1042: 'There are times when even justice brings harm.' Socrates, of course, dissents from the common view; see Denyer 2001: 132–4.

5 There is a marked resemblance to the staging of the opening scene of Sophocles' *Oedipus the King*.

6 Turner (2001: 28) argues that a 'suppliant may be in the right by virtue of striving toward a socially accepted goal ... or, more vaguely, by simply suffering hardship from a position of weakness,' but if both these criteria fail, the 'assumption of the suppliant's role is invalid.' This is, I think, to confuse supplication with the appeal to pity. Unlike the claim to pity, supplication, especially at an altar, has a ritual component, the efficacy of which is independent of a prior evaluation of right and wrong. Cf. Giordano 1999: 190–1: 'The inviolability of refugees extends not only to those who are truly in need, that is, the classical types of Homeric supplication, but also to murderers and those condemned to death, and to criminals of every kind.'

7 Cf. Euripides, *Hecuba* 799–801 for the gods as guarantors of *nomos*; Hogan 1972: 247.

8 Cf. the chorus' claim that their case is *endika*, 65. Perhaps there is a reference to justice also in 43–4, if the unintelligible *anomoi* conceals a reference to unlawful treatment of the corpses, as A.Y. Campbell (1950: 123) and Kovacs (1998, in the critical apparatus) have suggested, rather than an expression such as *ana moi* or the like, adopted by the Oxford Classical Text (Diggle 1981–4).

9 For further discussion, and comparison with Aeschylus's *Suppliant Women* and Euripides' *Children of Hercules*, see Konstan 2005c. Bernek (2004: 15–44) outlines the paradigm that informs the Greek suppliant tragedies (including Aeschylus's *Eumenides* and Sophocles' *Oedipus at Colonus*), and proposes a model for an intertextual interpretation; the result is an emphasis on Euripides' ironical

transformation of the Aeschylean pattern (cf. 236, 263 on the *Children of Hercules*, 306–7 on the *Suppliant Women*).

10 Stephen Halliwell (2002: 183) writes that the 'notion of sympathy, which underlies both pity and fear, is not a vaguely humanitarian instinct: it is the capacity to recognise a likeness between oneself and the object of one's emotions, a likeness which imports with it a sense that one could imagine suffering such things oneself.' Those who have suffered most, however, are presumably best able to imagine what another person is suffering, yet are least susceptible to feeling pity, according to Aristotle. Pity is not a matter of sympathetic identification. When misfortune is present rather than prospective, one does not fear it (fear is of future harm), and without the fear, there is no pity.

11 Would the gods, then, be capable of pity? On Aristotle's view, they should not be, and in general, the Greeks seemed not to have expected pity of them; see Konstan 2001a: 105–13.

12 Cf. Halliwell 2002: 208–11, who points out that 'it is an extraordinary feature of *Philoctetes* that it invites its audience to recognize the increasing aptness of pity ... without having access, until much later, to Neoptolemus's own reactions' (209).

13 The chorus's pity does not necessarily signify a disposition to help Philoctetes; Philoctetes himself mentions that merchants who from time to time took refuge on Lemnos pitied him (*eleousi*), indeed, but refused to take him aboard their ships (307–11). If Philoctetes' cries and the stench of his wound really were unbearable, as Odysseus claims (1–11), then perhaps it was not wrong to abandon him, and hence, despite the accidental nature of his affliction, he is not deserving of pity. But Neoptolemus moves to touch the wretched Philoctetes when his malady is at its most intense (756–62), thus intimating the hollowness of Odysseus's excuse.

14 Plato employs the term *sumpaskhô* at *Republic* 605D, but the sense is apparently to feel pain or pleasure along with someone (cf. *sunkhairô*) rather than to experience another person's emotion by a process of identification.

15 Modern ideas of sympathy are inspired by an epistemological question: how is it that human beings, each locked into his or her own private world of sensations, ever come to know and appreciate the feelings of other people? This is the so-called problem of other

minds, and it is a major issue in philosophy today. The ancients, however, are almost entirely silent on it. They took it for granted that we know what others feel, and were concerned principally with the ethical character of our responses. For a splendid analysis of the difference between ancient pity, as an emotion specific to a detached observer, and modern notions of identification, see Halliwell 2002: 207–16.

16 Stephen Halliwell (1998: 174) rightly points out that this latter condition 'cannot be held to have been a universal presupposition of Greek pity'; but as we have seen, it was widely shared.

17 See Apicella Ricciardelli 1971–2; Carey 1988: 137–9; and Zierl 1994: 24, 28, 138; cf. Aristotle *Poetics* 18, 1456a20–4.

18 In the *Nicomachean Ethics* (1108b1–10), where Aristotle exploits the threefold classification of virtues and emotions according to excess, mean, and deficiency, he offers the term *epikhairekakia* or pleasure at another's misery as the opposite to *phthonos*, with *nemesis* occupying the mean; the paradigm, however, is not entirely coherent (see chapter 5, pp. 114–15).

Chapter Eleven

1 Melanie Klein (1975b: 176) writes: 'By the sense of loneliness I am referring not to the objective situation of bieng deprived of external companionship. I am referring to the inner sense of loneliness – the sense of being alone regardless of external circumstances, of feeling lonely even when among friends or receiving love.'

2 Planalp refers here to Sharpsteen 1991, who argues that 'jealousy is cognitively organized as a blended emotion' (31); cf. also Caston 2000: 9, 'a nexus of emotions'; White and Mullen 1989: 9, 'a complex of thoughts, emotions, and actions'; Farrell 1980: 543: 'not some *one* affective state'; Marina 1996: 31: 'un complejo entramado de sentimientos'; Neu 1980: 425–6, citing Spinoza, *Ethics* Part 3, Proposition 35, and Freud 1955: 223. However, Duchenne arranged scenes to show passions, including 'three scenes of Lady Macbeth expressing "the aggressive and wicked passions, of hatred, of jealousy, of cruel instincts," modulated to various degrees by contrary feelings of filial piety' (Sobieszek 1999: 121, citing Duchenne de Boulogne 1862: part 3, 169–74 = Duchenne de Boulogne 1990: 120–2 [translation of preceding]).

3 Stearns (1989: xi–xii) notes that 'most students of human jealousy
have argued that jealousy is an amalgam of more basic emotions –
fear of impending loss, grief, and anger at the source of loss. As an
amalgam, jealousy is open to various socially determined combinations'; cf. 5–6. So too, in the case of shyness, Crozier (1999: 17)
suggests that 'shyness is not a unitary experience but refers to two
distinctive experiences, fear and wariness on the one hand and
shame and embarrassment on the other ... Whether or not it is the
case that the lay perspective tends to blur distinctions among
different emotions, the trend in psychological research is to emphasize the differences among the self-conscious emotions rather than
their similarities.'

4 Of the three earlier definitions, 'zeal against' and 'zeal in favour' are
described as obsolete; the third, 'solicitude,' is still in use but is
largely restricted, at least in the United States, to cultivated language. Farrell (1997: 167–9) observes that professional jealousy, like
sibling rivalry, may also take the form of a three-party relationship,
e.g., a performer displaced by another in the esteem of the public
(which acts as the third in the triangle). On the range of meanings of
the French 'jalousie,' see Lagache 1947: 2–3.

5 Cf. W.L. Davidson 1912: 322, '*three* persons are involved in the
situation'; Klein 1975c: 180: '[E]nvy implies the subject's relation
to one person only and goes back to the exclusive relation with the
mother. Jealousy is based on envy, but involves a relation to at least
two people'; Farrell 1980: 529–31 = Farrell 1989: 247–9; also Farrell
1997: 166, 170–1; Segal 1973: 40, cited in R. Lloyd 1995: 3. Psychologists sometimes see the origin of jealousy in competition
among siblings for the mother's affection, as well as in the rivalry
associated with the Oedipus complex (cf. Klein 1975c: 197–201).
These three-party relationships may indeed serve as models for the
experience of jealousy, but they will be activated in societies that
place particular emphasis on a romantic ideal of love.

6 Ben-Ze'ev 2000: 281; cf. Lagache 1947: 5, citing D'Alembert, *Oeuvres*
vol. 3: 320: 'On est jaloux de ce qu'on possède et envieux de ce que
possèdent les autres'; Neu 1980: 433; Stearns 1989: 12; Parrott 1991:
4; Caston 2000: 8.

7 As Caston (2000: 8) notes, 'Jealousy is most often about a person,
while envy is about a thing.' Modern Greek *zêlía* and *zêlophthonía*
mean both 'envy' and 'jealousy' (so too the verb *zêleuô* and adjective

zêliárês); cf. Stafilidis 1998 s.vv. Irini Christophoros points out to
me (personal communication) that Modern Greek does not distinguish lexically between the feeling that arises when something is
stolen, when someone has what you want, and when a person you
love goes off with another. Baumgart (1990: 82) reports that God's
jealousy, expressed by *'qineah* in the language of the Bible, *kinah* in
modern Hebrew,' is 'still semantically undifferentiated from "envy"'
(cf. p. 106).

8 Cf. Tov-Ruach 1980: 466; Farrell 1980: 535; Farrell 1989: 252; Neu
1980: 433, '[W]e may fear for their loss ... as feeling agents'; Farrell
1989: 261: 'A man who thought of his wife strictly as an object
wouldn't in fact feel jealousy, it seems to me, when he suspected her
of infidelity ... On the contrary, I should think he would feel
something more like indignation'; Marina 1996: 179: 'El amante no
desea poseer al amado como posee una cosa ...; quiere poseer una
libertad como libertad' ('A lover does not desire to possess the beloved as one possesses a thing ...; he desires to possess a freedom [in
the other] as such'); Farrell 1997: 172–3; Wierzbicka 1999: 99: '[T]he
jealousy scenario can be summed up in three key components ...: (1)
'I want this person to feel good feelings for me'; (2) 'I think this
person feels good feelings for someone other than me'; (3) 'this is
bad.' Everything else is variable'; Caston 2000: 177.

9 Cf. Parrott 1991: 15–16. Jealousy differs from envy also in that it is
concerned with a particular individual, not just any person: we may
envy someone who has a girlfriend or boyfriend when we do not; we
are jealous when we are in love with the woman or man in question;
cf. Caston 2000: 9; Farrell 1980: 534; Neu 1980: 433–4. Modern
theorists sometimes refer jealousy (and envy) to a generalized lack of
confidence; thus Rubin (1975 [a self-help manual]: 220): 'Jealousy
and envy are a function of insecurity and low self-esteem ... Envy
comes from feeling so deprived that it seems that everyone must
surely have more than we do. Jealousy is born of feeling that we
have so little to give compared to someone else'; Lagache 1947: 125:
'Le fond affectif de la jalousie vécue est l'anxiété' ('The affective
basis of jealousy as it is experienced is anxiety'). Farrell (1980: 551–3)
acknowledges insecurity as a factor in jealousy, but denies that it
constitutes a complete explanation; cf. Farrell 1989: 258–9; also Neu
1980: 433: 'At the center of jealousy is insecurity'; Tov-Ruach 1980:

467: 'A person is jealous only when the perceived deprivation makes him doubt himself'; Leguina 2002: 62: 'Al fin y al cabo, los celos, creo yo, son un producto más, el más doloroso quizá, de nuestra propia inseguridad' ('In the end, I believe that jealousy is one more product – perhaps the most painful – of our own insecurity'). Contrast Fuentes 2001: 54: 'Envy is a powerless poison: we want to be someone else. Jealousy is noble: we want the other to be mine' ('la envidia es una ponzoña impotente, queremos ser otro. El celo es generoso, queremos que el otro sea mío'). Another feature of jealousy is the passion to know, to be informed; Leguina 2002: 62: 'la angustia de los celos se produce, especialmente, por desconocimiento, por la necesidad de saber cómo, incluso en qué posturas y actitudes están en cada preciso momento los amantes ausentes' ('the anxiety associated with jealousy is produced especially by unawareness, by the need to know how – even in what positions and poses – the absent lovers are at each precise moment').

10 Neu (1980: 442) offers a more flexible version of the functionalist position: 'While social arrangements may vary, whatever the social arrangements, jealousy serves to reinforce them.' For a sophisticated defence of moderate jealousy as an Athenian mean, see Kristjánsson 2002: 136–69.

11 Cf. W.C. Green 1892: 77: 'Nay, says Chremylus, he wanted to keep your gifts to himself.'

12 Cf. Andronicus, *On the Emotions* 2, p. 12 Kreuttner; Cicero, *Tusculan Disputations* 4.18: 'Obtrectatio' autem est ea quam intellegi ζηλοτυπίαν volo, aegritudo ex eo, quod alter quoque potiatur eo, quod ipse concupiverit' ('*Obtrectatio* is what I understand by *zêlotupia*, that is, a pain arising from the fact that someone else also has what one has oneself wanted' [sc. 'and now has,' which is the force of 'also']); Graver 2002: 143: '[J]ealousy [on the Stoic definition] is when I am distressed that another has obtained what I wanted even though I have also obtained it.'

13 Aristotle treats *zêlos* as a positive emotion, and in this he is consistent with ordinary Greek usage; cf. Saïd 2003 on the use of the term in Isocrates, where *zêloun* (verb) is associated with such positive notions as *thaumazein* ('admire'), *epainein* ('praise'), *makarizein* ('felicitate'), *epithumein* ('desire'), *mimeisthai* ('imitate'), and *exisôsai* ('equal'); contrast *phthonein* ('to envy'), which occurs in the

company of *epitiman* ('reproach'), *diaballein* ('slander'),
blasphêmein ('speak ill of'), *loidorein* ('abuse' or 'insult'), and
epibouleuein ('plot against'). For *zêlos* as competition for excellence,
cf. *Panathenaïcus* 159, *Evagoras* 77, and *Demonicus* 11 (in the latter
two philosophy is the goal of such effort). In *Antidosis* 148–9,
Isocrates contrasts the *zêlos* of right-thinking people with a feeling
of pain and irritation at the goodness of others. Hesiod, *Theogony*
383–4 makes *Zêlos* the offspring of Night (like *Nemesis*); in *Works
and Days*, *zêlos* is positive at 23 and 313 (in verbal form), negative
at 195–6.

14 So too, Descartes notes that 'what one commonly calls envy is a
vice that consists in a perversity of nature, which makes certain
people angry at the good that they see coming into the possession of
other men' (262 art. 182), although he adds: 'But I use the word here
to mean a passion that is not always vicious.'

15 This cognitive approach is shared by modern investigators of
jealousy and related emotions, e.g. Parrott 1991: 4: 'In analyzing
envy and jealousy, I assume that the emotion people *experience* is
determined by the cognitive appraisals that they make and by the
aspects of those appraisals on which they focus their attention.'

16 Cf. the contrast between *phthonein* as a negative emotion and
hamillasthai as productive competition for excellence in Isocrates,
To Nicocles 59.

17 For *zêlotupia* in connection with political or public competition, cf.
Plutarch, *Pelopidas* 4.3, *Flamininus* 13.2, *Lucullus* 4.5 (the tension
between Pompey and Lucullus), 16.2, *Alexander* 71.5, *Cato Minor*
37.1, *Dion* 18.1, *Aratus* 54.7, etc. For the invidiousness (*zêlotupia*) of
eunuchs, who serve in royal courts, cf. Heliodorus, *Aethiopica* 8.6.2,
9.25.5 ('*zêlotupia* is native to the tribe of eunuchs, for they are
assigned to bar others from what they themselves lack'); of courtesans, 2.8.5.

18 *Epistle* 73; for jealousy of skill at painting, cf. Lucian, *On Not
Readily Believing in Slander* 2; for envy paired with *zêlotupia*, cf.
also Epictetus, *Enchiridion* 19.2 and Plutarch, *On Good Cheer* 468B;
for a younger brother's *zêlotupia* in regard to the hereditary right of
an older, in this case to a priesthood, Heliodorus, *Aethiopica* 1.25.6,
7.2.4.

19 Photius's definition (ζ 34) is identical to that of the Suda, apart from

textual corruption; see Theodoridis 1998: 243 with the apparatus criticus. So too for *zêlotupoun* (ζ 35), Photius gives *anti tou misou*, 'instead of hatred,' with reference to Aeschines 3.211.

20 Cf. Serrano Aybar 1977: 101; Burguière 1970; on the history of the major manuscript tradition and its early arrival in southern Italy, see Lucà 1994.

21 In a study of the origin of terms for jealousy in the romance languages (Provençal *gelos*, French *jaloux*, Italian *geloso*, Spanish *celoso*, etc.), Grzywacz (1937: 4) notes that this emotion was late in finding an unambiguous term to denote it (cf. R. Lloyd 1995: 4). Grzywacz argues that the romance terms arose as learned, rather than popular, formations and were based on occurrences of *zêlos* and *zêlotês* in the Bible; their modern significance thus owes something to their connection with the idea of a jealous God.

22 Cf. also Lucian, *On Sacrifices* 7; also *Dialogues of the Gods* 7.1, 8.1, 8.5, 12.2, 17.2, 22.2; Fantham 1986: 56.

23 Cf. Sissa and Detienne 2000: 105: 'Hera takes umbrage at every decision, every thought that her husband does not share with her. She wants to know everything and, indeed, has a knack of finding out all that Zeus does or wants to do. As we have seen, a detailed list of his amorous infidelities does not bother her ... But when Zeus hides his military complicity with Thetis from her, she cannot bear it.' This account of Hera's behaviour in the *Iliad* is perfectly just; I disagree with Sissa and Detienne only over characterizing it as jealousy. Cf. *Odyssey* 5.118, in which Calypso accuses the gods of being *zêlêmones*, 'spiteful,' because while they freely enjoy sex with mortal women, they begrudge goddesses coupling with mortal men.

24 Cf. Quintus of Smyrna, *Post-Homerica* 9.333–49, where the Lemnian women murder their husbands with a 'spiteful mind' (*zêlêmoni nousôi*, 348), because they slept with their maids rather than with their wives; what irks the wives is the dishonour (*ou tieskon*, 340), which roused them to anger (*thumon*, 345); there is no mention of alienation of affections.

25 Herodas's fifth mime (third century BC), which stages Bitinna's savage treatment of a slave whom she accuses of sexual infidelity, bears the title *Zêlotupos* (probably not assigned by Herodas himself). Plutarch reports (*Conjugal Precepts* 144B–C) that a certain Melanthius responded to a speech by Gorgias at Olympia concerning

concord among the Greeks: 'This fellow is counselling us on concord, while he can't persuade himself, his wife, and his maid – three private individuals – to get along. For I gather that Gorgias felt a passion [*erôs*] for the maid, while his wife felt *zêlotupia* towards her'; cf. also Ctesias 688 F 29 *FGrHist* (Jacoby 1923–54) on the *zêlotupia* of Artoxerxes' wife Parysatis towards Stateira. Arsace in Heliodorus, *Aethiopica* 7.7.7, in love with the hero Theagenes, is said to be 'not without *zêlotupia*' of Chariclea, to whom Theagenes is betrothed (cf. 7.8.6, 7.10.6, 7.21.5, 7.26.6–7); Arsace desires sex, not marriage, with Theagenes, but Theagenes, faithful to Chariclea, will not consent (cf. too Achaemenes' *zêlotupia* in respect to Chariclea at 7.27.4, 7.29.1, where each time the term is paired with *orgê* or 'anger').

In early modern times, 'jealousy was assumed to be a particularly masculine emotion in support of proper patriarchal governance' (Stearns 1989: 15); Baumgart (1990: 121) observes of the Middle Ages and the Renaissance: 'It is conspicuous how seldom jealous women appear not only in popular literature but also in the literature of the high culture.' J.B. Bryson (1991: 191) reports that a study of jealous responses in various European countries today, however, indicates that 'the profiles for males and females are quite similar,' the United States being exceptional in this respect. White and Mullen (1989: 127) note that despite the popular stereotype of the sexually posses-sive male, 'most research has reported no gender differences in the level of self-reported jealousy, and those studies finding a difference are not consistent in finding one gender to be more jealous than the other.'

26 Cf. Diogenes Laertius 7.131: 'They [the Stoics] are pleased that wives should be in common among the sages; a man will enjoy whatever woman he chances on, as Zeno says in his book *On the Republic* and Chrysippus in his *On the Republic*: "we shall love all the children equally like fathers, and *zêlotupia* over adultery will be eliminated."'

27 Cf. Cleopatra's resentment of honours bestowed on Octavia in Plutarch's *Life of Antony* 57.2. In a satirical context, a man may be reproached for exhibiting too little *zêlotupia*; thus, in Lucian's dialogue on the misanthrope Timon (16), the god Wealth offers an analogy for Timon's former promiscuity in regard to money: 'If

someone has lawfully married a young, pretty woman and then neither guards [*phulattein*] her nor has any *zêlotupia* at all, but lets her go walking where she pleases night and day and associate with whomever she wishes ...' For the expression *zêlotupôs phulattein*, cf. *On Men Hired for Salary* 7.19–20; cf. also Catullus 17.

28 Modern 'jealousy' is ideologically gendered as well; cf. Farber 1978: 182: 'A man is cuckolded; a woman is unfortunate.' Buss (2000: 3) asserts that women universally find 'emotional infidelity more upsetting,' while men 'find the prospect of a partner's sexual infidelity more agonizing'; the evidence he cites, however, does not unambiguously support his conclusion.

29 Cf. also Lucian, *Dialogues of Courtesans* 2.2, and contrast 8.1 on the legitimacy of male *zêlotupia*, which is taken as a sign of genuine love. Rademaker 2005: 158 notes that, in Euripidean tragedy, 'absence of jealousy, and absence of possesive infatuation with men, is indeed part of the ideology of female *sôphrosunê*'; female jealousy, I am arguing, was understood precisely as a form of possessive infatuation.

30 On the problematic nature of Hera's marriage and her vindictive temperament, see Clark 1998: 16–17.

31 This is a different matter from what Jon Elster (1999a: 101) calls a 'weak proto-emotion,' by which he means that the relevant concept is lacking in a given culture. Elster offers guilt (159) and boredom (258) as examples of proto-emotions in classical antiquity.

32 In *Odyssey* book 8.265–366, Hephaestus's response to the discovery that his wife Aphrodite has been sleeping with Ares is to shame the adulterers by trapping them in bed and exposing them to the mockery of the rest of the gods; Hephaestus does not try to conceal his humiliation – ensnaring Ares is vengeance enough, since he inflicts on him the same indignity that he suffered: there is no question of romantic jealousy. Cf. Bourdieu 1966: 220: 'If a Kabyle avenges his honour which has been impugned through his wife, this does not necessarily mean that he is impelled by jealousy or love; even if he was without either of these feelings he should neverthe-less carry out his duty, and in so doing he would increase his merit.'

33 Contra, e.g., Pucci (1999: 222), for whom Medea is 'tormented by an uncontrollable jealousy'; but see Bongie 1977; Knox 1977; Foley 1989; and Boedeker 1991. Note too that the chorus pray that they

themselves not be smitten by the arrow of desire (632–3), not that their husbands be faithful. There is a judicious survey of Medea's multiple or overdetermined motivation, including a significant element of resentment at Jason's betrayal of the marriage bed, in Mastronarde 2002: 16–22.

34 Dejanira's emotion, in Sophocles' *Women of Trachis*, when Hercules brings Iole into her home perhaps comes closer to jealousy, but again she is primarily concerned to protect her position in the household rather than being peeved at Hercules' infidelity; as she says (459–62), she has long endured his philandering (see chapter 2, p. 60).

35 The tyrant in Xenophon's *Hiero* (3.3–4) remarks that adulterers are punished by death because they corrupt 'the love [*philia*] of wives for their husbands; since when a woman has sex as a result of some mishap their husbands esteem them no less, provided that their love seems to remain uncontaminated'; although this account seems closer to the modern concern with the other's affective state, I suspect that Hiero's point is substantially the same as Lysias's. Hupka (1991) suggests that romantic jealousy may not arise in societies in which collective identification overrides the individual sense of self (cf. Marina 1996: 140–1). As Hupka puts it (1991: 265), '[D]ifferent motives for the arousal of jealousy raise the question of whether the predicaments are comparable and even can be regarded as jealousy situations. Are the Andalusian husband and the Kabyle husband, when avenging the honor that has been impugned by the liaisons of their wives, propelled by the same emotions as an American husband confronting his wife's affair?'

36 I do not mean to suggest that modern jealousy is uniform and lacks a history; as Stearns (1989: 4) remarks of this emotion in American experience, '[J]ealousy has changed significantly over time.'

37 Theocritus 6.25–8 might seem to suggest the arousal of a jealous response (so Gow 1950: 124 ad v. 27); the Cyclops, frustrated by Galatea's indifference towards him, sings: 'But I sting her back, and don't look at her, but say I have another as wife; when she hears this she feels *zêlos* [verb *zaloi*, in Doric] towards me, O Paean, and melts with love, and grows passionate as she looks out from the sea at my cave and my flocks.' But Polyphemus is not so much thinking of making Galatea jealous as of stimulating her interest in him by a show of unconcern – the principle of playing hard to get. As Daphnis

puts it earlier in the poem (17), 'She flees if you court her and pur-
sues if you do not.' In 3.50, the singer exclaims, 'I feel *zêlos* [*zalô*]
towards Iasion,' but here the point is that Iasion's lot as lover of
Demeter was enviable, even though he paid for it with his life
(*Odyssey* 5.125); so too Endymion is called *zalôtos*, 'enviable' (49).

38 It is a pity that his *Misoumenos* or 'Hated Man' is so fragmentary.

39 The theme of reciprocal love enters New Comedy with the role of
the young courtesan; see Konstan 1995: 146–7.

40 Jealousy may also have been inhibited by the prevalence of arranged
marriages and the availability of female slaves for sex, along with
the expectation that men were permitted such relations; for other
factors, see Konstan 1995: 148–52 on Menander's *Epitrepontes*. As
jealousy emerges as a possibility in a society previously governed by
communal restraint, popular literature may be reticent about
describing it; cf. Stearns 1989: 21–2 for the response to jealousy
during the Victorian era in the United States.

41 On elegy, however, cf. James 2003: 105–6, who notes that 'the
problem of the rival, which on its face seems to be about sexual
jealousy, turns out to be primarily about money ... Sexual jealousy is
merely a symptom of the real problem.' Cf. also magical binding
formulas, e.g. #28 in Gager 1992: 97–100 (Egyptian, third or fourth
century AD, accompanied by a female figurine pierced by thirteen
needles), in which Sarapammôn petitions that Ptolemais 'not be had
in a promiscuous way, let her not be had anally, nor let her do
anything for pleasure with another man, just with me alone,
Sarapammôn, to whom Area gave birth, and do not let her drink or
eat, that she not show any affection, nor go out, nor find sleep
without me ... Drag her by the hair and her heart until she no longer
stands aloof from me ..., and I hold Ptolemais herself ..., obedient for
all the time of my life, filled with love for me, desiring me, speaking
to me the things she has on her mind.' The formula is a common
type in this epoch. It may be doubted that Sarapammôn contem-
plates marriage with Ptolemais.

42 Catullus 109; cf. Reitzenstein 1940; Konstan 1972–3; Büchner 1974:
256–7.

43 Catullus 58; repetition of the beloved's name is more common in
exclamations of devotion than of despair, e.g. Anacreon 359, cited by
Nisbet and Hubbard 1970: 171 ad Horace 1.13.1–2.

44 Cf. *perpetuum*, v. 14. On the application of *vinculum, catena, foedus*, and the like to non-conjugal relations, see La Penna 1951: 187–95; and Nisbet and Hubbard 1970: 177–8 ad v. 18; for Horace's 'ambiguous acknowledgement and suppression of Catullus,' and his 'technique of inverting or reversing Catullan models,' see Hubbard 2000 (quotations on pp. 31, 36; bibliography on 25 n. 3).

45 See, e.g., Romano 1991: 535–6: 'La trattazione del tema della gelosia e la descrizione dei sintomi patologici di essa avevano un celebre archetipo, il carme 31 L.-P. di Saffo ..., che a Roma era stato imitato da Valerio Edituo ... e, sopratutto, da Catullo' ('The treatment of the theme of jealousy and the description of its pathological symptoms had a celebrated model – poem 51 L.-P. of Sappho ..., which was imitated in Rome by Valerius Aedituus and above all by Catullus'); Owens 1992: 241: '[I]n Catullus 51, the poet is jealous of another man who enjoys Lesbia's affections'; Dover 1994 [orig. 1971] 108: 'Sappho describes, with almost clinical precision, the symptoms of an anxiety state caused ... by homosexual jealousy'; and Toohey 2004: 75, who sees Sappho's jealousy as one manifestation of the disease of love-sickness. In 1711, Ambrose Philips translated:

> Blest as th'immortal gods is he,
> The youth who fondly sits by this,
> And hears and sees thee all the while
> Softly speak and sweetly smile.
> 'Twas this deprived my soul of rest,
> And raised such tumults in my breast, etc.

''Twas this' refers unambiguously to the communion of the other two as the source of the poet's emotion, but it is not in the Greek. See now Furley 2000 for a vigorous critique of this interpretation, and a defence of the view that the man opposite Sappho is godlike 'because he does *not* succumb to the girl's charms even when exposed to their full force at such close proximity ...; there is no question of Sappho feeling jealous of the foil she introduces merely to underline her own predicament' (13). Furley (2000: 13 n. 26) notes that Radt (1970: 340–3) and Bremer (1982: 114) had already anticipated this interpretation. Furley is disposed, however, to see jealousy at work in Catullus's adaptation of Sappho's poem, perhaps because he read Sappho this way 'or he may have deliberately refashioned the original to serve his own purposes' (14); for Furley, the rearrangement of sexual roles (Catullus's persona is male) is part of the reason why 'Catullus' poem invites interpretation along the lines of jealous love' (15).

46 Nisbet and Hubbard (1970: 173 ad v. 5) cite Callimachus, *Epigram* 43.1–2, Apollonius of Rhodes 3.297–8, Theocritus 2.106ff., Asclepiades, *Anthologia Palatina* 12.135, Lucian, *Jup. Trag.* 2, and Plutarch, *Life of Demetrius* 38.4 on the Greek side; on the Latin, Valerius Aedituus, *Epigram* 1.2ff. (cited in Aulus Gellius 19.9.10) and Ovid, *Metamorphoses* 9.535ff. Cf. Stendhal 1916 (orig. 1822): 124, who in the chapter 'Of Jealousy' remarks on the tendency of jealous lovers to 'exaggerate the happiness of your rival, exaggerate the insolence happiness produces in him ... The only remedy is, perhaps, to observe your rival's happiness at close quarters. Often you will see him fall peacefully asleep in the same *salon* as the woman, for whom your heart stops beating, at the mere sight of a hat like hers some way off in the street.' Though jealousy is at work, the contrast Stendhal draws here is between the nonchalance of the rival, whose deepest passions have not been stirred, and the experience of being profoundly in love.

47 Horace's speaker retains also his voice and capacity to argue; cf. Ancona 1994: 123, and contrast *Epodes* 11.9–10.

48 Cf. Ancona 1994: 123. A propos *lentis* (8), Nisbet and Hubbard (1970) note: 'The word indicates the prolonged agony of Horace's love' (cf. Gauly 1995: 93; D. West 1967: 65, followed by Radici Colace 1985: 53–9, imagines culinary imagery), and of *penitus*: 'love was believed to attack the bones, and particularly the marrow.' Concerning *uror* Nisbet and Hubbard (1970:) write: 'In erotic poetry *uri* normally refers to love, but there is no reason why it should not have been used of a more complicated set of feelings,' and they refer the reader to *Epistles* 1.2.12: *hunc amor, ira quidem communiter urit utrumque.*

49 Today, the scenario is a romantic commonplace; for an example, see Fragoulis 2001: 147: 'Ariadne put on some clothes, made some tea and then told the story of her six-day lovefest in intimate detail, as Medea sat pokerfaced, absorbing the information and watching her friend's changing expressions without blinking her envious, evil eye.' Earlier, on learning of her friend's affair, 'Medea shook with

jealousy and rage' (144). For an early example, see the description of
Chaereas's *zêlotupia* in Chariton's novel *Callirhoe* (1.3.4–6, 1.4.8);
Paglialunga (2000) notes that Chaereas's jealous symptoms resemble
those of lovesickness.

50 Quinn 1984: 149; cf. 150 ad vv. 15–16: 'confirming the suspicion
that Lydia was once H.'s mistress'; also Maleuvre 1990: 132–7.

51 Ancona (1994: 122–5) acknowledges the two different ideals of love,
but emphasizes the tension between Horace's desire to dominate
Lydia and the source of this desire in Lydia's relationship with
Telephus.

52 Two important moments in the evolution of the modern paradigm
of jealousy are manifested in the novel *Pandosto, The Triumph of
Time* (1588), by Robert Greene, and in Samuel Richardson's *Pamela*
(1740). In the first (the basis for Shakespeare's *Winter's Tale*), the
king Pandosto conceives a morbid jealousy over the relationship
between his wife, Bellaria, and his childhood friend, Egistus, who,
while Pandosto is occupied with affairs of state, have taken to
walking together in the garden, 'where they two in private and
pleasant devises would pass away the time to both their contents'
(para. 4). Pandosto is unable to believe that their affection can be
innocent. His suspicions recall the situation in Horace's ode, but
with a difference: in Greene's novella, the husband's passion is
represented as paranoid, since the wife is in fact faithful; as she says,
'[T]hat I loved Egistus I can not deny: that I honored him I shame
not to confess ... But as touching lascivious lust, I say Egistus is
honest, and hope my self to be found without spot' (para. 31). It is
the idea of jealousy as a disordered state of mind that is new: 'Ah
Jealousy,' Pandosto soliloquizes, 'a hell to the mind, and a horror
in the conscience, suppressing reason, and inciting rage: a worse
passion then frenzy, a greater plague than madness' (para. 34). In
Pamela, Mr B— suspects that Pamela harbours an affection for a
young clergyman that puts in question her loyalty to himself
(Richardson 1958: 227, 524–5). Here too, there are no grounds for Mr
B—'s anxiety, as Pamela has no amorous interest in the other man
(by contrast, the knowledge that Mr B--- has had a daughter by
another woman and continues to support the girl arouses in Pamela
the most generous sentiments, 458–9, 507–17). Here again, jealousy

is configured around a man's lack of trust in his wife's innocent friendship with another.

53 Stroh (1993: 170) remarks of this poem: 'an quisquam gravius ac copius illius affectus vim descripsit, qui cum apud Romanos proprio nomine careat, a posteris plurimis Graeca voce dicitur zelotypia (i.e. "Eifersucht," "gelosia")?' ('has anyone described the power of that emotion more seriously and fully – an emotion that lacked a name of its own among the Romans, but is called by many later writers by the Greek term *zelotypia* [i.e. "jealousy"]?').

Chapter Twelve

1 The quotation refers to Freud's (1957) distinction between mourning and melancholy. Cf. Brown 2003: 459: 'The irony of melancholia, of course, is that attachment to the object of one's sorrowful loss supersedes any desire to recover from this loss, to live free of it in the present, to be unburdened by it. This is what renders melancholia a persistent condition, a state, indeed, a structure of desire, rather than a transient response to death or loss.' For Freud, this suggested that melancholia was a response to 'an object-loss which is withdrawn from unconsciousness, in contradistinction to mourning, in which there is nothing about the loss that is unconscious' (Freud 1957: 245).

2 Some scholars attempt to capture the ambiguity of *lupê* in philosophical literature by resorting to the more inclusive English word 'distress' (e.g., Long and Sedley 1987).

3 On terms for pain in the Greek medical writers, see King 1988: 58–60; in addition to *lupê* and *algêma* or *algos*, King discusses *odunê*, commonly used (especially in the plural) of labour pains (60), but also of 'sharp pain, pain which pierces the body,' and *ponos* (plural *ponoi*), 'often used for long-lasting pain, dull pain' (58). *Ponos* refers more generally to hard work or toil, particularly in connection with agriculture; King sees its connection with 'pain in both war and childbirth' (59) as a sign that these are both valorized effortful activities that require struggle, and for this reason were not treated with painkillers.

4 For the close association between grief and pain, see Sophocles, *Ajax*

937, 940–1, 946–9, 951, 957, 972–3, 982, 993–4, and 1005, where the words *ania*, *algistos*, and *pathos* itself describe the reaction of his dear ones to Ajax's death. Tecmessa and the chorus also believe that Odysseus and the Atridae will show contempt for them, which Aristotle treats as an emotion in *Rhetoric* 2.11; but their grief itself is not so much an emotion as a state of pain.

5 A newpaper article under the headline 'Anglers Cast Doubts That Fish Feel Pain' (*Providence Journal*, 7 May 2003, A6, taken from the *New York Times*) reports: 'Eminent scientists have concluded that, despite anglers' long-standing protestations to the contrary, fish do indeed feel pain when hooked. Animal-rights activists ... now say they are encouraged in their insistence that anglers should desist from their pastime. "While fishing might seem fun, there's a terri-fied animal fighting for its life at the other end of the line," said Dawn Carr, an animal-rights activist.' That the fish feel pain is plausible, and it is reason enough to oppose sport fishing. But the inference from the animal's pain to the idea that it experiences the emotion of fear is unwarranted.

6 Grief might be said to differ from pain in its directedness or inten-tionality: we do not simply grieve but grieve for someone. But even in the case of physical pain, we often experience not just pain but, e.g., a pinprick: we say 'the needle hurts,' not 'there is pain.'

7 The anguish to which death, like any intensely felt loss or absence, gives rise is perhaps more like a desire or *epithumia* than a *pathos* in the narrow sense; compare the longing (in Greek, *pothos*) that we feel when we are deprived of the company of a loved one. For the analogy between grief and erotic pining, cf. Aristotle *Rhetoric* 1370b22–8.

8 Cf. Sophocles, *Ajax* 713–17; but in fact Ajax has not given over his anger, any more than Electra has.

9 So too Electra cites her mother's reproach: 'Are you the only one whose father has died? Is there no other mortal in mourning?' (289–90); cf. the chorus's comment at 1171–3 (by which time they should know better): 'Consider, Electra, that you were born of a mortal father, and Orestes was mortal. Do not groan too much, for we are all bound to suffer this.' On the topos that what is done cannot be remedied, cf. the chorus in Sophocles' *Ajax*, responding to the hero's

exclamations of anguish: 'Why are you suffering [*algoiês*] over what has been done; there is no way these things can be as though they were not so' (377–8). But Ajax is not simply lamenting a state of affairs; rather, he still harbours hopes of revenge by killing Agamemnon, Menelaus, and Odysseus (as he had intended) and then slaying himself (387–91). Ajax still believes that it is he who has been insulted and mocked, and his rage has as its object those who have, in his view, harmed him deliberately and unjustly (cf. chapter 4, p. 106).

10 Cf. L. MacLeod 2001: 45: 'To the Chorus, [Electra's] behaviour seems excessive and futile, and at the beginning it assumes that her lamentation has its source in purely personal reasons, grief for Agamemnon ...; the women do not understand why she continues to lament for a father now long dead.' Aristotle does concede that 'time ends anger,' *Rhetoric* 1380b6; see also the tragic poet Theodectes fragment 9, Snell 1971–: 'O wretched Thyestes, endure and bite back the bit of anger ... Infinite time obscures all.'

11 This might be the theme of a modern drama, in which the action consists chiefly in the manifestation of an interior condition or struggle; but such a plot was foreign to the ancient stage.

12 Leona MacLeod (2001: 39) observes that 'mourning need not mean that Elektra is governed solely by her passions. True, she hates the rulers and deeply grieves her father's murder, but there is an ethical basis to her lamentation ... Her passions contain an ethical truth.' The vehicle for the ethical dimension, I argue, is Electra's anger rather than her grief as such.

13 Helene Foley (2001: 151) observes: 'In these early scenes, Electra practices through her aggressive lamentation what I shall call an ethics of vendetta. Lamentation has a particular function to play in the jural system of cultures that practice feuds or vendetta justice; it aims to provoke revenge through the awakening of shared pain.' The pain, however, is not caused by grief but rather by an injustice, a point that remains implicit in Foley's analysis. On lamentation as a socio-political gesture, Foley cites Seremetakis 1991; I nevertheless wonder whether vendetta, as opposed to rectification of an injustice, is at stake in the play.

In *Prometheus Bound*, attributed to Aeschylus but probably completed and produced by his son after Aeschylus's death (M.L. West 1990: 67–72), Prometheus cries out in language reminiscent of Electra's apostrophe to heaven and earth: 'O bright air and swift winds, river streams and endless laughter of sea waves, and earth, mother of all and the all-seeing circle of the sun, I call on you to see what I, a god, suffer at the hands of gods' (88–92). Like Electra, Prometheus complains not about his pain as such but rather of the disgrace (*aikeia, aeikês*, 93, 97) to which Zeus is subjecting him. The daughters of Ocean who form the chorus reprove Prometheus for his headstrong resistance to Zeus's inexorable power (178–80), by which he augments his own suffering. Like Electra again, Prometheus concedes that he has brought Zeus's wrath upon himself ('I erred deliberately,' 266). But he is convinced that he is in the right (cf. 976, 1093), and his resolute hostility to Zeus is grounded in resentment at the unjust way he has been treated. The tension between Prometheus's physical pain and his anger are analogous, I suggest, to that between Electra's grief for her father and her rage at Agamemnon's murderers.

14 Cf. *Phaedrus* 258b for verb *penthein* = 'be sorry'; *penthos* has a somewhat formal register, like the English 'mourning' in comparison with 'grief'; three of the four occurrences in Demosthenes are in his funeral oration, six of the seven occurrences in Lysias are in his.

15 Bruns 1909: 2.334–5 = Paulus, *Opinions* 1.21.2–5, 8–14, as cited in Shelton 1998: 94. Shelton comments: 'A mother's grief for her child would undoubtedly extend well beyond a month ... The social demand that they suppress their grief may well have caused hysterical symptoms in many women.' Shelton adduces the medical writer Soranus (second century AD), who remarks in his *Gynecology* (3.26) that 'hysterical suffocation' is most often 'preceded by repeated miscarriage, premature childbirth, long widowhood, retention of menses, menopause, or inflation of the womb' (ibid., 302). But miscarriage scarcely counts as infant death, and I am not confident that this passage provides evidence for the harmful effects of suppressed grief.

16 Ancient Hebrew law restricted the period of mourning normally to seven days (e.g., Genesis 50:10, 1 Samuel 31:13), and at times to a single day or less (2 Samuel 1:12); thirty days is also indicated (Numbers 20:29). For discussion of the relationship between

mourning, which is a ritual act, and grief, which is a psychological function, see Olyan 2003.

17 Cf. the advice, in a treatise ascribed to Seneca (*On Remedies for Chance Events* 13.1), to a person who has lost his sons: 'You're a fool to weep over the mortality of mortals,' a sentiment that Rudolf Kassel (1958: 14) describes as 'shocking to the modern reader.'

18 In the case of the aged, death was understood to be less tragic. Thus, the Greek rhetorician Menander (third or fourth century AD) remarks that it is ridiculous to recite lamentations for the very old (436.23–4 Spengel 1854–85; translation in Russell and Wilson 1981).

19 In his treatise *On Memory and Recollection*, Aristotle observes that without time there can be no memory; consequently, 'only those animals remember that can perceive time' (449b28–9). The condition for memory – that its object no longer be present – is simultaneously what makes forgetting possible. As Glenn Most (2001: 149) observes, Virgil himself 'recognized that memory even presupposes forgetting and depends upon it.' Memory's desire to overcome forgetting would result in the cessation of time and hence the end of memory itself.

20 There is a similar tension in Virgil's *Aeneid* between Dido's resolution to remain faithful to her deceased husband, Sychaeus, and what may seem a perverse attachment to her grief for him. Her sister, Anna, treats it as the latter, and rehearses the commonplaces of consolation literature (4.31–5): 'You who are dearer than light to your sister, will you let your youth be consumed in grief, and not know sweet children or the rewards of love? Do you believe that ashes or buried ghosts care about that?' For further discussion, see Konstan 2003a.

21 Compare Mosley 2003: 11, in connection with the destruction of the World Trade Center in New York City on 11 September 2001: 'The thing I feared most was the healing quality that time has on the human heart. I knew that after a while I would fall back into complacency – that I would learn to accept that which I knew was unacceptable.'

22 This is not to deny that the two sentiments may mutually reinforce one another: the combination of grief and outrage at injustice forms a powerful motive, as the case of Electra herself testifies.

Conclusion

1 Striker (1996: 289) comments of the account of emotions in the *Rhetoric*: 'Book 2 focuses exclusively on emotions relating to other people.'

2 Neu (1980: 434) distinguishes between 'admiring envy' and 'malicious envy'; with malicious envy, 'one wants to lower the other (to one's own level or below); in the case of admiring envy, one wishes to raise oneself (to become like the other).' Neu adds that both sentiments involve 'a desire to overcome inequality, but the desire comes from different directions' (440).

3 Stocker (1996: 265–322), commenting on 'The Complex Evaluative World of Aristotle's Angry Man,' notes that, for Aristotle, anger is evaluative, and hence *orgê* is 'a moral notion' (266), deeply connected with honour. When Aristotle's man 'is not accorded the rank and respect he thinks due ... [h]e experiences the lack of respect as a deep wound to himself, that is, to his self' (268). Such dependency on others' reassurance suggests a narcissistic personality (269–70); but it may be that 'Aristotle's men and our narcissists cannot have the same structure of feelings' (271), and Stocker concedes he may be describing what *we* would be like if we were similar to Aristotle's men (272). Stocker affirms: 'The psyche of Aristotle's man is, further, constituted by a desire ... that he be a center, if not the center, of attention, concern, and understanding' (277), and this conditions his need for friendship (280); but the demand to be 'understood' is itself a modern phenomenon; see Konstan 1997a: 14–18, 152–3.

Bibliography

Abu-Lughod, Lila. 1999 (orig. 1986). *Veiled Sentiments: Honor and Poetry in a Bedouin Society*. Berkeley: University of California Press.

Adrados, Francisco R., et al. 1980–. *Diccionario Griego-Español*. Madrid: Consejo Superior de Investigaciones Científicas.

Ahmed, Sara. 2004. *The Cultural Politics of Emotion*. Edinburgh: Edinburgh University Press.

Alaux, Jean. 1995. *Le liège et le filet: Filiation et lien familial dans la tragédie athénienne du Ve siècle avant J.-C.* Paris: Éditions Belin.

Alexiou, Evangelos. 1999. 'Zur Darstellung der ὀργή in Plutarch's Βίοι.' *Philologus* 143: 101–13.

Allen, Christopher. 1998. 'Painting the Passions: The *Passions de l'Âme* as a Basis for Pictorial Expression.' In Stephen Gaukroger, ed., *The Soft Underbelly of Reason: The Passions in the Seventeenth Century*, 79–111. London: Routledge.

Allen, Danielle. 1999. 'Democratic Dis-Ease: Of Anger and the Troubling Nature of Punishment.' In Susan A. Bandes, ed., *The Passions of Law*, 191–214. New York: New York University Press.

Allen, Danielle. 2000. *The World of Prometheus: The Politics of Punishing in Democratic Athens*. Princeton: Princeton University Press.

Althoff, Gerd. 1998. '*Ira Regis*: Prolegomena to a History of Royal Anger.' In Rosenwein 1998: 59–74.

Ancona, Ronnie. 1994. *Time and the Erotic in Horace's Odes*. Durham, NC: Duke University Press.

Anderson, William S. 1964. *Anger in Juvenal and Seneca*. Berkeley: University of California Press.

André, Christophe, and François Lelord. 2002 (orig. French edition 2001). *La fuerza de las emociones*. Barcelona: Editorial Kairós.

Anonymus. 1896. *In Aristotelis artem rhetoricam commentarium*. Ed. Hugo Rabe. Berlin: Reimer = *Commentaria in Aristotelem Graeca*, vol. 21, part 2: 1–262.

Apicella Ricciardelli, Gabriella. 1971–2. 'Il φιλάνθωπον nella *Poetica* di Aristotele.' *Helikon* 11–12: 389–96.

Arndt, William F., and F. Wilbur Gingrich. 1957. *A Greek-English Lexicon of the New Testament and Other Early Christian Literature*. Cambridge: Cambridge University Press.

Arnim, J. von. 1921–4. *Stoicorum Veterum Fragmenta*. 3 vols. Leipzig: Teubner.

Arrowsmith, William, trans. 1958. 'Hecuba.' In David Grene and Richmond Lattimore, eds, *The Complete Greek Tragedies*. Chicago: University of Chicago Press.

Averill, James R. 1980. 'A Constructivist View of Emotion.' In Robert Plutchik and Henry Kellerman, eds, *Theories of Emotion*, 305–40. New York: Academic Press.

Aznárez, Juan Jesús. 2002. 'La defensa de los golpistas alega que Chávez reunció al poder.' *El País* 27, no. 9211 (15 August): 7.

Bailey, F.G. 1983. *The Tactical Uses of Passion: An Essay on Power, Reason, and Reality*. Ithaca: Cornell University Press.

Baird, Robert M., and Stuart E. Rosenbaum. 1999. 'Introduction.' In Baird and Rosenbaum eds 1999: 9–18.

Baird, Robert M., and Stuart E. Rosenbaum, eds. 1999. *Hatred, Bigotry, and Prejudice: Definitions, Causes and Solutions*. Amherst, NY: Prometheus Books.

Baker, R. 1996. *Sperm Wars*. London: Fourth Estate.

Baker, R., and M. Bellis. 1995. *Human Sperm Competition: Copulation, Competition and Infidelity*. London: Chapman and Hall.

Ball, Philip. 2001. *Bright Earth: Art and the Invention of Color*. New York: Farrar, Straus and Giroux.

Barbalet, J.M. 1998. *Emotion, Social Theory, and Social Structure: A Macrosociological Approach*. Cambridge: Cambridge University Press.

Barbaro, Ermolao, trans. 1545. *Aristotelis Rhetoricorum libri tres*. With commentary by Daniel Barbaro. Basel = *Aristotelis Rhetoricorum libri tres*, Hermolao Barbaro Patricio Veneto interprete, Danielis Barbari in eosdem libros commentarii. Basileae 1545.

Barkan, Elazar. 2000. *The Guilt of Nations: Restitution and Negotiating Historical Injustices.* New York: W.W. Norton & Co.

Barkow, Jerome H., Leda Cosmides, and John Tooby, eds. 1992. *The Adapted Mind: Evolutionary Psychology and the Generation of Culture.* New York: Oxford University Press.

Barnes, Jonathan. 1995. 'Rhetoric and Poetics.' In Jonathan Barnes, ed., *The Cambridge Companion to Aristotle,* 259–85. Cambridge: Cambridge University Press.

Barnes, Jonathan, ed. 1984. *The Complete Works of Aristotle.* Princeton: Princeton University Press.

Baron-Cohen, Simon. 2003. *The Essential Difference: Men, Women and the Extreme Male Brain.* London: Allen Lane.

Barton, Carlin A. 2001. *Roman Honor: The Fire in the Bones.* Berkeley: University of California Press.

Barton, Richard E. 1998. '"Zealous Anger" and the Renegotiation of Aristocratic Relationships in Eleventh- and Twelfth-Century France.' In Rosenwein 1998: 153–70.

Bartov, Omer. 2001 (orig. 1985). *The Eastern Front, 1941–45, German Troops, and the Barbarisation of Warfare.* 2nd edition. Houndmills: Palgrave.

Bauman, Zygmunt. 2001. 'El desafío ético de la globalización.' *El País* 26, no. 8823 (20 July): 11.

Baumgart, Hildegard. 1990 (orig. 1985). *Jealousy: Experiences and Solutions.* Trans. Manfred and Evelyn Jacobson. Chicago: University of Chicago Press.

Bavelas, Janet Beavin, and Nicole Chovil. 1997. 'Faces in Dialogue.' In Russell and Fernández-Dols eds 1997: 334–46.

Beauvoir, Simone de. 1974 (orig. 1949). *The Second Sex.* Trans. H.M. Parshley. New York: Random House.

Beazley, J.D. 1956. *Attic Black-Figure Vase-Painters.* Oxford: Clarendon Press.

Beck, Aaron T. 1999. *Prisoners of Hate: The Cognitive Basis of Anger, Hostility, and Violence.* New York: HarperCollins.

Belfiore, Elizabeth S. 2000. *Murder among Friends: Violation of Philia in Greek Tragedy.* New York and Oxford: Oxford University Press.

– 2001. 'Family Friendship in Aristotle's Ethics.' *Ancient Philosophy* 21: 113–32.

Benedict, Ruth. 1946. *The Chrysanthemum and the Sword: Patterns of Japanese Culture*. Boston: Houghton Mifflin.

Ben-Ze'ev, Aaron. 2000. *The Subtlety of Emotions*. Cambridge, MA: MIT Press.

Berlin, Brent, and Paul Kay. 1969. *Basic Color Terms: Their Universality and Evolution*. Berkeley: University of California Press.

Bernabé, Alberto, ed. 1987. *Poetarum epicorum graecorum*. Leipzig: Teubner.

Bernabé, Alberto, trans. 1998. *Aristóteles Retórica*. Madrid: Alianza Editorial.

Bernasconi, Robert. 1997. 'What Goes Around Comes Around: Derrida and Levinas on the Economy of the Gift and the Gift of Genealogy.' In Schrift 1997: 256–73.

Bernek, Rüdiger. 2004. *Dramaturgie und Ideologie: Der politische Mythos in den Hikesiedramen des Aischylos, Sophokles und Euripides*. Munich: K.B. Saur.

Bischof-Koehler, Doris. 1988. 'Über den Zusammenhang von Empathie und der Fähigkeit, sich im Spiegel zu erkennen.' *Schweizerische Zeitschrift für Psychologie* 47: 147–59. Available at http://verlag.hanshuber.com/Zeitschriften/SJP.

– 1989. *Spiegelbild und Empathie: Die Anfänge der Sozialen Kognition*. Repr. 1993. Bern: Hüber.

– 1991. 'The Development of Empathy in Infants.' In M.E. Lamb and H. Keller, eds, *Infant Development: Perspectives from German-Speaking Countries*, 245–73. Hillsdale, NJ: Lawrence Erlbaum Associates.

– 1994. 'Selbstobjektivierung und fremdbezogene Emotionen: Identifikation des eigenen Spiegelbildes, Empathie und prosoziales Verhalten.' *Zeitschrift für Psychologie* 202: 349–77. Available at http://www.hogrefe. de/zfp/zfp_idx.html.

– 2001. 'Zusammenhang von Empathie und Selbsterkennen bei Kleinkindern.' In M. Cierpka and P. Buchheim, eds, *Psychodynamische Konzepte*, 321–8. Berlin: Springer.

Blonder, Lee Xenakis. 1999. 'Brain and Emotion Relations in Culturally Diverse Populations.' In Hinton, ed. 1999: 274–96.

Blundell, Mary Whitlock. 1989. *Helping Friends and Harming Enemies: A Study in Sophocles and Greek Ethics*. Cambridge: Cambridge University Press.

Boedeker, Deborah. 1991. 'Euripides' Medea and the Vanity of *Logoi.*' *Classical Philology* 86: 95–112

Bollnow, Otto Friedrich. 1992. 'Über die Dankbarkeit.' In Josef Seifert, ed., *Danken und Dankbarkeit: Eine universale Dimension des Menschseins*, 37–62. Heidelberg: Carl Winter.

Bongie, Elizabeth B. 1977. 'Heroic Elements in the *Medea* of Euripides.' *Transactions of the American Philological Association* 107: 27–56.

Bons, Jeroen A.E., and R.T. Lane. 2003. 'Quintilian VI.2: On Emotion.' In Olga Tellegen-Couperus, ed., *Quintilian and the Law: The Art of Persuasion in Law and Politics*, 129–44. Leuven: Leuven University Press.

Borg, Alexander, ed. 1999. *The Language of Color in the Mediterranean: An Anthology of Linguistic and Ethnographic Aspects of Color Terms.* Stockholm: Almqvist and Wiksell International 1999 = Acta Universitatis Stockholmiensis, Stockholm Oriental Studies 16.

Borgeaud, Philippe. 1988 (orig. 1979). *The Cult of Pan in Ancient Greece.* Trans. Kathleen Atlass and James Redfield. Chicago: University of Chicago Press.

Borod, Joan C., ed. 2000. *The Neuropsychology of Emotion.* Oxford: Oxford University Press.

Bourdieu, Pierre. 1966. 'The Sentiment of Honour in Kabyle Society.' Trans. Philip Sherrard. In J.G. Peristiany, ed., *Honour and Shame: The Values of Mediterranean Society*, 193–241. Chicago: University of Chicago Press.

– 1977. *Outline of a Theory of Practice.* Trans. Richard Nice. Cambridge: Cambridge University Press.

– 1990. *The Logic of Practice.* Trans. Richard Nice. Stanford: Stanford University Press.

– 1997. 'Marginalia – Some Additional Notes on the Gift.' Trans. Richard Nice. In Schrift 1997: 231–41.

Brandstätter, Herman, and Andrzej Eliasz. 2001. 'Persons' Emotional Responses to Situations.' In Brandstätter and Eliasz eds. 2001: 3–19.

Brandstätter, Herman, and Andrzej Eliasz, eds. 2001. *Persons, Situations, and Emotions: An Ecological Approach.* Oxford: Oxford University Press.

Braund, Susanna, and Glenn W. Most, eds. 2004. *Ancient Anger: Perspectives from Homer to Galen* = *Yale Classical Studies* 32.

Braund, Susanna, and Giles Gilbert. 2004. 'An ABC of Epic *Ira*: Anger, Beasts, and Cannibalism.' In Braund and Most 2004: 250–85.

Bremer, Jan-Maarten. 1982. 'A Reaction to Tsagarakis' Discussion of Sappho fr. 31.' *Rheinisches Museum* 125: 113–16.

– 1998. 'The Reciprocity of Giving and Thanksgiving in Greek Worship.' In Gill, Postlethwaite, and Seaford 1998: 127–37.

Brilliant, Richard. 2000. *My Laocoön: Alternative Claims in the Interpretation of Artworks*. Berkeley: University of California Press.

Brinton, Alan. 1988. 'Pathos and the "Appeal to Emotion": An Aristotelian Analysis.' *History of Philosophy Quarterly* 5: 207–19.

– 1994. 'A Plea for the *Argumentum ad Misericordiam*.' *Philosophia* 23: 25–44.

Brooks, Cleanth. 1970. *The Well Wrought Urn: Studies in the Structure of Poetry*. San Diego: Harcourt Brace & Co.

Brown, Wendy. 2003. 'Resisting Left Melancholia.' In Eng and Kazanjian 2003a: 458–65.

Bruns, Carl Georg, ed. 1909. *Fontes iuris romani antiqui*. Tubingen: I.C.B. Mohr (P. Siebeck).

Bryson, Bill. 2000. *Down Under*. London: Black Swan.

Bryson, Jeff B. 1991. 'Modes of Response to Jealousy-Evoking Situations.' In Salovey 1991: 178–207.

Büchner, Karl. 1974. *Das Theater des Terenz*. Heidelberg: C. Winter.

Buck, Ross W. 2000. 'The Epistemology of Reason and Affect.' In Borod 2000: 31–55.

Bührer-Thierry, Geneviève. 1998. '"Just Anger" or "Vengeful Anger"? The Punishment of Blinding in the Early Medieval West.' In Rosenwein 1998: 75–91.

Bulman, Patricia. 1992. Phthonos *in Pindar*. Berkeley: University of California Press = University of California Publications: Classical Studies 35.

Burguière, Paul. 1970. 'Cyrilliana (III).' *Revue des Études Anciennes* 72: 364–84.

Burke, Edmund. 1990. *A Philosophical Enquiry into the Origin of Our Ideas of the Sublime and the Beautiful*. Oxford: Oxford University Press.

Buss, David M. 1994. *The Evolution of Desire: Strategies of Human Mating*. New York: Basic Books.

– 2000. *The Dangerous Passion: Why Jealousy Is as Necessary as Love and Sex.* New York: Free Press.

Butler, Joseph (Bishop). 1896. *The Works of Joseph Butler, D.C.L.* Ed. W.E. Gladstone. Volume 2: *Sermons, etc.* Oxford: Clarendon Press.

Cahoon, Leslie. 1985. 'A Program for Betrayal: Ovidian *Nequitia* in the *Amores.*' *Helios* 12: 29–39.

Cairns, Douglas L. 1993. *Aidôs: The Psychology and Ethics of Honour and Shame in Ancient Greek Literature.* Oxford: Clarendon Press.

– 1996. '*Hybris*, Dishounour, and Thinking Big.' *Journal of Hellenic Studies* 116: 1–32.

– 2003. 'The Politics of Envy: Envy and Equality in Ancient Greece.' In Konstan and Rutter 2003: 235–52.

Campbell, A.Y., ed. 1950. *Euripides: Helena.* Liverpool: University Press of Liverpool.

Campbell, Lily B. 1960. *Shakespeare's Tragic Heroines: Slaves of Passion.* Magnolia, MA.: Peter Smith.

Carawan, Edmund. 2000. 'Deianira's Guilt.' *Transactions of the American Philological Association* 130: 189–237.

Carey, Christopher. 1988. '"Philanthropy" in Aristotle's *Poetics.*' *Eranos* 86: 131–9.

Carroll, J.M., and J.A. Russell. 1996. 'Do Facial Expressions Signal Specific Emotions? Judging the Face in Context.' *Journal of Personality and Social Psychology* 70: 205–18.

Casimire, M.J., and M. Schnegg. 2003. 'Shame across Cultures: The Evolution, Ontogeny, and Function of a "Moral Emotion."' In H. Keller, Ype H. Poortinga, and Axel Scholmerich, eds, *Between Culture and Biology: Perspectives on Ontogenetic Development*, 270–302. Cambridge: Cambridge University Press.

Caston, Ruth Rothaus. 2000. 'Elegiac Passion: A Study of Jealousy in Roman Love Elegy.' Dissertation, Brown University, Providence, RI.

Cavallero, Pablo A. 2000–1. 'Philanthropía en los *Nombres divinos* de Pseudo Dionisio.' *Byzantion Nea Hellás* 19–20: 130–42.

Chapsal, Madeleine. 1977. *La jalousie.* Paris: Fayard.

Chichi, Graciela Marta. 2002. 'Las alusiones a la vergüenza en el *Gorgias* de Platón.' In María Marta García Negroni, ed., *La argumentación: Actas del congreso internacional, Buenos Aires 10–12 de julio de 2002.* Buenos Aires: University of Buenos Aires Press.

Chirassi Colombo, Ileana. 1994. 'Antropologia della *charis* nella cultura greca antica.' In Galli 1994: 85–104.

Citroni Marchetti, Sandra. 2000. *Amicizia e potere nelle lettere di Cicerone e nelle elegie ovidiane dall'esilio.* Florence: Università degli Studi di Firenze = Studi e Testi 18.

Clark, Isabelle. 1998. 'The Gamos of Hera: Myth and Ritual.' In Sue Blundell and Margaret Williamson, eds, *The Sacred and the Feminine in Ancient Greece*, 13–26. London: Routledge.

Clore, Gerald L., and Karen Gasper. 2000. 'Feeling Is Believing: Some Affective Influences on Belief.' In Frijda, Manstead, and Bem eds 2000: 10–44.

Cohen, David. 1991. *Law, Sexuality, and Society.* Cambridge: Cambridge University Press.

– 1995. *Law, Violence, and Community in Classical Athens.* Cambridge: Cambridge University Press.

Considine, Patrick. 1986. 'The Etymology of MHNIΣ.' In J.H. Betts, J.T. Hooker, and J.R. Green, eds., *Studies in Honour of T.B.L. Webster*, 53–64. Bristol: Bristol Classical Press.

Cooley, Charles Horton. 1983 (orig. 1902; 2nd ed. 1922). *Human Nature and the Social Order.* New Brunswick, NJ: Transaction Publishers.

Cooper, John M. 1996. 'An Aristotelian Theory of the Emotions.' In A.O. Rorty 1996: 238–57.

– 1997a. 'Aristotle on the Forms of Friendship.' *Review of Metaphysics* 30: 619–48 = Cooper 1999: 312–35.

– 1997b. 'Friendship and the Good in Aristotle.' *Philosophical Review* 86: 290–315 = Cooper 1999: 336–55.

– 1999. *Reason and Emotion: Essays on Ancient Moral Psychology and Ethical Theory.* Princeton: Princeton University Press.

Cooper, Lane, trans. 1932. *The Rhetoric of Aristotle.* New York: D. Appleton-Century.

Cope, Edward Meredith. 1877. *The Rhetoric of Aristotle, with a Commentary.* Rev. and ed. John Edwin Sandys. Cambridge: Cambridge University Press.

Corbeill, Anthony. 2002. 'Ciceronian Invective.' In James M. May, ed., *Brill's Companion to Cicero: Oratory and Rhetoric*, 197–217. Leiden: Brill.

– 2004. *Nature Embodied: Gesture in Ancient Rome.* Princeton University Press.

Cornford, Francis M. 1907. *Thucydides Mythistoricus*. London: E. Arnold.

Cosmides, Leda, and John Tooby. 2000. 'Evolutionary Psychology and the Emotions.' In Lewis and Haviland-Jones 2000: 91–115.

Cox, Cheryl Anne. 1998. *Household Interests: Property, Marriage Strategies, and Family Dynamics in Ancient Athens*. Princeton: Princeton University Press.

Crawford, Neta C. 2000. 'The Passion of World Politics: Propositions on Emotion and Emotional Relationships.' *International Security* 24: 116–56.

Creighton, Millie R. 1990. 'Revisiting Shame and Guilt Cultures: A Forty-Year Pilgrimage.' *Ethos* 18: 279–307.

Crozier, W. Raymond. 1999. 'Individual Differences in Childhood Shyness: Distinguishing Fearful and Self-Conscious Shyness.' In Schmidt and Schulkin 1999: 14–29.

Dale, A.M., ed. 1954. *Euripides Alcestis*. Oxford: Clarendon Press.

Damasio, Antonio R. 1994. *Descartes' Error: Emotion, Reason, and the Human Brain*. New York: Avon Books.

Darwin, Charles. 1998 (orig. 1872). *The Expression of the Emotions in Man and Animals*. 3rd edition, with introduction, afterword and commentary by Paul Ekman. London: HarperCollins.

David, Jean-Michel. 1992. *Le patronat judiciare au dernier siècle de la république romaine*. Rome: École Française de Rome.

Davidson, Richard J. 2000. 'Affective Style, Psychopathology and Resiliance: Brain Mechanisms and Plasticity.' *American Psychologist* 55: 1196–1214.

Davidson, Richard J., Katherine M. Putnam, and Christine L. Larson. 2000. 'Dysfunction in the Neural Circuitry of Emotion Regulation: A Possible Prelude to Violence.' *Science* 289: 591–4.

Davidson, William L. 1912. 'Envy and Emulation.' In James Hastings, ed., *Encyclopedia of Religion and Ethics*, vol. 4: 322–3. Edinburgh: T. & T. Clark.

Dawson, Christopher M., trans. and comm. 1970. *The Seven against Thebes by Aeschylus*. Englewood Cliffs, NJ: Prentice-Hall.

Dayton, John C. 2006. *The Athletes of War: An Evaluation of the Agonistic Elements in Greek Warfare*. Toronto: Edgar Kent.

Dean-Jones, Leslie. 1994. *Women's Bodies in Ancient Greek Science*. Oxford: Clarendon Press.

Delpierre, Guy. 1973. *La peur et l'être*. Toulouse: Laboureur.

Delumeau, Jean. 1978. *La peur en Occident (XIVᵉ–XVIIIᵉ siècles): Une cité assiégée*. Paris: Librairie Arthème Fayard.

Denham, Susanne A. 1998. *Emotional Development in Young Children*. New York: Guilford Press.

Denyer, Nicholas. 2000. 'Just War.' In Roger Teichmann, ed., *Logic, Cause and Action*, 137–51. Cambridge: Cambridge University Press and London: Royal Institute of Philosophy = Philosophy Supplement 46.

Denyer, Nicholas, ed. 2001. *Plato: Alcibiades*. Cambridge: Cambridge University Press.

Derrida, Jacques. 1995. *The Gift of Death*. Trans. D. Willis. Chicago: University of Chicago Press.

– 1997a. *Deconstruction in a Nutshell: A Conversation with Jacques Derrida*. Ed. J.D. Caputo. New York: Fordham University Press.

– 1997b. 'The Time of the King.' Trans. Peggy Kamuf. In Schrift 1997: 121–47.

Descartes, René. 1988 (orig. 1649). *Les Passions de l'âme: Précédé de La Pathéthique cartésienne par Jean-Maurice Monnoyer*. Paris: Gallimard.

Dickie Matthew W. 1981. 'The Disavowal of *Invidia* in Roman Iamb and Satire.' *Papers of the Liverpool Latin Seminar* 3: 183–208.

– 1987. 'Lo φθόνος degli dèi nella letteratura greca del quinto secolo avanti Cristo.' *Atene & Roma* 32: 113–25.

Diels, Hermann, and Walther Kranz, eds. 1951–2. *Die Fragmente der Vorsokratiker*. 6th ed. 2 vols. Berlin: Weidmann.

Diggle, James, ed. 1981–94. *Euripides Fabulae*. Oxford: Clarendon Press (Oxford Classical Texts).

Dilts, Mervin R., ed. 1986. *Scholia in Demosthenem*. Vol. 2. Leipzig: Teubner.

Dion, Jeanne. 1993. *Les passions dans l'oeuvre de Virgile: Poétique et philosophie*. Nancy: Presses Universitaires de Nancy.

Dixon, Suzanne. 1992. *The Roman Family*. Baltimore: Johns Hopkins University Press.

Dodds, E.R. 1951. *The Greeks and the Irrational*. Berkeley: University of California Press.

Donlan, Walter. 1980. *The Aristocratic Ideal in Ancient Greece: Atti-*

tudes of Superiority from Homer to the End of the Fifth Century B.C.
Lawrence, KA: Coronado Press.

Dover, Kenneth. 1994 (orig. 1974). *Greek Popular Morality in the Time of Plato and Aristotle.* Rev. ed. Indianapolis: Hackett Publishing Co.

Dover, Sir Kenneth J., ed. 1994 (orig. 1971). *Theocritus: Select Poems.* Wauconda, IL: Bolchazy-Carducci.

Dreyfus, Georges. 2002. 'Is Compassion an Emotion? A Cross-Cultural Exploration of Mental Typologies.' In Richard J. Davidson and Anne Harrington, eds, *Visions of Compassion: Western Scientists and Tibetan Buddhists Examine Human Nature*, 31–45. Oxford: Oxford University Press.

Duchenne de Boulogne, G.-B. 1862. *Mécanisme de la physionomie humaine, ou analyse électro-physiologique de l'expression des passions applicable à la pratique des arts plastiques.* Paris: Jules Renouard.

– 1990. *The Mechanism of Human Facial Expression.* Ed. and trans. R. Andrew Cuthbertson. Cambridge: Cambridge University Press.

Duff, Antony. 1987. 'Aristotelian Courage.' *Ratio* 29: 2–15.

DuFour, Médéric, ed. and trans. 1960. *Aristote Rhétorique.* Paris: Les Belles Lettres (Budé).

Dunbabin, K.M.D., and M.W. Dickie. 1983. 'Invidia rumpantur pectora: The Iconography of Phthonos/Invidia in Graeco-Roman Art.' *Jahrbuch für Antike & Christentum* 26: 7–37.

Durkheim, Émile. 1966. *Suicide: A Study in Sociology.* Trans. John A. Spaulding and George Simpson. New York: Free Press.

Eagleton, Terry. 2003. *Sweet Violence: The Idea of the Tragic.* Oxford: Blackwell's.

Edelstein, L., and I.G. Kidd, eds. 1972. *Posidonias.* Vol. 1. Cambridge: Cambridge University Press.

Ekman, Paul. 1980. *The Face of Man: Expressions of Universal Emotions in a New Guinea Village.* New York: Garland.

– 1984. 'Expression and the Nature of Emotion.' In Klaus Scherer and Paul Ekman, eds, *Approaches to Emotion*, 319–43. Hillsdale, NJ: Erlbaum.

– 1998. 'Afterword.' In Darwin 1998: 363–93.

Ekman, Paul, ed. 1973. *Darwin and Facial Expression: A Century of Research in Review.* New York: Academic Press.

- 1982. *Emotions in the Human Face.* 2nd edition. Cambridge: Cambridge University Press and Paris: Éditions de la Maison des Sciences de l'Homme.

Eloy Martínez, Tomás. 2002. *El vuelo de la reina.* Madrid: Alfaguara.

Else, Gerald F., trans. 1967. *Aristotle: Poetics.* Ann Arbor: University of Michigan Press.

Elster, Jon. 1999a. *Alchemies of the Mind: Rationality and the Emotions.* Cambridge: Cambridge University Press.

- 1999b. *Strong Feelings: Emotion, Addiction, and Human Behavior.* Cambridge, MA: MIT Press.

Emde, R.N. 1980. 'Toward a Psychoanalytic Theory of Affect: I. The Organizational Model and Its Propositions.' In S.I. Greenspan and G.H. Pollock, eds, *The Course of Life: Psychoanalytic Contributions towards Understanding Personality Development,* 66–83. Madison, CT: International University Press.

Emmons, Robert A. 2004. 'The Psychology of Gratitude: An Introduction.' In Robert A. Emmons and Michael E. McCullough, eds, *The Psychology of Gratitude,* 3–16. Oxford: Oxford University Press.

Eng, David L., and David Kazanjian, eds. 2003a. *Loss: The Politics of Mourning.* Berkeley: University of California Press.

- 2003b. 'Introduction: Meaning Remains.' In Eng and Kazanjian 2003a: 1–25.

Epstein, David F. 1987. *Personal Enmity in Roman Politics 218–43 BC.* London: Croom Helm.

Erikson, Erik H. 1950. *Childhood and Society.* New York: Norton.

Erickson, Keith. 1975. *Aristotle's Rhetoric: Five Centuries of Philological Research.* Metuchen, NJ: Scarecrow Press.

España, Ramón de. 2000. *El Odio: Fuente de vida y motor del mundo.* Barcelona: Ediciones Martínez Roca.

Evans, E.C. 1969. *Physiognomics in the Ancient World.* Philadelphia: American Philosophical Society.

Evans, H. Meurig, and W.O. Thomas. 1989. *Welsh-English, English-Welsh Dictionary.* New York: Saphrograph Corp.

Fantham, Elaine. 1986. 'ΖΗΛΟΤΥΠΙΑ: A Brief Excursion into Sex, Violence, and Literary History.' *Phoenix* 40: 45–57.

Farber, Leslie. 1978. *Lying, Despair, Jealousy, Envy, Sex, Suicide, Drugs, and the Good Life.* New York: Harper Colophon.

Farrell, Daniel M. 1980. 'Jealousy.' *Philosophical Review* 89: 527–59.

- 1989. 'Of Jealousy and Envy.' In George Graham and Hugh LaFollette, eds, *Person to Person*, 245–68. Philadelphia: Temple University Press.
- 1997. 'Jealousy and Desire.' In Roger E. Lamb, ed., *Love Analyzed*, 165–88. Boulder, CO: Westview Press.

Fernández-Dols, José Miguel, and James M. Carroll. 1997. 'Is the Meaning Perceived in Facial Expression Independent of Its Context?' In Russell and Fernández-Dols 1997: 275–94.

Fernández-Dols, José Miguel, and María-Angeles Ruiz-Belda. 1997. 'Spontaneous Facial Behavior during Intense Emotional Episodes: Artistic Truth and Optical Truth.' In Russell and Fernández-Dols eds 1997: 255–6.

Ferrari, Gloria. 2002. *Figures of Speech: Men and Maidens in Ancient Greece*. Chicago: University of Chicago Press.

Fischer, Agneta H., Antony S.R. Manstead, and P.M. Rodriguez Mosquera. 1999. 'The Role of Honor-related versus Individualistic Values in Conceptualizing Pride, Shame and Anger: Spanish and Dutch Cultural Prototypes.' *Cognition and Emotion* 13: 149–79.

Fisher, N.R.E. 1992. *Hybris: A Study in the Values of Honour and Shame in Ancient Greece*. Warminster: Aris and Phillips.
- 2003. '"Let Envy Be Absent": Envy, Liturgies and Reciprocity in Athens.' In Konstan and Rutter 2003: 181–215.

Fitness, J. 2000. 'Anger in the Workplace: An Emotion Script Approach to Anger Episodes between Workers and Their Superiors, Co-Workers, and Subordinates.' *Journal of Occupational Behavior* 21: 147–62.

Fitzgerald, Robert, trans. 1983. *The Aeneid of Virgil*. New York: Vintage Books.

Foley, Helene P. 1989. 'Medea's Divided Self.' *Classical Antiquity* 8: 61–85
- 2001. *Female Acts in Greek Tragedy*. Princeton: Princeton University Press.
- 2004. 'Bad Women: Gender Politics in Late Twentieth-Century Performance and Revision of Greek Tragedy.' In Edith Hall, Fiona Macintosh, and Amanda Wrigley, eds, *Dionysus since 69: Greek Tragedy at the Dawn of the Third Millennium*, 77–111. Oxford: Oxford University Press.

Fonseca, Isis Borges B. da, trans. 2000. *Retórica das Paixões: Aristóteles*. São Paulo: Martins Fontes.

Forgas, Joseph P. 2000. 'Feeling Is Believing? The Role of Processing

Strategies in Mediating Affective Influences on Beliefs.' In Frijda, Manstead, and Bem eds 2000: 108–43.

Forgas, Joseph P., and Patrick T. Vargas. 2000. 'The Effects of Mood on Social Judgment and Reasoning.' In Lewis and Haviland-Jones 2000: 350–67.

Fortenbaugh, William W. 2002 (orig. 1975). *Aristotle on Emotion.* 2nd edition. London: Duckworth.

– 2003–4. 'Aristotle and Theophrastus on the Emotions.' *Society for Ancient Greek Philosophy Newsletter* 2003/4.1.

Fortenbaugh, William W., Pamela Huby, Robert Sharples, and Dimitri Gutas, eds. 1992. *Theophrastus of Eresus: Sources for His Life, Writings, Thought, and Influence.* Leiden: E.J. Brill.

Foucault, Michel. 1985 (orig. 1984). *The Use of Pleasure: Volume 2 of The History of Sexuality.* Trans. Robert Hurley. New York: Pantheon Books.

Fragoulis, Tess. 2001. *Ariadne's Dream.* Saskatoon: Thistledown Press.

Franco, Cristiana. 2000–1. 'L'ingiustizia dei macellai: Vegetarianismo e rispetto della vita animale nell'antichità classica.' In *I viaggi di Erodoto* 43/44: 208–23.

Frank, Robert H. 1988. *Passions within Reason: The Strategic Role of the Emotions.* New York: W.W. Norton.

Frede, Dorothea. 1996. 'Mixed Feelings in Aristotle's *Rhetoric.*' In A.O. Rorty 1996: 258–85.

Frede, Dorothea, trans. 1997. 'Philebus.' In John M. Cooper and D. S. Hutchinson, eds, *Plato: Complete Works,* 398–456. Indianapolis: Hackett.

Freese, John Henry. 1926. *Aristotle: The Art of Rhetoric.* London: W. Heinemann (Loeb Classical Library).

Freud, Sigmund. 1955 (orig. 1922). 'Some Neurotic Mechanisms in Jealousy.' In *The Standard Edition of the Complete Psychological Works of Sigmund Freud,* trans. James Strachey in collaboration with Anna Freud, vol. 18: 221–32. London: Hogarth Press and Institute for Psycho-Analysis.

– 1957 (orig. 1917). 'Mourning and Melancholia.' In James Strachey, ed. and trans., *The Standard Edition of the Complete Psychological Works of Sigmund Freud,* vol. 14. London: Hogarth Press.

Friday, Nancy. 1997 (orig. 1985). *Jealousy.* 2nd edition (with new foreword). New York: M. Evans and Co.

Fridlund, Alan J. 1997. 'The New Ethology of Human Facial Expressions.' In Russell and Fernández-Dols 1997: 103–29.

Frijda, Nico H. 1993. 'The Place of Appraisal in Emotion.' *Cognition and Emotion* 7: 357–87 = Nico H. Frijda, ed., *Appraisal and Beyond: The Issue of Cognitive Determinants of Emotion*. Hove: Lawrence Erlbaum Associates.

Frijda, Nico H., Antony S.R. Manstead, and Sacha Bem. 2000. 'The Influence of Emotions on Beliefs.' In Frijda, Manstead, and Bem eds 2000: 1–9.

Frijda, Nico H., Antony S.R. Manstead, and Sacha Bem, eds. 2000. *Emotions and Beliefs: How Feelings Influence Thoughts*. Cambridge: Cambridge University Press.

Frijda, Nico H., and Batja Mesquita. 2000. 'Beliefs through Emotions.' In Frijda, Manstead, and Bem eds 2000: 45–77.

Frijda, Nico H., and Anna Tcherkassof. 1997. 'Facial Expressions as Modes of Action Readiness.' In Russell and Fernández-Dols 1997: 78–102.

Fuentes, Carlos. 2001. *Instinto de Inez*. Madrid: Alfaguara.

Furley, William D. 2000. '"Fearless, Bloodless ... Like the Gods": Sappho 31 and the Rhetoric of Godlike.' *Classical Quarterly* 50: 7–15.

Fürst, Alfons. 1996. *Streit unter Freunden: Ideal und Realität in der Freundschaftslehre der Antike*. Stuttgart and Leipzig: B.G. Teubner = Beiträge zur Altertumskunde 85.

Fusillo, Massimo. 1999 (orig. 1990). 'The Conflict of Emotions: A *Topos* in the Greek Erotic Novel.' In Simon Swain, ed., *Oxford Readings in the Greek Novel*, 60–82. Oxford: Oxford University Press.

Gage, John. 1995. 'Color and Culture.' In Lamb and Bourriau 1995: 175–93.

Gager, John G. 1992. *Curse Tablets and Binding Spells from the Ancient World*. New York: Oxford University Press.

Gainotti, Guido. 2000. 'Neuropsychological Theories of Emotion.' In Borod 2000: 214–36.

Galli, Giuseppe, ed. 1994. *Interpretazione e gratitudine. XIII coloquio sulla interpretazione (Macerata 30–31 Marzo 1992)*. Macerata: Università degli Studi di Macerata, Facoltà di Lettere e Filosofia Atti 22.

Garrison, Elise P. 1987. 'Some Contexts of Suicide in Greek Tragedy.' PhD dissertation, Stanford University.

- 1995. *Groaning Tears: Ethical and Dramatic Aspects of Suicide in Greek Tragedy*. Leiden: E.J. Brill = Mnemosyne supplement 147.
- 2004. 'Suicidal Males in Greek and Roman Mythology: A Catalogue.' Available at www.stoa.org/diotima/essays/garrison_essay2.shtml.

Gauly, Bardo Maria. 1995. '*Lentus amor*: Zu einer Metapher bei Tibull und Horaz und zum elegischen Pseudonym Marathus.' *Hermes* 123: 91–105.

Gauthier, René Antoine, and Jean Yves Jolif, eds. 1970. *L'éthique à Nicomaque*. 2nd edition. Vol. 2 (Commentary), part 1. Louvain: Publications Universitaires de Louvain.

Gaylin, Willard. 2003. *Hatred: The Psychological Descent into Violence*. New York: PublicAffairs.

Gewirth, Alan. 1978. *Reason and Morality*. Chicago: University of Chicago Press.

Gilbert, Paul, and Bernice Andrews. 1998. 'Preface.' In Paul Gilbert and Bernice Andrews, eds, *Shame: Interpersonal Behavior, Psychopathology, and Culture*, v–vii. New York: Oxford University Press.

Gill, Christopher. 1993. 'Panaetius on the Virtue of Being Yourself.' In Anthony Bulloch, Erich S. Gruen, A.A. Long, and Andrew Steward, eds, *Images and Ideologies: Self-Definition in the Hellenistic World*, 330–53. Berkeley: University of California Press.

- 1996. *Personality in Greek Epic, Tragedy, and Philosophy: The Self in Dialogue*. Oxford: Clarendon Press.

Gill, Christopher, Norman Postlethwaite and Richard Seaford, eds, 1998. *Reciprocity in Ancient Greece*. Oxford: Oxford University Press.

Giordano, Manuela. 1999. *La supplica: Rituale, istituzione sociale e tema epico in omero*. Naples: A.I.O.N. = Annali dell'Istituto Universitario Orientale di Napoli, Quaderni 3.

Gladman, Kimberly R., and Phillip Mitsis. 1997. 'Lucretius and the Unconscious.' In K.A. Algra, M.H. Koenen, and P.H. Schrijvers, eds, *Lucretius and His Intellectual Background*, 215–24. Amsterdam: Royal Netherlands Academy of Arts and Sciences.

Gohlke, Paul, trans. 1959. *Aristoteles Rhetorik*. Paderborn: Ferdinand Schöningh.

Goldhill, Simon. 1986. *Reading Greek Tragedy*. Cambridge: Cambridge University Press.

- 1990. 'Character and Action, Representation and Reading Greek Tragedy and Its Critics.' In Pelling 1990: 100–27.

Gordon, Robert M. 1987. *The Structure of Emotions: Investigations in Cognitive Philosophy*. Cambridge: Cambridge University Press.

Gould, John. 1974. 'Hiketeia.' *Journal of Hellenic Studies* 83: 74–103.

Gouldner, Alvin W. 1996. 'The Norm of Reciprocity: A Preliminary Statement.' In Komter 1996: 49–66.

Goulston, Theodore, ed. and trans. 1619. Ἀριστοτέλους τέχνης ῥητορικῆς βιβλία τρία *Aristotelis de Rhetorica seu Arte Dicendi libri tres*. London: Edward Hall. Frequently reprinted; see Erickson 1975.

Gow, A.S.F., ed. 1950. *Theocritus*. 2 vols. Cambridge: Cambridge University Press.

Grastyán, Endre. 1986 (orig. 1974). 'Human Emotion and Motivation' (Part 1: 'Emotion'). In *The New Encyclopedia Britannica*, vol. 18: 347–65. Chicago: William Benton.

Graver, Margaret, trans. 2002. *Cicero on the Emotions: Tusculan Disputations 3 and 4*. Chicago: University of Chicago Press.

Green, O.H. 1997. 'Is Love an Emotion?' In Roger E. Lamb, ed., *Love Analyzed*, 209–24. Boulder, CO: Westview Press.

Green, W.C. 1892. *The Plutus of Aristophanes*. Cambridge: Cambridge University Press (Pitt Press Series).

Greene, Ellen. 1998. *The Erotics of Domination: Male Desire and the Mistress in Latin Love Poetry*. Baltimore: Johns Hopkins University Press.

Grethlein, Jonas, 2003. *Asyl and Athen: Die Konstruktion kollektiver Identität in der griechischen Tragödie*. Stuttgart: Verlag J.B. Metzler = Drama: Beiträge zum antiken Drama und seiner Rezeption Beiheft 21.

Griffin, Jasper. 1985. *Latin Poets and Roman Life*. Chapel Hill: University of North Carolina Press.

Griffith, Mark, ed. 1983. *Aeschylus: Prometheus Bound*. Cambridge: Cambridge University Press.

Griffiths, Paul E. 1997. *What Emotions Really Are: The Problem of Psychological Categories*. Chicago: University of Chicago Press.

Grimaldi, William M.A., ed. 1988. *Aristotle Rhetoric II: A Commentary*. New York: Fordham University Press.

Grinker, Roy Richard. 1998. *Korea and Its Futures: Unification and the Unfinished War*. New York: St Martin's Press.

Grzywacz, Margot. 1937. *'Eifersucht' in den romanischen Sprachen*. Bochum-Langendreer: H. Pöppinghaus.

Guizzi, Francesco. 1998. 'Χάρις in Pericle e in Aristotele.' *Quaderni di Storia* 47: 75–102.

Hall, Edith. 1989. *Inventing the Barbarian: Greek Self-Definition through Tragedy*. Oxford: Oxford University Press.

Hall, Jonathan. 1997. *Ethnic Identity in Greek Antiquity*. Cambridge: Cambridge University Press.

Halliwell, Stephen. 1998 (orig. 1987). *The Poetics of Aristotle: Translation and Commentary*. Chapel Hill: University of North Carolina Press.

– 2002. *The Aesthetics of Mimesis: Ancient Texts and Modern Problems*. Princeton: Princeton University Press.

Hammer, Dean. 2002. 'The *Iliad* as Ethical Thinking: Politics, Pity, and the Operation of Esteem.' *Arethusa* 35: 203–35.

Handly, Robert, and Pauline Neff. 1985. *Anxiety and Panic Attacks: Their Cause and Cure*. New York: Fawcett Crest.

Hansen, Mogens Herman. 1993. 'The Battle Exhortation in Ancient Historiography.' *Historia* 42: 161–80.

Harkemanne, J. 1967. 'Φόβος dans la poésie homérique: Étude sémantique.' *Recherche de Philologie et Linguistique* 1: 47–94.

Harré, Rom, ed. 1986. *The Social Construction of Emotions*. Oxford: Basil Blackwell.

Harris, William V. 2001. *Restraining Rage: The Ideology of Anger Control in Classical Antiquity*. Cambridge, MA: Harvard University Press.

Harrison, James R. 2003. *Paul's Language of Grace in Its Greaco-Roman Context*. Tübingen: Mohr Siebeck = Wissenschaftliche Untersuchungen zu Neuen Testament 2.

Hatfield, Elaine, and Richard L. Rapson. 2000. 'Love and Attachment Process.' In Lewis and Haviland-Jones 2000: 654–62.

Heath, Malcolm. 1987. *The Poetics of Greek Tragedy*. Stanford: Stanford University Press.

– 2001. 'Aristotle and the Pleasures of Tragedy.' In O. Andersen and J. Haarberg, eds, *Making Sense of Aristotle: Essays in Poetics*, 7–23. London: Duckworth.

Hedges, Chris. 2003. 'A Skeptic about Wars Intended to Stamp Out Evil.' *New York Times*, 14 January: B2.

Heller, Steven. 2001. 'Designing Hate: Is There a Graphic Language of Vile Emotion?' In Steven Heller and Philip B. Meggs, eds, *Texts on Type: Critical Writings on Typography*, 42–4. New York: Allworth Press.

Herman, Gabriel. 1995. 'Honour, Revenge and the State in Fourth-Century Athens.' In Walter Eder, ed., *Die athenische Demokratie im 4. Jahrhundert v. Chr.: Vollendung oder Verfall einer Verfassungs-form?* 43–60. Stuttgart: Franz Steiner Verlag.

Herrmann, Fritz-Gregor. 2003. '*Phthonos* in the World of Plato's *Timaeus*.' In Konstan and Rutter 2003: 53–83.

Heylbut, Gustavus, ed. 1889. *Aspasii in Ethica Nichomachea quae supersunt commentaria*. Berlin: Reimer = Commentaria in Aristotelem graeca vol. 19, part 1.

Heylbut, H. 1887. 'Ptolemaeus περί διαφορᾶς λέξεων.' *Hermes* 22: 388–410.

Hickson Hahn, Frances. 2004a. 'Ut diis immortalibus honos habeatur: Livy's Representation of Gratitude to the Gods.' In Alessandro Barchiesi, Jörg Rüpke, and Susan Stephens, eds, *Rituals in Ink: A Conference on Religion and Literary Production in Ancient Rome held at Stanford University in February 2002*, 57–75. Stuttgart: Franz Steiner Verlag = Potsdamer Altertumswissenschaftliche Beiträger 10.

– 2004b. 'The Politics of Thanksgiving.' In C.F. Konrad, ed., *Augusto augurio: Rerum humanarum et divinarum commentationes in honorem Jerzy Linderski*, 31–51. Stuttgart: Franz Steiner Verlag.

Hillman, James. 1992 (orig. 1960). *Emotion: A Comprehensive Phenomenology of Theories and Their Meanings for Therapy*. Evanston, IL: Northwestern University Press.

Hinton, Alexander Laban. 1999. 'Introduction: Developing a Biocultural Approach to the Emotions.' In Hinton ed. 1999: 1–37.

Hinton, Alexander Laban, ed. 1999. *Biocultural Approaches to the Emotions*. Cambridge: Cambridge University Press.

Hinton, Isabel. 2003. 'Everybody Hates Somebody Somewhere.' Review of Stern 2003. *New York Times Book Review*, 16 November: 50.

Hochschild, Arlie Russell. 1975. 'The Sociology of Feeling and Emotion: Selected Possibilities.' In Marcia Millman and Rosabeth Moss Kanter, eds, *Another Voice: Feminist Perspectives on Social Life and Social Science*, 280–307. Garden City, NY: Anchor Doubleday.

Hogan, James C. 1972. 'Thucydides 3.52–68 and Euripides' Hecuba.' *Phoenix* 26: 241–57.

Hooker, J.T. 1987. 'Homeric Society: A Shame-Culture?' *Greece and Rome* 34: 121–5.

Hornum, Michael B. 1993. *Nemesis, The Roman State, and the Games*. Leiden: E.J. Brill = Religions in the Graeco-Roman World 117.

Horstmanshoff, Manfred. 1999. 'Les émotions chez Caelius Aurelianus.' In Philippe Mudry, ed., with Olivier Bianchi and Daniela Castaldo, *Le traité des Maladies aiguës et des Maladies chroniques de Caelius Aurelianus: Nouvelles approches* = Actes du colloque de Lausanne 1966. Nantes: Institut Universitaire de France, 1999.

Hubbard, Thomas K. 2000. 'Horace and Catullus: The Case of the Suppressed Precursor in *Odes* 1.22 and 1.32.' *Classical World* 94: 25–37.

Hume, David. 1906 (orig. 1739–40). *A Treatise of Human Nature*. Ed. L.A. Selby-Bigge. Oxford: Oxford University Press.

Hupka, R.B. 1991. 'The Motive for the Arousal of Romantic Jealousy: Its Cultural Origin.' In Salovey 1991: 252–70.

Hupka, Ralph B., Zbigniew Zaleski, Jürgen Otto, Lucy Reidl, and Nadia V. Tarabrina. 1996. 'Anger, Envy, Fear, and Jealousy as Felt in the Body: A Five-Nation Study.' *Cross-Cultural Research* 30: 243–64.

Iganski, Paul, ed. 2003. *The Hate Debate: Should Hate be Punished as a Crime?* London: Profile Books.

Irwin, Eleanor. 1974. *Colour Terms in Greek Poetry*. Toronto: Hakkert.

Irwin, Terence, trans. 1985. *Aristotle: Nicomachean Ethics*. Indianapolis: Hackett.

Isaac, Benjamin H. 2004. *The Invention of Racism in Classical Antiquity*. Princeton: Princeton University Press.

Isaacs, Kenneth S. 1998. *Uses of Emotion: Nature's Vital Gift*. Westport, CT: Praeger.

Isen, Alice M. 2000. 'Positive Affect and Decision Making.' In Lewis and Haviland-Jones 2000: 417–35.

Izard, Carroll E., 1977. *Human Emotion*. New York: Plenum.

Izard, Carroll E. and Brian P. Ackerman. 2000. 'Motivational, Organizational, and Regulatory Functions of Discrete Emotions.' In Lewis and Haviland-Jones 2000: 253–64.

Jackson, W.T.H. 1982. *The Hero and the King: An Epic Theme*. New York: Columbia University Press.

Jacoby, Felix von, ed. 1923–54. *Die Fragmente der griechischen Historiker*. Berlin: Weidmann.

Jacoby, Mario. 1991. *Shame and the Origins of Self-Esteem: A Jungian Approach*. Trans. Douglas Whitcher. London: Routledge.

James, Sharon L. 2003. *Learned Girls and Male Persuasion: Gender and*

Reading in Roman Love Elegy. Berkeley: University of California Press.

James, Susan. 1997. *Passion and Action: The Emotions in Seventeenth-Century Philosophy.* Oxford: Clarendon Press.

James, William. 1884. 'What Is an Emotion?' *Mind* 9: 188–205.

Jameson, Fredric. 1984. 'Postmodernism, or The Cultural Logic of Late Capitalism.' *New Left Review* 146: 53–91.

Jones, Christopher. 1999. *Kinship Diplomacy in the Ancient World.* Cambridge, MA: Harvard University Press.

Jones, Joseph M. 1995. *Affects as Process: An Inquiry into the Centrality of Affect in Psychological Life.* Foreword by Joseph D. Lichtenberg. Hillsdale, NJ: Analytic Press.

Kalogerakis, Michael G. 2004. 'Hostility in Adolescents: Genesis, Evolution and Therapeutic Challenge.' In *Adolescent Psychiatry* 28: 1–5.

Kamtekar, Rachana. 1998. 'ΑΙΔΩΣ in Epictetus.' *Classical Philology* 93: 136–60.

Kannicht, Richard, ed. 2004. *Tragicorum graecorum fragmenta,* vol. 5: Euripides. Göttingen: Vandenhoeck & Ruprecht.

Kant, Immanuel. 1981. *Observations on the Feeling of the Beautiful and Sublime.* Trans. John T. Goldthwait. Berkeley: University of California Press.

Kappas, Arvid. 2001. 'A Metaphor Is a Metaphor Is a Metaphor: Exorcising the Homunculus from Appraisal Theory.' In Scherer, Schorr, and Johnstone 2001: 157–72.

Karavites, Peter (Panayiotis). 1982. *Capitulations and Greek Interstate Relations: The Reflection of Humanistic Ideals in Political Events.* Göttingen: Vandenhoeck & Ruprecht = *Hypomnemata* 71.

Karpyuk, Sergei. 2000. 'Crowd in Archaic and Classical Greece.' *Hyperboreus* 6: 79–102.

Kassel, Rudolf. 1958. *Untersuchungen zur griechischen und römischen Konsolationsliteratur.* Munich: C.H. Beck'sche Verlagsbuchhandlung = *Zetemata* 18.

Kassel, Rudolfus, ed. 1976. *Aristotelis Ars rhetorica.* Berlin: Walter de Gruyter.

Kaster, Robert A. 1997. 'The Shame of the Romans.' *Transactions of the American Philological Association* 127: 1–19.

– 2003. 'Invidia, νέμεσις, φθόνος, and the Roman Emotional Economy.' In Konstan and Rutter 2003: 253–76.

- 2005. *Emotion, Restraint, and Community in Ancient Rome.* New York: Oxford University Press.

Kemper, Theodore D. 1978. *A Social Interactional Theory of Emotions.* New York: Wiley.

- 2000. 'Social Models in the Explanation of Emotions.' In Lewis and Haviland-Jones 2000: 45–58.

Kennedy, George A., trans. and ed. 1991. *Aristotle on Rhetoric: A Theory of Civic Discourse.* New York: Oxford University Press.

Kim, Jaegwon. 1996. *Philosophy of Mind.* Boulder, CO: Westview Press.

King, Helen. 1988. 'The Early Anodynes: Pain in the Ancient World.' In Ronald D. Mann, ed., *The History of the Management of Pain: From Early Principles to Present Practice,* 51–62. Carnforth: Parthenon Publishing Group.

Kirkwood, Gordon. 1984. 'Blame and Envy in the Pindaric Epinician.' In D. Gerber, ed., *Greek Poetry and Philosophy,* 169–83. Chico, CA: Scholars Press.

Klein, Melanie. 1975a. *Envy and Gratitude and Other Works 1946–1963.* London: Virago Press.

- 1975b (orig. 1963). 'On the Sense of Loneliness.' In Klein 1975a: 300–13.

- 1975c (orig. 1957). 'Envy and Gratitude.' In Klein 1975a: 176–235.

Knox, B.M.W. 1964. *The Heroic Temper: Studies in Sophoclean Tragedy.* Berkeley: University of California Press.

- 1977. 'The *Medea* of Euripides.' *Yale Classical Studies* 25: 193–225.

Knuuttila, Simo. 2004. *Emotions in Ancient and Medieval Philosophy.* Oxford: Clarendon Press.

Komter, Aafke, ed. 1996. *The Gift: An Interdisciplinary Perspective.* Amsterdam: Amsterdam University Press.

- 2004. 'Gratitude and Gift Exchange.' In Robert A. Emmons and Michael E. McCullough, eds, *The Psychology of Gratitude,* 195–212. Oxford: Oxford University Press.

Konner, Melvin. 2003. 'When Bad People Do Bad Things.' Review of Gaylin 2003. *New York Times Book Review,* 3 August: 12.

Konstan, David. 1972–3. 'Two Kinds of Love in Catullus.' *Classical Journal* 68: 102–6.

- 1973. *Some Aspects of Epicurean Psychology.* Leiden: E.J. Brill = Philosophia Antiqua 25.

- 1994. *Sexual Symmetry: Love in the Ancient Novel and Related Genres.* Princeton: Princeton University Press.

- 1995. *Greek Comedy and Ideology*. New York: Oxford University Press.
- 1996. 'Friendship, Frankness and Flattery.' In John Fitzgerald, ed., *Friendship, Flattery, and Frankness of Speech*, 7–19. Leiden: E.J. Brill, 1996.
- 1997a. *Friendship in the Classical World*. Cambridge: Cambridge University Press.
- 1997b. Review of Mossman 1995. *International Journal of the Classical Tradition* 4: 115–18.
- 1999. 'The Tragic Emotions.' In Luis R. Gámez, ed., *Tragedy's Insights: Identity, Polity, Theodicy*, 1–21. West Cornwall, CT: Locust Hill Press = *Comparative Drama* 33: 1–21.
- 2000a. 'Las emociones trágicas.' In Ana María González de Tobia, ed., *Actas del Congreso: Una nueva visión de la cultura griega antigua en el fin del milenio*, 125–43. La Plata: Editorial de la Universidad Nacional de La Plata.
- 2000b. 'οἰκία δ᾽ἐστί τις φιλία: Love and the Greek Family.' *Syllecta Classica* 11: 106–26
- 2000c. 'A raiva e as emoções em Aristóteles: As estratégias do status.' *Letras Clássicas* 4.4: 77–90.
- 2001a. *Pity Transformed*. London: Duckworth.
- 2001b. Review of Belfiore 2000. *American Journal of Philology* 122: 270–4.
- 2002a. Review of Peachin 2001. *Bryn Mawr Classical Review* 2002.04.29. Available at http://ccat.sas.upenn.edu/bmcr.
- 2002b. 'Enacting Eros.' In Martha Nussbaum and Juha Sihvola, eds, *The Sleep of Reason: Erotic Experience and Sexual Ethics in Ancient Greece and Rome*, 354–73. Chicago: University of Chicago Press.
- 2003a. 'El luto y el olvido, o cómo olvidarnos de los muertos.' In *Actas del XVII Simposio Nacional de Estudios Clásicos de Argentina*. Available at http://www.criba.edu.ar/snec/konstan.htm.
- 2003b. 'Before Jealousy.' In Konstan and Rutter 2003: 7–27.
- 2003c. '*Nemesis* and *Phthonos*.' In G. Bakewell and J. Sickinger, eds, *Gestures: Essays in Greek Literature, History, and Philosophy in Honor of Alan Boegehold*, 74–87. Oakville, CT: David Brown / Oxbow.
- 2003d. '*Praotês* as an Emotion in Aristotle's *Rhetoric*.' *Hyperboreus* 9: 318–29.
- 2003e. 'Translating Ancient Emotions.' *Acta Classica* 46: 5–19.

- 2003f. 'Shame in Ancient Greek.' *Social Research* 70.4.
- 2004. 'Aristotle on Anger and the Emotions: The Strategies of Status.' In Braund and Most 2004: 99–120.
- 2005a. 'The Emotion in Aristotle *Rhetoric* 2.7: Gratitude, not Kindness.' In D. Mirhady, ed., *The Influences on Aristotle's Rhetoric.* New Brunswick, NJ: Transaction Publishers = Rutgers University Studies in Classical Humanities 12.
- 2005b. 'Aristotle on the Tragic Emotions.' In Victoria Pedrick and Stephen Oberhelman, eds, *Of Constant Sorrow: The Soul of Tragedy* (Memorial Volume for Charles Segal), 13–25. Chicago: University of Chicago Press.
- 2005c. 'Pity and Power.' In Sternberg ed. 2005: 48–66.
- 2005d. 'Die Entdeckung der Eifersucht.' *Antike und Abendland* 51: 1–12.
- 2005e. 'La invencion de los celos.' *Aretê* 17: 45–58.
- 2006a. 'Friends in Tragedy.' In Eleni Karamalengou and Eugenia Makrigianni, eds, *Festschrift for John-Theophanes A. Papademetriou.* Athens: University of Athens Press.
- 2006b. *Lucrezio e la psicologia epicurea.* Trans. Ilaria Ramelli. Milan: Vitae Pensiero.
- 2006c. 'Anger, Hatred, and Genocide in Ancient Greece.' *Common Knowledge* 12.1.
- 2006d. 'War and Reconciliation in Greek Literature.' In Kurt A. Raaflaub, ed., *War and Peace in the Ancient World.* Oxford: Blackwell.
Konstan, David, and N. Keith Rutter, eds. 2003. *Envy, Spite, and Jealousy: The Rivalrous Emotions in Ancient Greece.* Edinburgh: Edinburgh University Press.
Kovacs, David. 1998. *Euripides.* Vol. 2. Cambridge, MA: Harvard University Press.
Kövecses, Zoltán. 2000. *Metaphor and Emotion: Language, Culture, and Body in Human Feeling.* Cambridge: Cambridge University Press and Paris: Éditions de la Maison des Sciences de l'Homme.
Kristjánsson, Kristján. 2002. *Justifying Emotions: Pride and Jealousy.* London: Routledge.
Kurihara, Asako. 2003. 'Personal Enmity as a Motivation in Forensic Speeches.' *Classical Quarterly* 53: 464–77.
Kurke, Leslie. 1991. *The Traffic in Praise: Pindar and the Poetics of Social Economy.* Ithaca: Cornell University Press.

Kyriakou, Poulheria. 1998. 'Menelaus and Pelops in Euripides' *Orestes*.' *Mnemosyne* ser. 4, 51: 282–301.

Kytzler, Bernhard. 2003. 'Der Regenbogen der Gefühle: Zum Kontrast der Empfindungen im antiken Roman.' *Scholia* 12: 69–81.

Lada, Ismene. 1993. 'Empathic Understanding: Emotion and Cognition in Classical Dramatic Audience-Response.' *Proceedings of the Cambridge Philological Society* n.s. 39: 94–140.

Lagache, Daniel. 1947. *La jalousie amoureuse: Psychologie descriptive et psychanalyse*. Vol. 2: *La jalousie vécue*. Paris: Presses Universitaires de France.

Lamb, Trevor, and Janine Bourriau, eds. 1995. *Color: Art and Science*. Cambridge: Cambridge University Press.

Landis, C. 1934. 'Emotion: II: The Expression of Emotion.' In C. Murchinson, ed., *Handbook of General Experimental Psychology*, 312–51. Worcester MA: Clark University Press, 1934.

Lansky, Melvin R. 1991. 'The Transformation of Affect in Posttraumatic Nightmares.' *Bulletin of the Menninger Clinic* 55: 470–90.

– 1992. *Fathers Who Fail: Shame and Psychopathology in the Family System*. Hillsdale, NJ: Analytic Press.

– 1996. 'Shame and Suicide in Sophocles' *Ajax*.' *Psychoanalytic Quarterly* 65: 761–86.

– 1997. 'Envy as Process.' In Melvin R. Lansky and Andrew P. Morrison, eds, *The Widening Scope of Shame*, 327–38. Hillsdale, NJ: The Analytic Press.

– 2001. 'Hidden Shame, Working Through, and the Problem of Forgiveness in *The Tempest*.' *Journal of the American Psychoanalytic Association* 49: 1005–33.

– Unpublished. 'Hate, the Ego-Ideal, and Forgiveness in Sophocles' *Philoctetes*: An Aspect of the Problem of Working Through.'

Lape, Susan. 2004. *Reproducing Athens: Menander's Comedy, Democratic Culture, and the Hellenistic City*. Princeton: Princeton University Press.

La Penna, Antonio. 1951. 'Note sul linguaggio erotico dell'elegia latina.' *Maia* 4: 187–209.

Larmour, David H.J., Paul Allen Miller, and Charles Platter, eds. 1998. *Rethinking Sexuality: Foucault and Classical Antiquity*. Princeton: Princeton University Press.

Lateiner, Donald. 2004. 'The Iliad: An Unpredictable Classic.' In Robert

Fowler, ed., *The Cambridge Companion to Homer*, 11–30. Cambridge: Cambridge University Press.

– 2005. ' The Pitiers and the Pitied in Herodotus and Thucydides.' In Sternberg 2005: 67–97.

Latte, Kurt, ed. 1966. *Hesychii Alexandrini lexicon*. Vol. 2. Hauniae: E. Munksgaard.

Lattimore, Richmond, trans. 1951. *Homer: The Iliad*. Chicago: University of Chicago Press.

Laughlin, Charles D., and Jason Throop. 1999. 'Emotion: A View from Biogenetic Structuralism.' In Hinton ed. 1999: 329–63.

Lawson-Tancred, H.C., trans. 1991. *Aristotle: The Art of Rhetoric*. Harmondsworth: Penguin.

Lazarus, Richard S. 1991a. 'Cognition and Motivation.' *American Psychologist* 46: 352–67.

– 1991b. *Emotion and Adaptation*. New York: Oxford University Press.

– 2001. 'Relational Meaning and Discrete Emotions.' In Scherer, Schorr, and Johnstone 2001: 37–67.

Lazarus, Richard S., Allen D. Kanner, and Susan Folkman. 1980. 'Emotions: A Cognitive-Phenomenological Analysis.' In Robert Plutchik and Henry Kellerman, eds, *Emotion: Theory, Research, and Experience*, vol. 1: Theories of Emotion: 189–217. New York: Academic Press.

Leaf, Walter, ed. 1888. *The Iliad*. Vol. 2: Books XIII–XXIV. London: MacMillan.

LeDoux, Joseph. 1996. *The Emotional Brain: The Mysterious Underpinnings of Emotional Life*. New York: Simon and Schuster.

LeDuff, Charlie. 2004. 'Budget Woes to the Wind as Schwarzenegger Takes to the Road.' *New York Times* (New England edition), 13 February: A12.

Leguina, Joaquín. 2002. *Cuernos*. Madrid: Alfaguara.

Lehane, Dennis. 1996. *Darkness, Take My Hand*. New York: Avon Books.

– 2001. *Mystic River*. New York: HarperCollins.

Leighton, Stephen R. 1987. 'Aristotle's Courageous Passions.' *Phronesis* 33: 76–99.

– 1996. 'Aristotle and the Emotions.' In A.O. Rorty ed. 1996: 206–37.

Levin, Jack. 2002. *The Violence of Hate: Confronting Racism, Anti-Semitism, and Other Forms of Bigotry*. Boston: Allyn and Bacon.

Lewis, Helen Block. 1971. *Shame and Guilt in Neurosis*. New York: International Universities Press.

– 1987a. 'Introduction: Shame – the "Sleeper" in Psychopathology.' In H.B. Lewis ed. 1987: 1–28.

– 1987b. 'The Role of Shame in Depression over the Life Span.' In H.B. Lewis ed. 1987: 29–50.

Lewis, Helen Block, ed. 1987. *The Role of Shame in Symptom Formation*. Hillsdale, NJ: Lawrence Erlbaum Associates.

Lewis, Michael. 1992. *Shame: The Exposed Self*. New York: Free Press.

– 2000. 'Self-Conscious Emotions: Embarrassment, Pride, Shame, and Guilt.' In Lewis and Haviland-Jones 2000: 623–36.

Lewis, Michael, and Jeannette M. Haviland-Jones, eds. 2000. *Handbook of Emotions*. 2nd edition. New York: Guilford Press.

Lewis, Thomas, Fari Amini, and Richard Lannon. 2000. *A General Theory of Love*. New York: Random House.

Li, Jin, Lianqin Wang, and Kurt W. Fischer. 2004. 'The Organization of Chinese Shame Concepts.' *Cognition and Emotion* 18: 767–97.

Liddell, Henry George, Robert Scott, and Henry Stuart Jones. 1940. *A Greek-English Lexicon*. 9th edition. Oxford: The Clarendon Press.

Lindheim, Sara. 2003. *Mail and Female: Epistolary Narrative and Desire in Ovid's Heroides*. Ann Arbor: University of Michigan Press.

Lintott, Andrew W. 1968. *Violence in Republican Rome*. Oxford: Clarendon Press.

Lloyd, Geoffrey E.R. 1966. *Polarity and Analogy: Two Types of Argumentation in Early Greek Thought*. Cambridge: Cambridge University Press.

Lloyd, Rosemary. 1995. *Closer and Closer Apart: Jealousy in Literature*. Ithaca: Cornell University Press.

Lloyd-Jones, Hugh. 1987. 'Ehre und Schande in der griechischen Kultur.' *Antike und Abendland* 33: 1–28.

Long, A.A., and David Sedley. 1987. *The Hellenistic Philosophers*. 2 vols. Cambridge: Cambridge University Press.

Lucà, Santo. 1994. 'Il lessico dello Ps.-Cirillo (Redazione V_1): De Rossano a Messina.' *Rivista di Studi Byzantini e Neoellenici* 31: 45–80.

Lutz, Catherine A. 1988. *Unnatural Emotions: Everyday Sentiments on a Micronesian Atoll and Their Challenge to Western Theory*. Chicago: University of Chicago Press.

Lyons, Deborah. 2003. 'Dangerous Gifts: Ideologies of Marriage and Exchange in Ancient Greece.' *Classical Antiquity* 22: 93–134.

Lyons, John. 1995. 'Color in Language.' In Lamb and Bourriau 1995: 194–224.

- 1999. 'The Vocabulary of Color with Particular Reference to Ancient Greek and Classical Latin.' In Borg 1999: 38–75.
Lyons, William. 1980. *Emotion*. Cambridge: Cambridge University Press.
Maass, Peter. 2003. 'Good Kills.' *New York Times Magazine*, 20 April: 32–7.
Mackay, E.A. 2002. 'The Evocation of Emotional Response in Early Greek Poetry and Painting.' In Ian Worthington and John Miles Foley, eds, *Epea and Grammata: Oral and Written Communication in Ancient Greece*, 55–69. Leiden: E.J. Brill.
MacLaury, Robert E. 1999. 'Basic Color Terms: Twenty-five Years After.' In Borg 1999: 1–37.
Macleod, C.W. 1977. 'Thucydides' Plataean Debate.' *Greek, Roman and Byzantine Studies* 18: 227–46; repr. in C.W. Macleod, *Collected Essays*, 227–46. Oxford: Clarendon Press, 1983.
MacLeod, Leona. 2001. *Dolos and Dike in Sophokles' Elektra*. Leiden: E.J. Brill = *Mnemosyne* supplement 219.
Maleuvre, J.-Y. 1990. 'Trois Odes d'Horace (I, 8, 13, 14).' *Les Études Classiques* 58: 129–42.
Mandelbaum, Allen, trans. 1981. *The Aeneid of Virgil*. New York: Bantam Books.
Mandler, George. 1997. 'Foreword.' In Russell and Fernández-Dols eds 1997: vii–x.
Manstead, Antony S.R., and Agneta H. Fischer. 2001. 'Social Appraisal: The Social World as Object of and Influence on Appraisal Processes.' In Scherer, Schorr, and Johnstone 2001: 221–32.
Margalit, Avishai. 1996. *The Decent Society*. Cambridge, MA: Harvard University Press.
Marguerite de Navarre. 1999. *Heptaméron*. Ed. Renja Salminen. Geneva: Librairie Droz.
Marina, José Antonio. 1996. *El laberinto sentimental*. Barcelona: Anagrama.
Marina, José Antonio, and Marisa López Penas. 2001 (orig. 1999). *Diccionario de los sentimientos*. Barcelona: Anagrama ('Compactos').
Marincola, John. 2003. 'Beyond Pity and Fear: The Emotions of History.' *Ancient Society* 33: 285–315.
Markus, H.R., and S. Kitayama. 1991. 'Culture and the Self: Implications for Cognition, Emotion, and Motivation.' *Psychological Review* 98: 224–53.

Marušič, Jera. 2000. 'Tragiški užitkiv Aristotelovi Poetiki.' *Keria* 2: 111–31.

Masaracchia, Agostino. 1995. *Isocrate: Retorica e politica.* Rome: Gruppo Editoriale Internazionale.

Mastronarde, Donald J., ed. 2002. *Euripides Medea.* Cambridge: Cambridge University Press.

Mattern-Parkes, Susan P. 2001. 'Seneca's Treatise *On Anger* and the Aristocratic Competition for Honor.' In Elizabeth Tylawsky and Charles Weiss, eds, *Essays in Honor of Gordon Williams: Twenty-five Years at Yale,* 177–88. New Haven: Henry R. Schwab Publishers.

McConnell, Terrance. 1993. *Gratitude.* Philadelphia: Temple University Press.

McCrone, John. 2004. 'Reasons to Forget: Scientists Count the Ways We Get It Wrong.' *Times Literary Supplement,* 30 January: 3–4.

Mendelsohn, Daniel. 2002. *Gender and the City in Euripides' Political Plays.* Oxford: Oxford University Press.

Mesquita, Batja, and Phoebe C. Ellsworth. 2001. 'The Role of Culture in Appraisal.' In Scherer, Schorr, and Johnstone 2001: 233–48.

Metcalf, Peter, and Richard Huntington. 1991. *Celebrations of Death: The Anthropology of Mortuary Ritual.* 2nd edition. Cambridge: Cambridge University Press.

Mignini, Filippo. 1994. '*Gratitudo,* tra *charis* e *amicitia*: Momenti di storia di un'idea.' In Galli 1994: 17–84.

Milhaven, J. Giles. 1989. *Good Anger.* Kansas City: Sheed and Ward.

Miller, Dean A. 2000. *The Epic Hero.* Baltimore: Johns Hopkins University Press.

Miller, William Ian. 1997. *The Anatomy of Disgust.* Cambridge, MA: Harvard University Press.

– 2000. *The Mystery of Courage.* Cambridge, MA: Harvard University Press.

Mills, M.J. 1980. 'The Discussion of *Andreia* in the Eudemian and Nicomachean Ethics.' *Phronesis* 25: 198–218.

Milobenski, Ernst. 1964. *Der Neid in der griechischen Philosophie.* Wiesbaden: O. Harrassowitz.

Mitchell, Lynette G. 1996. 'New for Old: Friendship Networks in Athenian Politics.' *Greece and Rome,* new ser., 43: 11–21.

Moliner, María. 1990. *Diccionario de uso del español.* Vol. 1. Madrid: Editorial Gredos.

Momigliano, Arnaldo. 1973. 'Freedom of Speech in Antiquity.' In Philip P. Wiener, ed., *Dictionary of the History of Ideas: Studies of Selected Pivotal Ideas*, vol. 2: 252–63. New York: Charles Scribner's Sons, 1973.

Montiglio, Silvia. 2000. *Silence in the Land of Logos*. Princeton: Princeton University Press.

Morrison, Andrew P. 1989. *Shame: The Underside of Narcissism*. Hillsdale, NJ: Analytic Press.

– 1996. *The Culture of Shame*. New York: Ballantine Books.

Mosley, Walter. 2003. 'An African-American Appeal for Peace.' *The Nation* 276.3 (27 January): 11–14.

Mossman, Judith. 1995. *Wild Justice: A Study of Euripides' Hecuba*. Oxford: Clarendon Press.

Most, Glenn W. 2001. 'Memory and Forgetting in the *Aeneid*.' *Virgilius* 47: 148–70.

– 2003. 'Epinician Envies.' In Konstan and Rutter 2003: 123–42.

Muellner, Leonard. 1996. *The Anger of Achilles: Mênis in Greek Epic*. Ithaca: Cornell University Press.

Müri, Walter. 1947. 'Beitrag zum Verständnis des Thukydides.' *Museum Helveticum* 4: 251–75.

Murukami, Haruki. 2002. 'Tony Takitani.' Trans. from Japanese by Jay Rubin. *The New Yorker*, 15 April: 74–81.

Narayan, Uma. 1997. *Dislocating Cultures: Identities, Traditions, and Third-World Feminism*. New York: Routledge.

Nathanson, Donald L. 1992. *Shame and Pride: Affect, Sex, and the Birth of the Self*. New York: W.W. Norton.

Neisser, Ulric, and L.K. Libby. 2000. 'Remembering Life Experiences.' In Endel Tulving and Fergus I.M. Craik, eds, *The Oxford Handbook of Memory*, 315–32. New York: Oxford University Press.

Neisser, Ulric, and Eugene Winograd, eds. 1988. *Remembering Reconsidered: Ecological and Traditional Approaches to the Study of Memory*. Cambridge: Cambridge University Press.

Nelli, María Florencia. 2002. 'La auto-aniquilación como muerte heroica: Un análisis del suicidio, desde la perspectiva del *hegemón*, en el *Áyax* de Sófocles.' In R.P. Buzón et al., eds, *Los estudios clásicos ante el cambio de milenio: Vida Muerte Cultura*, vol. 2: 196–204. Buenos Aires: University of Buenos Aires Press.

Nelson, Charles A., and Michelle de Haan. 1997. 'A Neurobiological

Approach to the Recognition of Facial Expressions in Infancy.' In Russell and Fernández-Dols eds 1997: 176–204.

Neu, Jerome. 1980. 'Jealous Thoughts.' In A.O. Rorty 1980: 425–63.

Newmyer, Stephen. 2006. 'Tool Use and Manufacture in Animals: Ancient and Modern Insights and Moral Consequences. *Scholia* 15.

Ničev, Alexandre. 1985. 'La notion de pitié chez Sophocle.' In Jacques Brunschwig, Claude Imbert, and Alain Roger, eds, *Histoire et structure: À la mémoire de Victor Goldschmidt*. Paris: J. Vrin.

Nisbet, R.G.M., and Margaret Hubbard, eds. 1970. *A Commentary on Horace* Odes, *Book I*. Oxford: Clarendon Press.

Nisbett, Richard E. 2003. *The Geography of Thought: How Asians and Westerners Think Differently ... and Why*. New York: Free Press.

Nusbaum, Martha Craven. 1986. *The Fragility of Goodness: Luck and Ethics in Greek Tragedy and Philosophy*. Cambridge: Cambridge University Press.

– 1996. 'Aristotle on Emotions and Rational Persuasion.' In A.O. Rorty 1996: 303–23.

– 2001. *Upheavals of Thought: The Intelligence of Emotions*. Cambridge: Cambridge University Press.

Oatley, Keith. 1992. *Best Laid Schemes: The Psychology of Emotions*. Cambridge: Cambridge University Press and Paris: Éditions de la Maison des Sciences de l'Homme.

– 2003. 'Writingandreading: The Future of Cognitive Poetics.' In Joanna Gavins and Gerard Steen, eds, *Cognitive Poetics in Practice*, 161–74. London: Routledge.

Ober, Josiah. 1989. *Mass and Elite in Democratic Athens: Rhetoric, Ideology, and the Power of the People*. Princeton: Princeton University Press.

O'Higgins, Laurie. 2003. *Women and Humor in Classical Greece*. Cambridge: Cambridge University Press.

Ohly, Friedrich. 1992 (orig. 1976). *The Damned and the Elect: Guilt in Western Culture*. Trans. Linda Archibald. Cambridge: Cambridge University Press.

Oliker, Stacey J. 1998. 'The Modernization of Friendship: Individualism, Intimacy, and Gender in the Nineteenth Century.' In Rebecca G. Adams and Graham Allan, eds, *Friendship in Context*, 18–42. Cambridge: Cambridge University Press.

Olyan, Saul. 2003. *'That Our Eyes Might Run with Tears': Ritual and*

Social Dimensions of Biblical Mourning. Oxford: Oxford University Press.

Ortega y Gasset, José. 1976 (orig. 1924). 'Las Atlántidas.' In *Las Atlántidas y Del imperio romano*, 35–97. Madrid: Ediciones de la Revista del Occidente.

Ortony, Andrew, Gerald L. Clore, and Allen Collins. 1988. *The Cognitive Structure of Emotions.* Cambridge: Cambridge University Press.

Orwin, Clifford. 1984. 'The Just and the Advantageous in Thucydides: The Case of the Mytilenaian Debate.' *American Political Science Review* 78: 485–94.

Owens, William M. 1992. 'Double Jealousy: An Interpretation of Horace *Odes* 1.13.' In Carl Deroux, ed., *Studies in Latin Literature and History 6*, 237–44. Brussels: Latomus = Collection Latomus 217.

Padel, Ruth. 1992. *In and Out of the Mind: Greek Images of the Tragic Self.* Princeton: Princeton University Press.

Paglialunga, Esther. 200. 'Amor y celos en los personajes masculinos de Caritón de Afrodisia.' *Florentia Iliberritana* 11: 181–94.

Pakaluk, Michael, trans. and comm. 1998. *Aristotle Nicomachean Ethics Books VIII and IX.* Oxford: Clarendon Press.

Panchenko, Dimitri. 2002. 'The City of the Branchidae and the Question of Greek Contribution to the Intellectual History of India and China.' *Hyperboreus* 8: 244–55.

Panoussi, Vassiliki. 1998. 'Epic Transfigured: Tragic Allusiveness in Vergil's *Aeneid*.' Doctoral thesis, Brown University, Providence, RI.

Parker, Holt N. 2000. 'Horace *Epodes* 11.15–18: What's Shame Got to Do with It.' *American Journal of Philology* 121: 559–70.

Parker, Robert. 1998. 'Pleasing Thighs: Reciprocity in Greek Religion.' In Gill, Postlethwaite, and Seaford 1998: 105–25.

Parkes, Colin Murray, Pittu Laungani, and Bill Young, eds. 1997. *Death and Bereavement across Cultures.* London: Routledge.

Parkinson, Brian. 1995. *Ideas and Realities of Emotion.* London: Routledge.

Parrott, W. Gerrod. 1991. 'The Emotional Experiences of Envy and Jealousy.' In Salovey 1991: 3–30.

Partridge, Eric. 1959 (orig. 1958). *Origins: A Short Etymological Dictionary of Modern English.* New York: Macmillan Company.

Pastoureau, Michel. 2001. *Blue: The History of a Color.* Trans. Markus I. Cruse. Princeton: Princeton University Press.

Pattison, Stephen. 2000. *Shame: Theory, Therapy, Theology*. Cambridge: Cambridge University Press.

Peachin, Michael, ed. 2001. *Aspects of Friendship in the Graeco-Roman World* (Proceedings of a conference held at the Seminar für Alte Geschichte, Heidelberg, 10–11 June 2000). Portsmouth: Journal of Roman Archaeology (JRA Supplementary Series 43).

Pears, David F. 1978. 'Aristotle's Analysis of Courage.' *Midwest Studies in Philosophy* 3: 273–85.

Pelling, Christopher, ed. 1990. *Characterization and Individuality in Greek Literature*. Oxford: Clarendon Press.

Perry, Ellen E. 2000. 'Rhetoric, Literary Criticism, and the Roman Aesthetics of Artistic Imitation.' In Elaine K. Gazda, ed., *The Ancient Art of Emulation: Studies in Artistic Originality and Tradition from the Present to Classical Antiquity*, 153–71. Ann Arbor: University of Michigan Press = *Memoirs of the American Academy in Rome*, Supplementary volume 1.

Planalp, Sally. 1999. *Communicating Emotion: Social, Moral, and Cultural Processes*. Cambridge: Cambridge University Press.

Plutchik, Robert. 1991. *The Emotions: Facts, Theories, and a New Model*. Rev. ed. Lanham, MD: University Press of America.

Polin, R. 1953. *Politique et philosophie chez Thomas Hobbes*. Paris: Presses Universitaires Françaises.

Price, Richard. 1974 (orig. 1797). *A Review of the Principal Questions in Morals*. Ed. D.D. Raphael. Oxford: Oxford University Press.

Pritchett, W. Kendrick. 1991. *The Greek State at War*. Part 5. Berkeley: University of California Press.

Prodger, Phillip. 1998. 'Photography and *The Expression of the Emotions*.' Appendix 3 in Darwin 1998: 399–410.

Provine, Robert R. 1997. 'Yawns, Laughs, Smiles, Tickles, and Talking: Naturalistic and Laboratory Studies of Facial Action and Social Communication.' In Russell and Fernández-Dols eds 1997: 158–75.

Pucci, Pietro. 1999. 'Écriture tragique et récit mythique.' In *Les Tragiques Grecs = Europe: Revue Littéraire Mensuelle* 77 nos. 837–8 (January/February).

Pujol Gebellí, Xavier. 2001. 'Científicos españoles descubren el factor genético que predispone a la ansiedad.' *El País* 26 no. 8844 (10 August 2001): 18.

Quinn, Kenneth, ed. 1984. *Horace: The Odes*. Corrected edition. London: St Martin's Press.

Raaflaub, Kurt A. 2004. *The Discovery of Freedom in Ancient Greece.* Trans. Renate Franciscono. Chicago: University of Chicago Press.

Rabe, Hugo, ed. 1896. *Stephanos. Commentaria in Aristotelem graeca.* Vol. 21, part 2. Berlin: Reimer.

Raccanelli, Renata. 1998. *L'amicitia nelle commedie de Plauto: Un'indagine antropologica.* Bari: Edipuglia.

Rademaker, Adriaan. 2005. Sophrosyne *and the Rhetoric of Self-Restraint: Polysemy and Persuasive Use of an Ancient Greek Value Term.* Leiden: E.J. Brill = *Mnemosyne* Supplement 259.

Radici Colace, P. 1985. 'Il poeta si diverte: Orazio, Catullo, e due esempi di poesia non seria.' *Giornale Italiano di Filalogia* 16: 53–71.

Radt, Stefan L. 1970. 'Sapphica.' *Mnemosyne* 23: 337–47.

Ramírez Trejo, Arturo E. 2002. *Aristóteles Retórica.* Mexico City: Universidad Nacional Autónoma de México.

Ranulf, Svend. 1933. *The Jealousy of the Gods and Criminal Law at Athens: A Contribution to the Sociology of Moral Indignation.* 2 vols. London: Williams & Norgate and Copenhagen: Levin and Munksgaard.

Rapp, Christof, trans. and ed. 2002. *Aristoteles Rhetorik.* Berlin: Akademie Verlag.

Rawls, John. 1971. *A Theory of Justice.* Cambridge, MA: Harvard University Press.

Reddy, William M. 2001. *The Navigation of Feeling: A Framework for the History of the Emotions.* Cambridge: Cambridge University Press.

Redfield, James M. 1975. *Nature and Culture in the Iliad.* Chicago: Chicago University Press.

Reginster, Bernard. 1997. 'Nietzsche on *Ressentiment* and Valuation.' *Philosophy and Phenomenological Research* 57: 281–305.

Reiken, Frederick. 2002. 'The Ocean.' *The New Yorker,* 9 September: 140–7.

Reitzenstein, R. 1940. *Terenz als Dichter.* Amsterdam: Pantheon = *Albae Vigiliae* 4.

Rendell, Ruth. 1981. *Death Notes.* New York: Ballantine Books.

Renehan, Robert. 1971. 'Greek Lexicographical Notes: Fourth Series.' *Glotta* 49: 65–85.

Rhodes, P.J. 1996. 'Personal Enmity and Political Opposition in Athens.' *Greece and Rome,* 2nd ser. 43: 21–30.

– 1998. 'Enmity in Fourth-Century Athens.' In Paul Cartledge, Paul

Millett, and Sitta von Reden, eds, *Kosmos: Essays in Order, Conflict and Community in Classical Athens*, 144–61. Cambridge: Cambridge University Press.

Richardson, Samuel. 1958. *Pamela or Virtue Rewarded*. Introduction by William M. Sale. New York: W.W. Norton & Company.

Richardson Lear, Gabriel. 2004. *Happy Lives and the Highest Good: An Essay on Aristotle's* Nicomachean Ethics. Princeton: Princeton University Press.

Riese, Alexander, ed. 1926. *Anthologia latina*. Vol. 2. Leipzig: Teubner.

Riezler, Kurt. 1943. 'Comment on the Social Psychology of Shame.' *American Journal of Sociology* 48: 457–65.

Roberts, Robert C. 2004. 'The Blessings of Gratitude: A Conceptual Analysis.' In Robert A. Emmons and Michael E. McCullough, eds, *The Psychology of Gratitude*, 58–78. Oxford: Oxford University Press.

Roberts, W. Rhys, trans. 1984. 'Rhetoric.' In Jonathan Barnes, ed., *The Complete Works of Aristotle*, vol. 2: 2152–69. Princeton: Princeton University Press (Bollingen Series 71.2).

Robertson, G.I.C. 1999. 'The Eyes of Achilleus: *Iliad* 1.200.' *Phoenix* 53: 1–7.

Rodriguez Mosquera, P.M., Antony S.R. Manstead, and Agneta H. Fischer. 2000. 'The Role of Honor-related Values in the Elicitation, Experience and Communication of Pride, Shame and Anger: Spain and the Netherlands Compared.' *Personality and Social Psychology Bulletin* 26, no. 7: 833–44.

Rolls, Edmund T. 1999. *The Brain and Emotion*. Oxford: Oxford University Press.

Romano, Elisa. 1991. *Q. Orazio Flacco: Le opere*. Vol. 1: *Le Odi, il Carme Secolare, gli Epodi*. Part 2: *Commento*. Rome: Libreria dello Stato.

Romilly, Jacqueline de. 1956. 'La crainte dans l'oeuvre de Thucydide.' *Classica et Mediaevalia* 17: 119–27.

– 1974. 'Fairness and Kindness in Thucydides.' *Phoenix* 28: 95–100.

Rorty, Amélie Oksensberg, ed. 1980. *Explaining Emotions*. Berkeley: University of California Press.

– 1996. *Essays on Aristotle's Rhetoric*. Berkeley: University of California Press.

Rorty, Richard. 1999 (orig. 1993). 'Human Rights, Rationality, and Sentimentality.' In Baird and Rosenbaum eds 1999: 263–81.

Rosaldo, Michelle Z. 1984. 'Toward an Anthropology of Self and Feeling.' In Shweder and LeVine 1984: 137–57.

Roseman, Ira J., and Craig A. Smith. 2001. 'Appraisal Theory: Overview, Assumptions, Varieties, Controversies.' In Scherer, Schorr, and Johnstone 2001: 3–19.

Rosenblatt, Paul C. 1997. 'Grief in Small-Scale Societies.' In Parkes, Laungani, and Young 1997: 27–51.

Rosenwein, Barbara H. 2003. 'Eros and Clio: Emotional Paradigms in Medieval History.' In Hans-Werner Goetz and Jörg Jarnut, eds, *Mediävistik im 21. Jahrhundert: Stand und Perspektiven der internationalen und interdisziplinären Mittelalterforschung*. Munich: Wilhelm Fink Verlag.

Rosenwein, Barbara H., ed. 1998. *Anger's Past: The Social Uses of an Emotion in the Middle Ages*. Ithaca: Cornell University Press.

Rowe, Christopher J., trans. 2002. *Aristotle: Nicomachean Ethics*. With commentary by Sarah Broadie. Oxford: Oxford University Press.

Rubin, Theodore I., M.D. 1975. *Compassion and Self-Hate: An Alternative to Despair*. New York: Simon and Schuster.

Russell, Donald A., and Nigel G. Wilson, eds and trans. 1981. *Menander Rhetor*. Oxford: Clarendon Press.

Russell, James A. 1997. 'Reading Emotions from and into Faces: Resurrecting a Dimensional-Contextual Perspective.' In Russell and Fernández-Dols eds 1997: 295–320.

Russell, James A., and José Miguel Fernández-Dols. 1997a. 'Preface.' In Russell and Fernández-Dols eds 1997: xi–xii.

Russell, James A., and José Miguel Fernández-Dols. 1997b. 'What Does a Facial Expression Mean?' In Russell and Fernández-Dols eds 1997: 3–30.

Russell, James A., and José Miguel Fernández-Dols, eds. 1997. *The Psychology of Facial Expression*. Cambridge: Cambridge University Press.

Rusten, J.S., ed. 1990. *Thucydides: The Peloponnesian War, Book II*. Cambridge: Cambridge University Press.

Rutherford, R.B., ed. 1992. *Homer: Odyssey Books XIX and XX*. Cambridge: Cambridge University Press.

Sabini, J., and M. Silver. 1986. 'Envy.' In Rom Harré, ed., *The Social Construction of the Emotions*, 167–83. Oxford: Basil Blackwell.

Saïd, Suzanne. 2003. 'Envy and Emulation in Isocrates.' In Konstan and Rutter 2003: 217–34.

Ste Croix, G.E.M. de. 1981. *The Class Struggle in the Ancient Greek World*. Ithaca: Cornell University Press.

Salovey, Peter, ed. 1991. *The Psychology of Jealousy and Envy*. New York: Guilford Press.

Sanders, Kirk R. Unpublished. 'The Conclusion of Philodemus's *De ira.*'

Sartre, Jean-Paul. 1996 (orig. 1943). *Being and Nothingness: A Phenomenological Essay on Ontology*. Trans. Hazel Barnes. New York: Washington Square Press.

Scheff, Thomas J. 1995. 'Editor's Introduction. Shame and Related Emotions: An Overview.' *American Behavioral Scientist* 38: 1053–9. Special issue, *Shame and Related Emotions: An Interdisciplinary Approach*.

– 1997. 'Shame in Social Theory.' In Melvin R. Lansky and Andrew P. Morrison, eds, *The Widening Scope of Shame*, 205–30. Hillsdale, NJ: Analytic Press.

– 2000. 'Shame and the Social Bond: A Sociological Theory.' *Sociological Theory* 18: 84–99.

– Unpublished. [2004.] 'Routines in Human Science: The Case of Emotion Words.' Available at http://www.soc.ucsb.edu/ faculty/ scheff/33.html.

Scherer, Klaus R. 1993. 'Studying the Emotion-Antecedent Appraisal Process: An Expert System Approach.' In Frijda 1993: 325–55.

Scherer, Klaus R., Angela Schorr, and Tom Johnstone, eds. 2001. *Appraisal Processes in Emotion: Theory, Methods, Research*. Oxford: Oxford University Press.

Schmidt, Louis A., and Jay Schulkin, eds. 1999. *Extreme Fear, Shyness, and Social Phobia: Origins, Biological Mechanisms, and Clinical Outcomes*. New York: Oxford University Press.

Schneier, Franklin R. 1999. 'Extreme Fear, Shyness, and Social Phobia: Treatment and Intervention.' In Schmidt and Schulkin 1999: 273–93.

Schoeck, Helmut. 1966. *Envy: A Theory of Social Behavior*. Trans. Michael Glenny and Betty Ross. Indianapolis: Liberty Press.

Schopenhauer, Arthur. 1995. *On the Basis of Morality*. Trans. E.F.J. Payne. Providence, RI: Berghahn Books.

Schorr, Angela. 2001. 'Appraisal: The Evolution of an Idea.' In Scherer, Schorr, and Johnstone 2001: 20–34.

Schrift, Alan D. 1997. *The Logic of the Gift: Toward an Ethic of Generosity*. London: Routledge.

Schwartz, Martin. 1982. 'The Indo-European Vocabulary of Exchange, Hospitality, and Intimacy (the Origins of Greek *ksénos, sún, phílos*; *Avestan xsnu-, xsanman-*, etc.): Contributions to Etymological Methodology.' *Proceedings of the Berkeley Linguistics Society* 8: 188–204.

Scott, Mary. 1995. 'The Character of Deianeira in Sophocles' "Trachiniae."' *Acta Classica* 38: 17–28.

Scruton, David L. 1986. 'The Anthropology of an Emotion.' In David L. Scruton, ed., *Sociophobics: The Anthropology of Fear*, 7–49. Boulder, CO: Westview Press.

Scullion, Scott. 2002. 'Tragic Dates.' *Classical Quarterly* 52: 81–101.

Scully, Matthew. 2002. *Dominion: The Power of Man, the Suffering of Animals, and the Call to Mercy*. New York: St Martin's Press.

Sedgwick, Eve Kosofsky. 1985. *Between Men: English Literature and Male Homosocial Desire*. New York: Columbia University Press.

– 1995. 'Shame and Performativity.' In David McWhirter, ed., *Henry James's New York Edition: The Construction of Authorship*, 207–39. Stanford: Stanford University Press.

Sedgwick, Eve Kosofsky, and Adam Frank. 1995. 'Shame in the Cybernetic Fold: Reading Silvan Tomkins.' In Tomkins 1995: 1–28.

Segal, Hanna. 1973. *Introduction to the Work of Melanie Klein*. London: Hogarth Press.

Seidensticker, B. 1982. *Palintonos Harmonia: Studien zu komischen Elementen in der griechischen Tragödie*. Göttingen: Vandenhoeck & Ruprecht = Hypomnemata 72.

Seidler, Günter Harry. 2000 (orig. 1995). *In Others' Eyes: An Analysis of Shame*. Trans. Andrew Jenkins. Madison, CT: International Universities Press.

Sen, Amartya K. 1990. 'Rational Fools: A Critique of the Behavioral Foundations of Economic Theory.' In Jane J. Mansbridge, ed., *Beyond Self-Interest*, 25–43. Chicago: University of Chicago Press, 1990.

Seremetakis, C.N. 1991. *The Last Word: Women, Death, and Divination in Inner Mani*. Chicago: University of Chicago Press.

Serrano Aybar, Concepción. 1977. 'Historia de la lexicografía griega antigua y medieval.' In F.R. Adrados et al., *Introducción a la lexicografía griega*, 61–106. Madrid: Instituto Antonio Nebrija.

Shackleton Bailey, D.R. 1982. *Anthologia latina*. Stuttgart: Teubner.

Sharpsteen, Don J. 1991. 'The Organization of Jealousy Knowledge: Romantic Jealousy as a Blended Emotion.' In Salovey 1991: 31–51.

Shay, Jonathan. 1994. *Achilles in Vietnam: Combat Trauma and the Undoing of Character*. New York: Athenaeum.

Shelton, Jo-Ann. 1998. *As the Romans Did: A Sourcebook in Roman Social History*. 2nd edition. New York: Oxford University Press.

Sherman, Nancy. 2000a. 'Emotional Agents.' In Michael P. Levine, ed., *The Analytic Freud: Philosophy and Psychoanalysis*, 154–76. London: Routledge.

– 2000b (pub. 2001). 'Is the Ghost of Aristotle Haunting Freud's House?' *Proceedings of the Boston Area Colloquium in Ancient Philosophy* 16: 63–81.

Shipp, George P. 1972. *Studies in the Language of Homer*. 2nd edition. Cambridge: Cambridge University Press.

Shweder, Richard A., and Jonathan Haidt. 2000. 'The Cultural Psychology of the Emotions: Ancient and New.' In Lewis and Haviland-Jones 2000: 397–414.

Shweder, Richard A., and Robert A. LeVine, eds. 1984. *Culture Theory: Essays on Mind, Self, and Emotion*. Cambridge: Cambridge University Press.

Sieveke, Franz G., trans. 1980 (3rd. ed. 1989). *Aristoteles Rhetorik*. Munich: Wilhelm Fink Verlag.

Simmel, Georg. 1996. 'Faithfulness and Gratitude.' In Aafke E. Komter, *The Gift: An Interdisciplinary Perspective*, 39–48. Amsterdam: Amsterdam University Press.

Sissa, Giulia, and Marcel Detienne. 2000 (orig. 1989). *The Daily Life of the Greek Gods*. Trans. Janet Lloyd. Stanford: Stanford University Press.

Smith, Adam, 1982. *The Theory of Moral Sentiments*. Ed. D.D. Raphael and A.L. Macfie. Indianapolis: Liberty Classics.

Smith, Craig A., and Richard S. Lazarus. 1993. 'Appraisal Components, Core Relational Themes, and the Emotions.' *Cognition and Emotion* 7: 233–69 = Nico H. Frijda, ed., *Appraisal and Beyond: The Issue of Cognitive Determinants of Emotion*. Hove: Lawrence Erlbaum Associates.

Smith, Craig A., and Heather S. Scott. 1997. 'A Componential Approach to the Meaning of Facial Expression.' In Russell and Fernández-Dols eds 1997: 229–54.

Smith, Martin Ferguson, ed. 1993. *Diogenes of Oenoanda: The Epicurean Inscription.* Naples: Bibliopolis.

Smith, Richard H. 1991. 'Envy and the Sense of Injustice.' In Salovey 1991: 79–99.

Smoes, Étienne. 1995. *Le courage chez les grecs, d'Homère à Aristote.* Brussels: Éditions Ousia = Cahiers de Philosophie Ancienne 12.

Snell, Bruno, ed. 1971–. *Tragicorum graecorum fragmenta.* Göttingen: Vandenhoeck & Ruprecht.

Sobieszek, Robert. 1999. '"Gymnastics of the soul": The clinical aesthetics of Duchenne de Boulogne.' In *Six Exposures: Essays in Celebration of the Opening of the Harrison D. Horblit Collection of Early Photography,* 107–29. Cambridge, MA: Harvard University Press (Houghton Library).

Sodano, Angelo Raffaele, ed. 1970. *Porphyry: Quaestionum Homericarum liber I.* Naples: Giannini.

Solomon, Robert C. 1984. 'Getting Angry: The Jamesian Theory of Emotion in Anthropology.' In Shweder and LeVine 1984: 238–54.

– 1993. *The Passions: Emotions and the Meaning of Life.* Revised edition. Indianapolis: Hackett Publishing Co.

– 2000. 'The Philosophy of Emotions.' In Lewis and Haviland-Jones 2000: 3–15.

– 2004. 'Foreword.' In Robert A. Emmons and Michael E. McCullough, eds, *The Psychology of Gratitude,* v–xi. Oxford: Oxford University Press.

Sorabji, Richard. 1993. *Animal Minds and Human Morals: The Origins of the Western Debate.* Ithaca: Cornell University Press.

– 1999. 'Aspasius on Emotion.' In Antonina Alberti and Robert W. Sharples, eds, *Aspasius: The Earliest Extant Commentary on Aristotle's Ethics,* 96–106. Berlin: Walter de Gruyter.

– 2000. *Emotion and Peace of Mind: From Stoic Agitation to Christian Temptation.* Oxford: Oxford University Press.

Spengel, Leonard, ed. 1854–85. *Rhetores Graeci.* 3 vols. Leipzig: Teubner.

Spinoza, Baruch. 1982. *The Ethics and Selected Letters.* Trans. Samuel Shirley. Ed. with Introduction by Seymour Feldman. Indianapolis: Hackett.

Spinoza, Baruch. 1989 (orig. 1677). *Ethica.* Trans. G.H.R. Parkinson. London: Everyman.

– 1992. *The Ethics; Treatise on the Emendation of the Intellect; Selected Letters*. Ed. Seymour Feldman. Trans. Samuel Shirly. Indianapolis: Hackett Publishing Co.

Stafford, Emma. 2000. *Worshipping Virtues: Personification and the Divine in Ancient Greece*. London: Duckworth and the Classical Press of Wales.

Stafilidis, Andreas D., ed. 1998. *Hyper Lexicon: English-Greek Greek-English*. 4th edition. Athens, Stafilidi Publishers.

Stahr, Adolf, trans. 1862. *Aristoteles: Drei Bücher der Rhetorik*. Stuttgart: Krais & Hoffmann.

Stanford, W.B., ed. 1959. *Homer: Odyssey Books I–XII*. 2nd edition. London: Macmillan.

Stearns, Peter N. 1989. *Jealousy: The Evolution of an Emotion in American History*. New York: New York University Press.

Steinlein, Walter. 1941. 'Φθόνος und verwandte Begriffe in der älteren griechischen Literatur.' Dissertation, Erlangen, Friedrich-Alexander-Universität.

Stendhal (Marie Henri Beyle). 1916 (orig. 1822). *On Love*. Trans. Philip Sidney Woolf and Cecil N. Sidney Woolf. New York: Brentano's.

Stenger, Jan. 2000. 'Nemesis.' In Hubert Cancik and Helmut Schneider, eds, *Der neue Pauly: Enzyklopädie der Antike*, vol. 8: cols. 818–19. Stuttgart: J.B. Metzler.

Stephanus of Alexandria. 1896. *In Artem rhetoricam commentaria*. Ed. Hugo Rabe. Berlin: Reimer = *Commentaria in Aristotelem Graeca* vol. 21, part 2: 263–322.

Stern, Jessica. 2003. *Terror in the Name of God: Why Religious Militants Kill*. New York: Ecco/HarperCollins.

Sternberg, Rachel. 1999. 'The Transport of Sick and Wounded Soldiers in Classical Greece.' *Phoenix* 53.3–4: 191–205.

– 2000. 'The Nurturing Male: Bravery and Bedside Manners in Isocrates' *Aegineticus* (19.24–9).' *Greece & Rome* 47: 172–85.

Sternberg, Rachel, ed. 2005. *Pity in Ancient Athenian Life and Letters*. Cambridge: Cambridge University Press.

Stocker, Michael (with Elizabeth Hegeman). 1996. *Valuing Emotions*. Cambridge: Cambridge University Press.

Strawson, P.F. 1974. *Freedom and Resentment and Other Essays*. London: Methuen & Co.

Striker, Gisela. 1996. 'Emotions in Context: Aristotle's Treatment of the Passions in the *Rhetoric* and His Moral Psychology.' In A.O. Rorty 1996: 286–302.

Stroh, Wilfried. 1993. 'De Horati poesi amatoria.' In *Atti del Convegno di Venosa 8–15 novembre 1992*, 151–79. Venosa: Edizioni Osanna.

SVF = *Stoicorum veterum fragmenta*. Ed. J. von Arnim. Leipzig: B.G. Teubner, 1921–4.

Swedenborg, Emanuel. 1928 (orig. 1768). *The Delights of Wisdom Pertaining to Conjugal Love, after which Follow the Pleasures of Insanity Pertaining to Scortatory Love*. Trans. Samuel M. Warren; rev. Louis H. Tafel. New York: Swedenborg Foundation.

Swift, Jonathan. 1963–5. *Correspondence*. Ed. Harold Williams. 5 volumes. Oxford: Clarendon Press.

Tangney, June Price, and Ronda L. Dearing. 2002. *Shame and Guilt*. New York: Guilford Press.

Taplin, Oliver. 1992. *Homeric Soundings: The Shaping of the* Iliad. Oxford: Clarendon Press.

Tavris, Carol. 1989. *Anger: The Misunderstood Emotion*. Rev. ed. New York: Simon and Schuster.

Taylor, Gabriele. 1985. *Pride, Shame and Guilt: Emotions of Self-Assessment*. Oxford: Oxford University Press.

Thalmann, William G. 1978. *Dramatic Art in Aeschylus'* Seven Against Thebes. New Haven: Yale University Press.

Theodoridis, Christos, ed. 1998. *Photii Patriarchae Lexicon*. Vol. 2. Berlin: Walter de Gruyter.

Thompson, R.A., ed. 1990. *Nebraska Symposium on Motivation*, vol. 36: *Socioemotional Development*. Lincoln: University of Nebraska Press.

Timpanaro, Sebastiano. 1975 (orig. 1970). *On Materialism*. Trans. Lawrence Garner. London: Verso.

Todd, Stephen C., trans. 2000. *Lysias*. Austin: University of Texas Press.

Tomeo, Javier. 1986. *Preparativos de viaje*. Barcelona: Anagrama.

Tomkins, Silvan. 1995. *Shame and Its Sisters: A Silvan Tomkins Reader*. Ed. Eve Kosofsky Sedgwick and Adam Frank. Durham, NC: Duke University Press.

Toohey, Peter. 2004. *Melancholy, Love, and Time: Boundaries of the Self in Ancient Literature*. Ann Arbor: University of Michigan Press.

Tovar, Antonio, trans. 1953. *Aristoteles Rhetorica*. Madrid: Instituto de Estudios Políticos.

Tov-Ruach, Leila. 1980. 'Jealousy, Attention, and Loss.' In A.O. Rorty 1980: 465–88.

Trümpy, H. 1950. *Kriegerische Fachausdrücke im griechische Epos: Untersuchungen zum Wortschatze Homers*. Basil: Helbing & Lichtenhahn.

Turner, Chad. 2001. 'Perverted Supplication and Other Inversions in Aeschylus' Danaid Trilogy.' *Classical Journal* 97: 27–50.

Tzanetou, Angeliki. 2005. ' A Generous City: Pity in Athenian Oratory and Tragedy.' In Sternberg ed. 2005: 98–122.

Tzifopoulos, Yannis Z. 1995. 'Thucydidean Rhetoric and the Propaganda of the Persian Wars Topos.' *La Parola del Passato* 50: 91–115.

– 1997. Ἡ ρητορική τῶν Περσικῶν πολέμων· ἡ ἐρμνεία τῆς Ἱστορίας στίς Ἱστορίες τοῦ Θουκυδίδη.' In Πράκτικα· Πρωτο Πανελληνιο και Διεθνες Συνεδριο Αρχαιας Ελληνικης Φιλολογιας 23–26 Μαϊου 1994. Ed. J.-Th. A. Papademetriou. Athens: Hellenic Society for Humanistic Studies and International Centre for Humanistic Research, 38.

Urmson, J.O. 1990. *The Greek Philosophical Vocabulary*. London: Duckworth.

Usher, Stephen. 1974–85. *Dionysius of Halicarnassus: The Critical Essays*. 2 vols. Cambridge, MA: Harvard University Press.

Valpy, A.J., trans. 1991 (orig. 1831). *The Characters of Theophrastus*. London: Open Gate Press.

van Hooff, Anton J.L. 1990. *From Autothanasia to Suicide: Self-Killing in Classical Antiquity*. London: Routledge.

Van Wees, Hans. 1998. 'The Law of Gratitude: Reciprocity in Anthropological Theory.' In Gill, Postlethwaite, and Seaford 1998: 13–49.

Veyne, Paul. 1978. 'La famille et l'amour sous le Haut-Empire romain.' *Annales: Économies Sociétés Civilisations* 33: 36–63.

Viano, Cristina. 2003. 'Competitive Emotions and *Thumos* in Aristotle's *Rhetoric*.' In Konstan and Rutter 2003: 85–97.

Walbank, Frank W. 1985. *Selected Papers: Studies in Greek and Roman History and Historiography*. Cambridge: Cambridge University Press.

Walcot, P. 1978. *Envy and the Greeks: A Study of Human Behavior*. Warminster: Aris and Phillips.

Walsh, George B. 1984. *The Varieties of Enchantment: Early Greek Views of the Nature and Function of Poetry*. Chapel Hill: University of North Carolina Press.

Walsh, Thomas R. 2005. *Feuding Words and Fighting Words: Anger and the Homeric Poems.* Lanham, MD: Rowman and Littlefield.

Wardman, Alan. 1974. *Plutarch's Lives.* Berkeley: University of California Press.

Wardy, Robert. 1996. *The Birth of Rhetoric: Gorgias, Plato and Their Successors.* London: Routledge.

Wartelle, Abbé André. 1989. 'Le sacré chez les apologistes grecs.' *Revue des Études Grecques* 102: 40–57.

Wassiliewsky, B., and V. Jernstedt, eds. 1984 (orig. 1896). *Cecaumeni strategicon et incerti scriptoris de officiis regiis Libellus.* In Deno John Geanakoplos, ed., *Byzantium: Church, Society, and Civilization Seen through Contemporary Eyes.* Chicago: University of Chicago Press.

West, David. 1967. *Reading Horace.* Edinburgh: Edinburgh University Press.

West, Martin L. 1990. *Studies in Aeschylus.* Stuttgart: Teubner.

Westermarck, E. 1908. *The Origin and Development of the Moral Ideas.* Vol. 2. London: Macmillan.

White, Geoffrey M. 2000. 'Representing Emotional Meaning: Category, Metaphor, Schema, Discourse.' In Lewis and Haviland-Jones 2000: 30–44.

White, Gregory L., and Paul E. Mullen. 1989. *Jealousy: Theory, Research, and Clinical Strategies.* New York: Guilford Press.

White, Stephen D. 1998. 'The Politics of Anger.' In Rosenwein ed. 1998: 127–52.

Wierzbicka, Anna. 1999. *Emotions across Languages and Cultures: Diversity and Universals.* Cambridge: Cambridge University Press.

Wilkins, John, ed. 1993. *Euripides: Heraclidae.* Oxford: Clarendon Press.

Williams, Bernard. 1993. *Shame and Necessity.* Berkeley: University of California Press.

Wilson, Donna F. 2002. *Ransom, Revenge, and Heroic Identity in the Iliad.* Cambridge: Cambridge University Press.

Wilson, Peter. 2000. *The Athenian Institution of the Khoregia: The Chorus, the City, and the Stage.* Cambridge: Cambridge University Press.

Winckelmann, Johann Joachim. 1968 (orig. 1764). *History of Ancient Art.* 4 volumes. Trans. G. Henry Lodge. New York: F. Ungar.

Winkler, John J., trans. 1989. 'Achilles Tatius.' In B.P. Reardon, ed., *Collected Ancient Greek Novels*, 170–284. Berkeley: University of California Press.

Wisse, Jakob. 1989. *Ethos and Pathos from Aristotle to Cicero.* Amsterdam: Adolf M. Hakkert.

Wissmann, Jessica. 1997. *Motivation und Schmähung: Feigheit in der Ilias und in der griechischen Tragödie.* Stuttgart: M und P Verlag für Wissenschaft und Forschung = *Drama* Beiheft 7.

Wistrich, Robert S., ed. 1999. *Demonizing the Other: Antisemitism, Racism and Xenophobia.* Amsterdam: Harwood Academic.

Wohl, Victoria. 1998. *Intimate Commerce: Exchange, Gender, and Subjectivity in Greek Tragedy.* Austin: University of Texas Press.

Wolf, Christa. 1986. *Casandra.* Trans. into Spanish by Miguel Sáenz. Madrid: Ediciones Alfaguara. German original published as *Kassandra: Erzählung* (Darmstadt: Luchterhand, 1983).

Wollheim, Richard. 1999. *On the Emotions.* New Haven: Yale University Press.

Wood, Linda A. 1986. 'Loneliness.' In Harré 1986: 184–208.

Wright, Christopher. 1984. *Poussin Paintings: A Catalogue Raisonné.* London: Jupiter Books.

Wurmser, Léon. 1981. *The Mask of Shame.* Baltimore: Johns Hopkins University Press.

Zaborowski, Robert. 2002. *La crainte et le courage dans l'Iliade et l'Odyssée.* Warsaw: Stakroos.

Zahn-Waxler, Carolyn, E. Mark Cummings, and Ronald Iannotti, eds. 1986. *Altruism and Aggression: Biological and Social Origins.* Cambridge: Cambridge University Press.

Zanker, Graham. 1994. *The Heart of Achilles: Characterization and Personal Ethics in the* Iliad. Ann Arbor: University of Michigan Press.

– 2004. *Modes of Viewing in Hellenistic Poetry and Art.* Madison: University of Wisconsin Press.

Zielbauer, Paul. 2001. 'The Latest Case: Inhaled Anthrax Suspected in Connecticut Woman, 94.' *New York Times*, 21 November: B6.

Zierl, Andreas. 1994. *Affekte in der Tragödie: Orestie, Oidipus Tyrannos und die Poetik des Aristoteles.* Berlin: Akademische Verlag.

Index

definition, 65–6; cause of (in Aristotle), 43, 45–6; as a cause of hatred, 192–3; and democracy, 75; vs. demonization of the other, 72; in Demosthenes, 67; diminishing of, 83–5; in Euripides' *Hecuba*, 57–9; in Euripides' *Medea*, 61–5; and gratitude, 164–6; vs. grief, 247–52, 257–8; and harm, 68; vs. hatred, 42–3, 46–8, 185–6, 191, 197; and hierarchy, 73; and honour, 73–4; and humility, 84; in the *Iliad*, 48–56; incompatible with fear, 46, 87–8; vs. indignation, 68, 128; and injustice, 65–8, 72–3; and judgment, 44–5; medieval, 290n66; as negative, 69–70; as personal, 47, 186; vs. pity, 67; and revenge, 41, 43, 54, 56–65; Seneca on, 65–6; in Sophocles' *Ajax*, 106, 110; in Sophocles' *Electra*, 248–52; in Sophocles' *Women of Trachis*, 59–61; and status, 55–6, 61; suppression of, 75; susceptibility to, 74; Theophrastus on, 65–6; Thucydides on, 67–70; and war, 70–3; of women, 56–61. See also *kholos*, *mênis*, *orgê*

animals: absence of emotions in, xii, 22; absence of reason in, 269n31

Antiphon: on anger, 69; on shame, 104

anxiety, 32; in Aristotle, 149–50; in Epicureanism, 149–50

apoina ('ransom'), 54

appetites vs. emotions, 39, 74, 314n6

appraisal theory of emotion, 23–4

Aristophanes: *Clouds*, 176; *Frogs*, 144; *Knights*, 188; *Wasps*, 68; *Wealth*, 222–3

Aristotle, 15–16, 21–2, 77, 137, and passim; on anger, 41–8; and anxiety, 149–50; on calmness or satisfaction, 77–90; on courage, 70; on definition, 36; definition of emotion, 27–8, 33–7, 41–2; on envy, 111–15, 120; on fear, 130–5, 138–9, 154–5; on friendship, 171–5, 182–4; on gratitude, 156–64; on hatred, 185–94, 198; on humaneness, 213–18; on indignation, 111–15, 120, 122, 125; on irascibility, 70; on love, 171–6, 178–84; on *nemesis* in the *Ethics*, 114–16; on *philanthrôpia*, 216–17; on physiology of emotion, 44; on pity, 204–18; —, conflicting view of, 203–4; on reason in animals, 269n31, on rivalrous emotions, 224–5; on shame, 98–105

Arrowsmith, William, 61–2

art and expression, 13–14, 29–30

Aspasius: on emotion, 131–2, 306n4; on *philia*, 332n10

automatisms not emotions, 25–6

autonomy vs. interdependency, 23–4

balance of power, role of fear in, 139–41

Barbaro, Daniel, 158–60